Plausible Legality

OXFORD STUDIES IN CULTURE AND POLITICS
Clifford Bob and James M. Jasper, General Editors

PLAUSIBLE LEGALITY

Legal Culture and Political Imperative in the Global War on Terror

Rebecca Sanders

OXFORD
UNIVERSITY PRESS

Oxford University Press is a department of the University of Oxford. It furthers
the University's objective of excellence in research, scholarship, and education
by publishing worldwide. Oxford is a registered trade mark of Oxford University
Press in the UK and certain other countries.

Published in the United States of America by Oxford University Press
198 Madison Avenue, New York, NY 10016, United States of America.

Library of Congress Cataloging-in-Publication Data
Names: Sanders, Rebecca, author.
Title: Plausible legality : legal culture and political imperative in the
global war on terror / By Rebecca Sanders.
Description: New York : Oxford University Press, 2018.
Identifiers: LCCN 2017059867 (print) | LCCN 2017060686 (ebook) |
ISBN 9780190870560 (updf) | ISBN 9780190870577 (epub) |
ISBN 9780190870553 (hardcover)
Subjects: LCSH: Terrorism—Prevention—Law and legislation—United States. |
Administrative responsibility. | Civil rights—Government policy—United States. |
Human rights—United States. | Rule of law. | International crimes. |
National security—Law and legislation—United States. |
War on Terrorism, 2001–2009.
Classification: LCC KF9430 (ebook) | LCC KF9430 .S26 2018 (print)
| DDC 344.7305/32517—dc23
LC record available at https://lccn.loc.gov/2017059867

9 8 7 6 5 4 3 2 1

Printed by Sheridan Books, Inc., United States of America

CONTENTS

ACKNOWLEDGMENTS

I am grateful to the Department of Political Science, the University Research Council, the College of Arts and Sciences, and the Taft Research Center at the University of Cincinnati for financially and institutionally supporting this project. Numerous people have provided essential assistance to me over the years, offering encouragement, insight, and advice on my research at various stages of development, including Steven Bernstein, Danielle Bessett, Jutta Brunnée, Erynn Masi de Casanova, Patricia Greve, Laura Dudley Jenkins, Teresa Kramarz, Anne Sisson Runyan, David Welch, and Rina Williams. I am especially indebted to Clifford Bob, whose support and feedback have proved invaluable. I am moreover obliged to the many human rights and legal experts who took the time to speak to me as I conducted my research as well as the colleagues, conference co-panelists and discussants, and anonymous peer reviewers who have helped me develop my ideas over the years. Most importantly, I am grateful to my family for their love and support—my mother, Jill, and father, John, my husband Jeffrey, and our daughter, Naomi.

Plausible Legality

CHAPTER 1
The Politics of Plausible Legality

On September 30, 2011, American armed drones attacked a vehicle convoy in the Yemeni desert. Among the dead that day was Anwar al-Awlaki, a New Mexico-born imam and propagandist for al-Qaeda in the Arabian Peninsula who aimed to recruit followers around the world to the cause of Islamist extremism. Carried out under the direction of the Central Intelligence Agency (CIA), the strike was the first known instance in which an American citizen was subject to a "targeted killing" by the US government.[1] While human rights critics decried the attack as an illegal assassination that violated core tenets of due process—al-Awlaki had neither been prosecuted nor convicted of a crime in a US court—American authorities deemed the operation necessary and justified not only on security grounds but also on legal grounds.

As evidenced by carefully crafted leaked and declassified memoranda, Obama administration lawyers went to considerable lengths to establish a legal basis for such strikes.[2] Efforts to construct legal cover for contentious security practices were not confined to targeted killing. Years before, the George W. Bush administration had produced the notorious "torture memos," legally rationalizing waterboarding and other "enhanced interrogation techniques," while additional legal opinions authorized indefinite detention, military commissions, and mass surveillance of Americans without a warrant in pursuit of the "global war on terror."[3]

The United States' post-9/11 engagement with legal rules raises several critical questions. Why would the most powerful state in the world bother to justify security policy in detailed legal terms? How have American legal rationales for torture, arbitrary deprivations of life and liberty, and surveillance changed over time, and what accounts for these changes? How did the Bush and Obama administrations interpret, reinterpret, and manipulate

legal norms in order to advance their preferred policies? What do these justificatory practices tell us about the capacity of law to constrain state violence and promote human rights principles? This book examines these
problems through the lens of international relations, international law, and
sociolegal theory. I analyze how political actors use law to achieve their political objectives and then situate these patterns within a broader theoretical
understanding of how law operates in contemporary politics.

I argue that legal cultures—what I define as collectively shared
understandings of legal legitimacy and appropriate forms of legal practice—
play a significant role in shaping state conduct.[4] Put differently, legal
cultures underwrite how political actors interpret, enact, and evade legal
norms.[5] While legal cultures generally encourage some degree of compliance, they become especially important for the purposes of this study when
state policy preferences strain or contradict legal rules. In such cases, legal
cultures routinize how authorities justify the uneven application or violation of the law. For instance, there are longstanding incongruities between
human rights law and national security policy in liberal democracies.[6] Legal
cultures mediate how political actors manage these tensions. They provide rationales for state violence, for ignoring legal constraints in certain
circumstances or in regard to certain populations. Legal cultures can thus
foster rule following, but they can also promote rule evasion and revision.

In this book, I examine how legal cultures have shaped justifications
for human rights violations by the United States. As I document in detail,
American approaches to security practices have changed over time. In some
instances, authorities have respected legal limits, choosing to treat prisoners
humanely, uphold due process, and protect the privacy of individuals. But
in others, they have undermined legal norms in the name of national security. My claim is not that authorities always break the law. Rather, it is
that when they do, they do so in particular ways that are informed by predominant legal culture. When political actors defend controversial policies
with justifications drawn from outside prevailing cultural logics, they may
begin to reshape legal culture, but they also risk pushback, scandal, and
even prosecution.

In the post-9/11 United States, officials have operated within a *culture
of legal rationalization*. While the Bush and Obama administrations preferred aggressive and unconstrained military and intelligence operations to
varying degrees, this culture encouraged them both to seek legal cover for
human rights violations. As a result, authorities habitually consulted lawyers
and solicited numerous legal memoranda throughout the policymaking
process. This strategy aimed to establish what I call the *plausible legality* of
contentious security practices.[7] Lawyers at the Department of Justice, the
Department of State, the Department of Defense, the National Security

Agency, the CIA, and elsewhere generated opinions that attempted to navigate through and around constraining rules in order to say "yes" to their political leaders as often as possible. To do so, they exploited and manipulated ambiguities and loopholes in the law, claiming that enhanced interrogation techniques, targeted killing, and other dubious practices were compatible with existing legal rules. Where extant norms were insufficient or courts rejected their legal arguments, policymakers pushed Congress to create more permissive legislation. In many cases, lawmakers acquiesced, institutionalizing plausibly legal policies in legislation.

The distinctive nature of this cultural formation becomes apparent in comparison with other historical instances when Americans have violated human rights in the service of national security. Legal culture in the United States has changed over time, contributing to varying patterns of state violence. In order to identify similarities and differences with these precedents, I examine how Americans have pursued torture (chapter 3), detention, trial, and lethal targeting (chapter 4), and surveillance (chapter 5) across time— the most controversial security practices associated with the global war on terror. My analysis of these cases reveals several distinct legal cultures in American history: A *culture of exception* legitimized widespread human rights abuses against African Americans, indigenous peoples, immigrants, and political subversives well into the twentieth century. The Cold War then helped usher in a *culture of secrecy* in which controversial operations were conducted primarily through covert and clandestine means. An aforementioned culture of legal rationalization has predominated throughout the post-9/11 period. Whether the administration of Donald J. Trump will operate within this culture or succeed in its apparent efforts to revive a culture of exception remains to be seen.

What do these trends mean for the capacity of law to shape state practice? I analyze this problem in light of contending theoretical accounts of state behavior found in international relations, international law, and sociolegal theory. While realists, decisionists, and various critical theorists emphasize the supremacy of sovereign power over law, or *law as permit*, liberals and constructivists identify the rationalist and normative pathways through which law shapes state practice, or *law as constraint*. In cultures of legal rationalization, political actors care more about law than the perspective of law as permit assumes, but law is also more easily manipulated and less substantively constitutive of state identity than the perspective of law as constraint admits. I thus propose a paradoxical reading of law as a *permissive constraint*—as a force that can be marshaled to serve cynical state interests, but that also deeply structures the boundaries of legitimacy. In the contemporary legal culture of the United States, legal rules form a normative terrain that strategic agents confront and navigate.

My project is both practically and theoretically significant. American security policy in the post-9/11 period is a matter of substantial domestic and international public concern. From a human rights perspective, accounting for how and why American authorities adopted controversial practices is key to designing more effective and robust formal and informal human rights mechanisms. By identifying the complex ways in which states that express rhetorical commitment to human rights evade legal standards, rights advocates will be better placed to react to such maneuvers. I also advance scholarly insight into the relationship between law and state practice, a foundational problem at the heart of contemporary global politics. This question is especially relevant considering the proliferation of irregular forms of violent conflict that strain traditional legal categories. This book contributes to greater understanding of this emerging and rapidly changing landscape.

THE CONCEPT OF LEGAL CULTURE

I argue that the contemporary American national security establishment operates within a culture of legal rationalization. As a result, authorities have attempted to justify torture, indefinite detention, military commissions, targeted killing, and warrantless surveillance in the global war on terror by constructing the plausible legality of these practices. In order to understand these dynamics, it is necessary to unpack the concept of legal culture: what it is and how it can be identified, how it influences political actors, and how it may change.

The letter of the law is not self-executing. Rather, it must be interpreted and enacted by agents. Law's impact on state policy is mediated by lawyers, judges, policymakers, politicians, experts, activists, and publics who decide and contest what legal rules mean and make judgments about whether rule following or rule breaking should be pursued in a given context. These actors are embedded in legal cultures, or collectively shared understandings of legal legitimacy and appropriate forms of legal practice.[8] Emphasizing legal culture directs our attention to social beliefs and social practices of law, what legal scholars have called "interactional law,"[9] "law in action," and "living law,"[10] and what international norm theorists call "meaning-in-use" or the contextual interpretation of norms.[11] Legal cultures create patterned ways of engaging law, including justifications for and denials of legal wrongdoing, that give predictable shape to these processes.[12]

Legal cultures can be identified by the ways in which law is consistently interpreted and enacted in a given sociopolitical context. Collectively shared understandings of what law is, why it is important, who it is for, how it applies to different subjects and situations, who determines and enforces legal compliance, the relationship between law and politics, and the conditions under which law can legitimately be altered or suspended all form legal culture.[13] Comparative legal theorists, legal anthropologists, and law and society scholars have explored these themes through a number of case studies, often focusing on processes of legal transplantation, borrowing, convergence, and pluralism in an increasingly globalized legal environment.[14] In this study, I focus on changing American legal culture over time in the national security field.

Layered and nested legal cultures may form at different locations across international, national, and organizational levels and in different issue areas of state practice. Generally speaking, the United States' current national legal culture is individualistic, litigious, and venerates constitutional rights. As a result, Americans frequently seek to resolve political disputes in courts. My primary focus, the American national security establishment—including military, intelligence, and law enforcement agencies, as well as the political and judicial institutions that govern them—is embedded in a national security legal culture that is preoccupied with the management and legitimacy of violence. While it overlaps with and is informed by broader national legal culture, security practice by its nature creates habitual tensions with legal norms, particularly human rights protections, meaning national security legal culture is intently focused on the line between permissible and impermissible security conduct. Distinctive organizational cultures may develop within the national security realm,[15] contributing to disagreements. For instance, as evidenced by post-9/11 debates among government lawyers over the legality of torture, military officers are trained to automatically parse decisions through the law of armed conflict and its legal restraints while CIA operatives are not.

While some American international law experts identify primarily with the national security establishment and its associated legal culture, many members of the international law community share a transnational legal culture. Acculturated through top law schools and professional opportunities, they tend to hold cosmopolitan commitments. Many work for human rights nongovernmental organizations (NGOs) and international organizations. They have played an important role in trying to encourage the American national security establishment to take their legal obligations more seriously, to adopt a *culture of human rights*, to which I return later. None of these cultures are entirely bounded or mutually exclusive. Legal cultures produce coherent patterns, but they may overlap.[16] Sometimes individuals may travel between cultures, resulting in cultural cross-pollination and influence.[17]

How do legal cultures emerge and change? I argue that they are created and altered through the interaction of purposeful human action, shifting social norms, and major historical events. Human agency drives the development and disruption of legal cultures as individuals seek to pursue their material interests and ideological commitments through their approach to law and convince others to follow their lead. Legal specialists such as lawyers and judges dominate what Pierre Bourdieu termed "the juridical field,"[18] but this professional "community of practice"[19] is not the exclusive agent of these processes. Politicians, bureaucrats, intellectuals, journalists, and civil society activists also participate in legal culture. In some cases, they perpetuate and reproduce cultural norms and practices; in others, they upset the status quo and demand change. When standard ways of engaging legal norms become controversial or costly, actors may promote new ways of interpreting and enacting law, resulting in conflict and contestation. Which preferences prevail within a given community, and thus become culturally dominant, may result from these struggles.

Broad and gradual shifts in the normative environment also drive cultural change by altering actors' perceptions of their interests and identity. In other cases, wars or elections may catalyze more rapid transformations in actor preferences and social power relations. In the United States, the rise of the civil rights movement, the growth of international law after the Second World War, and the strategic dynamics of the Cold War all contributed to shifting national security legal culture away from a culture of exception toward a culture of secrecy. Under the doctrine of plausible deniability, authorities avoided responsibility for illegal or immoral behaviors by delegating their dirty work to secretive security agencies and allies abroad. Later, ongoing human rights activism, the intelligence scandals of the 1970s and 1980s, and new forms of political oversight and media scrutiny pushed an increasingly risk averse national security establishment to embrace a culture of legal rationalization and the pursuit of plausible legality.

I document and map American national security legal culture as it relates to human rights violations using a variety of sources. Culture is not a discreet variable that can be measured in isolation from the people and artifacts that express it. In this case, the parameters of cultural beliefs about law, specifically human rights law and the laws of war, are found in legal white papers, memoranda, court rulings, policy statements, speeches, interviews, commentary, testimony, and arguments produced by actors engaged in legal processes. While the secretive and elite world of American national security is more difficult to observe than other more transparent legal cultures, a great deal of classified material has been leaked or declassified and posted on the Internet, providing a surprising level of access to primary data such as the torture memos. These sources become evidence of legal culture when they form patterned, routinized approaches to law.

Throughout chapters 3–5, I use interpretive methods including analysis of government documents, legal memoranda, speeches, and other public pronouncements to trace how historical and contemporary actors have translated their culturally informed beliefs about the legal legitimacy of state violence into national security practice.[20] This standpoint takes seriously actors' justificatory narratives about their legal engagements, which are often quite explicit and consistent. These justifications in turn shape patterns of state violence. How states maim, kill, and control reflects in part how policymakers understand the law and the legal environment. While it can be difficult to definitively falsify cultural arguments, the specific claims I make about American national security legal culture are subject to critical scrutiny. For example, if actors in what I identify as cultures of exception regularly comply with legal constraints on human rights abuses despite the cultural demonization and dehumanization of prospective victims, or if actors in cultures of legal legalization frequently engage in open acts of extra-legal violence, either I have incorrectly diagnosed prevailing legal culture or legal culture itself is not shaping outcomes.

My analysis demonstrates that different legal cultures produce and reproduce different patterns of legal practice. These variations help explain why political actors engage legal rules and pursue human rights abuses in disparate ways. Legal prohibitions that seem robust in some instances fail in others. Shared laws do not always translate into shared understandings.[21] For instance, international prohibitions on state violence found in international conventions on genocide, refugees, and torture among other treaties have not generated uniform state practice. Legal culture also helps account for change over time. The laws of war, such as the Geneva Conventions, have persisted through world wars, colonial emergencies, and contemporary counterterrorism, accompanied by both humanitarian and abusive state behavior. In the United States, chattel slavery, racial segregation, and the current era of de jure racial equality have existed since the introduction of the Bill of Rights. I do not mean to suggest that international and domestic human rights and humanitarian legal norms have not themselves changed over time, but they have consistently imposed some basic limits on state violence. Nonetheless, the interpretation and implementation of these limits have varied considerably.

Legal cultures bridge the gap between abstract legal principles and state action. Moreover, they help account for the changing ways in which actors address tensions between legal norms and security agendas. In the contemporary United States, legal culture illuminates the paradox of American national security practice, which simultaneously embraces and defies international human rights principles through a strategy of plausible legality that legally rationalizes human rights abuses.

Although aspects of American legal culture such as reverence for constitutional rights and suspicion of government overreach have remained relatively constant, political actors have adopted changing justifications for human rights violations in the name of national security. Through a detailed historical analysis of how authorities have engaged in torture, arbitrary deprivations of life and liberty, and warrantless surveillance practices, I identify here several distinct national security legal cultures that have operated in the United States at varying points in time: cultures of exception, cultures of secrecy, and cultures of legal rationalization. Through historical comparison, I show how legal logics of state violence have changed, producing distinct patterns of practice. I then reflect on what an alternative culture of human rights might look like.

Emerging Human Rights Norms

As I document in chapters 3–5, the eighteenth-century Enlightenment encouraged greater legal prohibitions on state violence in Europe and the United States. While the specific language of universal human rights is largely a product of the expansion of international law in the mid-twentieth century, increasingly influential concepts of individual rights to be free from church and state repression rendered problematic a variety of previously normal practices such as torture, indefinite detention, and intrusive searches and seizures of property. These rights were gradually institutionalized in law. The legal cultures I examine in this book thus emerged in tandem with expanding human rights legal norms. Expectations of legal compliance in liberal democracies such as the United States required political actors to develop justifications for human rights violations. When tensions between legal norms and policy preferences emerged, legal cultures helped bridge the divide.

Taking a long historical view, it is clear that what we today understand as torture, arbitrary deprivations of life and liberty, and warrantless surveillance were at one time considered legal and legitimate in the Western world. Not only were such practices permitted, they were deeply integrated into predominant modalities of political rule. Torture, for instance, was a normal feature of statecraft and criminal procedure in Europe from antiquity until the eighteenth century. And it was far from hidden: authorities conducted grotesque public torture spectacles to communicate their power. Similarly, contemporary notions of due process and privacy were not widely accepted. In the realm of armed conflict, war frequently saw prisoners put to death and noncombatants brutalized. In other words, human rights norms had yet to develop or influence states, their nascent judicial systems, and their associated legal cultures. The law did not protect individuals. Rather, it defended monarchical and church prerogatives. As a result, public authorities committed overt human rights violations without the need for exculpatory justification.

Eventually, rules emerged that did prohibit human rights abuses by the state. During the eighteenth century, philosophical ideas emphasizing humanism, individual rights, and the contractual obligations of governments toward their citizens increasingly questioned unbridled forms of oppression and cruelty. The English, French, and American revolutions challenged divine right and codified new conceptualizations of the "rights of man." In the field of armed conflict, rules protecting civilians as well as wounded and captured soldiers were progressively codified throughout the late nineteenth century. These developments culminated in a spate of human rights and humanitarian law treaties throughout the twentieth century, particularly after the founding of the United Nations in 1945.

As critical scholars have noted, human rights norms are not always inclusive or emancipatory. Historically, rights were not extended to women or colonized and enslaved populations. Even today these norms have tended to elevate white, property owning men as ideal rights bearers, often ignoring the differential challenges faced by women, people of color, poor people, and minorities.[22] For example, the public/private distinction at the heart of the liberal rights tradition does little to limit domestic and sexual violence, which remain endemic.[23] Human rights claims can be strategically deployed to advance a variety of political agendas, including the interests of powerful groups and states.[24] For its part, international humanitarian law legitimates certain forms of killing and destruction while limiting others.[25] Nonetheless, these legal norms play an important role in regulating state violence. How they have been interpreted, manipulated, and evaded to permit human rights abuses thus demands attention.

In this book, I examine the United States' paradoxical commitment to human rights and rule of law alongside the reality of ongoing American human rights violations. The discrepancy is often striking and has been accompanied by changing rationales. My findings may also help explain similar patterns in other liberal democracies that are grappling with tensions between legal norms and security imperatives. They may be less relevant for understanding countries that have rejected or failed to internalize core tenets of international human rights and humanitarian law. In such contexts, political and military leaders promote authoritarian legal cultures to justify impunity for human rights abuses.

Historically, states have frequently invoked the concept of exception to justify human rights violations. Exception denotes exclusion from the protection of otherwise operative legal norms. The law does not apply or may be suspended in reference to certain populations or situations. In cultures of exception, exceptional arguments and practices become routinized and widely accepted. In some instances, actors frame exceptions as temporally limited responses to emergencies. This is common in wartime. In others, exceptions are cast as normal and permanent features of the legal order. This is more likely in societies where targeted populations constitute a real or imagined threat to the security of the state or predominant groups. Public authorities engage in exceptional rhetoric that demonizes others as enemies, subversives, or subhumans who can be controlled or defeated only through abusive violence. Explicitly racist justifications for human rights violations are common. In extreme cases, the law itself may explicitly authorize human rights abuses that are prohibited against the general population.

Despite Enlightenment ideals, the advent of human rights principles did not prevent Western states from perpetrating exceptional human rights violations. The colonization of the global south from the sixteenth century on unleashed gratuitous horrors on subjugated populations. Enslavement, torture, and murder were justified through characterizations of subaltern others as lazy, dangerous, and animal-like. Legal scholars, philosophers, and theologians played an important role in the process, deeming indigenous peoples uncivilized and thus outside the requirements of emerging humanitarian restraints on state violence. These colonial and imperialist logics were underwritten by widespread societal racism, which denigrated the humanity of nonwhites. This exceptional imperialist violence continued well into the twentieth century.

Its founding ideological commitment to civil liberties failed to spare the United States from these pathologies. As colonial settlement expanded, indigenous peoples were subject to violence, displacement, and dispossession. Women were considered inferior to men and denied national suffrage until 1920. Nowhere was exclusion more starkly evident than in the practice of chattel slavery. That the founding fathers kept slaves while authoring the Bill of Rights speaks to the nature of the emergent American legal culture, which celebrated individual freedoms for propertied white men while creating vast rights-free zones for others. This disjuncture was especially acute in regard to the management of state violence. While rejection of British abuses helped spur nationalist sentiment, atrocities, including legally authorized torture, were frequently deployed to maintain racial hierarchy.

The evolution of American constitutional law, the eventual abolition of slavery, and the growth of international law did not do away with these exceptional practices. While the concept of human rights became more robust in the United States, excluded outsiders continued to face systematic violence. In some cases, their removal from legal protection could be de facto, such as lynchings of African Americans throughout the American South that persisted into the 1960s. Although technically illegal, authorities turned a blind eye or even participated. Exclusion could also be de jure, such as the denial of due process rights for immigrants deemed security threats throughout the twentieth century.

American counterterrorism policy after 9/11 often appears to perpetrate exceptional human rights abuses. However, as I argue here and throughout the book, I find important differences between the legal logics that shaped the global war on terror and past instances of American violence.

Cultures of Secrecy

In contrast to cultures of exception, cultures of secrecy are characterized by public commitments to *universal* human rights law. Instead of justifying human rights abuses, authorities deny wrongdoing by concealing their activities to the greatest extent possible. Cultures of secrecy thus encourage clandestine and covert security operations, extensive document classification, and habitual lying by public officials.

The aftermath of the Second World War saw the creation of the United Nations, the growth of international human rights and humanitarian law, and the emergence of the civil rights movement in the United States. These developments combined to undermine the legitimacy of exceptional state violence. As human rights norms became more inclusive and human rights advocates more organized and vocal, states became sensitive to accusations of wrongdoing. As a result, abusive practices by liberal democracies were increasingly pushed underground.

In the face of these developments, a distinctive culture of human rights abuses emerged in the United States in the latter half of the twentieth century. As it sought to present itself as the liberal democratic alternative to Communism and the leader of the "free world," American authorities worked to create a benevolent image of the United States at home and abroad. This image was not compatible with torture, extrajudicial killing, or mass surveillance. At the same time, the increasingly powerful national security establishment believed that Soviet influence throughout the global south posed a grave danger.[26] As a result, the United States allied with anti-Communist authoritarian leaders around the world. These relationships were maintained through the emerging American intelligence apparatus, particularly the CIA. In this context, covert action—operations for which the United States could plausibly deny responsibility—became a favored way of balancing public image and strategic objectives. Proxies in client regimes abused, imprisoned, and executed opponents while American officials feigned ignorance. Within the United States, a systemic program of illegal domestic spying against allegedly subversive Americans was conducted in secret.

This American national security ethos transcended partisan politics. Within the elite and secretive national security community, plausible deniability became emblematic of a Cold War national security legal culture focused on evading public, judicial, and legislative scrutiny. While plausible deniability is far from unique to the United States, the juxtaposition between the United States' covert and clandestine activities and its public embrace of democracy, individual rights, and the rule of law has been especially intense.

Cultures of Legal Rationalization

Exception and secrecy are historically prevalent logics of state violence. They remain attractive frameworks through which authoritarian states manage contradictions between their international human rights commitments and abusive behaviors. However, there are other more evasive ways in which political actors in liberal democracies pursue human rights violations. In what I call cultures of legal rationalization, public authorities produce detailed legal justifications for controversial policies. Of course, law may also be invoked in cultures of exception as outlined above. But cultures of legal rationalization differ in that they seek to obfuscate, not highlight, derogations and double standards. Rather than admit and defend human rights violations, authorities argue that abusive practices are normal, unexceptional, and compatible with existing legal rules. Hallmarks of cultures of legal rationalization include the proliferation of lawyers in national security policymaking, the constant production of legal memoranda and opinions, the use of legalistic discourses in justificatory rhetoric, and ongoing public debate and litigation over the legality of security operations. These legalistic processes may be undertaken in both good and bad faith, making it difficult to distinguish cynical from sincere legal justifications.

Post-9/11 American engagement with international law, specifically international human rights and humanitarian law, does contain elements of cultures of exception and secrecy. Officials authorized torture, indefinite detention, military commissions, targeted killing, and warrantless surveillance, employing emergency rhetoric and executive power claims. Secrecy has also played a critical role in post-9/11 policy. Controversial decisions were made behind closed doors, and many government policies remain classified. Moreover, the United States continues to partner with abusive allies around the world, echoing the dynamics of Cold War covert action and proxy war. However, I argue that the frameworks of exception and secrecy do not capture distinctive features of contemporary American national security legal culture. In particular, they do not fully account for the intense legal sensitivity of the national security establishment. For a variety of reasons, security and intelligence officials have become legally risk averse, generating extensive demands for legal cover.

Throughout the 1970s and 1980s, numerous scandals highlighted American illegality and malfeasance during the Cold War. The Pentagon Papers disclosed the dismal state of the war in Vietnam and the undeclared expansion of the conflict into neighboring countries. The Watergate affair revealed that President Richard Nixon had engaged in undemocratic dirty tricks against his political adversaries. The Senate's Church Committee compiled an extraordinary dossier on the intelligence community's bad behavior, ranging from assassination plots against foreign leaders to systemic surveillance and harassment of American citizens. Later, the Iran Contra scandal as well as various human rights investigations exposed American support for Central American death squads. Leaking and investigative journalism made secrecy increasingly difficult to maintain.

These scandals led to political rebukes, public outrage, and, in a few instances, legal prosecutions. New Senate and House oversight committees were established to monitor intelligence activities. Legislation, such as the Foreign Intelligence Surveillance Act of 1978 (FISA), clarified and checked the power of intelligence agencies. Meanwhile, human rights advocates and NGOs deepened their criticism of US alliances in the global south. After the Cold War, humanitarian intervention, peacekeeping, and human rights enforcement took center stage in international politics. The global juridification of politics undermined impunity for state leaders.[27] From universal jurisdiction cases, to international war crimes tribunals, to judicial enquiries and impeachment proceedings, legal investigations became increasingly common means of challenging political power.

These developments pushed the United States to reevaluate relationships with foreign partners and improve human rights practices. In this context, the American national security establishment could no longer rely on logics of exception or secrecy to reconcile tensions between human rights norms and security policy. Fearing social and legal sanctions, policymakers, military commanders, and intelligence agents began to solicit ever more detailed legal advice for security operations from their lawyers. Legal advisors played an increasingly prominent role in justifying American security practice, from broad policy initiatives to the minutiae of military and intelligence missions.[28] By the turn of the millennium, this way of doing things was taken for granted, taught in law schools and training academies and routinized in institutional practices. In other words, legal rationalization became and remains an entrenched cultural norm.

These trends are evident in the global war on terror. For the most part, the Bush and Obama administrations attempted to distance themselves from overtly racist discourses. They did not publically justify breaking the law. While they pursued policies in secret to the greatest extent possible, insider leaking, investigative journalism, and human rights monitoring created an expectation of eventual public disclosure. As a result, officials systemically sought legal cover for potentially illegal behaviors.

In response to demands for greater legal compliance, American national security lawyers produced a plethora of legal rationalizations for controversial practices. In the face of the most advanced human rights regime in world history, they resorted to complex argumentative maneuvers aimed at permitting abuses without overtly suspending or breaking binding legal rules. Unlike past attempts at pursuing national security under the doctrine of plausible *deniability*, post-9/11 plausible *legality* aimed to redefine, reinterpret, and, when possible, reconstruct the law to accommodate contentious practices. It cast cruel, inhuman, and degrading interrogation, indefinite detention, unfair trials, extrajudicial killing, and warrantless surveillance as legal and permissible. When existing laws proved inadequate to the task, policymakers sought new legislation.

Legal rationalizations for human rights abuses have been hotly contested. Human rights critics have decried the torture memos and related initiatives as criminal. Yet there remain differences between cultures of legal rationalization and those that have shaped human rights abuses in other contexts. These differences help account for the strangely legalistic character of post-9/11 security policy as well as the apparent impunity of American authorities for what might otherwise be considered grave violations of domestic and international law. Moreover, this culture has reverberated globally. Practices such as targeted killing and mass surveillance are becoming legally normalized. In an interactional legal environment, legal culture can be emulated, diffusing plausible legality and emboldening human rights violators around the world.

It is unclear whether President Trump will upend the culture of legal rationalization. The administration has made concerted attempts to create a more permissive legal culture that does not rely on plausible legality for justification. The president has repeatedly expressed disdain for international law, advocating a host of human rights violations, including torture.[29] At the same time, his hostility to legal rules has undermined his policy initiatives, most notably his ban on Muslim immigration. Courts, buoyed by public protest, have partially blocked his most controversial plans. Whether the administration adapts to the culture of legal rationalization in order to facilitate its agenda or continues to advocate exceptional legal logics remains to be seen.

Cultures of Human Rights?

In the absence of intense conflict between state policy preferences and legal rules, authorities in the United States generally attempt to achieve straightforward legal compliance. Even where such conflicts exist, there are many public officials who reject the plausible legality of human rights abuses. Human rights advocates aim to amplify these sentiments and promote greater allegiance to human rights principles in national security circles. In a culture of human rights, tensions between security policy and human rights norms would be resolved in favor of the latter. The national security establishment would be substantively constrained not by fears of prosecution but by widely shared commitments to human rights as appropriate guides to action. This culture remains aspirational in the United States, but it is not an impossible goal. I discuss pathways toward this end in chapter 6.

LAW AND STATE VIOLENCE

What does analysis of legal cultures tell us about the capacity of legal rules to limit human rights abuses? In chapter 2, I situate this problem in the landscape of international relations and international law theory. I summarize two overarching perspectives found in the literature—law as permit and law as constraint. Realist, decisionist, and critical scholarship informs the former. Because these approaches understand law as subordinate to politics, they tend to reject the possibility that legal rules can significantly curtail the behavior of powerful states. Moreover, in some cases, law itself serves as an instrument of abuse. In contrast, liberal and constructivist theories suggest law has potential to independently constrain state violence through a variety of complex material and sociological mechanisms.

I argue that law's impact on state practice is highly contextual and contingent. Legal cultures play an important role in mediating how legal norms translate law into practice. In cultures of exception, states appear to conform to the expectations of law as permit, ignoring law when it contradicts their interests and using law to persecute their enemies. However, in cultures of legal rationalization, the material and social consequences of law breaking drive policymakers toward legal compliance or the appearance of legal compliance. In this context, law is best characterized as a permissive constraint on state practice—permissive insofar as ambiguities and loopholes in the law can be manipulated to justify human rights abuses through plausible legality, but constraining in that law following remains an influential standard of appropriate conduct.

Law as permissive constraint has mixed implications for the realization of human rights. On the one hand, plausible legality is a highly effective exculpatory strategy for political actors because it frustrates accusations of illegality. Even when legal rationalizations are widely criticized, as in the case of the torture memos, the veneer of legal cover undercuts accountability efforts. On the other hand, because plausible legality accepts the legitimacy of universal human rights and humanitarian law, it provides opportunities for human rights advocates to entrap policymakers in their rhetorical commitments and push for deeper forms of legal compliance. Interpretive battles over the meaning of law are therefore key to making cultures of legal rationalization less permissive and more constraining.

The book's three case study chapters explore the aforementioned themes in depth. Chapter 3 traces the relationship between law and torture in the United States over time. Chapter 4 outlines changing justifications for abusive detention, trial, and targeted killing practices. Chapter 5 examines intelligence surveillance. Throughout my analysis, I highlight how varying legal cultures have helped produce distinctive patterns of state violence.

Across all issue areas, plausible legality has ensured impunity for contemporary American authorities. Legal rationalizations have eroded the efficacy of human rights and humanitarian norms, particularly in regard to due process and privacy rights. These developments have had domestic and international reverberations, creating a more permissive environment for state violence and possibly portending a reversion to more overtly exceptional human rights abuses. The book concludes by examining the growing challenge to human rights from far-right nationalists around the world and the Trump administration in the United States. I further explore whether the plausible legality of human rights violations can be limited or reversed, arguing that pushback and social pressure from human rights advocates holds most promise for doing so. While protests, lobbying, and litigation by NGOs, social movements, and human rights lawyers have not always succeeded, they have helped defend and advance pro-human rights understandings of legal rules. This ongoing contestation will continue to shape American engagement with law for the foreseeable future.

CHAPTER 2

Permissive Constraint

Law, Power, and Legal Culture

Post-9/11 American legal justifications for torture, indefinite detention, military commissions, targeted killing, and warrantless surveillance raise important questions about the capacity of legal rules to limit state violence. Can law prevent human rights abuses? What role does it play, if any, in regulating political life? As outlined in chapter 1 and elaborated in greater detail in chapters 3, 4, and 5, I argue that the development and progressive institutionalization of human rights norms have clearly not prevented human rights violations. Rather, expanding legal norms have generated new tensions between human rights and security practices in liberal democracies. How policymakers navigate these tensions largely determines whether law operates as an appendage of state power or fulfills an independent constraining function.

Throughout the book, I document how changing legal cultures have shaped the ways in which American authorities resolve contradictions between legal norms and state violence. These legal cultures—collectively shared understandings of legal legitimacy and appropriate forms of legal practice—inform how actors interpret, enact, and evade the law. In a national security *culture of exception*, actors suspend, break, and reconstruct law to serve perceived national interest. Individuals and groups deemed threatening or dangerous by those in power are excluded from the protection of legal norms and are subject to intense and open violence. In a *culture of secrecy*, actors attempt to conceal human rights abuses. They pursue plausible deniability in order to avoid public scrutiny and justification. However, in a *culture of legal rationalization*, policymakers construct what I call *plausible legality*, or legal cover for contentious practices. As evidenced by American justifications for controversial security policies in the global war on terror, legal arguments serve to immunize security officials from accusations of illegality and normalize human rights abuses.

In this chapter, I explore where legal cultures in general, and the culture of legal rationalization that characterizes contemporary American national security practice in particular, fit into the landscape of international relations and international law theory. Because these literatures grapple with the relationship between legal norms and political power, they provide a theoretical toolkit for interpreting the role of law in limiting state violence. For the purposes of this inquiry, I identify two broad heuristic categories. From the perspective of *law as permit*, commonly found in realist international relations theory as well as increasingly popular Schmittian legal theory and various critical approaches, states instrumentally invoke legal principles to serve their policy goals but will not comply with rules that contradict their sovereign interests, particularly their national security. In contrast, liberal and constructivist proponents of *law as constraint* argue that law serves rational and normative purposes, which pull states toward legal cooperation and sometimes compliance. I argue that while these optics enhance our understanding of how law operates in some circumstances, neither sufficiently accounts for contemporary American national security legal practice, which displays elements of both law as permit and law as constraint. I therefore advocate a hybrid perspective of *law as permissive constraint*.

Rather than theorize a universal logic of state legal engagement, I argue that the relationship between law and political power is historically and culturally contingent. The capacity of legal norms to limit state violence varies by time and place. It is therefore best determined by observing patterns in how political actors engage law in particular contexts. In cultures of exception, states act largely in accordance with the assumptions of law as permit. They ignore and flout legal norms or create discriminatory and oppressive legal rules to justify state violence. In cultures of secrecy, actors systematically conceal human rights abuses. As with cultures of exception, law fails to constrain. However, because patterns of exceptional violence and state secrecy are historically and culturally bounded, they do not confirm the inevitable supremacy of power over law, as many theorists of law as permit assert. On the contrary, different cultural formations point to the capacity of law to more deeply structure state practice.

In cultures of legal rationalization, actors' pursuit of plausible legality displays significant elements of both law as permit and law as constraint. While highly institutionalized legal rules do not necessarily translate into consistent compliance as suggested by law as constraint, powerful proponents of realpolitik seek legal conformity far beyond what is anticipated by law as permit. These dynamics are evident in contemporary American counterterrorism policy. After 9/11, authorities sought maximum freedom of action to protect national security but have been constrained by the risk of societal opprobrium, political scandal, and even legal prosecution that could result from authorizing human rights abuses. Accordingly, they have systematically manipulated legal norms to accommodate their policy preferences. Policymakers have permitted numerous abusive security practices, but have done so through convoluted legal arguments that claim they are lawful. This strategy has proved highly effective in foreclosing prosecution and undercutting opposition. Law as permissive constraint provides a framework for understanding how law functions in this environment.

In many ways, my analysis of legal cultures affirms constructivism's emphasis on the sociological dimensions of political and legal behavior. However, norm theorists have often neglected the reality of persistent violence by states that have embraced human rights principles. Constructivist research has tended to focus on successful cases of human rights and humanitarian norm diffusion and influence. It has therefore primarily contributed to understanding law as constraint. In contrast, I argue that ongoing human rights violations by liberal democracies are structured through legal cultures that facilitate rather than substantively prevent them. This does not mean that anarchy or sovereignty trump law; it does mean that patterns of human rights abuses, like human rights compliance, emerge from and become routinized through social processes.

There is nothing inherently progressive about legal culture. While activists and advocates continue to encourage American authorities to adopt a *culture of human rights* in which deeper commitment to international human rights and humanitarian legal norms would effectively preclude abuses, that future remains largely aspirational in the national security field. Political leaders, influential policymakers, and public attitudes continue to support the status quo or prefer forms of legal engagement that would reduce, not enhance, respect for human rights. In this regard, it is critical to remember that although the story of human rights is often one of progressive change, legal cultures do not always advance unidirectionally. The United States could revert to a culture of exception, a distinct possibility in light of the early rhetoric of the Trump administration. Doing so would create a security environment that conforms more to the pessimistic prognostications of law as permit than the optimistic expectations of law as constraint.

In the following pages, I further develop these arguments by outlining the perspectives of law as permit and law as constraint in more detail. I overview what realists, decisionists, and critical theorists on the one hand and liberals and constructivists on the other say about law's capacity to shape state security practice and then read post-9/11 American policy through the lens of these respective approaches. My intent is not to comprehensively summarize these vast theoretical literatures but to distill contending assumptions about the relationship between law and state violence in order to catalyze new and alternative frameworks. Doing so is necessarily a reductive exercise that glosses over complexity and nuance in the work of individual authors. I then highlight where law as permit and law as constraint accurately capture the legal politics of the global war on terror and where they do not. I conclude by elaborating the case for understanding the operation of contemporary American national security legal culture from the perspective of law as permissive constraint.

LAW AS PERMIT

It is not surprising that both realist and decisionist perspectives on law and politics were forged in the darkness of the interwar crisis in Europe. In the lead-up to the Second World War, the League of Nations stood by helplessly as fascists consolidated power, purged enemies, and began their rapacious conquest of the continent. In Germany, the Weimar Republic's liberal legalistic pretensions crumbled as political radicalism gripped the country. For an emerging group of realist scholars who would come to dominate the field of international relations, liberal internationalism's faith in collective security and international law proved dangerously idealistic. Instead, they developed a theoretical paradigm that placed material power at the heart of international politics. Contemporaneously, Weimar and later Nazi jurist Carl Schmitt developed his critique of constitutional liberalism. In reviewing these perspectives and their applicability to contemporary American legal practice, I argue that they aptly capture some aspects of American policy but not others.

For realists, the strong do what they can and the weak do what they must. Pervasive insecurity under anarchy forces states to maximize material power, often at the expense of morality. Actors seek survival, sometimes dominance, and in doing so approach law instrumentally to advance their interests and vanquish their enemies. States frequently ignore legal rules, even ones they helped create, or engage in legal cheap talk that pays lip service to rules while pursuing illegal behaviors. Because international law is largely unenforceable against the strong, impunity is common. In contrast, weak states may be coerced into rule following or punished for transgressions, highlighting the status of law as a form of hegemonic discipline.[1]

In addition to realist analysis, Schmitt's decisionist philosophy has emerged as a popular framework for interpreting the global war on terror. While realists decry the structural weakness of international law, Schmitt problematized the rule of law itself.[2] As articulated in his famous formulation "Sovereign is he who decides on the exception,"[3] legal rules are incapable of defining and regulating emergency.[4] Rather, sovereign power holds the fundamental "monopoly to decide."[5] For Schmitt, the sovereign's core political responsibility is distinguishing friend from enemy. The political enemy is "the other, the stranger; and it is sufficient for his nature that he is, in a specially intense way, existentially something different and alien."[6] Because political agency trumps norm-based legal formalism, sovereigns must act without legal constraint.[7] Read against Schmitt's Nazism, these ideas have odious implications. "The friend, enemy, and combat concepts receive their real meaning precisely because they refer to the real possibility of physical killing. War follows from enmity. War is the existential negation of the enemy," according to Schmitt[8]

Realists and decisionists are not the only ones to highlight law's subordination to power. A variety of critical theorists have analyzed how law frequently, although not exclusively, perpetuates imperialism and unequal global power relations,[9] naturalizes domination,[10] and universalizes hegemonic preferences.[11] The United States in particular has used and shaped international law to advance its interests and security.[12] Because law often does more to facilitate than to constrain state violence, its emancipatory capacity is limited if not illusory.[13]

Does what I have called law as permit accurately capture contemporary American legal politics? There is certainly reason to support this view. Post-9/11 counterterrorism policy evinced a particularly virulent form of American exceptionalism, characterized by intense unilateralism and double standards. In the absence of any counterbalancing power, the United States has eschewed international norms with few consequences, as realists would predict.[14] A vast swath of literature analyzes the global war on terror through the lens of decisionism.[15] According to Sanford Levinson, "the true *éminence grise* of the [George W. Bush] administration, particularly with regard to issues surrounding the possible propriety of torture, is Schmitt."[16] Scott Horton argues that "Schmitt's thinking and analysis—the weakness of liberalism, the utility of 'law-free' zones, the demonization of adversaries, the subordination of justice to politics" have been reflected in the Bush administration's "war on the rule of law."[17] For Jens David Ohlin, a small clique of "New Realists" formed the legal ideology of the Bush administration, combining rejection of international law with a Schmittian embrace of unchecked executive power.[18]

Italian political theorist Giorgio Agamben has become one of the most popular interlocutors in the Schmittian revival. He argues that the state of exception is the "dominant paradigm of government in contemporary politics."[19] In his biopolitical reading, exception reduces undesirables to *homo sacer*, or "bare life" that can be killed but not sacrificed, to objects stripped of what Hannah Arendt called the "right to have rights." The Nazi death camp epitomizes this condition as a place where "everything is possible," making the concept of juridical protection meaningless.[20] According to Agamben, "the prisoners in Guantánamo, and their situation is legally-speaking actually comparable with those in the Nazi camps. The detainees of Guantánamo . . . have absolutely no legal status. They are subject now only to raw power; they have no legal existence."[21] A similar view of the global war on terror is summed up by critical theorist Judith Butler: "The law is not that to which the state is subject nor that which distinguishes between lawful state action and unlawful, but is now expressly understood as an instrument, an instrumentality of power, one that can be applied and suspended at will."[22]

As I document throughout the book, the empirics of contemporary American legal politics lend themselves to such analysis. The Bush administration's "unitary executive" theory justified extensive presidential prerogative, even an "imperial presidency." As infamously asserted by Richard Nixon: "When the president does it, that means it's not illegal."[23] Echoing the language of exception several decades later, Justice Department lawyer John Yoo defended the absolute monopoly to decide: "The Framers . . . created an executive with its own independent powers to manage foreign affairs and address emergencies which, almost by definition, cannot be addressed by existing laws."[24] This aggressive assertion of executive power was evident in the executive orders and presidential signing statements issued by the Bush administration that purported to unilaterally impose the president's preferred legal interpretations.

While law as permit provides a compelling perspective, I argue that it does not account for the full range of American legal engagement in the global war on terror. The torture memos and related legal rationalizations suggest a more extensive concern with legality than realpolitik or sovereign decisionism would predict. Government lawyers took pains to construct a variety of exculpatory rationales for abusive policies, invoking rather than ignoring extant legal norms. They did not suspend the Constitution, dismiss court rulings, endorse crude racism, or cast domestic minorities as existential enemies. Instead, they selectively reinterpreted constraining provisions to facilitate controversial security practices. As Frédéric Mégret notes of American detention policy, "the US authorities' case is often not a case to simply violate or do away with the law, as much as it is a characteristically strict, almost legalistic interpretation of the law."[25] Fleur Johns argues that Guantánamo is "less an outcome of law's suspension or evisceration than of elaborate regulatory efforts by a range of legal authorities . . . . They are spaces where law and liberal proceduralism speak and operate *in excess.*"[26] "[G]iven this almost hyperlegality," asks Nasser Hussain, "does it then make any sense to continue to use the analytic idiom of the state of exception? After all, that category invokes a very specific idiom and imagery: one of exclusion or outsideness, abeyance or suspension, and of course decision."[27]

I suggest that while law as permit may indeed capture the dynamics of legal cultures of exception, contemporary American legal rationalizations of abusive security practices do not fully follow this logic.[28] Rather than suspend law or collapse power and norms, even the Bush administration and later the Obama administration were highly preoccupied with obtaining legal cover. The resultant legal authorizations were often deeply cynical, but they were not just rhetorical—they closely tracked existing laws and, in turn, dictated policy. This raises the question: Can we interpret American legal politics in light of, not just in spite of, the law? In the following section, I explore the alternative perspective of law as constraint, which is informed by liberal and constructivist scholarship.

LAW AS CONSTRAINT

For proponents of what I call law as constraint, legal norms can tame state power and limit state violence. Accordingly, much liberal and constructivist scholarship is devoted to theorizing how best to strengthen legal compliance in international politics. While these perspectives in no way assume that states always follow the law, they do hold out hope that deeper compliance is possible.

According to liberal theory, law enhances soft power, allowing states to attract allies and set international agendas.[29] For some liberal scholars, state–society relations, domestic ideologies, and interest groups shape legal behavior.[30] As a result, liberal democracies promote political commitments to individual rights and freedoms on the world stage, creating zones of liberal peace, but also conflict with nondemocracies.[31] For a variety of neoliberals and rational institutionalists, state calculations related to reputation, reciprocity, transaction costs, iterated games, and sanctions mitigate anarchy and incentivize cooperation, particularly in the context of well-designed legal regimes.[32] While liberals are more optimistic about the constraining capacity of international law than realists, they are not idealists. They understand that states violate their legal commitments, particularly when it comes to human rights.[33] In many instances, states cynically ratify human rights treaties to reduce international criticism. Nonetheless, human rights advocates and civil society can leverage legal norms to pressure states to improve behavior.[34]

The problem of compliance is also a core preoccupation of the constructivist international relations and international law literature. From this sociological perspective, legal regimes rest on legitimacy and shared social purpose, not simply material power.[35] Anarchy is "what states make of it."[36] Law functions as a normative system, creating standards of appropriate behavior.[37] Global governance, epistemic communities, and transnational advocacy networks diffuse norms.[38] As theorized by Martha Finnemore and Kathryn Sikkink's norm life cycle model, norm entrepreneurs promote their ideas through international organizations, eventually resulting in widespread norm adoption and internalization.[39] Legal scholars have posited other mechanisms of normative influence including transnational legal process, iterated legal interactions, and acculturation.[40] When norms fail to constrain states, this situation may be due to tensions between domestic and international norms, varying organizational cultures, or contestation over normative meaning.[41]

While law as permit provides an intuitive account of post-9/11 American legal politics, I argue that there is also evidence of law as constraint at work. Although the Bush administration was not particularly sensitive to the value of soft power, even it understood that Americans would not benefit from acquiring a reputation for torture or other gross human rights abuses. "We could neither lead the free world nor recruit new allies to our cause if we did not practice what we preached," acknowledged President Bush.[42] This understanding suggests concern with what Kelly Greenhill calls "hypocrisy costs"—"those symbolic political costs that can be imposed when there exists a real or perceived disparity between a professed commitment to liberal values and norms and demonstrated actions that contravene such a commitment."[43] Understood in this context, the torture memos and related legal rationalizations aspired to deflect criticism and preserve international standing.

The threat of legal sanctions, particularly at the level of individual criminal liability, influenced post-9/11 counterterrorism policy. Although there are few international mechanisms that could effectively hold Americans to account, violations of the Geneva Conventions, the UN Convention against Torture, and associated domestic legislation as well as other human rights and humanitarian laws are subject to prosecution in US courts. As a result, policymakers and security practitioners demanded legal cover. Law also arguably placed normative constraints on the global war on terror. Legal conformity is an important standard of appropriate behavior in the United States, reflecting longstanding liberal democratic commitments to rule of law and ongoing pushback by human rights activists against abusive policies. Legal justification remains a critical element of contemporary politics.[44] The extent to which political actors claim legal compliance, even when engaging in seemingly unlawful activities, is an important indicator of law's normative legitimacy.[45]

By drawing attention to the significance of reputation, material and social sanctions, and legitimacy, liberal and constructivist perspectives shed light on how legal norms constrained, at least to some extent, American counterterrorism policy. For rational and normative reasons, law must be taken seriously. These insights do not negate the dynamics of law as permit, but they do help provide a richer picture of why law matters, of why legalizing abuse was a necessary prerequisite for committing it.

At the same time, the strategy of plausible legality does not conform to the traditional expectations of liberal or constructivist scholarship. Simply feigning compliance to avoid sanctions adds little to realist assumptions. Moreover, while constructivist emphasis on legal legitimacy helps account for why actors would choose this mode of justification, it is not clear what work norms are really doing. Once internalized by states, legal norms should alter identity and behavior. If the torture prohibition, rights to life and liberty, and privacy norms really are standards of appropriate behavior in liberal democracies, they should prevent policymakers who have embraced these values from violating them in rhetoric and practice.

The perspective of law as permit explains why actors would break, ignore, or suspend the law and lie about it to deflect criticism, but not why they would bother to concoct convoluted legal rationales that downplay exceptionalism. The perspective of law as constraint explains why actors claim legal conformity but says less about why entrenched legal norms fail to substantively limit human rights violations. To understand this problem, I turn to the contradictory, even paradoxical, nature of legal constraint in contemporary American legal culture.

LEGAL THEORY, LEGAL CULTURE, AND STATE VIOLENCE

Law as permit and law as constraint are heuristic categories that highlight how different theoretical traditions have tended to think about the capacity of law to limit state violence. In the preceding discussion, I outlined where these respective approaches succeed and fail in accounting for contemporary American legal politics, which I argue is characterized by the pursuit of plausible legality. My purpose is not to test contending theories but to examine whether they provide useful conceptual tools for understanding this phenomenon. In doing so, I find that the global war on terror evinces aspects of both law as permit and law as constraint.

Throughout the book, I trace how varying cultures of exception, secrecy, and legal rationalization have shaped American torture, detention, trial, lethal targeting, and surveillance practices over time. Facing tensions between human rights and humanitarian legal norms and perceived national security imperatives, political actors engage in routinized forms of rule evasion that produce and reproduce predominant legal culture, or collectively shared understandings of legal legitimacy and appropriate forms of legal practice. Legal cultures emerge from a complex confluence of human agency, social norms, and historical events. By examining how political actors justify their behavior, we can identify different cultural patterns.

Analyzing legal practice through the lens of legal culture suggests that there can be no universal theory of legal politics. Like all sociological variables, legal culture is inherently contextual. The relationship between law and state violence changes because the legal cultures that mediate how political actors engage legal norms change. Law, in practice, is what states make of it. As David Nelkin notes: "The sort of investigations in which the idea of legal culture finds its place are those which set out to explore empirical variations in the way law is conceived and lived rather than to establish universal truths about the nature of law; to map the existence of different concepts of law rather than establish the concept of law."[46] Accordingly, frameworks such as law as permit, law as constraint, and law as permissive constraint shed light on the operation of some legal cultures but not all.

My contextual approach to understanding the relationship between law and power relies heavily on constructivist insights. Legal cultures promote different understandings of appropriate forms of legal practice, which in turn shape state behavior, including state violence. However, the socially constructed nature of state violence has been neglected by constructivist emphasis on law as constraint. While there "are no bad norms from the vantage point of those who promote the norm,"[47] most norm scholarship has been preoccupied with what many would consider "good norms" related to human rights, humanitarianism, and arms control.[48] As a result, we know less about how noncompliance and other forms of violent or oppressive behavior are themselves sociologically grounded, particularly in liberal democracies that have supposedly internalized legal norms.

Realism, decisionism, and related critical theories capture the reality of legal cultures characterized by interstate and intergroup competition and domination. For instance, cultures of exception generate extralegal responses to constraints on state violence, fulfilling many expectations of law as permit. They are hostile to the universality of law, justify human rights violations against enemies, outsiders, and minorities, and employ discourses of necessity. In addition to ignoring or suspending legal norms, actors in cultures of exception may reconstruct the law itself to facilitate greater human rights abuses. These cultural markers were evident during American slavery and segregation and in American wars with racial and ideological others well into the mid-twentieth century. They continue to be found in the legal politics of authoritarian regimes around the world.

As outlined in the following chapters, the expansion of international human rights and humanitarian law, the United States' strategic projection of its liberal democratic identity in the context of the Cold War, and intensifying pressure from the civil rights movement helped shift American national security legal culture away from a culture of exception and toward a culture of secrecy. In cultures of secrecy, actors attempt to avoid public scrutiny and criticism through clandestine and covert action. While less willing to justify overt human rights abuses, they still largely fulfill the expectations of law as permit. When faced with tensions between legal norms and political imperatives, authorities break the law with impunity by constructing plausible deniability and lying about their behavior. They act hypocritically, saying one thing and doing another. In other words, law as permit accurately highlights the reality of state violence and mendacity throughout history. However, these patterns of conduct are not, I argue, the inevitable product of anarchy or sovereignty. Rather, they reflect dominant forms of legal culture in particular contexts.

Law as permit proves less satisfying in capturing how states engage law in cultures of legal rationalization. While assuming that political actors will instrumentally marshal law to serve their interests, law as permit does not anticipate extensive efforts to assert plausible legality. Likewise, law as constraint does not predict that a longstanding liberal democracy would engage in torture, indefinite detention, targeted killing, and mass surveillance. Accordingly, I argue that the perspective of law as permissive constraint offers a more comprehensive framework for understanding the relationship between law and power in contemporary American national security practice.

In Table 2.1, I outline how law as permit aligns with cultures of exception and secrecy, how law as permissive constraint captures cultures of legal rationalization—the primary focus of this study—and how law as constraint allows for the possibility of cultures of human rights. Moreover, I note how these cultures manifest themselves in American approaches to torture, arbitrary deprivations of life and liberty, and mass surveillance, which I explore in greater depth throughout the book. While in reality dividing lines are often blurred, these categories help make sense of changing rationales for state violence.

Table 2.1 LEGAL THEORY, LEGAL CULTURE, AND STATE VIOLENCE

	Realism, Decisionism, Critical Theory			Liberalism, Constructivism
Relationship between law and human rights abuses	Law as permit: law subordinate to politics and fails to constrain human rights abuses		Law as permissive constraint: law shapes but does not prevent human rights abuses	Law as constraint: law substantively limits human rights abuses
National security legal cultures	Cultures of exception: human rights abuses publicly justified	Cultures of secrecy: human rights abuses denied	Cultures of legal rationalization: human rights abuses reframed as normal and lawful	Cultures of human rights: human rights norms prioritized
Torture	Antebellum torture of slaves; lynching; imperial torture	Cold War support for regimes that torture; secret CIA torture research	Post-9/11 enhanced interrogation techniques; torture memos	Torture never practiced or supported; perpetrators prosecuted
Deprivations of life and liberty	Colonial massacres; Red Scares; WWII internment	CIA assassination plots; cover-ups	Indefinite detention of unlawful enemy combatants; military commissions; targeted killing	Rights to habeas corpus and due process respected; extrajudicial killing never practiced or supported
Surveillance	Pervasive state surveillance of alleged subversives	Systematic illegal spying; intelligence agency dirty tricks	Domestic surveillance reclassified as foreign surveillance; exploitation of third-party surveillance and metadata	Warrants obtained for surveillance of citizens; incidental collection minimized

When law serves as a permissive constraint, it advances the political preferences of powerful actors, enabling their agendas, but simultaneously imposes material and normative limits. Legal norms are not simply epiphenomenal to power. Yet they cannot overcome the realities of power; they do not constitute actors all the way down. As captured by Martti Koskenniemi's classic characterization of international law's oscillation between "apology" and "utopia," this dualistic indeterminacy is pervasive in legal history.[49] The paradox of concurrently permissive and constraining law is especially acute today.

States that have signed on to the liberal rule of law project by ratifying and institutionalizing international legal norms operate in an environment deeply structured by law. Far from empty rhetoric, law breaking has substantial material and normative consequences. International and domestic judicial processes curb political power. They have the capacity to launch investigations, adjudicate disputes, impose sanctions, and prosecute individuals. Democratic checks and balances, the free press, and human rights NGOs also play a critical role in monitoring legal behavior and naming and shaming wrongdoing. At the same time, political actors face significant demands to protect national security. When this imperative is constrained by legal norms, such as human rights and humanitarian restrictions on state violence, policymakers may attempt to avoid and evade law, using legal maneuvers that blur the line between compliance and noncompliance.[50] However, they cannot overtly violate legal norms without incurring significant risk to their reputation, standing, and possibly freedom.

In this context, cultures of legal rationalization attempt to manage tensions between legal norms and political imperatives in ways that reinforce the dynamics of law as permissive constraint. Actors push legal boundaries but anticipate public disclosure and legal investigation. They therefore seek out legal cover to secure immunity and legitimacy for questionable policies. Post-9/11 American legal politics have reproduced this culture. The strategy of plausible legality exploits ambiguities, loopholes, and gaps in the law in order to cast American counterterrorism policy as legal and thus acceptable. Torture is framed as enhanced interrogation techniques; indefinite detention, military commissions, and targeted killing as compliant with the laws of war; and warrantless mass surveillance as legally legitimate foreign spying. Of course, plausibly legal arguments are not necessarily legally convincing. Indeed, some critics question whether the torture memos and related documents should be considered legal at all. This raises difficult questions about what exactly differentiates genuine legal claims from other types of political rhetoric that invoke law.

Many scholars suggest that legal argument is a distinct form of interaction based on deference to ordered, rule-bounded behavior.[51] Accordingly, "actors enter the realm of international law when they feel impelled not only to place reasoned argument ahead of coercion but also to engage in a distinctive type of argument in which principles and actions must be justified in terms of established, socially sanctioned, normative precepts."[52] Others posit more substantive standards. For instance, Jutta Brunnée and Stephen Toope argue that Lon Fuller's criteria of legality provide a framework for distinguishing legal norms and practice that are capable of generating a "compliance pull."[53] Jeremy Waldron suggests that not any norm can function as a legal norm. Basic conditions are required for liberal legality: "Law is not brutal in its operation. Law is not savage. Law does not rule through abject fear and terror, or by breaking the will of those whom it confronts. If law is forceful or coercive, it gets its way by nonbrutal methods which respect rather than mutilate the dignity and agency of those who are its subjects."[54]

While such accounts are ethically appealing and accurately capture how most contemporary international law professionals and international human rights advocates understand legal legitimacy, they may not be universally shared or reproduced by all political actors in all legal cultures. For instance, in cultures of legal rationalization, officials promote increasingly weak standards for what counts as legal. When post-9/11 American authorities claimed that waterboarding was lawful, they meant that government lawyers had written long legal memos infused with legal terms and references to treaties, legislation, and precedents deeming it so. They showed little concern for the conceptual coherence and accuracy of these opinions, let alone their brutal consequences.

What are the implications of law as permissive constraint for the capacity of legal norms to limit state violence? Cultures of legal rationalization pose as great a challenge to human rights and humanitarian law as cultures of exception and secrecy because plausible legality shifts shared understandings of legal rules, normalizing and legitimizing human rights abuses. These dynamics have the practical effect of blurring the line between law following and law breaking. States may appear to respect the letter of the law but actually violate its purpose, resulting in norm evasion.[55] By rhetorically adapting their language and framing, they minimize accusations of norm violation.[56] In these ways, plausible legality ensures impunity for human rights violations.

Three futures could emerge from this state of affairs. First, the American national security establishment could continue to operate within a culture of legal rationalization, soliciting legal cover to justify controversial policies. Alternatively, human rights activists could push policymakers toward developing a culture of human rights. In this scenario, authorities would place substantive respect for human rights and humanitarian legal norms first, even when these constraints limit their policy preferences. The law as constraint literature points to a variety of mechanisms to achieve this goal. Liberals highlight how reputational concerns and sanctions can push states to change their behavior in line with legal norms. Constructivists argue that transnational advocacy networks and other sources of normative influence can reshape how actors understand their interests and identities. It is indeed hypothetically possible that sustained international and civil society pressure could successfully promote deeper limitations on state violence.

Yet there is emergent evidence of a third future in which legal culture does not move toward greater human rights compliance but reverts to a culture of exception, triggering the dynamics of law as permit. The Trump era may portend a critical juncture in the development of American national security policy. In chapter 6, I elaborate on these possible futures, discussing pathways toward fostering a culture of human rights and analyzing the prospects for such a shift in light of contemporary political developments in the United States.

CONCLUSION

Legal and political scholars have long grappled with the relationship between law, power, and state violence. I have identified two divergent approaches: law as permit and law as constraint. The former, informed by realist, decisionist, and critical scholarship, emphasizes law's subordination to power. Sovereigns construct legal rules to enhance their agendas and violate law when it threatens their interests. Exceptional violence against deemed enemies is thus an omnipresent feature of political life. Law alternately legitimates power or is incapable of constraining it. In contrast, law as constraint, drawing from liberal and constructivist scholarship, holds hope that law can check state power. From a rationalist perspective, legal regimes reflect the preferences of interest groups but also create incentives for rule following and disincentives for rule breaking. From a normative perspective, law helps constitute actor identities and define legitimate conduct. I have argued that the efficacy of these contending perspectives is contingent on context, reflecting the dynamics of dominant legal cultures. Cultures of exception and secrecy manifest many features of law as permit, while a culture of human rights could potentially realize the aspirations of law as constraint.

I advocate an alternative perspective of law as permissive constraint for understanding the legal politics of the global war on terror. This framework captures the dynamics of cultures of legal rationalization. Political actors are strategic and goal seeking. When legal rules pose obstacles to perceived security imperatives, they attempt to avoid and manipulate them. At the same time, law creates a normative terrain that structures politics. To evade human rights and humanitarian norms, actors must develop justifications that take these rules into account or risk material and social sanction. As evidenced by post-9/11 American national security practice, authorities seek legal cover by asserting the plausible legality of contentious policies.

In the following chapters on torture, deprivations of life and liberty, and surveillance, I document how changing legal cultures in the United States have resulted in distinctive patterns of justification for these practices. The emergence of human rights norms during the Enlightenment and the subsequent expansion and institutionalization of human rights and humanitarian law generated significant tensions between the exercise of state violence and legal restrictions on that violence. This tension has been resolved in distinct ways across legal cultures, producing shifting logics of human rights abuse.

CHAPTER 3

Torture

Torture is universally prohibited by international law. Along with slavery, genocide, and other great evils, it violates basic human rights and humanitarian norms. In both peace and war, most countries have declared torture fundamentally wrong and illegal. However, this was not always the case. The story of torture is one of change—in norms, laws, and practices. Indeed, torture was once considered wholly legitimate, used openly in the service of the law. Even after the development of prohibitions, states continued to torture in order to instill terror and extract information. Rather than eliminate torture, legal constraints generated new justifications for rule violation. Despite a robust anti-torture legal regime, the administration of George W. Bush opted to pursue torture and other cruel, inhuman, and degrading practices in the global war on terror. In order to do so, it solicited numerous legal memoranda that recast torture as lawful "enhanced interrogation techniques." This attempt to construct legal cover for torture, or what I call *plausible legality*, helped shield officials from the legal consequences of their actions.

This chapter develops the necessary context for understanding these developments. It briefly reviews the history of torture in the West, describes the evolution of the torture prohibition in international and American law, and documents state sanctioned torture practices over time. It analyzes how shifts in legal culture have informed changing patterns of torture in the United States. A *culture of exception* justified gratuitous violence against African Americans at home and enemies abroad for much of early American history while a *culture of secrecy* pushed authorities to deny torture during the Cold War. I then turn to tracing how the contemporary American national security *culture of legal rationalization* has shaped torture in the post-9/11 period.

I argue that contemporary American policymakers' capacity to endorse torture is constrained by the normative hegemony and legal institutionalization of human rights principles. Moreover, human rights monitoring and press scrutiny make covert and clandestine torture difficult. While secrecy continues to play an important role in security decision making, officials are keenly aware that they cannot rely on plausible deniability to get away with systemic illegality. The risks of disclosure and prosecution are too high, spurring demand for legal cover that ensures immunity and even legitimacy for controversial programs. The fundamental character of the legal prohibition on torture in international law means that these efforts have been largely geared toward redefining torture. Despite harsh critiques from human rights advocates, the strategy of plausible legality has proved remarkably effective in creating impunity for torture in the global war on terror. The anti-torture legal norm in the United States and around the world has arguably been weakened as a result. Moreover, the pro-torture rumblings of the Trump administration suggest that regression to more exceptional logics of torture remains possible.

LEGAL TORTURE: OPEN SPECTACLES OF VIOLENCE

Not only was torture once widely practiced, it was considered legal and legitimate in Europe until the Enlightenment. While this history of torture in the "civilized West" is often neglected, it helped inspire the eventual development of legal prohibitions on torture in international and American law.

Torture to extract confessions and legal testimony played a key role in European judicial processes for hundreds of years. The ancient Greeks and Romans routinely tortured slaves. Later, the emergence of Roman-inspired public law in the twelfth century introduced complex civil procedures governing torture.[1] Torture techniques were intentionally gruesome; severe pain supposedly revealed truth.[2] Torture to obtain evidence in criminal investigations continued until its last vestiges were finally phased out on the continent between the mid-eighteenth and early nineteenth centuries.[3] In contrast, judicial torture was largely absent in England where common law rules of evidence did not require confessions. As William Blackstone explained, "trial by rack is utterly unknown to the law of England."[4] The Tower of London's infamous torturers operated according to royal prerogative rather than criminal procedure. The rack was an "engine of state, not of law."[5]

Torture was a common punishment for treason. For instance, the 1757 public torture and execution of Robert-Francois Damiens for regicide in France, painstakingly described in Michel Foucault's *Discipline and Punish*, points to a theatrical, didactic dimension of torture. Such practices "made the body of the condemned man the place where the vengeance of the sovereign was applied, the anchoring point for a manifestation of power, an opportunity of affirming the dissymmetry of forces."[6] Punitive spectacles of torture lasted until the nineteenth century, when they were replaced by the modern penal system.

Meanwhile, alongside judicial and state torture, canon law enacted its own torture protocol. In 1252, the Pope authorized torture of alleged heretics. The fifteenth- to eighteenth-century Spanish Inquisition increasingly relied on pain to extract confessions and recantations, preferring the *potro* (the rack), the *strappado* or *garrucha* (suspension), and the *toca*, more popularly known today as "waterboarding."[7] Contemporaneously, both Catholic and Protestant churches and states cooperated to identify and burn accused witches, mainly women. Witch hunts gained fervor in early modern Europe, especially in Germany. Torture was widespread and brutal, with detailed procedures documented in several demonology manuals.[8] These waves of religious persecution resulted in hundreds of thousands of deaths.

War created further opportunities for torture in Europe. Captured fighters were sometimes subject to various forms of punitive mutilation in detention. While torture was especially pervasive on all sides during the inter-religious battles of the eleventh- through thirteenth-century Crusades, it was also common in wars between Europeans throughout the Middle Ages. For instance, conflict between the English crown and Scottish, Welsh, and Irish rebels frequently included torture.[9]

Meanwhile, across the ocean, a distinct history was developing in what would become the United States. Although judicial torture never significantly took root in America, the Salem witchcraft trials of 1692–93 mark a limited reproduction of the European torture model. Torture practices were also inflicted on disgraced Puritans, who were branded with the letter marking their crime as punishment.[10]

This unpleasant history of torture confirms that for hundreds of years, torture formed a central component of legal culture in the West. With some national variation, torture was widely accepted as a legitimate means to divine truth and demonstrate political power. However, new philosophical ideas would eventually challenge the habitual use of torture, ushering in normative and legal limitations on this form of state violence.

Against Cruelty: The Emergence of Legal Prohibitions on Torture

During the eighteenth century, emerging Enlightenment thought progressively challenged the legitimacy of torture. Torture became characterized as uncivilized, irrational, and inhumane. In 1764, Cesare Beccaria argued in the highly influential *On Crimes and Punishments* that torture "is a sure route for the acquittal of robust ruffians and the conviction of weak innocents."[11] Voltaire concurred: "it is as absurd to inflict torture to acquire the knowledge of a crime, as it was formerly ridiculous to order a duel to decide the guilt of the accused party . . . a thousand fatal mistakes ought to induce legislators to put an end to this cruel practice."[12] These ideas helped change legal norms, leading to the eventual elimination of widespread state-sanctioned torture. In 1874, Victor Hugo declared that "torture has ceased to exist."[13]

Enlightenment ideals were especially important in shaping the American constitutional rights tradition. The Fifth Amendment to the US Constitution states that no one "shall be compelled in any criminal case to be a witness against himself, nor be deprived of life, liberty, or property, without due process of law"[14] and the Eighth Amendment that "[e]xcessive bail shall not be required, nor excessive fines imposed, nor cruel and unusual punishments inflicted."[15]

While acts of mob violence against loyalists were not uncommon in the revolutionary period, the American founding fathers rejected torture during the War of Independence. George Washington ordered the Continental army to treat Hessian and British soldiers "with humanity, and let them have no reason to Complain of our Copying the brutal example of the British" after the Battle of Princeton.[16] Later, during the Civil War, the *Instructions for the Government of Armies of the United States in the Field*, known as the Lieber Code, prohibited torture by Union forces.[17]

A substantial international anti-torture regime also emerged, which remains in effect today. The beginnings of international humanitarian law, which governs conduct in war, are found in the First Geneva Convention of 1864.[18] It was eventually followed by the Third Geneva Convention, which protects prisoners of war (POWs) in international armed conflicts from abuse. Common article 3 of the Geneva Conventions of 1949 reaffirmed the total prohibition on torture, stating in part: "Persons taking no active part in the hostilities, including members of armed forces who have laid down their arms and those placed 'hors de combat' by sickness, wounds, detention, or any other cause, shall in all circumstances be treated humanely" and that "violence to life and person, in particular murder of all kinds, mutilation, cruel treatment and torture . . . outrages upon personal dignity, in particular humiliating and degrading treatment" are forbidden.[19]

International human rights law, such as the 1948 Universal Declaration of Human Rights, the 1966 International Covenant on Civil and Political

Rights,[20] and the 1969 regional American Convention on Human Rights[21] clearly prohibit torture under all circumstances. The 1984 Convention against Torture and Other Cruel, Inhuman or Degrading Treatment or Punishment (CAT) later became the cornerstone of the international anti-torture regime.[22] Article 1 defines torture:

> For the purposes of this Convention, the term "torture" means any act by which se-vere pain or suffering, whether physical or mental, is intentionally inflicted on a person for such purposes as obtaining from him or a third person information or a confession, punishing him for an act he or a third person has committed or is suspected of having committed, or intimidating or coercing him or a third person, or for any reason based on discrimination of any kind, when such pain or suffering is inflicted by or at the instiga-tion of or with the consent or acquiescence of a public official or other person acting in an official capacity. It does not include pain or suffering arising only from, inherent in or incidental to lawful sanctions.

Article 2 clarifies: "No exceptional circumstances whatsoever, whether a state of war or a threat of war, internal political instability or any other public emergency, may be invoked as a justification of torture." Article 3 states: "No State Party shall expel, return ('*refouler*') or extradite a person to another State where there are substantial grounds for believing that he would be in danger of being subjected to torture." The Convention against Torture demands that state parties criminalize and prosecute torture within their jurisdiction and over their nationals and tasks the UN Committee against Torture with monitoring compliance.[23]

Article 16 of the Convention against Torture further prohibits "cruel, inhuman and degrading treatment": "Each State Party shall undertake to prevent in any territory under its jurisdiction other acts of cruel, in-human or degrading treatment or punishment which do not amount to torture as defined in article I, when such acts are committed by or at the instigation of or with the consent or acquiescence of a public official or other person acting in an official capacity." While the Convention against Torture doesn't clearly define cruel, inhuman, and degrading treatment, the Vienna Convention on the Law of Treaties, which provides guidelines for treaty interpretation, states: "A treaty shall be interpreted in good faith in accordance with the ordinary meaning to be given to the terms of the treaty in their context and in the light of its object and purpose."[24] Most re-cently, the 1998 Rome Statute of the International Criminal Court labels systematic torture and other inhumane acts as crimes against humanity and war crimes.[25]

Not only are there numerous legal treaties that forbid torture, the pro-hibition is widely considered to hold jus cogens or nonderogable status in international law alongside crimes such as slavery and genocide.[26] This is reflected in several universal jurisdiction cases that attempted to prosecute torture. Most notably, in *Pinochet No. 3* (1999), the British Law Lords nullified former Chilean dictator Augusto Pinochet's head of state immunity, permitting extradition proceedings to Spain for the international crime of torture.[27] While the case was eventually aborted due to Pinochet's failing health, it symbolized strong international opposition to torture and the growing willingness of states to enforce the torture prohibition beyond their sovereign borders.

Torture is also clearly prohibited in American law. The United States is party to the Geneva Conventions, International Covenant on Civil and Political Rights, and the Convention against Torture. Not only has it internalized these international rules, it has independently generated and institutionalized a robust anti-torture regime of its own. In addition to general constitutional protections, torture is banned in numerous statutes.

American military law has long prohibited torture. The Uniform Code of Military Justice, which covers military personnel and persons serving with or accompanying armed forces in the field in a time of war, states: "Any person subject to this chapter who is guilty of cruelty toward, or oppression or maltreatment of, any person subject to his orders shall be punished as a court-martial may direct."[28] Detainees must be given food, water, and prompt medical treatment.

While the United States ratified the Convention against Torture, the Senate's advice and consent interpreted the treaty so that " 'cruel, inhuman or degrading treatment or punishment' means the cruel, unusual and inhumane treatment or punishment prohibited by the Fifth, Eighth, and/or Fourteenth Amendments to the Constitution of the United States." The Senate further asserted:

> (1) (a) That with reference to Article 1, the United States understands that, in order to constitute torture, an act must be specifically intended to inflict severe physical or mental pain or suffering and that mental pain or suffering refers to prolonged mental harm caused by or resulting from: (1) the intentional infliction or threatened infliction of severe physical pain or suffering; (2) the administration or application, or threatened administration or application, of mind altering substances or other procedures calculated to disrupt profoundly the senses or the personality; (3) the threat of imminent death; or (4) the threat that another person will imminently be subjected to death, severe physical pain or suffering, or the administration or application of mind altering substances or other procedures calculated to disrupt profoundly the senses or personality.[29]

In 1994, the United States passed the Federal Anti-Torture Statute, which mirrors definitions in the Senate's advice and consent regarding the Convention against Torture while the 1996 War Crimes Act prohibits and makes punishable grave breaches of the Geneva Conventions when the victim or perpetrator is American.[30]

Private tort remedies also complement criminal law. For instance, the Torture Victim Protection Act supplements the 1789 Alien Tort Claims Act. It states: "An individual who, under actual or apparent authority, or color of law, of any foreign nation . . . subjects an individual to torture shall, in a civil action, be liable for damages to that individual."[31] In other words, torture victims can sue their torturers in US courts.

The torture prohibition is integrated into American immigration law. Well-founded fear of torture is grounds for claiming refugee status. Reaffirming the United States' position on torture, the State Department annually reviews the human rights practices of other countries, including torture practices, using the "internationally recognized individual, civil, political, and worker rights, as set forth in the Universal Declaration of Human Rights" as a guide.[32] The reports document torture and cruel, inhuman, and degrading treatment, frequently citing local and international NGO reports for evidence of abuse. The Torture Victims Relief Act provides funding for the medical treatment of torture victims from around the world while the United States Agency for International Development's Victims of Torture Program collaborates with NGOs and regional human rights bodies to rehabilitate and seek justice for torture victims. The United States is a donor to the UN Voluntary Fund for Victims of Torture.

Moving from normative condemnation to international treaties to the domestic institutionalization of anti-torture rules, torture was completely illegal in international and American law by the turn of the millennium. Yet despite these robust prohibitions, torture has stubbornly persisted around the world and in the United States. Legal proscription has not eliminated torture, even in liberal democracies that purport to respect human rights. As explained in chapters 1 and 2, I argue that changing legal cultures shape how authorities address tensions between human rights constraints and perceived national security imperatives. In the following sections, I review legal cultures of exception and secrecy before turning to the influence of the United States' post-9/11 culture of legal rationalization on patterns of American torture.

CULTURES OF EXCEPTION: SOUTHERN HORRORS AND COLONIAL FRONTIERS

Cultures of exception arise in response to normative and legal limits on state violence. Evidence of such cultures includes the creation of laws that legitimate otherwise proscribed behaviors, the suspension of normal legal rules, or the systemic failure to enforce the law. Cultures of exception are distinguished by their justificatory logics, which are often rooted in racism and other forms of bigotry, removing demonized and dehumanized populations from the protection of the law. In other cases, authorities invoke emergencies, particularly national security crises and war, to justify exceptional measures. Because cultures of exception legitimize human rights abuses, perpetrators enjoy impunity for crimes. Cultures of exception often traverse domestic and international politics and policy, encouraging exceptional violence both at home and abroad.

While Enlightenment human rights ideals helped forge American political ideology, they were notably absent in several areas of state practice for large swathes of American history. Most obviously, race-based chattel slavery was governed by parallel rules that allowed extensive abuse of African Americans. American lawmakers considered slaves property, not human beings entitled to emergent human rights protections. Deepening prohibitions on torture in Western legal culture in general and the nascent United States in particular therefore did not extend to enslaved people. Instead they were subject to a dehumanizing body of law, which formalized their exceptional lack of rights in slave codes.

The legitimacy of slave torture is apparent in early American legal texts. For instance, the colonial government of Virginia in 1705 forbade whipping "a christian white servant naked" without judicial permission but decreed that torturing a slave to death "shall not be accounted felony; but the master, owner, and every such other person so giving correction, shall be free and acquit of all punishment and accusation for the same, as if such incident had never happened."[33] 1723 legislation encoded additional atrocities, echoed in subsequent law throughout the South. For instance, slaves who gave false testimony were "to have one ear nailed to the pillory, and there to stand for the space of one hour, and then the said ear to be cut off; and thereafter, the other ear nailed in like manner, and cut off, at the expiration of one other hour; and moreover, to order every such offender thirty-nine lashes, well laid on, on his or her bare back, at the common whipping-post."[34]

Evolving slave codes sometimes prohibited excessive cruelty, relatively defined. However, these laws were rarely upheld throughout the antebellum South. Gratuitous violence against slaves was framed as a property crime, not human rights abuse.[35] For example, Henry Utz, a Louisiana overseer, tortured a runaway slave named Ginger Pop to death by "nailing the privates of Said negro to the bedstead and then inflicting blows upon him until Said negro pulled loose from the post to which he had been pinned by driving an iron tack or nail through his penis."[36] Despite ample evidence and witnesses, Utz was not only acquitted of criminal charges by a jury of his peers, he won back pay from the plantation owners who had fired him. While an 1856 appellate court ruling decided that Utz was justifiably terminated and should forfeit his wages for "revolting brutality" and "abuse of the plaintiffs [sic] property," it also declared that "we must acquit the defendant of homicide" and that "Ginger Pop is proved to have been a very vicious & worthless subject."[37] Whatever laws existed to protect slaves from torture on paper were entirely meaningless in practice.

In 1857, the infamous *Dred Scott v. Sandford* Supreme Court decision reaffirmed that African Americans were not citizens and were excluded from constitutional rights protections: "In the opinion of the court, the legislation and histories of the times, and the language used in the Declaration of Independence, show, that neither the class of persons who had been imported as slaves, nor their descendants, whether they had become free or not, were then acknowledged as a part of the people, nor intended to be included in the general words used in that memorable instrument."[38] The stability of the Southern plantation economy required that slaves be subject to perpetual terror. The racist legal culture of the time permissively tolerated and encouraged violence against blacks.

While slavery ended after the Civil War and the 1868 Fourteenth Amendment finally guaranteed African Americans equal protection under the law, state-sanctioned brutality persisted. As the hopes of Reconstruction faded throughout the South, the prevailing legal culture continued to resist extending rights. Systemic police and judicial racism created de facto impunity for extensive abuses. Most notably, lynchings were widespread in the late nineteenth- and early twentieth-century United States. Just as monarchs once tortured traitors to assert their power, these "Southern horrors" were public and disciplinary.[39] Torture functioned as part of a widespread terrorist campaign to "restore the balance of racial power to approximate pre-war conditions"[40] and to "shame a threatening 'other' into abject submission."[41]

The Ku Klux Klan (KKK) targeted men, women, and children, including whites who transgressed the color line. Violence often took the form of sexualized voyeuristic rituals including stripping, sexual posturing, bucking (in which a person was tied to a log for whipping), rape, rape in front of intimates, gang rape, child rape, genital torture and mutilation of men and women, tarring and feathering, skinning, burning, and hanging.[42] Such performative acts of "extra-lethal" violence allowed participants and onlookers to participate in an exciting "spectacle," pointing to the cultural acceptance and legitimacy of lynching.[43] Law enforcement did little to stop the atrocities—either because they sympathized with the perpetrators or because the KKK held sufficient power to immobilize local authorities. Police condoned and often participated in violence. As James Clarke explains,

"Since lynching enhanced the objectives of social control, and was not a punishable crime in the South, it flourished virtually unchecked by the law or community pressure."[44] The Equal Justice Initiative has documented 4,084 lynchings of African Americans between 1877 and 1950 in twelve Southern states and more than 300 lynchings in other states during this period.[45] These acts of torture and murder were not prosecuted as crimes, despite an otherwise functioning local justice system.

The racist legal culture that encouraged exceptional violence against African Americans also fueled impunity for torture in armed conflict. Although the Civil War-era Lieber Code remained in effect and eschewed torture, the United States' late nineteenth-century imperial expansion triggered exceptional justifications for torture against racialized others. Like the better-known cases of French colonial torture in Algeria[46] and British colonial torture in Kenya in the mid-twentieth century,[47] Americans used systemic torture against national liberation insurgents during the Philippine War (1899–1902).

Despite promising to bring "civilization," American troops and their local collaborators tortured and murdered prisoners, burned villages, and interned and killed civilians in their attempt to repress Philippine independence.[48] Long before waterboarding was employed in the global war on terror, Filipino prisoners were subject to the "water cure," whereby victims were pumped full of water, which was then forcefully expelled.[49] Torture was accompanied by racist characterizations of Filipino "niggers" as "barbaric," "savage," and prone to "Asiatic treachery."[50] A satirical song published in a contemporaneous soldier's newspaper sums up the scene:

Get the good old syringe boys and fill it to the brim
We've caught another nigger and we'll operate on him
Let someone take the handle who can work it with a vim
Shouting the battle cry of freedom

Hurrah, hurrah, we bring the jubilee
Hurrah, hurrah, the flag that makes him free
Shove in the nozel deep, and let him taste of liberty
Shouting the battle cry of freedom . . .[51]

Torture was widespread and well known up the chain of command. For General James Bell, "a short and severe war" was better than "a benevolent war indefinitely prolonged."[52] Major Edwin F. Glenn, a respected legal expert and notorious torture ringleader opined that "every man, woman, and child in the islands was an enemy, and . . . always will be."[53]

Eventually, American anti-imperialists pushed the US Senate's Committee on the Philippines to investigate abuses. The resulting exposure of atrocities proved scandalous, suggesting that public appetite for torture was more limited than in ardent imperialist circles. In response to recriminations, the McKinley administration attempted to minimize the extent of torture, placing blame on wayward soldiers and Filipino allies. Several officers were court-martialed for violations of the laws of war. Foreshadowing arguments that would appear in more organized fashion after 9/11, some claimed the water cure did not amount to torture. Punishments for those found guilty were exceedingly weak. For instance, despite being convicted of torture, Glenn received several promotions and ironically went on to author the military's *Rules of Land Warfare*.[54]

At the turn of the century, American legal culture evinced a hesitant tolerance for torture on the nation's colonial frontier. The imperialist military and political establishment did little to stop torture by American forces. Like the torture of African Americans at home, bigotry legitimized violence. However, this culture of exception was tempered by the United States' historical antipathy to military torture and growing anti-imperialist political sentiment. While torture occurred in several subsequent conflicts, the Philippine War was the most notable instance in which the United States systemically countenanced torture.[55] In future wars, Americans would prove increasingly concerned with legal restrictions on torture.

These brief snapshots highlight how legal cultures of exception justify torture. Notwithstanding Enlightenment values and the progressively layered constitutional, human rights, and humanitarian legal regimes prohibiting torture, American authorities permitted torture against dehumanized others, eroding the constraining capacity of law. While racism is not the only logic of exception, it is a powerful and pervasive one that echoes through history.

CULTURES OF SECRECY: COVERT AND PROXY TORTURE

Like cultures of exception, cultures of secrecy emerge in response to normative and legal constraints. However, they reflect more limited tolerance for overtly exceptional justifications for unlawful actions. In cultures of secrecy, human rights abuses are not codified in law or celebrated in public. Instead, they are conducted through clandestine and covert means. Public authorities must work harder to deny wrongdoing and hide evidence of crimes than they do in cultures of exception. Accordingly, cultures of secrecy are characterized by official lying and cover-ups. They generally become evident once journalists or other investigators expose wrongdoing, resulting in scandal.

In the United States, controversies over atrocities in the Philippines portended growing distaste for exceptional violence, which would deepen in the subsequent decades. In the aftermath of the horrors of the Second World War, Americans championed the Nuremberg Tribunals and Universal Declaration of Human Rights. The expanding architecture of international law provided a powerful new vocabulary for human rights advocates. The emerging Cold War cast American liberal values against Communist oppression. Meanwhile, the civil rights movement gained increasing momentum at home, forcing the United States to reckon with the injustice and cruelty of white supremacy.

The growing hegemony and institutionalization of international human rights principles did not end torture. However, it did limit the public legitimacy of torture, forcing human rights abuses into the shadows. As the Cold War accelerated, the United States increasingly favored proxy wars that deflected responsibility for unsavory practices. While condemning Soviet abuses, the United States tolerated and actively supported allies who engaged in extensive torture while American intelligence agencies also engineered their own clandestine torture operations. These patterns of secrecy evince awareness of the distinction between legality and illegality, as well as the risk of sanction, embarrassment, and blowback that could result from the latter.

The United States' Cold War intelligence operations are indelibly tied to the doctrine of plausible deniability, often via covert action. As outlined in historical US national security documents, covert action denies agency. For instance, NSC 1012 explained that covert operations should be "so planned and executed that any U.S. Government responsibility for them is not evident to unauthorized persons and that if uncovered the U.S. Government can plausibly disclaim any responsibility for them."[56] US law defines covert action as "an activity or activities of the United States Government to influence political, economic, or military conditions abroad, where it is intended that the role of the [government] will not be apparent or acknowledged publicly."[57]

For much of the Cold War, American authorities pursued plausible deniability for human rights abuses. For security hawks, morality lost out to political necessity. Exceptional logics were thus embedded within a broader culture of secrecy. As the classified 1954 Doolittle Report put it, the Soviet Union was an "implacable enemy whose avowed objective is world domination by whatever means and at whatever cost. There are no rules in such a game. Hitherto acceptable norms of human conduct do not apply." Accordingly, it argued, "If the United States is to survive, long-standing American concepts of 'fair play' must be reconsidered," and "no one should be permitted to stand in the way" of the "fundamentally repugnant philosophy" of ruthless covert action.[58]

Avoiding Soviet retaliation, conflict escalation, and counterespionage were pragmatic motives for secrecy. But Americans also proved sensitive to their image and reputation. "Backfire," Secretary of State William Rogers told Henry Kissinger in the context of anti-Allende efforts in Chile, implied *"getting caught* doing something. After all we have said about elections, if the first time a Communist wins the U.S. tries to prevent the constitutional process from coming into play *we will look very bad*."[59] Through omission and commission, plausible deniability facilitated intelligence activities that violated other countries' sovereignty, promoted antidemocratic forces, engaged in paramilitary violence, or were implicated in illegal, immoral, or hypocritical behaviors.

American covert policy took many forms over the years. The CIA secretly manipulated elections and distributed propaganda in postwar Europe.[60] They backed coup attempts in Iran, Guatemala, Indonesia, Vietnam, Cuba, Congo, Chile, Greece, and Pakistan.[61] Assassination plots targeted Fidel Castro, Rafael Trujillo, and Patrice Lumumba.[62] As characterized by the ground-breaking Church Committee reports of the mid-1970s: "Previous excesses of drug testing, assassination planning, and domestic activities were supported by an internal structure that permitted individuals to conduct operations *without the consistent necessity or expectation of justifying or revealing their activities*."[63] Secrecy helped create an atmosphere of amoral impunity.

Many of these activities involved torture. Torture was common in Cold War conflicts waged in Central America, southern Africa, southeast Asia, and Afghanistan, where Americans oversaw, colluded with, and failed to prevent torture by their proxy allies. For example, the United States Agency for International Development's Office of Public Safety trained police in harsh interrogation in dozens of countries through the 1960s, focusing increasingly on South Vietnam. As the war intensified, the CIA-run Phoenix Program aimed to rout the elusive National Liberation Front, or Viet Cong. Provincial Reconnaissance Units brought prisoners to Provincial Interrogation Centers where torture was ubiquitous.[64] In 1967, police, military, and counterinsurgent units were coordinated into a "centralized pacification bureaucracy," Civil Operations and Rural Development Support. Phoenix increasingly relied on assassination and torture. By 1972, Phoenix operatives had "neutralized" 81,740 suspected guerillas, killing 26,369.[65]

Despite army instructions to "always treat your prisoner humanely,"[66] American military torture also occurred in Vietnam. In 1967, Master Sergeant Donald Duncan testified to the International War Crimes Tribunal (a nonlegal investigation led by philosophers Bertrand Russell and Jean-Paul Sartre) that the US Army Special Warfare School at Fort Bragg, North Carolina implicitly encouraged torture while publically disavowing it. The guerilla warfare curriculum covered "the NKVD manual, the manual used by the secret police in Russia, where are detailed quite specifically any number of methods of torture." Duncan went on to explain:

> This is a very highly classified class.... Other methods, of course, are discussed beyond the NKVD manual, but again, you know, it's always the other person supposed to be doing it. Now there's a very important reason for this—why they have to be so careful even in their own classrooms .... They are very conscious, first of all, of the *Rules of Land Warfare*. And very conscious that they can be brought to task for these things. So they bend over backwards to at least give the outward appearance of legality and adherence to ... the laws of land warfare .... They were not trying to justify it .... But in fact it was presented in such a way that it left no doubt in anybody's mind that, if you need the information, these are other methods and you certainly can use them. ... For the official record, if somebody said: 'You're teaching methods of torture,' they say, 'No, no, no, no, all we're teaching is what the enemy does.' Again, it's for the official record. There's no doubt left in the student's minds.[67]

Duncan sums up the evasive approach to torture training as "we cannot teach you that because the mothers of America would not approve."

The same racism and frustration with irregular warfare that had fueled torture in the Philippines decades earlier motivated American troops in Vietnam. While never official policy, torture spread horizontally, creating an "underground subculture of military interrogators who shared techniques tolerated and shielded by midlevel commanders."[68] Electric torture using field telephones was common. As a veteran of the Ninth Military Police Company of the Ninth Infantry Division stationed at Dong Tam recounted: "We would pretty much do anything as long as we didn't leave scars on the people." Another veteran recalled: "It was Military Intelligence [MI] that done it, them and the ARVNs [the Army of the Republic of Vietnam]. The ARVNs are the ones that hooked the wire up and did the cranking, but it was with the blessing of the MI .... They didn't want anybody else to see it ... we would keep our mouth shut."[69] Jon Burge, who went on to torture numerous African Americans using similar methods as a police officer in Chicago, also worked for the Ninth Military Police Company in Vietnam.[70]

When crimes risked exposure, cover ups mounted. In 1968, American soldiers murdered hundreds of women, children, and elderly Vietnamese villagers during the My Lai massacre. The army initially denied the incident. As noted by the Peers Inquiry: "It is evident that efforts to suppress and withhold information concerning the Son My incident were made at every level .... If there had been real concern in the chain of command, if anyone had taken action to ask questions, they would have had full and complete answers."[71] The report further notes the destruction of records and documents to conceal wrongdoing. While whistleblowers and aggressive investigative reporting did succeed in publicizing the massacre, subsequent criminal sentences were limited.

In this culture of secrecy, American officials primarily sought to deny and hide rather than justify atrocities. For instance, after Lieutenant Colonel Anthony B. Herbert, a highly decorated officer, denounced torture and murder by the 173rd Airborne Brigade, he was suddenly relieved of his command. The army aggressively sought out discrepancies in his account. "This package . . . provides sufficient material to impeach this man's credibility; should this need arise, I volunteer for the task," declared the commander of the army's Criminal Investigation Division.[72] The 1971 Winter Soldier Investigation, a public media event organized by Vietnam Veterans Against the War, produced further testimony of war crimes.[73] As the Pentagon pushed to win the war through body counts, horrendous violence against Vietnamese civilians remained common, not aberrant.

During and after the Vietnam War, the United States provided extensive financial and political support for dictatorial allies throughout Latin America. In some cases, Americans directly aided torture, applying lessons learned in Vietnam to Project X, a comprehensive exportable training program. According to the Pentagon, one manual "provided training regarding use of sodiopentathol compound in interrogation, abduction of adversary family members to influence the adversary, prioritization of adversary personalities for abduction, exile, physical beatings and execution."[74] Throughout the 1960s, the CIA trained Brazilians in using field telephones for electric torture.[75] It shipped electric needles used for torture to Uruguay.[76] Dan Mitrione, head of the American Office of Public Safety in Montevideo, advised on torture techniques, a fact that became widely publicized after he was kidnapped by Tupamaro guerillas.[77]

Several torture manuals were used by Project X, distributed by advisors on the ground and via officer training at places like the School of the Americas (SOA) at Fort Benning, Georgia.[78] The 1963 KUBARK Counterintelligence Training Manual (KUBARK was the CIA's codename for itself) is best known. The manual evinces constant awareness of the legal problems that might result from the exposure of torture:

> Interrogations conducted under compulsion or duress are especially likely to involve illegality and to entail damaging consequences for KUBARK. Therefore prior Headquarters approval at the KUDOVE level must be obtained for the interrogation of any source against his will and under any of the following circumstances:
>
> 1. If bodily harm is to be inflicted.
>
> 2. If medical, chemical, or electrical methods or materials are to be used to induce acquiescence.[79]

The manual goes on to explain the most efficacious techniques: "The following are the principal coercive techniques of interrogation: arrest, detention, deprivation of sensory stimuli through solitary confinement or similar methods, threats and fear, debility, pain, heightened suggestibility and hypnosis, narcosis, and induced regression."[80] To detect feigned illness and malingering, KUBARK recommends threatening electric shock treatment and frontal lobotomy.[81]

The KUBARK Manual's preoccupation with concepts such as "regression" and "self-induced pain" reflected decades of CIA experimentation. Americans were alarmed as zombie-like prisoners confessed in Stalinist show trials. They became increasingly concerned with the psychology of torture when robotic American POWs appeared on television during the Korean War. To uncover the secrets of mind control, the CIA launched a secret program that combined outlandish experiments with hallucinogenic drugs in the early 1950s along with more standard psychological research until 1963.[82] Early investigations were consolidated under the secret MKUltra program, run by the macabre character Sidney Gottlieb, whose other interests included assassination methods.[83]

MKUltra's experimental projects included the administration of LSD to unsuspecting subjects.[84] The CIA built on pioneering experiments into the effect of sensory deprivation by McGill University researchers Donald Hebb and Eugene Cameron. It further utilized the findings of prominent American behavioral scientists who worked under direct and indirect CIA and other government contracts and "advised the agency about the role of self-inflicted pain in Communist interrogation."[85] Instead of interrogators inflicting direct violence, which often spurred resistance from victims, this approach to torture leveraged the psychological damage wrought by extreme isolation, exhaustion, and confinement. CIA research frequently violated the rights and dignity of its subjects, many of whom were "undesirables": mental patients, foreigners, drug addicts, and prisoners.[86] The cumulative result was a new paradigm of psychological torture that eschewed obvious physical torture in favor of the methods advocated by KUBARK, methods that would reappear in the global war on terror.[87]

Despite the post-Church Committee creation of new House and Senate intelligence oversight committees in the 1970s, many problematic CIA practices persisted. Throughout the 1980s, the agency actively supported and empowered violent Islamist extremists against the Soviets in Afghanistan. Returning to the Americas, security officials reformulated the KUBARK Manual as the 1983 Human Resource Exploitation Manual to aid the Central American Contras, who were notorious for torture and indiscriminate killing.[88] In 1986, the Iran-Contra scandal revealed an illegal plot by members of President Ronald Reagan's National Security Council to sell arms to Iran and funnel payments to the Contras. While plausible deniability helped save the president from disgrace, the episode resulted in extensive investigations and multiple indictments.

By the 1990s, American alliances with human rights abusers were subject to mounting condemnation. Human rights campaigns such as SOA Watch, launched in response to revelations that SOA-trained operatives were implicated in the 1981 El Mozote massacre in El Salvador, were increasingly successful. A 1992 Defense Department report deemed objectionable seven Spanish-language training manuals distributed between 1987 and 1991.[89] In the mid-1990s, American lawyer Jennifer Harbury exposed a widespread terror campaign by SOA-trained, CIA-paid Guatemalan officers after her husband, a Mayan activist, was captured, brutally tortured, and murdered.[90] By 2001, SOA was compelled to rebrand itself as the Western Hemisphere Institute for Security Cooperation and offer an improved human rights curriculum.[91]

Throughout the Cold War, the United States never publically endorsed or advocated torture. On the contrary, American political narratives contrasted liberal democratic values with Soviet despotism and repression. However, the United States often failed to realize its rhetorical embrace of human rights in practice. Rather, where strategic calculations demanded torture or alliances with torturers, abusive behavior was driven underground. American Cold War national security legal culture promoted human rights principles in public while tolerating abuses carried out in secret by military and intelligence agents or foreign proxies. This trend persisted until growing human rights criticism, leaking, and investigative journalism reduced the viability of plausible deniability and increased public awareness of questionable activities.

CULTURES OF LEGAL RATIONALIZATION: 9/11 AND
THE REDEFINITION OF TORTURE

The institutionalization of international human rights law, the growth of accountability mechanisms, and the end of the Cold War meant that by the 1990s, torture was largely obsolete in American security practice. Bracketing police brutality cases and ongoing problems in the penal system, the United States did not employ torture for political, military, or intelligence purposes at the turn of the millennium. Certainly, it maintained close relationships with many states known to torture, but it began to press more strongly for improved human rights standards.

The 9/11 attacks triggered new demand for torture. For the first time since Pearl Harbor, the United States was directly attacked. The public was fearful and angry. Security officials were desperate to prevent further strikes. The Bush administration's hawkish predilection for military aggressiveness and executive power,[92] American inexperience with direct intelligence interrogation and detention in the post-Vietnam era, and the frustratingly asymmetrical, amorphous nature of al-Qaeda created a ripe environment for the growth of abusive practices. As a consequence, detainees at Guantánamo Bay, Abu Ghraib, Iraqi and Afghan prisons, and CIA "black sites" were subject to systemic, officially authorized torture.

While torture was far from unprecedented in American history, a national security culture of legal rationalization shaped torture policy in the global war on terror in distinctive ways. Seeking legal cover, policymakers and their lawyers redefined law and torture to construct the plausible legality of enhanced interrogation techniques. As a strategy, plausible legality aimed to foreclose political condemnation and legal prosecution for what would otherwise be illegal practices. It used legal language and legalistic argumentation to justify human rights abuses within existing legal frameworks by selectively interpreting legal rules and manipulating legal concepts. In doing so, it protected policymakers and security agents from legal jeopardy.

None of this is to say that the Bush administration's legal rationalization of torture was plausible in an objective sense. It was subject to intense criticism and pushback by human rights advocates and courts. Photographic evidence undermined its euphemistic discourse. Nonetheless, plausible legality proved an effective exculpatory strategy for post-9/11 American security and intelligence officials, who continue to enjoy impunity for torture.

Echoes of Exception and Secrecy

Before discussing novel aspects of the United States' contemporary national security culture of legal rationalization, it is important to acknowledge the traces of exception and secrecy that run through counterterrorism practice. After 9/11, President Bush declared his intent to "rid the world of the evildoers."[93] Pundits, academics,[94] and even television shows such as Fox's *24* fueled support for torture with "ticking bomb" scenarios.[95] For critics, this emergent atmosphere evinced "historical echoes" of fascism.[96] Others drew parallels between Nazi jurists and Bush administration lawyers,[97] arguing that American policy cast detainees into a lawless void akin to a Schmittian state of exception.[98] While there is some validity to this view, I suggest that it is empirically and theoretically problematic. As I document throughout the remainder of this chapter, neither the Bush administration nor that of his successor, Barack Obama, were eager to overtly justify illegal human rights abuses.[99]

There are also similarities to and differences from legal cultures of secrecy. Undoubtedly, covert operations to influence political outcomes around the world continue today. More importantly, counterterrorism activities have increasingly come to resemble covert action, blurring the line between intelligence and paramilitary activities.[100] As Vice President Dick Cheney explained in language invoking earlier eras:

> We also have to work, though, sort of the dark side, if you will. We've got to spend time in the shadows in the intelligence world. A lot of what needs to be done here will have to be done quietly, without any discussion, using sources and methods that are available to our intelligence agencies, if we're going to be successful. That's the world these folks operate in, and so it's going to be vital for us to use any means at our disposal, basically, to achieve our objective.[101]

According to Jane Mayer, Cheney closely studied the Vietnam Phoenix Program as a model.[102]

Notable post-9/11 versions of the "repugnant philosophy" of covert action included the practice of extraordinary rendition, which outsourced brutal torture of alleged terrorists to proxies during the early years of the global war on terror.[103] Victims were captured or kidnapped and put on secret CIA flights to countries well known to torture. In numerous cases, European states facilitated rendition flights.[104] Secrecy was key for all parties. The United States could not justify blatant torture, cooperating European states could not admit their complicity, and receiving Muslim countries feared the political consequences of close cooperation with America.

American officials have attempted to cover up evidence of torture at various points. The CIA destroyed videotapes that documented the reality of waterboarding.[105] At Camp Nama in Iraq, Mayer reports, the walls "were posted with placards warning against leaving marks on the detainees, with the motto 'No Blood, No Foul.'"[106] Without the photographic evidence that emerged at Abu Ghraib, it would have been nearly impossible to establish the extent of abuses.

The Bush administration attempted to limit inquiries into counterterrorism policy. It overclassified and reclassified documents, denied access to critical journalists, and punished leakers.[107] While President Obama increased openness by declassifying several important memos and investigative reports, secrecy persisted throughout his administration.

For example, he reversed his earlier decision to make more Abu Ghraib photographs publically available.[108] The Obama administration repeatedly invoked the "state secrets privilege," which allows the executive to exclude evidence from legal cases on national security grounds. It stalled the declassification of the Senate Select Committee on Intelligence's unflattering 6,700-page investigation into post-9/11 CIA torture, dragging its heels under pressure from the intelligence community and reportedly attempting to redact the document beyond comprehension.[109] Completed in September 2012, the report's executive summary was finally released in December 2014, although the complete version remains classified.[110]

Despite these patterns of secrecy, public scrutiny has proved inevitable. As James Olson notes: "The U.S. intelligence community has been under a magnifying glass: second-guessed at every turn, criticized in Congress, and lambasted in the press. Long gone are the days when American spies could do whatever they needed to do 'quietly, without any discussion.'"[111] Journalists and human rights investigators have revealed an extraordinary amount of information about torture practices. "I knew that an interrogation program this sensitive and controversial would one day become public," notes President Bush in his memoir.[112] Indeed, the details of enhanced interrogation techniques, including waterboarding, were publically available long before President Obama's April 2009 declassification of the prior administration's legal memoranda.

The Bush administration's embrace of extensive executive powers, including its authorization of torture, points to exceptional legal logics, and both the Bush and Obama administrations sought to minimize oversight. However, neither exception nor secrecy is a wholly effective means of facilitating human rights violations in contemporary American politics. These logics of rule evasion are out of sync with predominant legal culture, which relies on legal rationalization to justify human rights abuses.

Constructing a Golden Shield

Despite echoes of exception and secrecy, I argue that post-9/11 American security practice was shaped primarily by a culture of legal rationalization. Demand for legal rationalization emerges in contexts where compliance with rule of law is an important standard of political legitimacy, universal human rights principles enjoy normative hegemony, independent institutions can sanction law breaking, and security policy is subject to high levels of political and social monitoring.

In cultures of legal rationalization, policymakers seek legal cover. Law is neither suspended nor simply ignored. Rather, authorities task national security lawyers with constructing the plausible legality of controversial practices. As Jack Goldsmith suggests, lawyers were heavily involved in post-9/11 counterterrorism because "war itself was encumbered with legal restrictions as never before. Everywhere decision makers turned they collided with confining laws that required a lawyer's interpretation and—in order to avoid legal liability—a lawyer's sign-off."[113] He attributes this to three Washington pathologies: "the criminalization of warfare, the blame game, and the cover-your-ass syndrome . . . . Everyone wants cover."[114] Plausible legality thus combines desire to break with existing norms found in cultures of exception with awareness of reputational and legal risks found in cultures of secrecy. It attempts to legalize the exception without publically suspending the existing order, to permit the impermissible without fully admitting the move.

In the global war on terror, the Office of Legal Counsel (OLC), at the Department of Justice, which provides legal advice to the executive branch, anchored the production of plausibly legal arguments. OLC lawyers' numerous analyses, most infamously the August 1, 2002 torture memos, played a key role in constructing policy. Notwithstanding their often wildly permissive conclusions, these opinions claimed conformity with American obligations under both international and domestic law and previous precedent.[115] The memos became the CIA's "golden shield."[116] As former CIA counsel John Rizzo explains, they provided "legal cover." They were something "we could keep, and wave around if necessary, in the months and years to come . . . eventually and inevitably, there would be those . . . who would charge that the EITs [enhanced interrogation techniques] were not only barbaric but lapsed into criminality. An OLC legal memorandum . . . would protect the Agency and its people for evermore. It would be as good as gold."[117]

The Torture Memos

The torture memos provide voluminous evidence of American authorities' attempt to construct the plausible legality of various abusive interrogation techniques. Because law serves as a *permissive constraint* in cultures of legal rationalization and not simply as a permit, torture practices could not be justified by the legal logic of exception alone. However, the universal, nonderogable nature of the torture prohibition makes torture difficult to legalize within the framework of extant law. Lawyers therefore had to engage in extensive interpretive manipulation and maneuvering in order to rationalize torture.

On September 17, 2001, President Bush signed a covert action memorandum of notification authorizing CIA Director George Tenet to initiate a global campaign to capture and detain suspected terrorists.[118] However, the CIA was poorly prepared to hold prisoners. Throughout the following months, numerous questions emerged about what rules should govern detentions. In early 2002, the National Security Council Principals Committee debated whether al-Qaeda and Taliban fighters were eligible for Geneva Conventions protections, such as POW status or treatment according to common article 3 standards. In a January 9, 2002 OLC memo, Deputy Assistant Attorney General John Yoo and special counsel Robert Delahunty argued that because Afghanistan was a failed state, the Geneva Conventions did not apply there. Moreover, because terrorists were not state parties to the Geneva Conventions and broke the laws of war, they were not covered.[119]

In a January 25, 2002 memo, White House counsel Alberto Gonzales noted that rejecting the Conventions "substantially reduces the threat of domestic criminal prosecution under the War Crimes Act."[120] In a February 1, 2002 letter, Attorney General John Ashcroft argued that "a Presidential determination against treaty applicability would provide the highest assurance that no court would subsequently entertain charges that American military officers, intelligence officials, or law enforcement officials violated Geneva Convention rules relating to field conduct, detention conduct or interrogation of detainees."[121] Several officials, including State Department legal advisor William Taft[122] and Secretary of State Colin Powell, voiced opposition to these arguments.[123] Despite their protests, President Bush issued a February 7, 2002 decision declaring the nonapplicability of the Geneva Conventions to the emerging global war on terror, while promising humane treatment as a matter of policy.[124] In addition to rejecting the Geneva framework, the administration claimed that other laws did not apply: constitutional protections were limited to the sovereign territory of the United States; the Uniform Code of Military Justice did not cover the CIA; and only international humanitarian law, not international human rights treaties, were relevant to conduct in war. Yet despite these assertions, authorities were clearly cognizant of limitations on legal interrogation. In particular, they were keenly aware that international and American law prohibited torture.

In March 2002, suspected al-Qaeda ringleader Abu Zubaydah was captured in Pakistan. In anticipation of his interrogation, the CIA sought to develop an interrogation protocol. To do so, they eschewed experienced FBI and military interrogators, relying instead on advice from two psychologists, James Mitchell and John "Bruce" Jessen. Mitchell and Jessen had worked with the military's Survival, Evasion, Resistance, and Escape (SERE) program, part of the Joint Personnel Recovery Agency, which trained American soldiers to withstand interrogation. The psychologists recommended interrogation methods that would induce "learned helplessness." Despite the fact that neither "had experience as an interrogator, nor did either have specialized knowledge of al Qa'ida, a background in terrorism, or any relevant regional, cultural, or linguistic expertise,"[125] they met several times with administration officials and continued to advise, construct, and even conduct interrogations throughout 2002. They eventually formed a private corporation, which would garner $81 million in CIA contracts.[126] Several torture victims sued Mitchell and Jessen under the Alien Tort Statute for their role in orchestrating the program, settling for an undisclosed sum in August 2017.[127]

In July 2002, the CIA proposed escalating Abu Zubaydah's interrogation. Toward this end, Mitchell and Jessen suggested twelve SERE-inspired coercive techniques: (1) the attention grasp, (2) walling, (3) facial hold, (4) facial slap, (5) cramped confinement, (6) wall standing, (7) stress positions, (8) sleep deprivation, (9) waterboard, (10) use of diapers, (11) use of insects, and (12) mock burial.[128] CIA Acting General Counsel Rizzo met with National Security Council and Department of Justice lawyers to assess the legality of the techniques. National Security Advisor Condoleezza Rice and her deputy, Stephen Hadley, asked the CIA to provide additional information to the Department of Justice before a decision was rendered. Zubaydah's CIA interrogators contemporaneously requested assurances that he would "remain in isolation and incommunicado for the remainder of his life."[129] Moreover, they requested legal approval before deploying the waterboard. Between July 24 and July 26, 2002, the attorney general provided verbal authorization for all methods except mock burial.[130]

Legal rationalizations for enhanced interrogation techniques were formalized in two August 1, 2002 OLC memos largely written by Yoo and signed by Assistant Attorney General Jay Bybee.[131] The first torture memo, Bybee I, notoriously argued that torture "must be equivalent in intensity to the pain accompanying serious physical injury, such as organ failure, impairment of bodily function, or even death."[132] It went on to explore how a necessity defense might immunize interrogators from legal prosecution. More telling is the second memo, Bybee II. Building on Bybee I's broad evaluation of what constitutes "severe physical or mental pain or suffering," it examines eleven proposed techniques in detail, ultimately determining that none constituted the illegal crime of torture as defined by the Convention against Torture and the Federal Anti-Torture Statute.

Without citing any rationale, Bybee II opined that "any pain associated with muscle fatigue is not of the intensity sufficient to amount to 'severe physical pain or suffering' under the statute, nor, despite its discomfort, can it be said to be difficult to endure."[133] Neither confinement in a box nor sleep deprivation were thought to do so either. "Even those techniques that involve physical contact between the interrogator and the individual do not result in severe pain."[134] As to waterboarding, it stated, "the procedure does not inflict actual physical harm. Thus, although the subject may experience the fear or panic associated with the feeling of drowning, the waterboard does not inflict physical pain."[135] Rather, "[t]he waterboard is simply a controlled acute episode, lacking the connotation of a protracted period of time generally given to suffering."[136] Assuming an absence of undefined "substantial repetition," the memo declared: "Even when all of these methods are considered combined in an overall course of conduct, they would still not inflict severe physical pain and suffering."[137]

As to mental pain and suffering, the memo concluded that "it is plain that none of these procedures involves a threat to any third party, the use of any kind of drugs, or for the reasons described above, the infliction of severe physical pain."[138] Thus the legal question hangs on whether the conduct "constitutes a threat of severe physical pain or suffering, a procedure designed to disrupt profoundly the senses, or a threat of imminent death"[139]—assuming that the subject is a "reasonable person." No threats, concluded the memo, can be inferred from the actions themselves—"the type of actions that could be reasonably anticipated would still fall below anything sufficient to inflict severe physical pain or suffering."[140]

In a characteristic twist of logic, the memo argued that although the waterboard "constitutes a threat of imminent death," this is not severe mental pain and suffering because "based on your research into the use of these methods at the SERE school and consultation with others with expertise in the field of psychology and interrogation, you do not anticipate that any prolonged mental harm would result from the use of the waterboard."[141] The same rationale applied to the use of the techniques in an escalating fashion. Even if they were reasonably inferred to constitute a threat of severe physical pain or death, no prolonged mental harm is anticipated. If no severe physical or mental pain or suffering or prolonged mental harm is anticipated in good faith, there is no crime: "Because specific intent is an element of the offense, the absence of specific intent negates the charge of torture."[142]

In a particularly convoluted passage referring to the introduction of an insect into a confinement box, the direct advisory role of the memos in shaping and guiding interrogation practices becomes clear:

> As we understand it, you plan to inform Zubaydah that you are going to place a stinging insect into the box, but you will actually place a harmless insect in the box, such as a caterpillar. If you do so, to ensure that you are outside the predicate act requirement, you must inform him that the insects will not have a sting that would produce death or severe pain. If, however, you were to place the insect in the box without informing him that you are doing so, then, in order to not commit a predicate act, you should not affirmatively

lead him to believe that any insect is present which has a sting that could produce severe pain or suffering or even cause his death.[143]

This was not detached analysis; it was specific advice.

Interestingly, lawyers did evince awareness that certain methods might amount to cruel, inhuman, and degrading treatment.[144] However, Bybee I argued that the Convention against Torture requires criminal penalties for torture alone, indicating that it is a graver offense.[145] Moreover, the executive branch had long held that only "the most extreme acts" constitute torture.[146] Ultimately, there was just one proposed interrogation technique that the OLC refused to authorize. "[S]everal days prior to the issuance of the OLC memo of August 1, 2002," testified Rizzo, Yoo "called me to say that they were having, I believe he said a difficulty getting there, in terms of the torture statute on mock burial."[147] The CIA sought a declination of prosecution (i.e., a promise not to prosecute) from the Department of Justice for unapproved interrogation methods, which it refused to grant. "I was just asking because I wanted to secure maximum legal protection for the agency, in any feasible and legitimate form," explained Rizzo.[148]

In authorizing enhanced interrogation techniques, the torture memos frequently invoked their own set of covers to enhance their legitimacy and shield lawyers from accusations of bad faith. For instance, they cite the medical opinions of on-site doctors and psychologists associated with the CIA's Office of Medical Services. While the Office of Medical Services informed the CIA inspector general that its approval of techniques was exaggerated,[149] the plausible legality of enhanced interrogation techniques relied on highly questionable medical monitoring and assessments. Disturbing revelations that detainees were subject to "rectal feeding" and "rectal rehydration," humiliating and painful practices with no genuine medical purpose, further compound concerns that medical personnel behaved unethically.[150] Physicians for Human Rights argues that medical staff engaged in "human experimentation" that not only helped legitimize abuses but also actively sought to improve their effectiveness.[151] Debates over acceptable medical protocols have continued in recent years with the force-feeding of hunger-striking prisoners at Guantánamo Bay, a practice characterized by many as gratuitously painful and punitive.[152]

Notwithstanding their advocacy of executive prerogative and declaration of the nonapplicability of the Geneva Conventions, Bush administration lawyers remained aware that torture is universally prohibited, placing policymakers and interrogators in potential legal jeopardy. While hypothesizing necessity defenses for torture, OLC opinions asserted that enhanced interrogation techniques did not meet the legal definition of torture in international or American law. These findings shaped American interrogation practice throughout the global war on terror.

Torture in the Global War on Terror

There is clear and substantial evidence that post-9/11 American torture techniques directly reflected the torture memos. By reinterpreting the torture prohibition, these legal authorizations undermined legal constraint, giving a green light to numerous abusive practices.

Not surprisingly, Abu Zubaydah was subjected to the techniques outlined in the torture memos. He was held for months at a CIA black site in Thailand. The Senate Select Committee on Intelligence documents the "aggressive phase" of his interrogation, which began shortly after the OLC authorizations were issued:

> The use of the CIA's enhanced interrogation techniques—including "walling, attention grasps, slapping, facial hold, stress positions, cramped confinement, white noise and sleep deprivation"—continued in "varying combinations, 24 hours a day" for 17 straight days, through August 20, 2002. When Abu Zubaydah was left alone during this period, he was placed in a stress position, left on the waterboard with a cloth over his face, or locked in one of two confinement boxes.... Abu Zubaydah was also subjected to the waterboard "2–4 times a day ... with multiple iterations of the watering cycle during each application." ... Over the course of the entire 20 day "aggressive phase of interrogation," Abu Zubaydah spent a total of 266 hours (11 days, 2 hours) in the large (coffin size) confinement box and hours in a small confinement box, which had a width of 21 inches, a depth of 2.5 feet, and a height of 2.5 feet. The CIA interrogators told Abu Zubaydah that the only way he would leave the facility was in the coffin-shaped confinement box.[153]

A 2007 investigation by the International Committee of the Red Cross (ICRC) into the treatment of fourteen "high value" detainees suggests that the same methods were applied to others. According to the report, continuous solitary confinement, incommunicado detention, prolonged use of stress positions, forced nudity, forced shaving, diapering, walling, slapping, kicking, punching, extensive sleep deprivation, exposure to cold temperatures and loud noises, confinement in a box, prolonged shackling, denial of solid food, dousing with cold water, and waterboarding were experienced by various detainees, sometimes constantly for months at a time.[154] The Senate Select Committee on Intelligence identifies 119 known individuals held in CIA custody at multiple secret detention sites around the world.[155] In 2002, Gul Rahman died of hypothermia after being shackled partially naked to a freezing concrete floor.[156] In 2003, Khalid

Shaykh Muhammad was waterboarded 183 times. He was subsequently kept awake for seven and a half days straight.[157]

Enhanced interrogation techniques had overt OLC approval. However, interrogators went beyond authorized practices in several instances, employing threats, mock executions, and various forms of unapproved physical abuse. "Agency personnel reported a range of improvised actions that interrogators and debriefers reportedly used at that time to assist in obtaining information from detainees."[158] In addition to poor training, the permissive atmosphere created by the torture memos contributed to this state of affairs. Because the line between OLC-authorized techniques such as waterboarding, walling, and stress shackling and illegal torture is not legally or morally intuitive, it is not surprising that guidelines were transgressed.

Interrogation practices also developed in accordance with the SERE-inspired repertoire at Guantánamo Bay (often referred to as GTMO in military parlance). Department of Defense General Counsel William Haynes, White House legal advisors Gonzales and David Addington, and CIA counsel Rizzo visited Guantánamo in September 2002, where they received briefings on "Intel successes, Intel challenges, Intel techniques, Intel problems and future plans for facilities."[159] Throughout the fall, there were ongoing debates over interrogation methods at the base. "We will need documentation to protect us," opined Staff Judge Advocate Diane Beaver at one meeting. "Yes, if someone dies while aggressive techniques are being used . . . the backlash of attention would be severely detrimental. Everything must be approved and documented," proffered CIA lawyer Jonathan Fredman.[160] In October, Major General Mike Dunlavey requested that United States Southern Command approve a list of eighteen enhanced interrogation techniques, divided into three levels.[161] The "Haynes memo" followed on December 2, declaring that all eighteen techniques may be "legally available," but only level I and II methods should be employed as a matter of policy. Secretary of Defense Donald Rumsfeld approved, annotating the memo with his handwritten comments: "I stand for 8–10 hours a day. Why is standing limited to 4 hours?"[162] On December 10, Joint Task Force GTMO compiled a draft "SERE Interrogation Standard Operating Procedure," which provided detailed guidance on approved enhanced interrogation techniques such as the shoulder slap, stomach slap, stripping, stress positions, hooding, manhandling, and walling.[163] SERE trainers travelled to the base to instruct interrogators.[164]

Mohammed al-Qahtani became the first victim of a Special Interrogation Plan at Guantánamo. Interrogators created a detailed eighty-four-page log to document al-Qahtani's interrogation.[165] As summarized by attorneys at the Center for Constitutional Rights, abuses included extensive sleep deprivation, multiple twenty-hour interrogations, threats against family, religious and sexual humiliation, forced nudity, psychological degradation, stress positions, exposure to dogs, exposure to noise and temperature manipulation, and medical abuse.[166] While the log is most striking when read as a cumulative experience, accounts such as the following are illustrative:

> 0400: P/E down. Showed detainee banana rats standard of life vs his standard of life in his wooden booth. Compared his life in a wooden booth to the life he could have with his brothers in Cuba.
>
> 0430: Detainee was walked for 10 minutes. Detainee refused water.
>
> 0450: Detainee listened to white noise.
>
> 0530: Detainee required to sit and watch as interrogator and linguist played checkers. Laughed and mocked detainee throughout game. White noise present in background.
>
> 0630: 10 minute exercise period and used bathroom. Detainee refused water and stated that he was on a food/water strike. However, he stated that he was not on an interrogation strike. Detainee reminded of his low self worth and that this life he has chosen here in this wooden box will not cease until he has come to terms that lying is not an option. Detainee was instructed to clean room. Interrogator told detainee that he will not be allowed to leave trash all around and live like the pig that he is. He picked up all the trash from the floor while hands were still cuffed in front of him and interrogator swept the trash towards him. He was told that it is his responsibility to make sure the room is kept clean and he would have to clean it daily.
>
> 0650: Corpsman drew detainee's blood.
>
> 0700: Detainee instructed to go to sleep.
>
> 1100: Detainee awakened by music, taken to bathroom and walked 10 minutes.[167]

On several occasions, the log notes that water was poured on al-Qahtani's head. He was frequently threatened with enemas. At times he was forced to wear a dog collar and perform dog tricks.[168]

Female interrogators were used to humiliate detainees at Guantánamo. For example, allegations include incidents where a woman sat on a detainee's lap, "making sexual affiliated movements with her chest and pelvis while again speaking sexually oriented sentences" and where "a female military interrogator . . . wiped what she told the detainee was menstrual blood on a detainee's face and forehead."[169] Such incidents are indicative of the gendered politics of the global war on terror, which saw American authorities perversely mobilize feminist critiques of Islamist misogyny to justify sexualized violence against detainees.[170]

Military lawyers challenged the legality of these abusive interrogation methods on several occasions. This points to variation within the United States' post-9/11 national security culture of legal rationalization. Judge advocate general (JAG) corps training and acculturation made military lawyers less open to the Bush administration's legal acrobatics, particularly regarding torture. Between December 2002 and January 2003, Navy General Counsel Alberto Mora raised multiple concerns about interrogation at Guantánamo, threatening to send a legal memo asserting that "the majority of the proposed category II and all of the proposed category III techniques were violative of domestic and international legal norms in that they constituted, at a minimum, cruel and unusual treatment and, at worst, torture."[171] On January 15, 2003, Rumsfeld withdrew his previous authorization and the enhanced al-Qahtani interrogation was suspended.

Secretary Rumsfeld created a Detainee Interrogation Working Group to assess the legality of interrogation techniques. Despite objections from JAG lawyers,[172] the OLC continued to drive Department of Defense policy. On March 14, 2003, Yoo issued an expanded version of the August 1, 2002 torture memos, this time focused on military interrogation.[173] Without consent of all members, the Working Group echoed many of Yoo's findings in an April 4, 2003 report. It recommended thirty-five interrogation techniques as lawful and appropriate including hooding, environmental manipulation, isolation, prolonged interrogation, forced grooming, prolonged standing, sleep deprivation, physical training, face slap, stomach slap, removal of clothing, and use of aversion including intimidation with dogs.[174] On April 16, 2003, Rumsfeld authorized twenty-four techniques for use at Guantánamo including dietary and environmental manipulation, sleep adjustment, false flag, and isolation.[175] He also left the door open for commanders to request additional techniques on a case-by-case basis.[176]

The role of the torture memos in shaping military interrogation in Afghanistan and Iraq is somewhat more elusive. After the Abu Ghraib scandal broke, the Bush administration denounced the abuses, labeling the perpetrators "bad apples" and "rogue" criminals. As former Undersecretary of Defense for Policy Douglas Feith claimed, "the abuse [the photos] recorded was, in fact, a matter of personal sadism by a small number of individuals. The abuse had not been inflicted as an interrogation technique. It had not been done on orders from higher authorities. It violated the Defense Department's policies requiring the proper treatment of prisoners."[177] However, considering that torture at Abu Ghraib involved systemic use of previously approved enhanced interrogation techniques such as stress positioning, humiliation, and use of military dogs, this argument is misleading. In fact, interrogation in Afghanistan and Iraq was influenced by OLC legal advice, albeit in a considerably confused and arbitrary fashion. Methods designed for the CIA migrated to the combat theatre, producing a series of highly ambiguous rules. Legal directives were recycled through a broken telephone chain, promoting a permissive subculture where abuses flourished.

In fall 2002, members of the Special Mission Unit Task Force Afghanistan visited Guantánamo to learn about SERE methods. Upon their return, they proposed new interrogation techniques similar to those under consideration at Guantánamo "such as the use of strip searches for 'degradation;' hoods for 'sensory deprivation;' 'sensory overload' through lights, darkness, noises, and dogs; and manipulation of the detainees' environment through 'cold, heat, wet, discomfort, etc.'"[178] An October 27 follow-up memo recommended "imaginative but legal use of non-lethal psychological techniques (i.e., battlefield noises/chaos, barking dogs, etc.)" as well as stress techniques such as "sensory deprivation (hoods, silence, flex cuffs), sensory overload (shouting, gun shots, white noise, machinery noise) and manipulation of the environment (hot, cold, wet, windy, hard surfaces)."[179] In December 2002, two detainees, Habibullah and Diliwar, were killed in custody at the Bagram military base. "Army investigators concluded that the use of stress positions and sleep deprivation combined with other mistreatment at the hands of Bagram personnel, caused or were direct contributing factors in the two homicides."[180] Nonetheless, these interrogation methods, which were directly influenced by Rumsfeld's December 2, 2002 memo, were progressively codified in standard operating procedures. As the Special Mission Unit Task Force Afghanistan legal advisor explained, "the fact SECDEF [Secretary of Defense] approved use of the [CAT I/II/III] techniques at GTMO, subject to the same laws, provides an analogy and basis for use of these techniques [in accordance with] international and U.S. law."[181]

Techniques also migrated to Iraq. Prior to the March 2003 invasion, Special Mission Unit Task Force Iraq obtained Special Mission Unit Task Force Afghanistan's interrogation standard operating procedures, changing the letterhead and adopting them verbatim.[182] In July 2003, Special Mission Unit Task Force Iraq drafted its own standard operating procedures, including methods such as "'vary comfort positions' (sitting, standing, kneeling, prone); presence of military working dogs; 20-hour interrogations; isolation; and yelling, loud music, and light control."[183] Soon thereafter, Captain Carolyn Wood, in charge of the newly established Abu Ghraib prison, received a copy of these guidelines and submitted it to her chain of command as policy.[184] In early September, Guantánamo Commander Major General Geoffrey Miller visited Iraq. Despite clearly deplorable conditions, Miller reportedly accused the Iraq Survey Group, charged with finding weapons of mass destruction, of "running a country club" for detainees and recommended they "GTMO-ize" interrogations.[185] Contemporaneously, SERE trainers were sent to

Iraq to aid interrogations, resulting in the further use of enhanced interrogation techniques.[186]

On September 14, 2013, Lieutenant General Ricardo Sanchez, commander of Combined Joint Task Force 7, which directed conventional forces in Iraq, issued "Interrogation and Counter-Resistance Policy," aimed at addressing the American military's intelligence deficit in the emerging counterinsurgency. The standard operating procedures were based on methods approved by Secretary Rumsfeld earlier that winter and those proposed by Wood, which in turn drew from practices authorized in Afghanistan and Guantánamo. While recognizing that enemy prisoners of war (EPWs) in Iraq were entitled to Geneva Conventions protections that prohibited coercive interrogations, Sanchez argued that "with few exceptions, persons captured after May 1, 2003 were not entitled to EPW status as a matter of law." Captain Wood claimed that no EPWs were at Abu Ghraib.[187] The policy generated legal debate at US Central Command, with some lawyers emphasizing its incompatibility with Geneva rules. As a result, Sanchez issued new guidance on October 12, 2003 that removed offending techniques. Interrogators had to sign Interrogation Rules of Engagement forms, but these rules did not always match policy guidance. A few weeks later on October 25, the standard operating procedures were revised yet again. "Techniques included controlled fear (muzzled dogs), stress positions, sleep deprivation/adjustment, environmental manipulation, yelling, loud music, and light control, removal of comfort items, isolation, false documents/report, multiple interrogator, and repeat and control."[188]

The abuses committed by military police and military interrogators at Abu Ghraib in fall 2003 in many ways reflected these guidelines. Military police were put in the unorthodox role of preparing prisoners for interrogation. Use of military dogs, stress positions, forced exercise, forced nudity, sleep deprivation, sensory deprivation, and isolation were commonly practiced.[189] Nudity was "standard operating procedure," Lynndie England explained regarding the infamous image of her leading a naked man on a leash.[190] Amazingly, many of the same techniques were continually reauthorized in multiple interrogation standard operating procedures for Iraq and Afghanistan until May 2004, well *after* the Abu Ghraib scandal broke.[191]

Some things that occurred at Abu Ghraib, such as beating detainees to death, were not authorized. Prison personnel were young, ignorant, angry, and fearful. There doubtlessly were "bad apples." But there are unmistakable similarities between the techniques requested by the CIA and authorized by the OLC in August 2002, approved by Secretary Rumsfeld in December

2002 for use at Guantánamo Bay, and those caught on film in Iraq. As the Senate Armed Services Committee report summarizes:

> The abuse of detainees at Abu Ghraib in late 2003 was not simply the result of a few soldiers acting on their own. Interrogation techniques such as stripping detainees of their clothes, placing them in stress positions, and using military working dogs to intimidate them appeared in Iraq only after they had been approved for use in Afghanistan and at GTMO. Secretary of Defense Donald Rumsfeld's December 2, 2002 authorization of aggressive interrogation techniques and subsequent interrogation policies and plans approved by senior military and civilian officials conveyed the message that physical pressures and degradation were appropriate treatment for detainees in U.S. military custody. What followed was an erosion in standards dictating that detainees be treated humanely.[192]

Just as Guantánamo interrogators logged their activities, soldiers in Iraq did too. But unlike the former, the Abu Ghraib photos were impossible for anyone to defend openly. No one, not even Yoo or Cheney, would support techniques that appeared so obviously wrong. Abuses at Abu Ghraib violated international law and the Uniform Code of Military Justice. Yet they mirrored practices that in the abstract had been vetted and approved by the United States' leading policymakers and their lawyers.

Extraordinary Rendition to Proxy Torture

So far, I have traced how the CIA sought legal cover for torture, which was granted by the OLC. Enhanced interrogation techniques were subsequently approved by Secretary Rumsfeld and migrated throughout American military prisons. The torture memos played a critical role in facilitating abuse. American torture practices in the global war on terror frequently followed legal guidelines established by the OLC. However, other patterns of American counterterrorism strayed from the logic of legal rationalization. As previously noted, the practice of extraordinary rendition, in which detainees were secretly transferred to states such as Afghanistan, Egypt, Jordan, Libya, Morocco, Tunisia, Pakistan, and Syria for brutal, unconstrained torture, could not easily be reconciled with the law. Prominent rendition victims included Canadian citizen Maher Arar, who faced months of horrific interrogation in Syria after he was secretly deported by American authorities. In another infamous instance, CIA officers snatched Osama Moustafa Hassan Nasr off a Milan street, sending him to Egypt for torture.[193] An Open Society Foundation investigation tracked 136 extraordinary rendition cases involving the cooperation of 54 countries, which contributed to American efforts in a variety of ways, including facilitating detention and transport and imprisoning and torturing detainees.[194]

Why some high-value suspects were rendered while others were interrogated directly by the CIA is not entirely clear. From a practical standpoint, the CIA was overstretched and lacked capacity for a vast influx of detainees.[195] Moreover, Americans preferred others do their dirtiest work for them. As one official put it: "We don't kick the [expletive] out of them. We send them to other countries so they can kick the [expletive] out of them."[196] Enhanced interrogation techniques were torture, but these methods were distinct from Pakistani or Egyptian torture, a difference that reflects legal guidelines designed to minimize legal risks for interrogators. When Americans cognizant of constraints wanted to go further, they generally preferred to outsource interrogation.[197]

Extraordinary rendition rested on minimal legal grounds at best. The program was shrouded in secrecy. The Bush administration generally denied rather than defended it. However, the OLC did issue relevant opinions. While reiterating that the Geneva Conventions do not apply to al-Qaeda and that the Convention against Torture does not govern extraterritorial detention, a March 2002 memo acknowledged that conspiracy to commit torture abroad is a crime in US law:

> Thus, to fully shield our personnel from criminal liability, it is important that the United States not enter into an agreement with a foreign country, explicitly or implicitly, to transfer a detainee to that country for the purpose of having the individual tortured. . . . So long as the United States does not intend for a detainee to be tortured post-transfer, however, no criminal liability will attach to a transfer, even if the foreign country receiving the detainee does torture him.[198]

Moreover, it argued that the Convention against Torture forbids extradition from the United States when there is substantial grounds to believe that a person would be tortured, a provision interpreted by the Senate to mean "it is more likely than not that he would be tortured."[199] Extraordinary rendition to proxy torture thus did not entirely lack legal justification, although the exculpatory legal rationales developed by the OLC were even flimsier than those proffered in defense of enhanced interrogation techniques. Even if Americans hand delivered detainees and provided interrogators with questions, as long as they did not ask that detainees be tortured, and requested hollow assurances that detainees would not be tortured, they would not be criminally liable according to this logic. This reasoning was echoed in public pronouncements. As the US periodic report to the UN Committee against Torture stated: "The United States continues to recognize its obligation not to expel, return ('refouler') or extradite a person to another state . . . where the United States believes it is 'more likely than not' that they will be tortured."[200]

To sum up, Americans engaged in several systematic types of torture in the global war on terror. There was torture specifically designed to meet OLC authorizations. There was torture that built on the memos but often went beyond authorized techniques because of confusion, misunderstandings, and poor leadership. Lastly, some torture practices were so beyond the pale that they were outsourced to proxies. In all these cases, a national security culture of legal rationalization pushed officials to seek legal cover for torture.

Public Scrutiny and Policy Shifts

After the gruesome Abu Ghraib photographs appeared on *60 Minutes II* in April 2004, the Bush administration's interrogation policies became increasingly unsustainable. In June 2004, one of the August 1, 2002 torture memos was leaked to the press, resulting in a flurry of outraged condemnation from human rights advocates. One week later, Goldsmith, then acting head of the OLC, withdrew it. However, legal rationalizations for enhanced interrogation did not disappear from subsequent OLC opinions. "While we have identified various disagreements with the August 2002 Memorandum," wrote OLC lawyer Daniel Levin, "we have reviewed this Office's prior opinions addressing issues involving treatment of detainees and do not believe that any of their conclusions would be different under the standards set forth in this memorandum."[201] The OLC did not clearly renounce waterboarding, despite rejection of some of the original authorization's rationales.[202] In 2005, OLC lawyer Steven Bradbury continued to argue that the CIA's enhanced interrogation techniques neither constituted torture nor violated the CAT's article 16 prohibition on cruel, inhuman, and degrading treatment, defined relative to the Fifth, Eighth, and Fourteenth Amendments to the US Constitution.[203]

The Detainee Treatment Act of 2005 sought to close potential jurisdictional loopholes in the law, banning Americans from inflicting cruel, inhuman, and degrading treatment on detainees anywhere in the world. Later, the Supreme Court ruled in *Hamdam v. Rumsfeld* (2006) that common article 3 of the Geneva Conventions, and by implication the War Crimes Act, did in fact protect detainees who were not POWs. As a result, the CIA requested additional legal assessments. Bradbury opined that the CIA's "conditions of confinement" were legal under both the Detainee Treatment Act[204] and Geneva Conventions common article 3 standards.[205] In a highly detailed 2007 memo, he also reauthorized six techniques proposed by the

CIA—prolonged sleep deprivation, dietary manipulation, the "facial hold," the "attention grab," the "abdominal slap," and the "insult slap."[206] While waterboarding was dropped from the list of interrogation techniques, the memo was ambiguous about whether it would be prohibited under the new rules.[207]

President Bush always insisted that he did not authorize torture: "I had asked the most senior legal officers in the U.S. government to review the interrogation methods, and they had assured me they did not constitute torture. To suggest that our intelligence personnel violated the law by following the legal guidance they received is insulting and wrong."[208] Nonetheless, increased public scrutiny took its toll on administration policy. As summed up by the Senate Select Committee report: "By 2006, press disclosures, the unwillingness of other countries to host existing or new detention sites, and legal and oversight concerns had largely ended the CIA's ability to operate clandestine detention facilities . . . . The CIA last used its enhanced interrogation techniques on November 8, 2007. The CIA did not hold any detainees after April 2008."[209] Upon taking office, President Obama rescinded the torture memos and mandated conformity with the US Army Field Manual.[210] However, cooperation with torturers in countries such as Egypt, Pakistan, and Saudi Arabia and controversial practices such as force-feeding detainees at Guantánamo persisted.[211]

Impunity for Torture

The Bush administration's attempt to assert the plausible legality of torture was widely rejected by human rights experts. Major NGOs such as Amnesty International, Human Rights Watch, the Center for Constitutional Rights, and the American Civil Liberties Union (ACLU) vigorously advocated against American interrogation policy and filed numerous lawsuits to halt abuses. OLC lawyers were subject to intense criticism. The torture memos and related legal opinions were obviously in bad faith; they intentionally obscured the law, distorted precedent, and were part of a "criminal conspiracy," argued human rights lawyer Michael Ratner. The purpose of this "illegal lawyering" was to aid and abet human rights violations, making the lawyers as guilty as the perpetrators.[212] For Philippe Sands, legal decisions reflected a "preordained policy of aggression that came from the very top." Lawyers "gave their names as jurists to cloak the policy with a veneer of legality" and, as such, "bear direct responsibility for decisions."[213] While law always invites a range of plausible interpretations, "[i]t is the consistent pattern of result-oriented reasoning, insistently maintained in secret over several years by multiple lawyers—even as both the statutory law and the administration's own public statements seemed to become more restrictive—that is ultimately the most compelling evidence of bad-faith lawyering," argues David Cole.[214]

After European cooperation with extraordinary rendition flights came to light, European parliamentarians strongly denounced American policy: "[T]he United States has introduced new legal concepts, such as 'enemy combatant' and 'rendition,' which were previously unheard of in international law and stand contrary to the basic legal principles that prevail on our continent."[215] The UN Special Rapporteur on torture suggested "diplomatic assurances with regard to torture are nothing but attempts to circumvent the absolute prohibition of torture and refoulement."[216] Groups such as the International Commission of Jurists argued that the legal rationalization of abuse contributed to the erosion of international human rights and humanitarian legal regimes around the world.[217]

In some instances, members of the national security establishment itself criticized American policy. As previously noted, JAG lawyers urged Secretary Rumsfeld to reject enhanced interrogation techniques. Eventually, State Department legal advisors such as John Bellinger pushed back against OLC claims that interrogation methods were compliant with common article 3 standards: "We believe that the reasonable person, as well as world opinion, would consider such acts to constitute humiliation and degradation of a level to be considered an outrage upon personal dignity. We believe that the world would find these acts particularly revolting."[218] According to the Office of Professional Responsibility at the Department of Justice, the torture memos contained "errors, omissions, misstatements, and illogical conclusions... their cumulative effect compromised the thoroughness, objectivity, and candor of the OLC's legal advice."[219] In particular, the Office of Professional Responsibility found that memos ignored and misrepresented relevant precedents, mischaracterized the law, and omitted important information.

American torture policy was thus contested from without, by human rights advocates who sought to push the United States toward a culture of deeper compliance with international human rights and humanitarian norms. But it was also contested from within, by establishment lawyers who generally operated in accord with the United States' national security culture of legal rationalization but could not countenance patently fallacious arguments. Put differently, the torture memos were rejected not only because they violated the substantive spirit and intent of international human rights law, but also because torture is extremely difficult to convincingly legally rationalize vis-à-vis the letter of the law. The plausible legality of torture was simply not plausible, even to those who might otherwise be sympathetic to pushing the bounds of legal justification in the service of national security.

At the same time, widespread rejection of OLC arguments did not undermine the broader exculpatory purpose of the torture memos. Despite external and internal critiques, the strategic construction of plausible legality proved remarkably effective in fulfilling its goals. American policymakers avoided accountability for authorizing torture. The Abu Ghraib scandal exemplifies the striking hypocrisy of the national security establishment in this regard. The Bush administration successfully propagated its "bad apple" theory, placing sole blame on low-level soldiers who perpetrated abuses despite the direct line that ran from officially authorized interrogation methods designed for the CIA, to their employment at Guantánamo, to their diffusion in Afghanistan and Iraq.[220]

While several soldiers implicated in Abu Ghraib abuses were jailed, plausible legality made possible formal immunity for interrogators who more closely followed OLC guidance. The Detainee Treatment Act accepted "good faith reliance on advice of counsel" as a legitimate defense for human rights violations:

> In any civil action or criminal prosecution against an officer, employee, member of the Armed Forces, or other agent of the United States Government who is a United States person, arising out of the officer, employee, member of the Armed Forces, or other agent's engaging in specific operational practices, that involve detention and interrogation of aliens who the President or his designees have determined are believed to be engaged in or associated with international terrorist activity that poses a serious, continuing threat to the United States, its interests, or its allies, and that were *officially authorized and determined to be lawful at the time* that they were conducted, it shall be a defense that such officer, employee, member of the Armed Forces, or other agent did not know that the practices were unlawful and a person of ordinary sense and understanding would not know the practices were unlawful.[221]

The torture memos proved to be a "golden shield." The authority of their legal form survived despite widespread criticism of their content. Plausible legality worked, even in the absence of consensus about substantive validity.

It is highly unlikely that any members of the Bush administration will ever be prosecuted for authorizing torture. After his election, President Obama preferred to move on. Attorney General Eric Holder appointed a special prosecutor to investigate CIA abuses, but his mandate was confined to acts conducted outside of legal guidelines. In summer 2011, save for two ongoing murder investigations, the agency was exonerated.[222] The remaining cases were dropped in summer 2012 after the Department of Justice found insufficient evidence to obtain convictions.[223] While reflecting a failure of political will, the cover of plausible legality helped facilitate this limited scope of recrimination. If Yoo had recommended electrocution, rape, or ripping out fingernails, if the CIA had created black sites without Department of Justice sign off, it would be much harder to grant them a legal pass.

Reticence toward domestic prosecutions shifted accountability efforts out to foreign legal proceedings and universal jurisdiction cases and down to professional ethics boards and civil suits. However, with the exception of the 2009 conviction of twenty-three American agents tried in absentia in Italy for their role in kidnapping and rendition,[224] foreign investigations have achieved few successes. Evidence suggests that extensive American diplomatic force was leveraged to undercut German charges against CIA agents accused of kidnapping and rendering Khaled el-Masri to Afghanistan for torture.[225] While Judge Balthazar Garzon of Spain, famed for his investigation of Pinochet, was willing to proceed, his investigation of high-ranking White House, OLC, and Department of Defense figures was cut short, due at least in part to heavy American pressure.[226] Domestic civil suits have also fared poorly.[227]

Many human rights advocates hoped that the release of the Department of Justice Office of Professional Responsibility Report would contribute to accountability, yet it disappointed.[228] Despite being highly critical of legal opinions, the report focused more on the process of memo writing than the substance of memo conclusions. Accordingly, Yoo was lambasted for putting "his desire to accommodate the client above his obligation to provide thorough, objective, and candid legal advice,"[229] but Bradbury's more thorough reasoning process was deemed professionally appropriate, despite ultimately authorizing most of the same techniques approved in the Bybee memos.[230] In all cases, the Department of Justice declined to recommend further censure or punishment.[231] As a result, the lawyers appear to have escaped any serious legal consequences for their actions.

CONCLUSION

Legal restrictions on torture have proved an elusive check on state violence in the United States. Through most of its early history, foundational commitments to Enlightenment values and civil liberties were not enough to overcome the powerful logic of racial exclusion. Instead, a culture of exception legitimized systematic state-tolerated torture of African Americans as well as indigenous peoples at the nation's imperial frontiers. Eventually, developing international human rights and humanitarian law, the emerging civil rights movement, and the strategic dynamics of the Cold War reduced the legitimacy of exceptional violence and ushered in a culture of secrecy.

Seeking to simultaneously project the United States' liberal democratic image and defeat the Soviet Union, officials authorized clandestine torture experiments, covered up torture scandals, and covertly supported abusive proxies throughout the global south. Plausible deniability aimed to avoid accusations of hypocrisy. Both these cultures, of exception and of secrecy, largely reinforced the assumptions of *law as permit*. Sometimes, law itself facilitated abuses against dehumanized others; in other instances, authorities ignored legal rules that impeded their national security agendas.

The intelligence scandals of the 1970s and 1980s, growing human rights activism, and deepening oversight and media scrutiny combined to encourage new cultural patterns. By 9/11, the American national security establishment operated within a culture of legal rationalization. Fearing recrimination, risk-sensitive security agencies demanded the production of legal cover—or plausible legality. As a result, government lawyers wrote numerous legal memoranda that manipulated ambiguities and loopholes in the law in order to deem enhanced interrogation techniques lawful.

Notwithstanding invocations of executive prerogative and claims that legal prohibitions on torture did not apply to the global war on terror, the Bush administration's core exculpatory position was that enhanced interrogation techniques did not meet the legal definition of torture. As torture is a universally proscribed practice, they could not openly admit or defend it. Nor could they evade public scrutiny. Instead, they feigned conformity with the law in order to avoid consequences for breaking it. While their legal arguments were subject to extensive critique, they succeeded in constructing impunity for post-9/11 torture.

These observations point to contradictory conclusions about law's ability to constrain state violence in contexts where states profess allegiance to human rights norms. Realists may be right that law cannot impose morality on states. However, in cultures of legal rationalization, legal rules do shape how they go about doing their dirty work. Law acts as a permissive constraint—it can be manipulated to allow abuse, but it imposes at least some limits on the possible. Even when bent to the breaking point, it still serves as an important boundary marker. Policymakers care about law because in cultures of legal rationalization, law matters a great deal. In chapter 6, I further examine how this pattern of practice erodes legal norms, creating space for renewed justifications for exceptional state violence foreshadowed in the early rhetoric of the Trump administration, as well as how human rights pushback could move American national security legal culture toward deeper compliance with legal norms.

CHAPTER 4

Deprivations of Life and Liberty

Detention, Trial, and Targeted Killing

The contemporary liberal rule of law requires that individuals enjoy rights to life and liberty unless they have been convicted of a crime through fair and neutral legal proceedings. In order to safeguard these rights, the American justice system includes a variety of due process requirements aimed at preventing wrongful incarceration, conviction, and punishment. Even in wartime, where detention, trial, and killing standards are modified by the exigencies of combat, international humanitarian law and American law restrict who can be imprisoned and killed. Targeting noncombatants is a serious war crime. As with the prohibition on torture, these rules evolved over centuries of normative, legal, and practical change, reflecting the growing importance of human rights in international and domestic law.

Time and again, American security policy in the global war on terror has challenged prohibitions on arbitrary (i.e., not legally justified) deprivations of life and liberty. After 9/11, the George W. Bush administration used immigration and material witness laws to detain hundreds of mostly Muslim men en masse, sometimes secretly and incommunicado. It interpreted the Geneva Conventions as allowing the indefinite detention of prisoners at Guantánamo Bay while denying them POW status. It created military commissions to prosecute accused terrorists, proceedings that lacked evidentiary and other standards normally associated with fair trials. It authorized targeted killing, straining prohibitions on extrajudicial assassination and murdering civilians. The Obama administration maintained some of these policies, extending Guantánamo detention despite promises to close the prison, and rapidly accelerated the American targeted killing program.

These seemingly disparate practices are linked together through what they deny—namely, rights to life and liberty in the absence of lawfully justified limitations on those rights.

The United States' post-9/11 human rights violations were not unprecedented. When torture occurred, as discussed in chapter 3, due process was clearly absent. More broadly, rights to life and liberty have often been early victims of national security crises. As I have argued, patterns of state violence shift over time. Changing national security legal cultures have legitimized certain justifications for human rights abuses while limiting others. A national security *culture of exception* shaped much of the United States' early history, permitting otherwise proscribed atrocities against "others," most often racialized others. In this chapter, I highlight examples of these exceptional detention, trial, and killing practices, including war crimes against indigenous peoples during the Indian Wars, post-Civil War peonage and convict leasing of African Americans, Japanese internment during the Second World War, and several iterations of Red Scares that culminated in McCarthyism. Social and political changes eventually tempered the United States' appetite for exception, yet perceived national security imperatives did not disappear. As a *culture of secrecy* deepened during the expanding Cold War, the United States partnered with abusive foreign regimes, providing tacit and sometimes explicit support for widespread extrajudicial detention and murder abroad.

There are echoes of exception and secrecy in post-9/11 American counterterrorism policy. However, a contemporary *culture of legal rationalization* has pushed American policymakers to construct legal cover for contentious practices. Whereas the purported *plausible legality* of torture manipulated the definition of torture to exclude enhanced interrogation techniques, legal justifications for detention, trial, and targeted killing policy have been facilitated by the uneven nature of laws governing these practices. Individuals' immigration status, combatant or civilian status, and geographical location, along with the presence or absence of a legal state of armed conflict, all contribute to the precise nature of the legal protections to which they are entitled. Loopholes and gaps within and among American law, international human rights law, and international humanitarian law governing armed conflict have created opportunities for plausibly legal arguments in support of indefinite detention, military commissions, and targeted killing. Accordingly, policies condemned as illegal by human rights advocates were repeatedly defended in public by the Bush and Obama administrations. In contrast to the case of torture, many of these policies continue to enjoy widespread support from the national security establishment.

Liberal democracies hold due process to be a cornerstone of the rule of law. People must not be detained without cause and must be able to contest their detention in front of a neutral examiner—the right to habeas corpus. Defendants in criminal proceedings must know the charges and evidence against them and have access to independent counsel. The law must be applied equally to similarly situated people and not be used in a discriminatory or biased fashion. Rights to just and fair treatment do not disappear during wartime. While due process standards are considerably weaker in contemporary military contexts, international humanitarian law dictates that prisoners who have not been accused of a crime may be detained only to remove them from the battlefield and must be treated humanely at all times. Certain combatants are eligible for a variety of additional rights related to POW status. Detainees charged with crimes must have access to regularly constituted courts. Outside the conduct of lawful warfare, killing is considered illegal murder and may amount to a war crime.

These human rights and humanitarian legal rules are relatively recent developments. As discussed in chapter 3, officially sanctioned cruelty was built into European legal procedure for hundreds of years. Prior to the Enlightenment and concomitant political revolutions, victims of church and state persecution faced extreme violence without recourse to a neutral justice system. Human rights norms as we understand them today did not inform the law or legal culture.

Wartime captives did not fare any better. Historically, prisoners were executed or otherwise abused with impunity. The ancient Greeks and Romans enslaved the civilian populations of conquered lands. During the eleventh- through thirteenth-century Crusades, defeated populations were often massacred and prisoners tortured or used as human shields. Rather than restrain such violence, zealous religious faith, which was beginning to regulate some forms of warfare within Christendom, legitimized violence against nonbelievers as absolute enemies.[1] Cruelty also persisted in intra-European conflict, such as Henry V's famous order to kill French prisoners after the 1415 Battle of Agincourt.

Reflecting the chaotic, segmented political situation in early modern Europe, no single norm governed treatment of prisoners in war. Massacres were common, particularly in cases of ethnic or confessional conflict. Defeated towns and villages were often subject to reprisals, hostage taking, and extortion by victorious armies. The ancient practice of holding captives for slavery or ransom persisted. In other cases, prisoners were forced to join their captor's ranks.[2] Instead of internment, prisoner redistribution through re-enlisting detainees on the other side, bloc prisoner exchange "cartels," and the practice of "parole" (release on the promise not to return to hostilities) were common ways of dealing with prisoners prior to the nineteenth century.[3] In this context, contemporary international humanitarian principles were not particularly relevant. With some limited exceptions, polities lacked an effective, consistent, constraining legal structure to limit the exploits of bloodthirsty rulers and soldiers.

In the following sections, I describe the emergence of legal norms that challenged these practices and laid the groundwork for contemporary legal rules governing detention, trial, and targeted killing policy in the United States. I begin by outlining the development of due process rights in peacetime and go on to discuss legal constraints on state violence during wartime. The complex relationship between these two distinct but intertwined bodies of law forms a significant point of legal contention in the global war on terror. Human rights advocates argue that counterterrorism policy should primarily be grounded in human rights law, while American policymakers argue that the law of armed conflict permits controversial practices.

EVOLVING HUMAN RIGHTS AND CIVIL LIBERTIES PROTECTIONS

The American civil liberties tradition emerged both from and in contrast to political and legal developments in Europe, especially England. In the case of the latter, early precedents for modern due process rights date back to the thirteenth century, when the English monarchy granted concessions to noblemen in the Magna Carta: "No free man shall be seized or imprisoned, or stripped of his rights or possessions, or outlawed or exiled, or deprived of his standing in any other way, nor will we proceed with force against him, or send others to do so, except by the lawful judgment of his equals or by the law of the land."[4] Nonetheless, Westminster's infamous Star Chamber court was increasingly used to repress political opposition and religious dissent. It was eventually abolished with the Habeas Corpus Act of 1640, followed by further legislation in 1679, some of whose provisions would be echoed in American law.[5]

Many American founders were deeply committed to just detention and fair trials, at least for white men. As John Adams wrote of his unpopular but ultimately successful legal advocacy on behalf of British soldiers accused in the 1770 Boston Massacre: "It was . . . one of the most gallant, generous, manly and disinterested Actions of my whole Life, and one of the best Pieces of Service I ever rendered my Country. Judgment of Death against those Soldiers would have been as foul a Stain upon this Country as the Executions of the Quakers or Witches, anciently."[6] Alexander Hamilton, quoting William Blackstone, also emphasized the importance of habeas corpus:

> To bereave a man of life ... or by violence to confiscate his estate, without accusation or trial, would be so gross and notorious an act of despotism, as must at once convey the alarm of tyranny throughout the whole nation; but confinement of the person by secretly hurrying him to gaol [jail], where his sufferings are unknown or forgotten, is a less public, a less striking, and therefore *a more dangerous engine* of arbitrary government.[7]

Due process rights were considered sufficiently important that they were integrated into the suspension clause of article I of the US Constitution: "The Privilege of the Writ of Habeas Corpus shall not be suspended, unless when in Case of Rebellion or Invasion the public Safety may require it."[8]

Multiple aspects of due process rights were more extensively guaranteed by the Bill of Rights. The Fifth Amendment mandates grand juries, precludes double jeopardy, provides rights against self-incrimination, and states that no person shall "be deprived of life, liberty, or property, without due process of law."[9] The Sixth Amendment further declares that:

> In all criminal prosecutions, the accused shall enjoy the right to a speedy and public trial, by an impartial jury of the State and district wherein the crime shall have been committed, which district shall have been previously ascertained by law, and to be informed of the nature and cause of the accusation; to be confronted with the witnesses against him; to have compulsory process for obtaining witnesses in his favor, and to have the Assistance of Counsel for his defence.[10]

The Eighth Amendment states: "Excessive bail shall not be required, nor excessive fines imposed, nor cruel and unusual punishments inflicted."[11] After the Civil War, the Fourteenth Amendment universalized these rules for all Americans regardless of race, clarifying: "No State shall make or enforce any law which shall abridge the privileges or immunities of citizens of the United States; nor shall any State deprive any person of life, liberty, or property, without due process of law; nor deny to any person within its jurisdiction the equal protection of the laws."[12] These constitutional protections have been enhanced over time with legislation and court rulings.

Multiple international human rights instruments mandate due process rights. The Universal Declaration of Human Rights states: "No one shall be subjected to arbitrary arrest, detention or exile" and "Everyone is entitled in full equality to a fair and public hearing by an independent and impartial tribunal, in the determination of his rights and obligations and of any criminal charge against him."[13] Article 6 of the International Covenant on Civil and Political Rights further states: "No one shall be arbitrarily deprived of his life," and articles 9, 14, and 15 lay out extensive due process requirements.[14] In sum, American constitutional and international law guarantee due process of law for all people.

INTERNATIONAL HUMANITARIAN STANDARDS

Human rights are constricted by the realities of war. Even when war is conducted lawfully, people are maimed and killed, their property and communities destroyed. Nonetheless, international humanitarian law, or the law of armed conflict, has long sought to regulate wartime violence, placing limitations on states' ability to legally kill and detain their adversaries. International humanitarian law is *lex specialis*, meaning that it is the primary, although not exclusive, framework governing war. International legal obligations found in international human rights law continue to apply but must be interpreted through the lens of the law of armed conflict. For example, human rights restrictions on the arbitrary deprivation of life should be assessed relative to rules governing the lawful use of lethal force in war. To provide a simple example, soldiers can kill other soldiers on the battlefield without violating human rights law.

In the United States, the Civil War-era Lieber Code developed early regulations to govern ethical military conduct. "Military necessity does not admit of cruelty," it declared, "that is, the infliction of suffering for the sake of suffering or for revenge, nor of maiming or wounding except in fight, nor of torture to extort confessions."[15] It forbade targeting civilians: "as civilization has advanced during the last centuries, so has likewise steadily advanced, especially in war on land, the distinction between the private individual belonging to a hostile country and the hostile country itself, with its men in arms. The principle has been more and more acknowledged that the unarmed citizen is to be spared in person, property, and honor as much as the exigencies of war will admit."[16] It freed the slaves.[17] It laid out standards for the treatment of POWs: "A prisoner of war is subject to no punishment for being a public enemy, nor is any revenge wreaked upon him by the intentional infliction of any suffering, or disgrace, by cruel imprisonment, want of food, by mutilation, death, or any other barbarity."[18] However, not everyone was a public enemy. The Lieber Code excluded what we might today call insurgents or guerilla fighters: "such men, or squads of men, are not public enemies, and, therefore, if captured, are not entitled to the privileges of prisoners of war, but shall be treated summarily as highway robbers or pirates."[19] Certain provisions of the Lieber Code, such as those allowing retaliation and bombardment of cities without notice to civilians, are obsolete. Moreover, its suggestion that "[p]rotection was, and still is with uncivilized people, the exception" is incompatible with contemporary law.[20] Nonetheless, it helped lay the groundwork for subsequent articulations of international humanitarian law.

In 1863, the ICRC was founded to provide humanitarian aid for victims of war. In 1864, it convinced several governments to adopt the original Geneva Convention on the condition of the wounded, which mandated care for injured soldiers. Further agreements followed including the St. Petersburg Declaration (1868), the Brussels Declaration on Laws and Customs of War (1874), the Hague Conventions (1899 and 1907), and further elaborations of the Geneva Conventions in 1929, 1949, and 1977. Emerging through a confluence of state practice and *opinio juris* (state beliefs about their legal obligations), customary international law compliments these treaties. The ICRC has compiled the customary laws of war in two lengthy volumes.

The 1949 Geneva Conventions remain the single most important set of regulations governing armed conflict. American soldiers are expected to comply with the Geneva Conventions under the Uniform Code of Military Justice. I later elaborate on these rules in the context of contemporary American efforts to legally legitimize indefinite detention and targeted killing of alleged terrorists. Here I outline the broad parameters of international humanitarian law as it applies to *jus in bello*, or the just conduct of hostilities. My analysis does not focus on *jus ad bellum*, or the just initiation of war, although Americans have also developed plausibly legal arguments in this regard to justify the post-9/11 invasions of Afghanistan and Iraq. In brief, *jus ad bellum* criteria are largely defined in contemporary international law by the Charter of the United Nations, which authorizes armed intervention in another state in two instances: as an article 51 measure of individual or collective self-defense against armed attack or pursuant to a chapter VII Security Council resolution.[21] States are generally understood to have a right to suppress insurgency within their own territories, provided they comply with legal limitations.

Customary international humanitarian law and a variety of treaties promote four central principles to govern the conduct of hostilities: distinction, necessity, prevention of unnecessary suffering, and proportionality.[22] Regarding the first, civilians are protected persons. They must never be direct targets of military attack, although they may become what is colloquially known as "collateral damage," or the unintended but not necessarily unanticipated victims of attack, provided commanders take adequate precautions to minimize civilian casualties. Combatants who no longer pose a threat due to capture, injury, or surrender are protected persons. Civilian objects such as homes, schools, and hospitals are also protected as long as they are not being used for military purposes. Failure to respect the principle of civilian distinction is a serious war crime. In many irregular or unconventional conflicts, combatants fail to distinguish themselves from the civilian population, making the task of legal compliance difficult.

The principle of necessity justifies military measures that are required to secure the defeat of the enemy as quickly as possible. Acts of violence that are not necessary to win are not permitted. However, necessity does not permit prohibited acts (e.g., torture) even if they would aid swift victory. International humanitarian law also prohibits the infliction of unnecessary suffering on combatants, banning weapons that cause superfluous injury. This concept has historically applied to restrictions on serrated bayonets, exploding bullets, and poison gas.[23] Finally, the principle of proportionality demands that attacks not be "excessive in relation to the concrete and direct military advantage anticipated."[24] While it is challenging to define what constitutes an excessive loss of life, this provision restricts violence that incidentally causes extensive civilian suffering while achieving limited military gains, but it permits limited incidental civilian suffering to achieve substantial military advantage. Once again, collateral damage is sometimes permissible. Calculations become most difficult when both anticipated harm and military gains are high.

In addition to the Geneva Conventions, a variety of historical precedents inform legal standards of behavior in armed conflict. The post–Second World War Nuremberg International Military Tribunals helped develop international criminal law aimed at holding individuals accountable for atrocities. Nuremberg inspired later ad hoc tribunals for the former Yugoslavia and Rwanda and the creation of the International Criminal Court. These courts have produced extensive case law that helps clarify the application of both international human rights and humanitarian law in practice, especially in noninternational armed conflicts.

Prohibitions on arbitrary deprivations of life and liberty are entrenched in American constitutional law and international human rights and humanitarian law. Nonetheless, as with torture, this developing body of law has often found itself in tension with state security agendas. Varying national security legal cultures have pushed policymakers to resolve this tension in different ways: through overt exceptions, secret violations, and efforts to reinterpret legal rules to facilitate contentious policies.

CULTURES OF EXCEPTION: MINORITIES, ALIENS, AND SUBVERSIVES

Legal cultures of exception are characterized by the exclusion of demonized others from the protection of the law. In the United States, there is a long history of formally and practically suspending legal rights to life and liberty in both peacetime and war for indigenous peoples, racial minorities, foreigners, and political subversives. Exceptions were justified through appeals to overt bigotry in some cases and to more measured claims of national security and military necessity in others.

Colonialism was firmly rooted in a legal culture of exception. The international humanitarian legal rules that developed throughout the late nineteenth century were not extended to "savages." Arguing that only high contracting parties (i.e., Western states) could engage in reciprocity, Europeans invoked a profoundly racist imaginary to deem African, Arab, Asian, and indigenous peoples "uncivilized" and incapable of restraint.[25] As a result, otherwise prohibited means and methods of warfare were freely applied in the global south. As discussed in chapter 3, the United States was not immune from these patterns, as evidenced by tolerance for imperial torture and other atrocities in the Philippine War.

Colonial violence also raged on the United States' internal frontiers. From the original encounter between indigenous peoples and colonists to later conflicts fueled by westward settlement expansion and the doctrine of Manifest Destiny, American soldiers deviated from nascent human rights and humanitarian norms, committing a variety of abuses, from killing prisoners to forcefully relocating civilians. Indian resistance, Americans believed, was best controlled with punitive brutality. As George Washington explained: "Our future security will be in their inability to injure us . . . and in the terror with which the severity of the chastisement they receive will inspire them."[26] In his fifth annual message, President Andrew Jackson defended the necessity of Indian removal: tribes "have neither the intelligence, the industry, the moral habits, nor the desire of improvement . . . . Established in the midst of another and a superior race, and without appreciating the causes of their inferiority or seeking to control them, they must necessarily yield to the force of circumstances and ere long disappear."[27]

The 1864 Sand Creek Massacre is illustrative of the legal culture of exception that shaped American conduct during the Indian Wars. Whatever the limitations of the emergent laws of war at the time, the actions of American forces were in obvious contravention of contemporaneous norms. A year after the Lieber Code had declared that "[m]ilitary necessity does not admit of cruelty," 675 volunteers from the Colorado First and Third Cavalry under the command of Colonel John Chivington attacked a peaceful Cheyenne and Arapaho Indian village, murdering 230 people, mostly women, children, and elderly civilians. Captain Silas S. Soule refused to participate and recounted the gruesome horrors in subsequent letters:

> The massacre lasted six or eight hours, and a good many Indians escaped. I tell you
> Ned it was hard to see little children on their knees have their brains beat out by men

professing to be civilized. . . . They were all scalped, and as high as half a dozen taken from one head. They were all horribly mutilated. One woman was cut open and a child taken out of her, and scalped.

White Antelope, War Bonnet and a number of others had Ears and Privates cut off. Squaw's snatches were cut out for trophies. You would think it impossible for white men to butcher and mutilate human beings as they did there, but every word I have told you is the truth, which they do not deny. It was almost impossible to save any of them.[28]

The letters initiated two congressional committees and an army investigation. For his testimony, Soule was shot dead in Denver. Despite evidence of their guilt, his murderers went free.[29] While chastised by Congress for executing a "foul and dastardly massacre," neither Chivington nor his men faced criminal charges. Promised reparations were never paid. Colorado sites were named in the perpetrators' honor. The events were memorialized as a battle, not a war crime.

Colonial violence continued across the Great Plains, culminating in the better-known massacre at Wounded Knee, South Dakota in 1890.[30] Writing decades later, Theodore Roosevelt would opine: "All men of sane and wholesome thought must dismiss with impatient contempt the plea that these continents should be reserved for the use of scattered savage tribes, whose life was but a few degrees less meaningless, squalid, and ferocious than that of the wild beasts . . . . It is . . . *idle to apply to savages the rules of international morality which obtain between stable and cultured communities.*"[31] While Americans were reluctant to justify wanton acts of violence against unarmed civilians in the immediate wake of massacres, they were equally reticent to do anything about it. Racist and dehumanizing depictions of American Indians were widely disseminated. Impunity for exceptional violence on the United States' internal frontiers reigned.

During the Civil War, authorities invoked exceptional necessity to justify brutal tactics of war. Prevailing norms articulated in the Lieber Code midway through the conflict permissively suggested that "[t]he more vigorously wars are pursued, the better it is for humanity. Sharp wars are brief."[32] Yet the Lieber Code also proscribed "wanton devastation." It is difficult to describe episodes such as General William Tecumseh Sherman's infamous March to the Sea as anything else. Intentional destruction and pillage of civilian property was widespread. "You cannot qualify war in harsher terms than I will. War is cruelty, and you cannot refine it; and those who brought war into our country deserve all the curses and maledictions a people can pour out . . . . You might as well appeal against the thunder-storm as against these terrible hardships of war," declared Sherman regarding the evacuation and burning of Atlanta in 1864.[33] Such acts were tolerated in order to shorten the war and save the Union. The Civil War thus proved

paradoxical as federal authorities transgressed the restrictions they themselves had championed.

Controversial challenges to constitutional norms also occurred during
the Civil War. President Abraham Lincoln, concerned about "the enemy in
the rear," suspended the writ of habeas corpus in 1861 without seeking congressional authorization. "Under cover of 'Liberty of speech,' 'Liberty of the
press' and 'habeas corpus' they hoped to keep on foot amongst us a most
efficient corps of spies, suppliers, and aiders and abettors of their cause in
a thousand ways," he wrote, explaining the need for speedy, unreviewable
detentions.[34] The suspension sparked a legal confrontation with judge
Roger Taney, who rebuked Lincoln's unilateral action.[35] Subsequently,
the federal government tried accused Confederate saboteurs by military
commission, a move that was eventually rejected by the Supreme Court in
situations where normal courts were open.[36] Over the course of the war, at
least 4,271 cases were heard before military commissions, many involving
"bushwhackers" or pro-Confederate irregular gangs, a great deal of whom
were summarily tried and executed.[37] POWs were also mistreated, subject to horrific conditions and abysmal mortality rates in both Union and
Confederate prison camps.

Although the Lieber Code's admonitions were often violated in practice during the Civil War, it is important to note that the countercivilian
massacres that characterized the Indian Wars were not directed at Southern
white women and children during the conflict, nor was there blanket impunity for war crimes. For instance, Union forces were court-martialed for
sexual violence against white and in a few cases black women in the South.[38]
Cultural tolerance for extra-legal violence thus varied considerably, the
parameters of which were often defined along racial lines.

Legal exceptionalism did not end with the cessation of the Civil War.
Instead, it continued to justify abuses in peacetime. For much of American
history, the pursuit of national security was as much a matter of protecting
social, political, and economic white supremacy as military security.
Accordingly, the 1868 Fourteenth Amendment guaranteeing equality before the law did not translate into the realization of equal justice for African
Americans. On the contrary, the persistence of racism in the American judicial system meant that blacks were habitually denied habeas corpus rights,
the presumption of innocence, access to counsel, and a jury of their peers.
For decades after the end of slavery, authorities throughout the postbellum
South unjustly imprisoned African Americans for alleged petty crimes and
then sold incarcerated inmates into forced labor. Fined and subject to peonage, prisoners became part of a convict leasing system and were sent to
mines, lumber camps, quarries, farms, and factories, many owned by major
corporations, where they toiled in horrific conditions, were tortured, and

sometimes worked to death.[39] As discussed in regard to exceptional torture in chapter 3, lynchings were also common phenomenon. Extreme acts of racial violence flourished virtually unchecked between Reconstruction and the Second World War.

African Americans were not the only victims of de jure and de facto legal exclusion. American authorities, with the approval of the courts, frequently used plenary power to deny basic due process rights to immigrants and citizens deemed foreign and threatening. For instance, the Alien Enemies Act (1798) authorized the president to unilaterally expel citizens of countries with which the United States was at war.[40]

Immigration and naturalization law further legalized discrimination. In 1882, Congress enacted the first Chinese exclusion laws. Racist double standards and xenophobia characterized numerous pieces of legislation during the First World War. The 1917 Immigration Act restricted entry based on political beliefs and excluded migrants from the "Asiatic zone."[41] The 1918 Immigration Act extended plenary powers, making resident aliens deportable for anarchist beliefs, regardless of their length of residency.[42] President Woodrow Wilson, an unrepentant white supremacist despite his liberal internationalism, legitimized the antialien frenzy with his public pronouncements. Foreigners "poured the poison of disloyalty into the very arteries of our national life"; such "disloyalty . . . must be crushed," he declared.[43] He authorized extensive profiling of Germans and Austro-Hungarians during the First World War: 6,300 enemy aliens were arrested, 2,300 interned.[44]

Meanwhile, other rights were increasingly curtailed for native and foreign-born Americans alike. The Espionage Act of 1917 outlawed information that could interfere with the success of the US armed forces. The Sedition Act of 1918 criminalized "any disloyal, profane, scurrilous, or abusive language . . . as regards the form of government of the United States, or the Constitution, or the flag." As a result, labor organizer Eugene Debs was sentenced to ten years in prison for praising draft resistance, while two thousand people were prosecuted, half convicted, for speaking out against the war.[45]

The Palmer Raids of 1919–20 marked the high point of the due process exceptionalism of the first Red Scare. After a series of terrorist bombings targeting prominent Americans, Attorney General A. Mitchell Palmer ordered dragnet detention and deportation of foreign nationals based on loose political associations. Investigations were led by J. Edgar Hoover, newly appointed to the Justice Department's Bureau of Investigation. The raids targeted Russian immigrant anarchists and communists, resulting in four thousand to ten thousand arrests, often without warrants and without provision for access to counsel.[46] Considering Palmer's order an egregious violation of rights, Assistant Secretary of Labor Louis Freedland Post, who held ultimate authority over the issuance of deportation orders, denounced the raids and reduced deportations to the hundreds.[47] The legal culture of exception proved subject to contestation.

Political and nativist animus also reared its head in criminal trials. For instance, Italian immigrants Nicola Sacco and Bartolomeo Vanzetti were executed in 1927 for an alleged anarchist inspired murder-robbery after several dubious trials and failed appeals. The atmosphere in which Sacco and Vanzetti were tried was rife with "anti-alien hysteria . . . . Aliens were presumably 'Reds' and 'Reds' were outside the pale of the law," explained activist Elizabeth Glendower Evans.[48]

The Second World War initiated profound new challenges to legal norms in the United States. In battle, civilians became the direct object of attack. The Allies invoked exceptional necessity to justify widespread incendiary area bombing of German and Japanese cities, which intentionally terrorized civilians.[49] Along with the eventual nuclear destruction of Hiroshima and Nagasaki, such actions directly undermined civilian distinction. "I suppose if I had lost the war, I would have been tried as a war criminal," Air Force General Curtis LeMay, American commander of Pacific bombing, candidly noted.[50] Lawyers played almost no role in advising generals during the war.[51] For the national security establishment, considerations of military necessity predominated.

On the home front, President Franklin Delano Roosevelt targeted Japanese and later Italian and German Americans with the Alien Enemies Act. Up to nine hundred thousand people were classified as enemy aliens and ordered to comply with registration measures, travel restrictions, and searches without probable cause.[52] Japanese people were subject to curfew, exclusion from certain areas, and relocation, with forty thousand foreign-born and seventy thousand American-born Japanese eventually interned pursuant to Executive Order 9066 (1942).[53] No interned Japanese person was ever charged or convicted of espionage or sabotage.[54] These discriminatory actions sparked some of the most infamous legal rulings in American history. In what are today considered shameful legal episodes, the Supreme Court upheld race-based internment in several key cases.[55] For instance, in *Korematsu v. United States* (1944), the court ruled that exclusion of American citizens due solely to their Japanese ancestry was constitutional in light of military necessity.[56] Dissenting judges made clear exactly what was at stake. As Justice Frank Murphy put it:

> Being an obvious racial discrimination, the . . . order deprives all those within its scope
> of the equal protection of the laws as guaranteed by the Fifth Amendment. . . . In
> excommunicating them without benefit of hearings, this order also deprives them of all

their constitutional rights to procedural due process . . . . [It] is one of the most sweeping and complete deprivations of constitutional rights in the history of this nation in the absence of martial law.[57]

"Once a judicial opinion rationalizes such an order," wrote Justice Robert Jackson, "the Court for all time has validated the principle of racial discrimination in criminal procedure and of transplanting American citizens. The principle then lies about like a loaded weapon, ready for the hand of any authority that can bring forward a plausible claim of an urgent need."[58]

After the Second World War, legal exceptionalism persisted in the United States. As the Cold War emerged, a second Red Scare gripped the nation. Throughout the 1940s and 1950s, numerous programs and laws restricted constitutional rights for both citizens and aliens. Fearing Soviet infiltration, the FBI developed several iterations of "custodial detention lists" and "security indexes" aimed at identifying subversives for possible detention.[59] The 1940 Smith Act continued to outlaw subversive political advocacy. In 1947, President Harry Truman initiated a Federal Employee Loyalty Program, which subjected federal workers to loyalty testing. The Internal Security Act of 1950, or McCarran Act, and the Immigration and Nationality Act of 1952, or McCarran-Walter Act, extended preventative detention powers and racially discriminatory immigration rules.[60]

Alleged Communists were blacklisted, often based on rumor and guilt by association. Those who fell victim to the witch hunts were fired from their jobs and shut out of their professions. The House Un-American Activities Committee (HUAC) and Senate Permanent Subcommittee on Investigations of the Committee on Government Operations under the leadership of Republican Senator Joseph McCarthy led the anti-Communist charge. Under congressional rules, those forced to testify had few options. As one representative explained of HUAC: "The rights you have are the rights given you by this Committee. We will determine what rights you have and what rights you have not got before this Committee."[61] Witnesses were confronted with secret evidence, denied counsel, and barred from cross-examining testimony.

As McCarthy's allegations became ever more sweeping, including an accusation that the army was "soft" on Communism, his political legitimacy faded. In March 1954, respected journalist Edward R. Murrow criticized McCarthy on his popular television show, *See It Now*:

We must not confuse dissent with disloyalty. We must remember always that accusation is not proof and that conviction depends upon evidence and due process of law . . . . We can deny our heritage and our history, but we cannot escape responsibility for the result. . . . We proclaim ourselves, as indeed we are, the defenders of freedom—what's left of it but we cannot defend freedom abroad by deserting it at home.[62]

In June 1954, McCarthy bullied army lawyer Joseph Welch during a televised hearing. "Until this moment, Senator, I think I never really gauged your cruelty or your recklessness . . . Have you no sense of decency?" asked Welch in the now-famous exchange.[63] By the end of 1954, the Senate censured McCarthy. This did not end blacklisting, but it did mark its eventual decline. All told, between 1947 and 1957, up to 13.5 million workers were subjected to some variety of loyalty test. Around 11,000 employees were fired from government jobs, 6,300 from private ones.[64]

The second Red Scare perpetuated the legal exceptionalism that characterized previous national security crises. However, many ordinary Americans and members of the national security establishment became increasingly reticent to endorse crude red-baiting and televised attacks on free expression and due process. Contemporaneously, the Supreme Court began to rule in favor of desegregation in *Brown v. Board of Education of Topeka* (1954). While the court did little to intervene in anti-Communist repression, civil rights were becoming part of the national conversation in new and important ways.[65] If the United States was going to lead the "free world," it had to practice what it preached, at least at home and in public. The dirty work of fighting the Cold War would persist for decades, particularly overseas, but image-conscious authorities would to try harder to shield human rights abuses from critical scrutiny.

Legal cultures of exception have pervaded much of American history. I have provided snapshots of a variety of instances in which violations of American, human rights, and humanitarian legal norms have been justified either by invocations of military necessity or by excluding demonized others from the protection of the law. These violations have ranged from unlawful indiscriminate killing in war, to unfair trials and unjust imprisonment, to expulsion, internment, and blacklisting. In a country where national security has meant not just conventional military defense but maintaining social hierarchy, abuses have cut across war and peacetime. In all these instances, people have been denied rights to life, liberty, and due process not because of their individual guilt, but because of their racial, ethnic, or political identities.

CULTURES OF SECRECY: DISAPPEARING ENEMIES

I have argued that national security legal cultures shape how political actors engage legal norms, thus mediating the capacity of law to constrain state violence. Cultures of exception tolerate widespread human rights abuses against demonized others. However, the declining legitimacy of open state violence does not guarantee deeper human rights compliance. As the Cold War progressed, Americans embraced an emerging culture of secrecy. The rapidly expanding national security state sought to advance American interests, as it understood them, through covert and clandestine action. Secrecy allowed authorities to publically champion liberal democracy while using decidedly illiberal means to combat the Soviet Union. In particular, the United States tacitly and actively supported numerous repressive regimes around the world. From Indonesia to Pakistan to South Africa, American officials at best turned a blind eye and at worst encouraged abuses in the name of anti-Communism. In some cases, American agents directly participated in extrajudicial detention, assassination, and coup attempts.

As I discussed at greater length in chapter 3, Americans committed, facilitated, and covered up Cold War torture and other war crimes in Vietnam and Central America. Unfortunately, when it comes to extrajudicial disappearances and killing, the list of examples is also long.[66] For instance, the United States supported Operation Condor, a multinational kidnapping and assassination campaign by the anti-Communist, Southern Cone dictatorships of South America throughout the 1970s. "Practices of secret detention were first used against armed movements, later against left-wing groups, Marxist and non-Marxist, and ultimately against all groups suspected of political opposition. The latter were labeled as 'subversives,' 'terrorists' or 'communists,'" notes a UN investigation.[67] Condor architects created a "vast parallel infrastructure of secret detention centers and clandestine killing machinery."[68] These predatory parastatal structures "allowed military and intelligence forces to carry out illegal acts that were visible on the one hand, and deniable on the other . . . and avoid the damage that accompanied world criticism of widespread, public human rights abuses."[69] Despite being well aware of systemic illegal human rights violations,[70] American intelligence officials provided preparatory, logistical, and direct operational support for Condor activities.[71]

Condor was just one example of a Cold War security program that resulted in violations of rights to life, liberty, and due process. As with all such initiatives, the United States was wary of getting caught and looking bad for its role in supporting human rights abuses. Yet it proved impossible to avoid growing public scrutiny. The Senate's Church Committee investigations in the mid-1970s were indicative of secrecy's unsustainability. Among the committee's many findings, discussed in greater detail in chapter 5 in the context of surveillance, investigations revealed that the CIA had engaged in multiple covert plots to assassinate several national leaders, including Patrice Lumumba of the Congo, Fidel Castro of Cuba, Rafael

Trujillo of the Dominican Republic, Ngo Dinh Diem of South Vietnam, and Rene Schneider of Chile.[72] In response, President Gerald Ford issued Executive Order 11905 (later 12333) banning assassination, which was renewed by subsequent presidents and remains in effect today. Section 2.11 of Executive Order 12333 (1981) states: "No person employed by or acting on behalf of the United States Government shall engage in, or conspire to engage in, assassination," while section 2.12 further restricts indirect participation in assassination: "No agency of the Intelligence Community shall participate in or request any person to undertake activities forbidden by this Order." Declassified CIA commentary suggests that the agency did not interpret the prohibition to inhibit covert training and arming of allied forces to engage in activities that would predictably result in the killing of individuals.[73] However, as I will discuss later in this chapter, there are notable differences between the CIA's Cold War tolerance for assassination and contemporary targeted killing, which are indicative of shifting approaches to contentious security practices.

Cultures of exception and secrecy in many ways affirm assumptions of what I have called *law as permit*. Authorities ignored, flouted, and reconstructed law to justify various forms of state violence. By the turn of the century, these cultures were displaced by a culture of legal rationalization.

CULTURES OF LEGAL RATIONALIZATION: LEGALIZING EXTRALEGALITY

After 9/11, American policymakers sought to identify and neutralize further plots. Believing that legal norms created bureaucratic obstacles to efficient deportations, interrogations, and other preventative national security measures, authorities redesigned detention and trial procedures to evade normal rules. Toward the end of the Bush administration and throughout the Obama administration, Americans used targeted killing in order to execute alleged terrorists without judicial process. These activities are contemporary manifestations of the broad range of policies and practices employed in the past that I have so far highlighted in this chapter. They involve the interpretation and application of the rules of war as they apply to detention and killing as well as American constitutional law, immigration law, and international human rights law.

Many global war on terror policies denied Arabs and Muslims in the United States and enemy fighters abroad full protection of the law in ways that revived the exclusionary tradition of legal cultures of exception. However, advancements in domestic and international legal rules combined with increased pressure to comply with human rights norms reduced the legitimacy of overtly racist rationales for contentious security practices. Moreover, covert detention and extrajudicial killing, like covert and proxy torture, proved difficult to sustain in the contemporary human rights and media environment. Public scrutiny was inevitable, requiring policymakers to defend their actions or risk political blowback and legal sanction.

As I have argued, the United States' post-9/11 counterterrorism policy emerged from a culture of legal rationalization, which sanitized rights violations. Through a strategy of what I call plausible legality, government lawyers produced legal interpretations that stripped alleged terrorists of substantive due process protections without relying on exceptional legal logics. Because detention, trial, and lethal targeting procedures are governed by distinct bodies of law in peacetime and war—laws that apply differently to citizens and foreigners, regular and irregular combatants, and persons inside and outside the United States—lawyers were able to exploit gaps and loopholes in legal rules. Despite political controversy over counterterrorism policy, these arguments effectively insulated Americans from prosecution and publically legitimized many of their policies.

Several episodes illuminate the strategy of plausible legality as it applies to detention, trial, and lethal targeting policy. First, after 9/11, hundreds of Arab and Muslim men were rounded up and detained incommunicado in the United States. While seemingly an act of racial discrimination echoing previous exceptional internments, authorities legitimized this move under existing immigration and material witness laws. Second, American policymakers constructed the category of "unlawful enemy combatant" to hold prisoners outside of Geneva Conventions protections and domestic constitutional standards at places like Guantánamo Bay. American officials took pains to rationalize this practice in light of rules governing armed conflict. Third, policymakers created military commissions to try detainees, portraying them as just, appropriate, and backed by legal precedent. Finally, both the Bush and Obama administrations defended targeted killing as normal, lawful killing in warfare. I will now discuss each of these in turn.

Immigration Detention, Material Witness Laws, and Watch Lists

Although potentially subject to change, the naked racism and xenophobia that justified lynching, Red Scares, and Japanese internment during the Second World War lack broad legitimacy in contemporary American politics. The successes of the civil rights movement and changing normative beliefs about equality prevented most, although not all, national security officials from advocating similarly harsh measures against Arabs and Muslims in the wake of 9/11. Indeed, policy pronouncements from the Bush and Obama administrations were rife with calls for intercommunal cooperation. "[T]he war against terrorism is not a war against Muslims, nor is it a war against Arabs," declared President Bush in 2001. "Islam is a vibrant faith. Millions of our fellow citizens are Muslim. We respect the faith. We honor its traditions. Our enemy does not. Our enemy doesn't follow the great traditions of Islam. They've hijacked a great religion," he said in 2002.[74]

Yet, in practice, there is no doubt that Arabs and Muslims were targeted for arrest, detention, and deportation, resulting in high levels of racial profiling and significant due process violations. Authorities relied on immigration, material witness, and other plenary and prosecutorial powers in order to carry out these actions. By stretching and manipulating existing laws, they advanced discriminatory ends through seemingly neutral legal processes. In other words, they pursued a strategy of plausible legality.

Laws governing immigrant detention in the United States grant authorities extensive discretion, often at the expense of basic fairness.[75] Americans took advantage of this state of affairs after 9/11. In the two months following the attacks, 1,200 citizens and aliens were detained for questioning by law enforcement nationwide, while 762 aliens were detained as part of the FBI's Pentagon/Twin Towers bombing investigation.[76] Between September 2001 and August 2002, the latter were placed on an "INS Custody List" while the FBI attempted to ascertain their relationship to terrorism.[77] This process took an average of eighty days, during which detainees were held on "no bond" orders. People who were tangentially encountered in the investigation but not suspected of any particular criminal activity continued to be held for immigration violations such as overstaying visas or entering the country illegally.[78]

Many of those detained were denied due process: "[D]etainees were not informed of the charges against them for extended periods of time; were not permitted contact with attorneys, their families, and embassy officials; remained in detention even though they had no involvement in terrorism; or were physically abused, verbally abused, and mistreated in other ways while detained."[79] Although most detainees were technically guilty of immigration violations, their immigration status was a pretext. In essence, American authorities exploited the low due process standards of immigration law to engage in preventative detention of ethnically and religiously profiled suspects.

A variety of other security initiatives also utilized immigration law. In fall 2001, the Department of State put mandatory holds on visa applications by men aged eighteen to forty-five from twenty-six mainly Arab and Muslim countries.[80] Subsequently, the Department of Justice announced its intent to interview 8,000 primarily Arab and Muslim nonimmigrant visa holders.[81] In January 2002, the Immigration and Naturalization Service accelerated efforts to deport 6,000 Middle Eastern "absconders" who had evaded deportation orders.[82] In July 2002, immigration agents began to aggressively enforce rules that required aliens to register changes of address. This was followed by the announcement of a Special Registration program in fall 2002, later dubbed the National Security Entry and Exit Registry System, which required many Arab and Muslim visitors to register with Homeland Security and undergo further screening. By June 2003, almost 128,000 people had registered at a port of entry, while almost 83,000 had been "specially registered" through domestic call in, 13,434 of whom were "placed in removal proceedings for visa violations, though *none* of them was charged with terrorism, terrorist affiliations, or otherwise suspected of terrorist affiliations."[83] There are numerous other examples of programs that selectively targeted Arabs and Muslims using immigration law, even though they constituted only 1 percent of "out of status" aliens in the United States. As a result, more Arabs and Muslims were removed from the United States post-9/11 than aliens were deported after the Palmer Raids.[84]

The Bush administration did not have to radically derogate from legal norms because the law grants broad discretion to detain and deport foreign nationals.[85] As Attorney General John Ashcroft summed up in an October 2001 speech:

> Robert Kennedy's Justice Department, it is said, would arrest mobsters for "spitting on the sidewalk" if it would help in the battle against organized crime. It has been and will be the policy of this Department of Justice to use the same aggressive arrest and detention tactics in the war on terror. Let the terrorists among us be warned: If you overstay your visa—even by one day—we will arrest you. If you violate a local law, you will be put in jail and kept in custody as long as possible. We will use every available statute. We will seek every prosecutorial advantage. We will use all our weapons within the law and under the Constitution to protect life and enhance security for America.[86]

In cultures of legal rationalization, spitting on sidewalks enforcement is a critical national security strategy.

After 9/11, security agencies were increasingly concerned with domestic terrorist sleeper cells in addition to threats from foreign nationals. However, there are more legal obstacles to detaining American citizens than detaining aliens. While the 2001 PATRIOT Act, a controversial piece of legislation discussed at length in chapter 5 in regard to surveillance, allowed detention up to seven days without charges for terrorism suspects, American law lacked the long-term preventative detention powers adopted by other countries.[87] As a result, policymakers sought a legal basis to hold suspects who had not committed crimes eligible for normal arrest warrants. To do this, they utilized material witness warrants. These warrants were originally designed to force witnesses, who might otherwise fail to appear, to testify in court proceedings. In 2001, Ashcroft authorized their use in terrorism cases to allow the detention and interrogation of suspects on the fraudulent pretext that they were required as witnesses in a prosecution. Detainees subject to material witness warrants had limited access to counsel and complained of shackling, strip searches, and other harsh detention conditions.[88] In response, human rights advocates attempted to establish the unconstitutionality of misusing material witness warrants[89] and make Ashcroft liable for abuses.[90] However, these efforts were unsuccessful.[91]

Finally, Arab and Muslim foreigners and citizens found themselves disproportionately targeted by post-9/11 terrorist watch lists. The most prominent example is the No Fly List, which bars listed individuals from airplane travel. Such lists have been rife with errors.[92] Because rules for listing and redress are opaque and inefficient, it is difficult to be removed from a watch list. Watch listing arguably violates individuals' rights to contest alleged wrongs. However, like other administrative and bureaucratic programs in the global war on terror, the watch list phenomenon erodes rights in a discriminatory fashion without appealing to overt exceptionalism or bigotry. While potentially similar in effect, watch lists have not emerged in the same dramatic frenzy as Cold War blacklists.

It is important to note that cultures of legal rationalization are not necessarily better than cultures of exception or secrecy. They simply function differently. Moreover, cultural change is not unidirectional or irreversible. As I discuss in chapter 6, President Donald J. Trump in 2017 introduced immigration restrictions that directly target Muslims. He has eschewed rhetorical outreach to Islam employed by the Bush and Obama administrations. In other words, exceptional logics may once again be emerging in American legal politics.

Unlawful Enemy Combatants

While American authorities exploited immigration and material witness laws to facilitate detentions within the United States, they relied on controversial interpretations of international humanitarian law to detain and, as I will discuss later, kill alleged terrorists abroad. In order to legally rationalize these contentious policies, the United States claimed that 9/11 was an act of war triggering armed conflict and that the attackers and their allies were combatants. As stated in the 2001 Authorization for Use of Military Force: "The President is authorized to use all necessary and appropriate force against those nations, organizations, or persons he determines planned, authorized, committed, or aided the terrorist attacks that occurred on September 11, 2001, or harbored such organizations or persons, in order to prevent any future acts of international terrorism against the United States by such nations, organizations or persons."[93] Because the global war on terror was conceived as first and foremost a *war*, it would be regulated by the rules of armed conflict, not the constitutional due process or international human rights constraints that govern law enforcement and criminal justice proceedings. Like the Civil War, Indian Wars, and two world wars as well as US military campaigns in the Philippines, Korea, and Vietnam, Americans sought primarily to defeat and neutralize their enemy.

In order to understand the legal arguments posited by the Bush and later Obama administrations, it is necessary to review the Geneva Conventions of 1949 at some length. Rules vary based on whether a war is an international armed conflict or a noninternational armed conflict. In an international armed conflict—a conflict between "high contracting parties" (i.e., states) or involving occupation by a high contracting party—all four conventions apply (I, II, III, and IV),[94] covering two general categories of persons: combatants and civilians. All persons are one or the other; there is no in-between category.[95] According to the ICRC, civilians are defined negatively as all persons who are not members of armed forces or a *levée en masse*.[96] Combatants are members of the armed forces of one party to a conflict, including irregular militias, volunteer corps, and organized resistance movements, or a *levée en masse*. In the context of armed conflict, combatants may lawfully kill each other as long as they follow the laws of war.

Combatants are required to meet four criteria to maintain their immunity under the combatant's privilege (i.e., the right to fight and kill the enemy without sanction) and qualify as POWs upon capture: "(a) that of being commanded by a person responsible for his subordinates; (b) that of having a fixed distinctive sign recognizable at a distance; (c) that of carrying arms openly; (d) that of conducting their operations in accordance with the laws and customs of war."[97] Enumerated in the Third Geneva Convention Relative to the Treatment of Prisoners of War, detaining powers must provide a number of special rights for POWs, such as treatment based on military rank, the right to wear badges and decorations, and access to canteens and recreational sports and games.[98] Detaining POWs is preventative—to stop them from returning to battle—not punitive. Fighters who fail to meet the requirements of a privileged combatant can be tried for war crimes or other criminal offences under domestic or international law. At all times, all detainees must be treated humanely. Secret and incommunicado detention is strictly prohibited by the Geneva Conventions.[99]

Reflecting the changing character of war and the growing influence of third-world national liberation guerilla movements, the 1977 First

Additional Protocol to the Geneva Conventions expanded the combatant's privilege and associated protections applicable to international armed conflicts to nonstate fighters engaged in "armed conflicts in which peoples are fighting against colonial domination and alien occupation and against racist régimes in the exercise of their right of self-determination."[100] Additional Protocol I, article 75 further clarified detention and trial standards for all detainees in international armed conflicts:

> 3. Any person arrested, detained or interned for actions related to the armed conflict shall be informed promptly, in a language he understands, of the reasons why these measures have been taken. Except in cases of arrest or detention for penal offences, such persons shall be released with the minimum delay possible and in any event as soon as the circumstances justifying the arrest, detention or internment have ceased to exist.
>
> 4. No sentence may be passed and no penalty may be executed on a person found guilty of a penal offence related to the armed conflict except pursuant to a conviction pronounced by an impartial and regularly constituted court respecting the generally recognized principles of regular judicial procedure.[101]

Strenuously objecting to the expansion of privileged combatancy to insurgents, the United States has not ratified the Additional Protocols. It has, however, recognized many aspects of Additional Protocol I as customary international law since 1986.[102]

There are far fewer rules governing noninternational armed conflicts, or "conflict[s] not of an international character occurring in the territory of one of the High Contracting Parties," which are covered by common article 3 of the 1949 Geneva Conventions.[103] For example, most civil wars fall into this category. All armed conflicts are either international or noninternational. According to the ICRC, "organized armed violence failing to qualify as an international or non-international armed conflict remains an issue of law enforcement, whether the perpetrators are viewed as rioters, terrorists, pirates, gangsters, hostage-takers or other organized criminals."[104]

Noninternational armed conflicts include a range of actors: civilians who assist armed groups in varying ways, civilians who engage in sporadic acts of belligerency, organized armed groups, dissident armed forces, state armed forces of the national government, and foreign forces operating at the invitation of the host national government. Nonstate actors are not expressly prohibited from engaging in hostilities by international law, but they are subject to domestic law, which criminalizes nonstate violence.[105] They may be punished within the bounds of international human rights law for crimes such as treason, murder, assault, and destruction of property. For states that rejected Additional Protocol I, Geneva POW rules apply only to international, not noninternational armed conflicts.

In international armed conflicts, civilians may be temporarily detained under some limited circumstances, as governed by the Fourth Geneva Convention.[106] However, in both international and noninternational contexts, the rights of civilians who engage in military operations are subject to considerable debate, a topic to which I will return when I discuss targeted killing rationales. Moreover, beyond the basic requirements of humane treatment found in common article 3, there are no clear international standards for preventative detention (i.e., removal from the battlefield) of anyone in noninternational armed conflicts.[107] Many law of war experts insist that states may detain members of organized armed groups until the cessation of hostilities, just as combatants are detained in international armed conflicts.[108] However, human rights advocates argue that there is no preventative detention authority via the Geneva Conventions in these conflicts. In their view, detainees should be held only for as long as they pose an immediate threat or if they are subject to prosecution for crimes. Where international humanitarian law is silent, international human rights law fills the void.[109] For its part, the ICRC suggests that "imperative reasons of security" are acceptable grounds for interning or administratively detaining persons not charged with crimes provided that detainees are registered, held in recognized locales, and are able to seek legal counsel and contest their detention. Recognizing that these obligations "are not clearly expressed in any IHL [international humanitarian law] treaty applicable to NIAC [noninternational armed conflict]," it has convened international consultations to address the ambiguity of rules governing noninternational detention.[110]

Compared to international human rights law, international humanitarian law is relatively permissive. In particular, it allows states to hold POWs for the duration of hostilities in international armed conflicts. However, it does not grant a carte blanche. Rather, the Geneva Conventions outline universally accepted standards for the treatment of both POW and non-POW detainees. After 9/11, American policymakers believed that these rules would restrict their ability to efficiently capture and interrogate suspected terrorists. Yet unlike past wars and national security crises, in which racism and logics of exceptional necessity justified extralegality, American officials were keen to solicit legal cover for contentious counterterrorism policies. In the prevailing culture of legal rationalization, lawyers helped forge legal arguments to permit abusive detention policies. Specifically, they claimed that al-Qaeda and Taliban fighters were ineligible for POW status, that constitutional and international human rights provisions did not apply to the global war on terror, and that detention facilities outside of the United States were not subject to American law.

The war in Afghanistan was an international armed conflict from the initial invasion in October 2001 until the United States and its coalition allies became guests of the newly installed Afghan government in June 2002.[111] Nonetheless, OLC lawyers argued that the Geneva Conventions did not govern detention operations in Afghanistan during this period. They claimed that al-Qaeda and Taliban members were not eligible for POW rights granted to enemy soldiers or associated militias of high contracting parties because they failed to wear insignia, carry arms openly, and obey the laws of war.[112] Lawyers further argued that "the Taliban militia would not even qualify as the *de facto* government of Afghanistan. Rather, it would have the status only of a violent faction or movement contending with other factions for control of Afghanistan's territory, rather than the regular armed forces of an existing state."[113]

While denying POW status to al-Qaeda and Taliban fighters was not hugely controversial, lawyers also made the more contentious claim that common article 3 protections did not apply either. Instead, they argued that common article 3 governs only noninternational armed conflicts: "As the Afghanistan war is international in nature, involving as it does the use of force by state parties—the United States and Great Britain—which are outside of Afghanistan, common article 3 by its very terms would not apply. Common article 3, as we have explained earlier, does not serve as a catch-all provision that applies to all armed conflicts."[114] When the war became noninternational in 2002, lawyers continued to reject the application of common article 3, arguing that the Geneva Conventions did not apply to transnational armed conflict with nonstate parties.

The notion that common article 3 did not apply to conflict between the United States and al-Qaeda and associated forces represented a break with American military precedent, which had previously—in theory although not always in practice, as we have seen—applied Geneva rules as a matter of policy in armed conflict.[115] According to this novel post-9/11 view, common article 2 of the Geneva Conventions governed international armed conflict between high contracting parties, while common article 3 governed noninternational armed conflict in the territory of *one* high contracting party: "common article 3 addresses only non-international conflicts that occur within the territory of a single state party, again, like a civil war. This provision would not reach an armed conflict in which one of the parties operated from multiple bases in several different states."[116] This argument contradicts the ICRC's and most international lawyers' understanding of international humanitarian law, but it has a quasi-legal quality all the same. In other words, it manifests the strategy of plausible legality.

The Bush administration also argued that the reciprocal responsibilities at the heart of international humanitarian law would erode if combatants who violate the laws of war enjoyed rights. As Vice President Dick Cheney opined, "terrorists intentionally attack civilians, thus putting themselves outside the realm of those whom Geneva is meant to protect."[117] To grant terrorists Geneva status would reward them without creating inducements to alter behavior.

The aforementioned arguments came under intense criticism in the early years of the global war on terror, including from within the national security establishment. For instance, State Department legal advisor William Taft warned: "The President should know that a decision that the Conventions do apply is consistent with the plain language of the Conventions and the unvaried practice of the United States in introducing its forces into conflict over fifty years."[118] Nonetheless, President Bush adopted many OLC positions, deciding that while Afghanistan was a Geneva theatre, the Taliban did not qualify for POW status and that neither al-Qaeda nor Taliban prisoners would be covered by common article 3 protections. However, "[a]s a matter of policy, the United States Armed Forces shall continue to treat detainees humanely and, to the extent appropriate and consistent with military necessity, in a manner consistent with the principles of Geneva."[119]

To classify fighters not covered by Geneva protections under these interpretations, the Bush administration constructed the category of "unlawful enemy combatant." As eventually codified by the Military Commissions Act of 2006 an unlawful enemy combatant is "a person who has engaged in hostilities or who has purposefully and materially supported hostilities against the United States or its co-belligerents who is not a lawful enemy combatant (including a person who is part of the Taliban, al Qaeda, or associated forces)."[120] In contrast, a lawful enemy combatant was defined as a member of state armed forces or associated militias that follow the laws of war. Ironically, while denying unlawful enemy combatants Geneva Conventions rights, American officials claimed that their combatant status made them eligible for military detention, prosecution, and lethal targeting. This paradoxical argument lies at the heart of efforts to construct the plausible legality of the global war on terror. Alleged terrorists were excluded from international humanitarian law protections while this very same body of law purportedly legitimized capturing, holding, and killing them.

The United States initially conducted no or highly unsatisfactory review hearings to determine the individual status of detainees captured in Afghanistan. As a result, prisoners were allocated blanket designations as lawful, unlawful, or noncombatants. Once labeled an unlawful enemy combatant, detainees were subject to indefinite detention without charge and without access to independent counsel or regularly constituted courts. Moreover, the Bush administration asserted its right to detain unlawful enemy combatants beyond the active military theatre of Afghanistan, deeming the global war on terror geographically and temporally boundless. With no clear way to gauge the edges of the battlefield and the end of the conflict, detention was hypothetically forever.

In addition to classifying suspected captured foreign al-Qaeda operatives as unlawful enemy combatants, the United States took the extraordinary measure of applying this designation to its own citizens. For example, Jose Padilla, an American citizen captured within the United States, not in a military theatre, was first held on a material witness warrant and then labeled an unlawful enemy combatant and held without charge in a military brig for several years. He was eventually criminally charged and sent to civilian court, but only after years of criticism and multiple habeas cases.[121] By invoking war powers to justify Padilla's detention, authorities implied the battlefield extended to US territory.[122]

In the post-9/11 national security culture of legal rationalization, American officials sought legal cover for contentious detention policies. To construct the plausible legality of denying Geneva rights to detainees, they exploited purported gaps in international humanitarian law, particularly between rules governing international and noninternational armed conflicts, claiming that transnational counterterrorism was not constrained by the Geneva framework. Because international law does not provide clear definitions of protagonists in war beyond privileged combatants and protected civilians, they also advanced the concept of unlawful enemy combatants, or persons who could be detained and killed like combatants but did not enjoy combatant rights. Although the Bush administration's efforts to permissively reinterpret the Geneva Conventions were highly controversial, there are some real instabilities in the law that facilitated their efforts. In particular, the law lacks clear standards for who can be detained and for how long without criminal charge in noninternational armed conflicts.[123] Classifying combatants, civilians, and those that fall somewhere in between is a genuinely difficult exercise.

The following sections will explore the concept of unlawful enemy combatant and related ideas as they played out in practice and in law at Guantánamo Bay, in military commission proceedings, and in lawsuits brought by human rights advocates.

Guantánamo Bay

Guantánamo Bay is a forty-five-square-mile American military base on the coast of Cuba. It became one of the primary symbols of the global war on terror when alleged terrorists were first brought there in January 2002. Since then, 779 prisoners have been held at the base for varying amounts of time.[124]

For critics, these detentions are emblematic of American disdain for the rule of law. This is in many ways true. Unlawful enemy combatants were denied Geneva Conventions protections. National security officials claimed American law did not apply at the base, removing the ability of detainees to seek relief in American courts. However, pushback from human rights advocates made Guantánamo a site of extensive legal contestation, forcing authorities to repeatedly legally rationalize their detention policies and practices.

Guantánamo's unique status is a legacy of American imperialism.[125] After the 1898 Spanish-American War, the United States occupied Cuba. Subsequently, the Senate passed the Platt Amendment (1901), which restricted Cuba's foreign relations with other countries, secured a semicolonial role for the United States in Cuban affairs, and required the lease of Guantánamo Bay to the Americans. The amendment was accepted by Cuba in 1902 and further formalized in the Cuban-American Treaty, granting Cuba self-government in 1903. According to this unusual agreement, the United States controls Guantánamo Bay, while Cuba retains technical sovereignty.[126] In 1934, the Treaty of Relations between the countries abrogated the Platt Amendment but reaffirmed the lease of Guantánamo.[127] To the displeasure of Cuba's government since the 1959 revolution, the United States has been unwilling to break the agreement.

The global war on terror is not the first instance in which Guantánamo Bay has been used as an extraterritorial detention facility. Prior to 1991, citizens and aliens on the base were offered full American constitutional protections.[128] After the 1991 coup against Haitian President Jean-Bertrand Aristide, Haitian refugees attempted to reach the Florida coast in makeshift boats. Instead, they were interdicted by the US Coast Guard and brought to Guantánamo Bay. By 1992, thousands of refugees were held at the base. Those deemed ineligible for asylum were repatriated to Haiti, never having had access to a lawyer or normal American legal procedure. American authorities at Guantánamo actively urged Haitians to return home, insisting it was safe, and provided inaccurate legal advice to detainees.[129] They further declared their intention to indefinitely detain HIV-positive refugees at Guantánamo. Before being closed in 1993, this "HIV prison camp" was surrounded by barbed wire and provided inadequate health and living standards.[130] In 1994, the base was revamped as a permanent "safe haven" for Cuban boat people, although migrants were eventually allowed into the United States or returned to Cuba.

In response to this legal situation, American lawyers sought to provide legal advice and representation to migrants at the base. However, courts rejected their attempts, concluding that "Haitians at Guantánamo had no constitutional rights whatever ... the Bill of Rights does not bind the federal government in its dealings with aliens at Guantánamo."[131] For Gerald

Neuman, these developments resulted in the creation of a troubling rights-free zone: "Guantánamo may then be seen as an example of what I will call an 'anomalous zone,' a geographical area in which certain legal rules, otherwise regarded as embodying fundamental policies of the larger legal system, are locally suspended."[132]

It is widely accepted that detainees in the global war on terror, like the Haitians and Cubans before them, were brought to Guantánamo to keep them out of reach of the American justice system. Because sovereignty infers certain legal obligations such as the extension of constitutional rights, the base's extraterritorial status increased its utility.

Once again, the OLC played a key role in legally rationalizing post-9/11 Guantánamo detentions. In arguing for the extraterritorial nonapplicability of American due process rights to Guantánamo prisoners, the OLC invoked the Second World War case of *Johnson v. Eisentrager* (1950):

> The basis for denying jurisdiction to entertain a habeas petition filed by an alien held at GBC [Guantánamo Bay, Cuba] rests on Johnson v. Eisentrager, 339 U.S. 763 (1950). In that case, the Supreme Court held that federal courts did not have authority to entertain an application for habeas relief filed by an enemy alien who had been seized and held at all relevant times outside the territory of the United States . . . Eisentrager involved several German soldiers who had continued to aid the Japanese in China after Germany had surrendered in April 1945. They were seized, tried by military commission in Nanking, China and subsequently imprisoned in Germany. From there, they filed an application for habeas corpus in the District Court for the District of Columbia, naming as respondents the Secretary of Defense, Secretary of the Army, and the Joint Chiefs of Staff. . . . The Court concluded that the federal courts were without power to grant habeas relief because the plaintiffs were beyond the territorial sovereignty of the United States and outside the territorial jurisdiction of any U.S. court.[133]

Accordingly, OLC lawyers John Yoo and Patrick Philbin concluded that Cuba's de jure sovereignty over Guantánamo and the lack of any explicitly constructed US federal court jurisdiction meant detainees had no habeas rights in American courts. Despite this finding, they remained sensitive to the importance of legal cover, cautioning that a "detainee could make a non-frivolous argument that jurisdiction does exist" and that there "remains some litigation risk."[134] Reflecting the national security culture of legal rationalization that shaped post-9/11 American counterterrorism policy, they noted: "You have also asked us about the potential *legal exposure* if a detainee successfully convinces a federal district court to exercise habeas jurisdiction. There is little doubt that such a result could interfere with the operation of the system that has been developed to address the detainment and trial of enemy aliens."[135]

In the absence of a successful legal challenge, the Guantánamo prison remained outside domestic US jurisdiction, creating what many critics labeled a "legal black hole."[136] Their exclusion from constitutional rights, combined with the Bush administration's permissive reading of the Geneva Conventions, meant that detainees had almost no meaningful opportunities to challenge their designation as unlawful enemy combatants and their resultant indefinite detention in the early years of the global war on terror. While this state of affairs was partially altered by habeas litigation, Guantánamo's ambiguous legal geography continues to provide a controversial legal framework for detention at the base. Indefinite detention appears poised to continue for the foreseeable future.

Military Commissions

Shortly after 9/11, the Bush administration introduced military commissions to try unlawful enemy combatants for war crimes. Not to be confused with military courts-martial used in the military justice system, military commissions are tribunals created by executive order pursuant to presidential war powers. As Harold Koh explained in 2002: "However detailed its rules and procedures may be, a military commission is not an independent court, and its commissioners are not genuinely independent decision makers.... Commissioners are not independent judges, but usually military officers who are ultimately answerable to the secretary of defense and the president, who prosecute the cases."[137] While military commissions are not inherently unfair, they lack the due process safeguards that operate in established court systems.

There are important precedents for military commissions. In 1942, eight German agents were captured off the coasts of Long Island and Florida. President Roosevelt ordered the saboteurs to be tried by military commission.[138] In *Ex parte Quirin*, lawyers attempted to argue that such commissions were illegitimate as civilian courts were still functioning. [139] They failed. The Supreme Court upheld the tribunals and the defendants were found guilty, some executed.

On November 13, 2001, President Bush similarly authorized military commissions via military order. The decision was made without consulting the national security advisor, Condoleezza Rice, who notes that the Department of State, Department of Defense, and even attorney general found themselves "outflanked on occasion" by Vice President Cheney, his counsel David Addington, and OLC attorneys who were "determined to push the boundaries of executive authority."[140] Individuals subject to military commissions were non-American citizens accused of membership in al-Qaeda or who "engaged in, aided or abetted, or conspired to commit, acts of international terrorism" or who harbored such persons.[141] Military commissions were designed to allow the government to prosecute unlawful enemy combatants using rules that protect national security information and allow evidence and procedures not generally permitted in a normal trial. As President Bush's order stated, "it is not practicable to apply in military commissions under this order the principles of law and the rules of evidence generally recognized in the trial of criminal cases in the United States district courts."[142] Moreover, defendants subject to these procedures had no right "to seek any remedy or maintain any proceeding, directly or indirectly, or to have any such remedy or proceeding sought on the individual's behalf, in (i) any court of the United States, or any State thereof, (ii) any court of any foreign nation, or (iii) any international tribunal."[143] Military commissions were governed by minimal procedural rules that privileged the prosecution.[144]

Human rights advocates have criticized post-9/11 military commissions for ignoring extensive developments in international humanitarian and human rights law since the Second World War.[145] There is no doubt that military commissions as originally envisioned by the Bush administration lacked due process safeguards. However, for all their efforts to evade legal restrictions on detention and trial procedures, American authorities did not reject or suspend the rule of law. Rather, they permissively interpreted existing rules to facilitate maximum freedom of action. Their legal logics were subject to ongoing contestation as lawyers for detainees engaged in a flurry of litigation on behalf of their clients—cases that forced the United States to continually amend its policies.

Habeas Litigation, the Supreme Court, and Legislative Adaptation

Numerous habeas cases were brought on behalf of Guantánamo detainees over the years. The resulting court rulings have checked, but not entirely undermined, the government's attempt to deny due process protections to prisoners. These cases are important not only for their substantive impact on security policy, but also for their broader role in shaping the terrain of post-9/11 American national security legal culture. While often leaving great discretion to legislators, the contemporary American judiciary has not been willing to approve the racialized exceptionalism that legally legitimized Japanese internment. Instead, authorities have been compelled to revise their policies to conform, to a minimal degree, with contemporary constitutional, human rights, and humanitarian norms.

In *Hamdi v. Rumsfeld* (2004), the Supreme Court ruled on whether the detention of Yaser Hamdi—an American citizen seized in Afghanistan and held at Guantánamo as an unlawful enemy combatant—was appropriate.[146] It decided that while the 2001 Authorization for Use of Military Force granted the executive the implicit power of wartime detention, American citizens must be subject to a basic, fair procedure to determine the legality of their detention even if they are captured in combat overseas.[147] In *Rasul v. Bush* (2004), the court further ruled that alien detainees at Guantánamo did in fact have the right to challenge the legality of their detention in US federal court.[148] In response to these rulings, the Bush administration initiated Combatant Status Review Tribunals to determine the appropriate status of detainees. These tribunals allowed detainees some participation in proceedings but denied them access to counsel, classified information, witnesses, and evidence.[149] Congress then passed the Detainee Treatment Act of 2005, which stripped federal judges of habeas jurisdiction over unlawful enemy combatants.[150]

In *Hamdam v. Rumsfeld* (2006), the Supreme Court rejected the Bush administration's contention that there were categories of transnational armed conflict not subject to Geneva rules.[151] Rather, it ruled that common article 3 of the Geneva Conventions operates relative and in "contradistinction" to article 2, closing the alleged gap between international and noninternational armed conflicts.[152] Any armed conflict thus immediately triggered basic obligations of humane treatment. Furthermore, while agreeing that al-Qaeda prisoners were not entitled to POW status, the court ruled that trial procedures were governed by common article 3, which prohibits "the passing of sentences and the carrying out of executions without previous judgment pronounced by a regularly constituted court, affording all the judicial guarantees which are recognized as indispensable by civilized peoples." To comply with this requirement, the court ruled that military commissions should be conducted in conformity with the "barest" fair trial procedures found in international customary law.[153] Finally, the decision invalidated the denial of habeas rights to Guantánamo inmates with pending claims that predated the Detainee Treatment Act.[154] "I disagreed strongly with the Court's decision, which I considered an example of judicial activism," writes President Bush in his memoir. "But I accepted the role of the Supreme Court in our constitutional democracy. . . . Whether presidents like them or not, the Court's decisions are the law of the land."[155]

After *Hamdam*, "high-value" detainees held at CIA black sites, which I discussed in chapter 3, were transferred to Department of Defense control at Guantánamo. However, the Supreme Court left a loophole. The concurrence with *Hamdam* stated: "Nothing prevents the President from returning to Congress to seek the authority he believes necessary."[156]

Despite its apparent challenge to the Bush administration, the court did not reject military commissions. Rather, it allowed Congress to authorize them through new legislation.

In response to the Supreme Court's ruling, Congress passed the Military Commissions Act of 2006. The law granted limited rights for detainees, in essence legislating what the Bush administration had attempted to achieve through executive decree. "It contained everything we asked for," states Bush.[157] It included numerous controversial provisions. All commissions established under the act were declared to automatically comply with Geneva standards by definition. Hearsay evidence was permitted. While information gleaned from torture was prohibited, evidence based on cruel, inhuman, and degrading treatment was barred only retroactive to the Detainee Treatment Act of 2005. Like the Detainee Treatment Act, the Military Commissions Act provided retroactive immunity for American personnel who had relied on legal authorizations to conduct abusive interrogations. The president was authorized to authoritatively interpret the "meaning and application" of the Geneva Conventions. The Military Commissions Act amended the War Crimes Act so that "grave breaches" of common article 3 were outlawed under US law.[158] However, only nine such acts were listed: torture, cruel treatment, performing biological experiments, murder, mutilation or maiming, intentionally causing serious bodily injury, rape, sexual assault or abuse, and taking hostages. Failure to try suspects in a "regularly constituted court" and inflicting "humiliating and degrading treatment" were omitted.

The Military Commissions Act institutionalized the category of unlawful enemy combatant, defined as persons alleged to be engaging in "material support" of terrorism, a vague and undefined concept that could range from fundraising to ideological support. The act furthermore invented new categories of crimes like "murder in violation of the laws of war," as opposed to ordinary murder, which is normally dealt with in criminal procedure. As explained by Jack Beard, "a common criminal offense such as murder, for which an unlawful enemy combatant may be tried under ordinary domestic law, may be difficult to characterize as a war crime in the context of an attack on military personnel because combatants who are engaged in hostilities are not generally protected from attack under the law of war."[159] Finally, the Military Commissions Act denied recourse to the Geneva Conventions as a source of unlawful enemy combatant rights and revoked the right of federal courts to hear habeas petitions from alien detainees.[160]

Reflecting push-pull dynamics between branches of government, the Supreme Court partially checked the Military Commissions Act in *Boumediene v. Bush* (2008), which ruled that alien Guantánamo detainees could claim habeas rights in US courts. [161] Finding that the United States had "practical" and "de facto" sovereignty and continuous "plenary control" over the base, it rejected the government's argument premised on extraterritoriality.[162] Combatant Status Review Tribunals were deemed an inadequate substitute for habeas review, therefore violating the suspension clause of the Constitution. Because it was practical to conduct habeas review for Guantánamo detainees, other mechanisms were unnecessary. However, the court did not lay out clear parameters for long-term preventative detention of non-POWs who have not been convicted of a crime.[163] There are still few guidelines to govern this process.

Debates persisted over whether the *Boumediene* principles extended to detention sites beyond Guantánamo.[164] In a 2009 court ruling, detention review at the Bagram military base in Afghanistan was deemed insufficient.[165] However, the decision was reversed on appeal. Among the appeal court's findings was that "[i]n Bagram, while the United States has options as to duration of the lease agreement, there is no indication of any intent to occupy the base with permanence, nor is there hostility on the part of the 'host' country. . . . While it is certainly realistic to assert that the United States has *de facto* sovereignty over Guantanamo, the same simply is not true with respect to Bagram."[166] Nonetheless, as Jack Goldsmith reports, senior legal advisors in Afghanistan remained concerned that the Supreme Court could require habeas review. As one lawyer stated, "we must perform customary military legal operations in a combat zone with an eye toward defensive litigation [and] must be concerned how a civilian court will view our legal actions and decisions."[167]

In sum, US Supreme Court and other judicial rulings form an important part of the post-9/11 legal landscape. While far less conclusive than human rights advocates would prefer, these decisions forced American authorities to perpetually reaffirm the plausible legality of security policy through amending practices and legislation.

The Obama Administration

The Obama administration continued to apply the war paradigm to American counterterrorism policy. It cited the Authorization for Use of Military Force informed by international law, as the source of its powers. Although rejecting the terminology of the global war on terror, it emphasized the United States' right of self-defense against al-Qaeda.[168] For critics, the administration's rhetorical shifts did not ultimately amount to substantive changes in legal logic.[169] Indefinite detention, military commissions, and, increasingly, targeted killing, traversed partisan politics and presidencies.

This is not to say there were not important differences between administrations. As discussed in chapter 3, President Obama repudiated enhanced interrogation techniques upon taking office. Moreover, he promised to close the Guantánamo prison within a year. Toward this end, he appointed a task force to review remaining detainees.[170] However, he not only failed in this timeline, he all but embraced the reality of permanent imprisonment. This was partly due to congressional intransigence. Despite early talk of establishing a "Guantánamo North," legislators blocked transfer of Guantánamo detainees to the United States. Yet a deeper problem persisted. The Obama administration believed there were detainees who could not be tried or released.[171] Whether held at Guantánamo or a new, less symbolic, location, the implication remained the same: indefinite detention.[172] As of late 2017, forty-one men remained at the base, including several top alleged 9/11 conspirators.[173]

President Obama and Attorney General Eric Holder did attempt to improve the detention and military commissions systems. They raised detention standards in Afghanistan in summer 2009.[174] They advocated reforming military commissions to increase procedural safeguards, such as prohibitions on statements obtained through cruel, inhuman, and degrading treatment. In 2009, the Military Commissions Act was successfully amended. However, some changes were largely cosmetic. For instance, the much-criticized terminology of unlawful enemy combatants was replaced with "unprivileged enemy belligerents."[175] The revised act did not prevent the controversial trial of Omar Khadr, charged with "murder in violation of the law of war" for acts committed at the age of fifteen. Khadr eventually entered a plea bargain that returned him to Canada to serve his remaining sentence. In addition to his young age, critics noted that Khadr was abused after capture and kept in unlawful detention conditions, which fundamentally undermined the fairness of his trial.[176] Khadr's case is one of only seven cases to be concluded by military commission since 9/11.[177]

In other instances, the Obama administration attempted to funnel captured terrorists into the domestic legal system. In a highly symbolic move, Attorney General Holder announced in fall 2009 that 9/11 mastermind Khalid Sheik Mohammed would be tried in civilian court in New York City. The political backlash was powerful and immediate. Congressional Republicans introduced legislation that would permanently bar the transfer of any detainee to the United States. In May 2011, military prosecutors refiled charges against Mohammed for trial by military commission, quashing any hope for a civilian trial.[178]

In December 2011, bipartisan legislators overwhelmingly passed the ambiguously worded National Defense Authorization Act for fiscal year 2012, which mandated indefinite military detention of al-Qaeda or Taliban suspects and associated forces without recourse to civilian justice. While the bill allowed accused Americans to be tried in the criminal justice system, such allowances were based on presidential discretion. In essence, the legislation limited civilian law enforcement's control over processing terror charges. Under pressure to ensure adequate defense appropriations, President Obama quietly signed the bill on New Year's Eve. While issuing a signing statement promising to uphold the rights of Americans, his acquiescence ushered in one of the most important pieces of post-9/11 legislation.[179]

The Obama administration tried to distance itself from some Bush administration policies. However, it often failed: "Barack Obama campaigned and began his presidency with a pledge to shut down Guantánamo, support federal trials for terrorism suspects, respect human rights and restore the rule of law," notes the Center for Constitutional Rights. "Guantánamo and the military tribunal system are no longer an inheritance from the Bush administration—they will be President Obama's legacy."[180]

Targeted Killing

Civilian casualties in war remain a vexing problem. Collateral damage or the incidental death of civilians is inevitable. Such deaths are not necessarily unlawful provided that military commanders consider proportionality and take adequate precautions. The United States claims to minimize civilian suffering through the use of "smart" weapons technologies and the employment of population-centric counterinsurgency that wins "hearts and minds" and respects distinction. When American soldiers and contractors wantonly violate the principle of distinction, such as the Mahmudiyah gang rape of a fourteen-year-old girl and murder of her family (2006) and Haditha (2005) and Nisour Square (2007) massacres in Iraq, the United States, under pressure from human rights advocates, usually investigates and prosecutes offenders, although convictions and meaningful sentences are rare. Rather than invoke exceptional necessity or overtly racist characterizations of their victims, defendants in such cases often successfully argue that they did not intentionally target civilians.[181] Yet the result is frequently the same: impunity. As with torture, failure to aggressively sanction unlawful killing of civilians erodes constraining norms and creates an increasingly permissive environment.

Perhaps because of its novel character, targeted killing has proved the most contentious form of lethal force in the global war on terror. While decried as extrajudicial killing by human rights advocates, American authorities have consistently defended the practice as lawful killing in warfare. In this sense, it differs markedly from instances where soldiers massacre civilians or intelligence agencies secretly assassinate enemies. Instead, it rests within the United States' increasingly legalized way of war.

According to Philip Alston, the former UN Special Rapporteur on extrajudicial, summary, or arbitrary executions: "A targeted killing is the intentional, premeditated and deliberate use of lethal force, by States or their agents acting under color of law, or by an organized armed group in armed conflict, against a specific individual who is not in the physical custody of the perpetrator."[182] Although there is no inherent link between military robotics and targeted killing, targeted killing strikes are often carried out by what are alternately called unmanned aerial vehicles or remotely piloted aircraft and are more commonly known as drones.

Preludes to contemporary American targeted killing emerged in the 1980s and 1990s. While denying an attempt on the dictator's life, President Ronald Reagan authorized a 1986 aerial assault on Muammar Gaddafi's Tripoli compound in response to a terrorist bombing in Germany.[183] In the wake of al-Qaeda attacks in the1990s, the Bill Clinton administration authorized use of lethal force against Osama bin Laden, but only if necessary for "self-defense," an initiative that proved controversial at the time. Jane Mayer reports that Attorney General Janet Reno was reluctant to allow targeted killing. As a result, "the line between sanctioned and illegal killing remained murky. Unless it was clarified by a new presidential finding, the CIA's lawyers were not about to let the Agency step on the wrong side of the law."[184]

In a fall 2001 presidential finding, "the Bush administration . . . concluded that executive orders banning assassination do not prevent the president from lawfully singling out a terrorist for death by covert action."[185] Drones were deployed toward this end. While they had commonly been used for surveillance and military support, CIA-controlled drone strikes out of theatre in the service of "hunter killer missions" was new.[186] Qaed Senyan al-Harithi, an al-Qaeda leader linked to the USS Cole bombing, became the first victim of targeted killing by drone on November 3, 2002 in Yemen.[187]

The Bush administration was not primarily focused on targeted killing, preferring to concentrate on its interrogation and detention program. Ultimately, the Obama administration accelerated the practice. With torture off the table and detention policy in flux, capturing alleged terrorists posed increased legal complications. Moreover, the Taliban and al-Qaeda were successfully routed in much of Afghanistan, reappearing in neighboring Pakistan where an American military presence on the ground was politically untenable. Faced with this geographical limitation, targeted killing by drones in inaccessible regions proved attractive. Statistics tell the story of the campaign's rapid expansion. Under President Bush, there were 48 drone strikes in Pakistan from 2004–2009. Under President Obama, there were 52 strikes in 2009, 122 in 2010, 72 in 2011, 48 in 2012, 26 in 2013, 22 in 2014, 10 in 2015, and 3 in 2016. Strikes from 2004–16 killed approximately 2,333–3,634 people, including 1,877–3,009 suspected militants and 245–299 civilians.[188] Other sources suggest 2,499–4,001 people were killed in Pakistan during this time period, including 424–966 civilians.[189] Yemen, Somalia, Libya, and eventually Syria also became targets, both with and without the acquiescence of their governing regimes. While the CIA managed much of the out-of-theatre drone program, the Department of Defense's Joint Special Operations Command has conducted strikes in Yemen and dominated operations in Syria.[190]

Targeted killing has taken on additional forms beyond drone strikes. For instance, Special Forces killed Osama bin Laden. On May 1, 2011, US Navy SEAL Team 6 executed Operation Neptune Spear, dropping from stealth helicopters into bin Laden's Abbottobad, Pakistan compound. During a brief firefight, bin Laden was shot dead along with several other adults. Not surprisingly, the Obama administration not only defended the operation, but also presented it as the core achievement of the president's counterterrorism policy. According to their logic, bin Laden was a combatant and thus a legitimate military target.[191]

The most contentious dimension of the targeted killing program involves its application to Americans. On September 30, 2011, an American drone strike killed American citizen Anwar al-Awlaki along with several associates in Yemen. While human rights organizations attempted to challenge al-Awlaki's placement on the "kill list" in American courts as a fundamental violation of his constitutional due process rights, their efforts failed.[192]

Despite widespread diplomatic and human rights criticism, the United States has publically justified the legal legitimacy of targeted killing. Most importantly, Americans have argued that the 9/11 attacks constituted acts of war triggering armed conflict between the United States and al-Qaeda and associated forces. Under this framework, military rules of engagement governed by the law of armed conflict, not criminal procedure, become the appropriate guide for action. Because the law of war imposes considerably lower standards for the application of deadly force than human rights provisions governing law enforcement operations, it creates a far more permissive environment for states. This law of war paradigm underlies the legal rationalization of indefinite detention, military commissions, and targeted killing.

At all times, all persons have the right under international human rights law to not be arbitrarily deprived of life.[193] "Any intentional use of lethal force by state authorities that is not justified under the provisions regarding the right to life, will, by definition, be regarded as an 'extra-judicial execution,'" notes David Kretzmer.[194] In peacetime, self-defense against immediate attack or the application of a lawfully applied death penalty meets this justificatory criteria, provided strict due process conditions are respected. In wartime, the arbitrary killing threshold is distinct.[195] States aim to incapacitate their enemy to the extent demanded by military necessity; killing is not contingent on law enforcement standards, due process, or conviction by a court. By labeling al-Qaeda operatives combatants in war, American officials rationalized a distinct set of practices that would otherwise be illegal.

In a 2010 speech, State Department legal advisor Koh outlined the administration's legal position:

> The United States agrees that it must conform its actions to all applicable law. As I have explained, as a matter of international law, the United States is in an armed conflict with al-Qaeda, as well as the Taliban and associated forces, in response to the horrific 9/11 attacks, and may use force consistent with its inherent right to self-defense under international law. As a matter of domestic law, Congress authorized the use of all necessary and appropriate force through the 2001 Authorization for Use of Military Force (AUMF). As recent events have shown, al-Qaeda has not abandoned its intent to attack the United States, and indeed continues to attack us. Thus, in this ongoing armed conflict, the United States has the authority under international law, and the responsibility to its citizens, to use force, including lethal force, to defend itself, including by targeting persons such as high-level al-Qaeda leaders who are planning attacks.[196]

Adding to this picture, Attorney General Holder clarified that the laws of war govern military action:

> Of course, any such use of lethal force by the United States will comply with the four fundamental law of war principles governing the use of force. The principle of necessity requires that the target have definite military value. The principle of distinction requires that only lawful targets—such as combatants, civilians directly participating in hostilities, and military objectives—may be targeted intentionally. Under the principle of proportionality, the anticipated collateral damage must not be excessive in relation to the anticipated military advantage. Finally, the principle of humanity requires us to use weapons that will not inflict unnecessary suffering.[197]

However, even when limiting principles are applied, the war paradigm is a great deal more permissive than law enforcement standards of conduct.

The messiness of applying the war paradigm to transnational terrorism is evidenced by a 2011 Department of Justice white paper, leaked in February 2013, that outlines the president's authority to kill American citizens such as al-Awlaki who are deemed "senior operational leader[s] of al-Qa'ida or its associated forces who pose an imminent threat of violent attack against the United States."[198] Echoing numerous public pronouncements by administration officials, it claims that kill authority exists under the nation's legal right to self-defense against armed attack. While its employment of an imminent threat standard may seem narrower than a general invocation of the right to use lethal force in war, the white paper suggests otherwise. An " 'imminent' threat of violent attack against the United States does not require the United States to have clear evidence that a specific attack on U.S. persons and interests will take place in the immediate future," it declares.[199] Rather, it could simply mean that a targeted individual is involved "in activities posing an imminent threat of violent attack against the United States" or has not renounced such activities.[200] Not only does the white paper imply that terrorist attacks by nonstate actors meet a level of violence triggering armed conflict, it asserts an even more expansive preemptive proposition that participation in possible future attacks does likewise. Indeed, it goes so far as to claim "that the U.S. government may not be aware of all al-Qa'ida plots as they are developing and thus cannot be confident that none is about to occur."[201] In this sense, its repeated invocation of imminence as a limiting principle is deceptive.

Efforts to legally rationalize targeted killing also generated interpretative debates over the status of belligerent civilians and the geographical scope of armed conflict. To understand these arguments, it is necessary to once again review the Geneva Conventions. When it comes to killing, the law is clear that civilians can be lethally targeted only for as long as they engage in direct participation in hostilities, but there is little consensus on how this standard should be applied. In 2009, the ICRC produced a contested interpretive guidance on this question. It uses three criteria to characterize direct participation in hostilities, defined as "specific acts": "The act must be likely to adversely affect the military operations or military capacity of a party to an armed conflict or, alternatively, to inflict death, injury, or destruction on persons or objects protected against direct attack," and there must be "a relationship of direct causation between the act and the expected harm" and "a belligerent nexus between the act and the hostilities."[202] Direct participation is differentiated from indirect participation. Acts such as imposing financial sanctions; supplying a party to a conflict; the design, production, and transport of weapons; and recruitment and training may not qualify as direct participation unless they are conducted "for the execution of a predetermined hostile act."[203] The interpretive guidance emphasizes that lethal targeting "is not a sanction for criminal behavior but a consequence of military necessity in the conduct of hostilities."[204]

According to the ICRC's interpretation, members of organized armed groups in noninternational armed conflicts who consistently engage in direct participation in hostilities hold a "continuous combat function" and are not civilians for the purposes of distinction. They can therefore be lethally targeted like members of armed forces. This loss of protection from direct attack is demarcated by function, not simply group affiliation:

> Continuous combat function requires lasting integration into an organized armed group acting as the armed forces of a non-State party to an armed conflict. Thus, individuals whose continuous function involves the preparation, execution, or command of acts or operations amounting to direct participation in hostilities are assuming a continuous combat function. An individual recruited, trained and equipped by such a group to continuously and directly participate in hostilities on its behalf can be considered to assume a continuous combat function even before he or she first carries out a hostile act.[205]

Civilians that do not meet continuous combat function criteria cannot be targeted when they are not directly participating in hostilities.

The ICRC guidance has ignited extensive controversy among scholars and military lawyers, particularly over the merits of its construction of continuous combat function and its "revolving door" approach to direct participation in hostilities that allows civilians to lose and regain protected status.[206] It can be difficult to apply to real-time, real-world targeting decisions. Whatever its flaws, it offers one of the few publically promulgated sets of international standards governing the status of belligerent civilians in armed conflict.

After 9/11, the United States rejected the Geneva dichotomy between combatants and civilians, claiming that there are lawful combatants, civilians, and a distinct third category of unlawful enemy combatants. As with detention and military commissions policy, this designation created a class of people who were purportedly subject to military justice and military targeting, but who were denied the rights owed to lawful combatants by the Geneva Conventions.

American authorities have failed to disclose criteria for identifying civilians involved in direct participation in hostilities. The Justice Department white paper merely states that an "operation against a senior operational leader of al-Qa'ida or its associated forces who poses an imminent threat of violent attack against the United States would target a person who is taking 'an active part in hostilities' and therefore would not consti-tute a 'grave breach' of Common Article 3."[207] This hardly clarifies much, particularly as critics have alleged many targeted killings are so-called sig-nature strikes, where targets are selected based not on their specific per-sonal identity but on their association with certain intelligence patterns and indicators. These signatures may include a range of variables from attending an al-Qaeda training camp, to associating with armed men, to geographic location and age.[208] According to researchers: "It is unclear what, if any, process is in place for decisions regarding the so-called 'signature strikes,' which are particularly problematic and open to abuse and mistake."[209] Such ambiguity, notes Alston, "is deeply problematic because it gives no trans-parency or clarity about what conduct could subject a civilian to killing."[210]

Targeted killing occurs outside of traditionally recognizable battlefields. Legal rationales for this practice are intimately linked to a legal theory of transnational and borderless warfare, in which the war paradigm follows terrorist suspects to locales around the world. Indeed, American authorities have invoked the right to use lethal military force against al-Qaeda and as-sociated forces anywhere in the world "without a geographic limitation."[211] The rules of armed conflict accompany alleged terrorists, extending wher-ever they travel. Attorney General Holder elaborated on this view:

> Our legal authority is not limited to the battlefields in Afghanistan. Indeed, neither Congress nor our federal courts has limited the geographic scope of our ability to use force to the current conflict in Afghanistan. We are at war with a stateless enemy, prone to shifting operations from country to country . . . This does not mean that we can use military force whenever or wherever we want. International legal principles, including re-spect for another nation's sovereignty, constrain our ability to act unilaterally. But the use of force in foreign territory would be consistent with these international legal principles if conducted, for example, with the consent of the nation involved—or after a determination that the nation is unable or unwilling to deal effectively with a threat to the United States.[212]

Whether the battlefield extends to the United States is ambiguous. Jeh Johnson, former general counsel of the Department of Defense and later Secretary of Homeland Security, noted that "when we attempt to extend the reach of the military on to U.S. soil, the courts resist, con-sistent with our core values and our American heritage—reflected, no less, in places such as the Declaration of Independence, the Federalist Papers, the Third Amendment, and in the 1878 federal criminal statute, still on the books today, which prohibits willfully using the military as a posse comitatus unless expressly authorized by Congress or the Constitution."[213] However, while clearly rejecting domestic targeted killing as a matter of policy, Holder answered a question about hypothetical domestic drone strikes by stating that, as a matter of law, the US government does not have the authority to extrajudicially kill Americans "not engaged in combat" on American soil.[214] He did not explain what engaged in combat means.

The ambiguities surrounding the identification of combatants subject to lethal targeting and the borders of armed conflict have expanded with the United States' growing engagement in conflicts in Syria and throughout Africa. The Authorization for Use of Military Force references al-Qaeda, not the so-called Islamic State in Iraq and al-Sham (ISIS), or "Daesh" as it is called by many, a distinct, rival organization. Although ISIS-affiliated individuals have carried out attacks in the United States, the problem of qualifying the existence of armed conflict with this group remain.[215] The legal wrangling that has accompanied debates over the targeted killing of al-Qaeda members will likely intensify as transnational conflict with ISIS deepens.

What is clear is that the United States continues to openly defend the legality of targeted killing, using rationales that overlap with indefinite detention and military commissions policies. Far from exceptional derogations from or covert violations of the law, lawyers have consistently sought to establish the plausible legality of these policies under American and international law.

CONCLUSION

Americans have placed rights to life, liberty, and due process at the center of their legal system. International human rights and humanitarian law restrict state violence, protect civilians, and require that detainees be treated fairly. Nonetheless, indiscriminate killing, indefinite and secret detention, racial and religious profiling, mass internment, ideological witch hunts, and assassination all have an unfortunate place in American history. Despite the perennial nature of such practices, changing trends can be observed. The overt racism and xenophobia that once justified abuses against indigenous peoples, African Americans, minorities, and immigrants became increasingly illegitimate after the Second World War in the face of thickening human rights norms. The contemporary laws of war make clear that exceptional necessity cannot justify war crimes. Moreover, Cold War clandestine and covert operations are difficult to sustain in the contemporary human rights and media monitoring environment. Authorities have little expectation of sustainable secrecy. Security and intelligence officials are subject to high levels of scrutiny and criticism, creating demand for legal cover for controversial policies. As with torture, in the contemporary national security culture of legal rationalization, government lawyers have played a key role in constructing plausibly legal justifications for rounding up immigrants, permanent detention, military commissions, and targeted killing programs.

As I have documented throughout this chapter, post-9/11 American legal rationalizations for detention, trial, and targeting policies have rested on strategic interpretations of legal rules. Legal norms have functioned as a *permissive constraint*, limiting overt exceptionalism and extralegality, yet simultaneously facilitating abusive policies. Officials exploited their extensive discretion in applying immigration and material witness laws. They identified alleged gaps in the Geneva Conventions framework between international and noninternational armed conflicts and combatants and civilians that enabled them to reframe detainees as unlawful enemy combatants ineligible for protection. They utilized extraterritorial prisons to avoid American jurisdiction, invoked executive war powers to create military commissions, and revised domestic legislation in response to pushback from the Supreme Court. Many of these legal maneuvers transcended administrations, particularly in regard to targeted killing, which Obama administration lawyers argued is a form of lawful killing in war. The substantive impact of these policies has been to arbitrarily deny many detainees and targets of the global war on terror of their rights.

One of the most troubling aspects of this story is the apparent vulnerability of legal norms to interpretive disagreement, manipulation, and revision. As summed up by former State Department legal advisor John Bellinger: "It is very easy for all to agree that the fight against transnational terrorism must be conducted in accordance with the rule of law, but it is much harder to say what the law exactly is, and how it should be applied in this context."[216] By arguing that legal rules were unclear or inapplicable to the changing conflict environment, American policymakers effectively exploited ambiguities and jurisdictional loopholes to justify abuses. In doing so, they established legal cover.

Unlike the case of torture, there has been little serious discussion of prosecuting politicians or lawyers for civil rights violations and war crimes related to post-9/11 detention, trial, and targeting policies. Rather, ongoing debate concerns whether such policies should be limited or expanded. Support for indefinite detention and targeted killing cuts across party lines. The courts have checked abuses on occasion, but policymakers have continually adapted, reflecting the flexibility of the contemporary American national security culture of legal rationalization.

CHAPTER 5
Surveillance

In contrast to universal and nonderogable prohibitions on torture and legal restrictions on arbitrary deprivations of life and liberty, the regulation of intelligence surveillance in the United States has been relatively limited. While the concept of individual privacy is central to the American civil liberties tradition, it is not considered an inviolable human right in all circumstances. All forms of spying are not inherently illegal or normatively transgressive. As with the other security practices I have examined in previous chapters, surveillance norms, laws, and policies, and the relationships among them, have shifted over time. What does and does not constitute a legitimate infringement of privacy has changed historically.

Edward Snowden's dramatic disclosure of controversial National Security Agency (NSA) programs in summer 2013 led many critics to conclude that contemporary American surveillance operates within an extralegal national security *culture of exception*, in which powerful actors ignore and suspend legal rules with impunity. NSA surveillance evinces further parallels with a *culture of secrecy*, in which illegal activities are pursued behind closed doors with the aim of evading public scrutiny. However, I argue that historical comparisons highlight important differences between post-9/11 surveillance and previous episodes of exceptional, unlawful, and clandestine spying, many of which were extensively documented and criticized by Senate investigations in the 1970s. Those revelations spurred the creation of the Foreign Intelligence Surveillance Act of 1978 (FISA). This law, which allows extensive foreign surveillance while limiting domestic surveillance, continues to structure American surveillance in critical ways.

I suggest that what many civil libertarians frame as exceptional spying does not directly challenge the dominant legal paradigm governing surveillance in the United States. Rather, authorities have maneuvered through and around legal rules. In this chapter, I trace shifts in the meaning of legitimate and illegitimate surveillance from historically unconstrained surveillance to the limited restraints that define the current surveillance regime. I argue that surveillance remains subject to highly dualistic legal norms that permit and even celebrate foreign spying while curtailing domestic surveillance. Reflecting a national security *culture of legal rationalization*, contemporary American security policy reinforces rather than challenges this framework. The intelligence community's demand for legal cover for controversial programs means that surveillance in the global war on terror remains wedded to the foreign versus domestic legal dichotomy, even as surveillance policy radically stretches these concepts, sometimes to the breaking point.

While flirting with exceptional derogations from legal constraints, post-9/11 American policymakers have employed a strategy of *plausible legality* in order to reconstruct the boundary between foreign and domestic intelligence targets. Instead of rejecting the wall between these two spheres, the administrations of George W. Bush and Barack Obama expanded the meaning of "foreign," a move predicated on this foundational dichotomy. This process has been facilitated by the changing nature of new communications technologies, which objectively render tenuous the boundary between foreign and domestic, as well as a preexisting "third-party disclosure" doctrine, which limits privacy regarding increasingly common forms of data. Although similar to attempts to legalize enhanced interrogation techniques and various controversial deprivations of life and liberty, surveillance policy has met with significantly less resistance. This is partly because of the weakness of privacy norms compared to other human rights values. Moreover, the primarily domestic character of surveillance law makes it vulnerable to frequent revision through the legislative process. There are thus limited obstacles to reinterpreting and rewriting surveillance restrictions to facilitate the plausible legality of government spying.

CONCEPTUALIZING PRIVACY AND SURVEILLANCE

Before delving into the history of privacy rights and privacy violations and the practice and regulation of surveillance, it is important to understand key concepts. Privacy has several dimensions. Most viscerally, it may involve bodily privacy or freedom from unwanted invasive procedures such as physical searches of one's person or medical testing. Territorial privacy applies to physical spaces such as one's home or workplace. Video surveillance and ID checks may infringe on one's privacy in the public sphere. Privacy also extends to information and data, such as personal papers, government records, and financial and consumer data held by corporations. Communications privacy covers mail, email, telephone calls, and other new forms of communication technology.

Various forms of surveillance, search, and seizure may occur in all of the aforementioned domains of privacy. There is domestic surveillance, generally associated with criminal law enforcement, and foreign surveillance, including military and intelligence surveillance, usually employed in relation to security threats. Intelligence surveillance collects information about adversaries while counterintelligence aims to identify double agents and espionage. Surveillance methods include human intelligence (HUMINT), whereby infiltrators or informers engage in surveillance, as well as signals intelligence (SIGINT), whereby technical interception of communication technologies is the primary means of conducting intelligence gathering.[1]

It is additionally possible to differentiate between government surveillance conducted by state security and policing agencies, government data collection for nonsecurity purposes, and corporate surveillance that occurs in the context of business transactions. Various dimensions of this complex landscape become more important than others throughout the history of surveillance. In the following discussion, I trace shifts from unconstrained to exceptional to covert surveillance before analyzing how American authorities legally rationalized mass surveillance in the global war on terror.

FROM THE KING'S PREROGATIVE TO CONSTITUTIONAL RIGHTS

English legal developments laid the groundwork for what would eventually become the American privacy regime. While monarchs exercised prerogative power to stamp out treason, some minimal rules governed surveillance in early modern England. For instance in 1604, jurist Sir Edward Coke famously ruled, "the house of everyone is to him as his castle and fortress, as well for his defence against injury and violence, as for his repose." However, he also concluded "in all cases when the King is party, the sheriff (if the doors be not open) may break [into] the party's house, either to arrest him or to do other execution of the King's process, if otherwise he cannot enter. But before he breaks [into] it, he ought to signify the cause of his coming and to make request to open the door."[2] In other words, privacy was valued but subject to lawful violation. Notions of just cause were vaguely defined. To conduct searches, English authorities increasingly utilized "general warrants," which were open-ended and nonspecific.[3]

General warrants travelled to eighteenth-century America, where they tended "to give their enforcers every discretion."[4] Broad suspicions justified searches without legal procedure to ensure just cause. Mail communications were especially insecure. For instance, Thomas Jefferson and Benjamin Franklin worried that their letters would be intercepted by the British.[5] However, it was search and seizure related to tax collection that became a lightning rod in the colonies. Concerned over declining revenues, England imposed a variety of measures that allowed customs officers to utilize the writ of assistance, a general warrant that demanded peace officers and subjects assist in the execution of the writ. "The writ, once issued, lasted for the life of the sovereign and therefore constituted a long-term hunting license for customs officers on the lookout for smugglers and articles imported in violation of the customs law."[6]

After the death of King George II, customs officers petitioned the court in *Paxton's Case* (1761) to have the writ extended. A group of American merchants led by James Otis Jr. strenuously objected. Although they eventually lost the challenge, the incident inspired John Adams' revolutionary fervor: "Otis was a flame of fire! . . . Then and there was the first scene of the first Act of Opposition to the arbitrary claims of Great Britain."[7] Over the years, British attempts to expand the writ met with increasing popular hostility, often resulting in physical confrontations.

British search and seizure policy was a major rallying point for American colonists. Not only did it offend the founding fathers' opposition to political tyranny, it challenged private property rights, which are closely associated with privacy rights in liberal thought.[8] In the late eighteenth century, several legal cases laid the groundwork for American surveillance law. In 1762, Englishman John Entick's home was forcibly raided and his papers were seized by the king's messengers, who had been sent to hunt down the author of a seditious pamphlet. In the precedent-setting case, *Entick v. Carrington* (1765), the English court ruled: "The great end, for which men entered into society, was to secure their property. That right is preserved sacred and incommunicable in all instances."[9] Invasions of this right could be justified only where there was an established just cause in the law.

These sentiments were adopted by the new American Bill of Rights, specifically the Fourth Amendment: "The right of the people to be secure in their persons, houses, papers, and effects, against unreasonable searches and seizures, shall not be violated, and no Warrants shall issue, but upon probable cause, supported by Oath or affirmation, and particularly describing the place to be searched, and the persons or things to be seized."[10] The Fourth Amendment did not prohibit search and seizure. Instead, it required authorities to produce evidence of a legitimate suspicion of criminal wrongdoing. However, the meanings of "unreasonable" and "probable cause" have not always been obvious. Numerous court cases and legislation have interpreted the Fourth Amendment, granting more and less weight to government and individual interests. For example, important historical cases include *Ex parte Jackson* (1878),[11] which required a warrant for the government to open first class mail, and *Boyd v. United States* (1886),[12] which ruled that authorities could not compel production of private papers to establish a criminal charge.[13] In *Olmstead v. United Sates* (1928),[14] the Supreme Court took a more permissive stance, deciding that warrantless wiretapping of a Prohibition-era bootlegger was legal because there was no physical trespass. Justice Louis Brandeis dissented, arguing that "writs of assistance and general warrants are but puny instruments of tyranny and oppression when compared with wiretapping."[15] As I will discuss later, evolving technologies and surveillance scandals prompted a flurry of new legislation in the late 1960s and 1970s.

SPYING AND THE NATIONAL SECURITY STATE

While the Bill of Rights and subsequent court cases created progressive legal restrictions on domestic surveillance, foreign military and intelligence operations have never been similarly constrained. George Washington took interest in intelligence during the Revolutionary War, requesting funds for continued intelligence activities in his first State of the Union message, which were granted under the Secret Service Fund.[16] Years later, President Abraham Lincoln encouraged growing surveillance, as did generals on both sides of the Civil War. In addition to HUMINT, Lincoln became an enthusiast of telegraph surveillance and early overhead reconnaissance using hot air balloons.[17]

After the Civil War, interest in military surveillance faded in the United States. By the First World War, American intelligence power was poorly developed, lagging far behind other countries. Many Americans were suspicious of peacetime espionage, believing it conflicted with open and limited government. In 1919, the Cipher Bureau, or "Black Chamber," headed by eccentric cryptologist Herbert O. Yardley, sought to expand American intelligence gathering capacity. However, it failed to gain widespread political acceptance. "Gentlemen do not read each other's mail," opined Secretary of State Henry Stimson. Deeming interception of foreign diplomatic communications "highly unethical," he quickly moved to disband the Black Chamber in 1929.[18]

The Second World War created new and urgent demands for foreign intelligence. The Office of Strategic Services led by "Wild Bill" Donovan pursued HUMINT in occupied Europe. Meanwhile, the United States' cryptanalysts reassembled to conduct SIGINT, forming the army's Signal Security Agency and the Naval Communications Intelligence Organization.[19] Their intercepts and decrypts were crucial to defeating

Japanese forces in the Battle of Midway. Meanwhile, the British Ultra program captured a German enigma machine, allowing decryption of Nazi communications and saving the Allied war effort in the Atlantic.[20]

While the intelligence community would be reorganized several times over the subsequent years, by the end of the Second World War, the political norms and technological naïveté that had fueled American reticence toward foreign intelligence in previous decades disappeared. Foreign intelligence surveillance, which had been frowned on but not considered illegal, was finally accepted as a core feature of the emerging national security state.

Foreign intelligence surveillance became permanently institutionalized after the Second World War. The CIA was tasked with pursuing HUMINT collection abroad by the National Security Act of 1947, while foreign SIGINT was initially delegated to the Armed Forces Security Agency, established in 1949. The latter was replaced by the NSA in 1952, headquartered at Fort Meade, Maryland. The CIA's mandate explicitly prohibits domestic spying. The National Security Act makes clear that "the Agency shall have no police, subpoena, law-enforcement powers, or other internal-security functions."[21] The NSA was originally authorized by executive order, which mandated it to "provide an effective, unified organization and control of the communications intelligence activities of the United States conducted against foreign governments."[22]

The CIA and NSA were joined by an emerging alphabet soup of surveillance agencies focusing on various aspects of military and technical intelligence. In addition, intelligence sharing between allied intelligence services was institutionalized via the United Kingdom-United States Agreement (UKUSA) or the "Five Eyes" agreement, which also included Canada, Australia, and New Zealand. The resultant partnership required the respective Anglo-American SIGINT agencies to exchange all nonexempt intelligence products.[23]

None of this intelligence gathering was illegal. On the contrary, foreign spying was and continues to be considered a heroic profession by many, celebrated in books and films. The legitimacy of international intelligence is reinforced by international norms, which formally limit but provide tacit green lights for foreign spying.

AMBIGUOUS AND CONTRADICTORY INTERNATIONAL LEGAL STANDARDS

International law addresses surveillance in two ways: as a violation of the privacy rights of individuals and as a violation of state sovereignty. Regarding the former, there are some prohibitions on surveillance in international human rights law. For example, article 12 of the Universal Declaration of Human Rights states: "No one shall be subjected to arbitrary interference with his privacy, family, home or correspondence, nor to attacks upon his honour and reputation. Everyone has the right to the protection of the law against such interference or attacks."[24] Article 12 of the International Covenant on Civil and Political Rights has almost identical wording.[25] However, unlike prohibitions on torture, derogations from these privacy rights are permitted. The European Convention on Human Rights outlines nonarbitrary grounds for limiting privacy including national security, public safety, national economic well-being, prevention of disorder or crime, protection of health or morals, and protection of the rights and freedoms of others.[26] A variety of other European declarations and protocols govern data privacy.

The extent to which international law prohibits foreign intelligence operations is subject to debate. Spying on other counties and their citizens violates national sovereignty norms. However, because most states regularly engage in foreign intelligence surveillance, some argue that it has become a customary lawful practice. Either way, there are few international rules specifically governing these practices.[27]

International humanitarian law treaties such as the Hague and Geneva Conventions are ambiguous about spying. The law of armed conflict permits "ruses of war" necessary to gain information about the enemy but not clandestine spying to obtain it. It is not a crime for states to seek secret information, but individuals caught spying are subject to arrest, trial, and even execution if convicted.[28] These contradictions extend to peacetime foreign intelligence gathering. States enjoy sovereignty over their airspace, limiting unwanted foreign aerial reconnaissance. However, space-based satellites are not similarly restricted.[29] The Vienna Convention on Diplomatic Relations forbids spying by and on diplomats and instructs against violating the privacy of diplomatic communications, yet diplomatic spying has been a longstanding feature of normal statecraft.[30] The United States continues to instruct its diplomatic staff to collect intelligence information as a matter of course.[31] Such intelligence gathering was a habitual feature of the Cold War, when norms of reciprocity governed relations between the United States and the Soviet Union. This game was and continues to be epitomized by the exchange of captured secret agents.[32]

Perhaps most interesting is the role of intelligence surveillance in arms control treaties. The Strategic Arms Limitation Talks resulted in agreements that called for "national technical means of verification" including surveillance monitoring.[33] They not only authorized intelligence to ensure compliance with treaty terms but forbade states from enacting countermeasures to block this surveillance. Subsequent arms control agreements have included similar provisions.[34] Beyond treaty-based monitoring, states have assumed that surveillance of other states' military capacities is legitimate. The United States publically announced that U2 spy planes had identified missiles in Cuba in 1962. Forty years later, Colin Powell based allegations that Iraq had weapons of mass destruction on American intelligence sources in his presentation to the UN Security Council. Within the context of the United Nations, secret intelligence continues to be used to implement financial sanctions and to prosecute international war crimes trials.[35] The result of these developments is ambiguous, even contradictory law. While spies are not protected from punishment, spying is a part of the "organized hypocrisy" of international politics.[36]

Considering this state of affairs, it is fair to suggest that while international human rights law cautions states against spying on their citizens, and while sovereignty norms prohibit states from human and technical intelligence gathering in other states, the laws of war and arms control treaties recognize that states do spy on each other as a normal, legitimate practice. Accordingly, most controversies over the legality and legitimacy of surveillance focus on domestic surveillance. In the following sections, I outline how these debates played out in varying national security legal cultures in the United States.

CULTURES OF EXCEPTION: "AN EXCESS OF ZEAL"

In previous chapters, I argued that a legal culture of exception shaped much of the United States' early history. Racism, imperialism, and wartime necessity legitimized discriminatory legal practice, either in the form of exclusionary legal rules or impunity for human rights abuses. Law thus did little to constrain state violence and was at times an engine of repression. These patterns also appear in surveillance practice.

Throughout the late nineteenth and early twentieth centuries, American authorities sought to undermine emergent socialist and labor movements. The Justice Department's Bureau of Investigation (BI), which would become the FBI in 1935, engaged in an aggressive campaign of countersubversion during and immediately after the First World War that included extensive surveillance and warrantless search and seizure. For instance, authorities allowed the American Protective League, a corps of two hundred and fifty thousand volunteer spies, to conduct vigilante harassment against suspected opponents of the war.[37] They increasingly engaged in "slacker raids" aimed at rounding up draft dodgers. On several occasions in 1918, police, soldiers, and volunteers swept into American cities, demanding proof of draft status from every man they encountered.[38] While acknowledging that "excess of zeal for the public good" had unfortunately led to unlawful conduct, Attorney General Thomas Gregory declared that "some such dragnet process is necessary."[39] Simultaneously, the BI continued to monitor thousands of pacifists, trade unionists, leftist politicians, and citizens whose sole crime was opposition to the war.[40] In this legal culture of exception, constitutional rights fell by the wayside.

Following several anarchist bombings in 1919, BI Director William Flynn declared that they were "connected with Russian Bolshevism, aided by Hun money."[41] The BI Radical Division, led by a young J. Edgar Hoover, stepped up efforts to identify dissidents and accumulated hundreds of thousands of case records in a massive index card depository. In line with the due process violations of the Palmer Raids and first Red Scare discussed in chapter 4, the BI made no effort to verify the accuracy of accusations, which were based on rumors, informers, and records of attending public meetings or subscribing to radical papers. By 1921, four hundred and fifty thousand index cards had been compiled.[42] Other ventures included extensive cooperation between private American communications companies and the short-lived Cipher Bureau to surveil suspected dissidents throughout the 1920s.

In 1924, Attorney General Harlan Fiske Stone moved to check abuses, introducing the "Stone line," which mandated "that the FBI not be concerned with the opinions of individuals, political or otherwise," but only with conduct that contravened American law.[43] However, Hoover was appointed to head the BI. Rejecting the Stone line, he authorized agents to abandon the criminal standard and utilize all possible sources of information in monitoring subversives.[44] Whatever reticence the national security establishment harbored toward reading gentlemen's mail, it did not extend to political radicals, many of whom were immigrants.

Although the Federal Communications Act of 1934 ordered "no person not being authorized by the sender shall intercept any communication and divulge or publish the existence, contents, substance, purport, effect, or meaning of such intercepted communications," the outbreak of the Second World War generated increased demand for information, including domestic intelligence.[45] Military censors were authorized to screen all telegraph traffic.[46] President Franklin Delano Roosevelt granted Hoover explicit permission to conduct national security surveillance, directed "insofar as possible" at aliens.[47] This restriction proved feckless over the years. Hoover went on to wiretap hundreds of American political adversaries, activists, Supreme Court justices, professors, celebrities, and writers without warrants.[48]

While American national security officials publically defended exceptional surveillance against alleged subversives during the world wars and Red Scares, spying on political rivals, civil rights campaigners, and ordinary citizens was more difficult to justify. As I have discussed at various points throughout the book, expanding human rights norms, deepening legal restrictions, and the need to maintain the United States' liberal democratic image in the context of the Cold War pushed the United States to embrace a national security culture of secrecy in the latter half of the twentieth century. In order to pursue an undemocratic and illegal campaign of systematic political spying, American intelligence agencies depended on secrecy to shield their activities from criticism.

Presidents had long utilized surveillance to pursue their political agendas, but the abuse of intelligence power by the administration of Richard Nixon took illegality to reckless new heights. In 1971, a small circle of Nixon insiders formed the so-called "plumbers" unit. Led by Howard Hunt, a former CIA agent, and G. Gordon Liddy, a former FBI agent, they used unlawful surveillance, searches, and leaks to attack the president's political opponents. In 1972, a group of conspirators acting under the auspices of the Committee to Re-Elect the President organized a botched robbery of the Democratic National Committee headquarters office at the Watergate Hotel complex in Washington, DC. *Washington Post* journalists Bob Woodward and Carl Bernstein eventually uncovered links between the Watergate burglary, the subsequent cover up, and the Nixon White House—revelations that led to congressional investigations, multiple indictments, and the resignation of the president in 1974.[49]

In the wake of Watergate and other emerging intelligence scandals, the Senate Select Committee to Study Governmental Operations with Respect to Intelligence Activities (1975–76), better known as the Church Committee after its chairman, Senator Frank Church of Idaho, launched a major investigation. The committee's final reports document extensive abuses by the FBI, CIA, NSA, and military intelligence including covert action and domestic spying. The findings were shocking. The FBI held over 500,000 domestic intelligence files and a list of 26,000 people subject to round up in an emergency, the NSA obtained copies of every international cable sent out of the United States between 1947 and 1975, the army investigated 100,000 Americans for political reasons throughout the 1960s and early 1970s, and the CIA's illegal mail opening created a database of 1.5 million people.[50] According to former Attorney General Edward Levi, from 1940 to 1974, 8,350 warrantless domestic wiretaps and 2,450 warrantless microphone installations were authorized by federal agencies.[51] By the early 1970s, nearly 250,000 Americans were under active surveillance.[52]

The seven volumes and six books published by the Church Committee run several thousand pages long and describe in great detail the dangers posed by unaccountable intelligence activities. *Volume 2: Huston Plan* documents President Nixon's authorization of FBI, CIA, and military intelligence surveillance of anti-Vietnam war protesters in 1970. "Did any person, other than Mr. Hoover in the footnotes, suggest or argue that the activities being proposed ought not to be done because they were either unconstitutional or illegal?" asked counsel Frederick A. O. Schwarz Jr. "No," answered White House aide Tom Huston in his committee testimony.[53] Officials seemed more concerned about getting caught than violating the law. As CIA Director Richard Helms wrote Henry Kissinger concerning a domestic intelligence dossier: "This is an area not within the charter of this Agency . . . . Should anyone learn of its existence it would prove most embarrassing for all concerned."[54]

Volume 3: Internal Revenue Service (IRS) describes how the IRS gathered financial and personal data on political activists. Amongst its eight thousand individual and three thousand organizational targets were the ACLU, the American Library Association, the Conservative Book Club, the Ford Foundation, the National Association for the Advancement of Colored People, the Lawyers Committee for Civil Rights Under Law, the National Urban League, and the University of North Carolina.[55] According to Church Committee testimony, the IRS used aggressive tax enforcement to single out and punish perceived dissidents as well as to pass on intelligence data to other agencies, especially the FBI: "Tax return confidentiality has eroded to the point where our Federal Government has turned these supposedly private documents into instruments of harassment used against citizens for political reasons."[56]

Similar concerns are echoed in *Volume 4: Mail Opening,* which covers the extensive interception of Americans' mail under Project HTLINGUAL. Starting in 1952, the CIA systematically screened over 28 million pieces of mail destined to and from the Soviet Union and other suspect destinations, secretly opening 215,820 envelopes.[57] This mail opening continued for two decades despite the fact that it was clearly illegal. As Senator John Tower explained: "There has never been any serious question regarding the legality of indiscriminate mail openings. Most of those associated with these invasions of privacy have flatly acknowledged the illegality of their actions. The closest we have come to justification for these mail openings is that they proved to be an invaluable source of national security information."[58] Once again, authorities were primarily concerned with avoiding publicity and "flap potential."[59] According to CIA Inspector General's Office staff member John Glennon, "we assumed that everyone realized it was illegal. The very point we were trying to make was the Agency would be in deep embarrassment if they were caught in this activity."[60] Of additional concern to the Church Committee was the lack of centralized responsibility and documentation for the program, which some senators interpreted as an attempt to establish "plausible deniability" so that "should it become public knowledge . . . certain persons could be exempted from any blame."[61]

Volume 5: The National Security Agency and Fourth Amendment Rights discusses the role of the NSA in monitoring citizens' electronic communications under Project MINARET. The head of the NSA, Lieutenant General Lew Allen, testified that "our communications intelligence activities are solely for the purpose of obtaining foreign intelligence in accordance with the authorities delegated by the President stemming from his constitutional power to conduct foreign intelligence."[62] Yet he also admitted that the NSA monitored communications of American citizens based on "watch lists."[63] Further details of MINARET were declassified in 2013, revealing that civil rights leaders Martin Luther King Jr. and Whitney Young, boxer Muhammad Ali, *New York Times* journalist Tom Wicker, and *Washington Post* columnist Art Buchwald, as well as Senator Church and Senator Howard Baker were on watch lists.[64] There is no evidence that these individuals posed a threat to national security. Accordingly, surveillance was conducted in a clandestine and covert manner. "Clearly recognizing that Minaret was illegal, the NSA analysts working on the program printed all reports derived from these intercepts on plain bond paper without the NSA's logo or any classification markings," explain Matthew Aid and Robert Burr. "They then had them hand-carried by NSA couriers to the very few individuals at the White House and elsewhere in Washington who were cleared to see these highly classified documents."[65]

Revelations concerning Project SHAMROCK were also shocking. The operation stretched from the 1940s to the 1970s, during which time the NSA and its predecessor agencies received copies of every international telegram transmitted via the United States from three telegraph companies: RCA Global, ITT World Communications, and Western Union International. The companies were assured of their immunity in 1947 and again in 1949. Neither the government nor the companies kept documentary records of their operational arrangements.[66] While originally focused on foreign intelligence, the communications of American citizens were increasingly targeted. The NSA selected 150,000 messages a month from the vast volume of incoming data for analysis.[67] As summed up by Senator Gary Hart, SHAMROCK

> resulted in companies betraying the trust of their paying customers who had a right to
> expect that the messages would be handled confidentially. It was undertaken without
> the companies first ascertaining its legality. It was not disclosed to the Congress until
> this year. Finally, it continued without interruption for nearly 30 years, even though ap-
> parently no express approval of the project was obtained from any President, Attorney
> General, or Secretary of Defense after 1949.[68]

In so doing, the NSA blatantly violated the Fourth Amendment. The conduct of both MINARET and SHAMROCK suggests that the NSA had little concern for legality for several decades. These secret programs largely ignored the law. Only when faced with political scrutiny were they reviewed and cancelled.

Operation CHAOS was the CIA's domestic spying program, conducted in direct defiance of its statutory role as laid out in the 1947 National Security Act. Initiated by President Lyndon Johnson in 1967 to seek out foreign influence over the antiwar, black power, and new left movements, CHAOS infiltrated domestic organizations with undercover agents and cooperated with the NSA's illegal surveillance. Lasting almost seven years, the operation created a CIA database of 300,000 names with extensive files on 7,200 citizens.[69]

Perhaps the most infamous of all the illegal Cold War projects was the FBI's Counterintelligence Program (COINTELPRO), discussed in *Volume 6: Federal Bureau of Investigation.* Throughout the 1960s and early 1970s, the FBI surveilled the antiwar movement, the civil rights movement, the student movement, the new left, communist groups, and right-wing organizations such as the KKK, developing 500,000 intelligence dossiers.[70] Methods included about 100 warrantless wiretaps a year, mail opening, break-ins, and the extensive use of informants.[71] COINTELPRO also engaged in harassment and sabotage, including "use of what is called misinformation to prevent dissenters from meeting or engaging in protest activity... efforts to neutralize people by breaking up their marriages or ruining their jobs . . . [and] intentionally exacerbating tensions between groups known to be violence prone and known to have a desire to injure each other." [72] The FBI was particularly preoccupied with King and the Southern Christian Leadership Conference, which it labeled a "black hate group." Hoover bugged King's home and office in order to dig up dirt on the civil rights leader.[73]

While the FBI did have some legitimate intelligence gathering powers, there is substantial evidence that it understood COINTELPRO to be unlawful. Its primary aim was to avoid public scrutiny. As David Cole explains, "because COINTELPRO was almost entirely illegal, it required a whole new level of secrecy, not so much to protect national security as to protect the Bureau itself from embarrassing disclosures."[74] For instance, after Hoover's death, the FBI destroyed the majority of his personal files, which included "do not file" and "black bag job" documents.[75]

The Church Committee's conclusions regarding domestic abuses are described in *Book II: Intelligence Activities and the Rights of Americans* and *Book III: Supplementary Detailed Staff Reports on Intelligence Activities and the Rights of Americans*. Together the reports paint a disturbing picture of the political abuse of intelligence, the failure of accountability mechanisms, and a "vacuum cleaner" approach that indiscriminately monitored lawful activity. These illegal practices had profoundly harmful consequences, including the destruction of personal and professional lives, the distortion of public policy, and, most basically, "the values of privacy and freedom which our constitution seeks to protect."[76] These observations foreshadow debates and fears that continue today over intelligence power, particularly in regard to electronic surveillance: "In an era where the technological capability of Government relentlessly increases, we must be wary about the drift toward 'big brother government.' The potential for abuse is awesome and requires special attention to fashioning restraints which not only cure past problems, but which anticipate and prevent the future misuse of technology."[77]

In sum, historical analysis sheds light on the varying ways in which public authorities have conducted surveillance. Foreign surveillance has long been conducted legally. In contrast, domestic surveillance has been subject to restrictions. In the face of these limitations, authorities have at times opted to ignore the law in the name of emergency necessity, targeting foreigners and alleged subversives for intrusive monitoring. In other cases, concerns about legal sanction and public embarrassment have pushed surveillance practices underground, resulting in eventual scandal. Post-9/11 surveillance shares similarities with some aspects of these precedents but also manifests important differences.

EVOLVING LAWS AND NEW TECHNOLOGIES

Over the latter decades of the twentieth century, judicial rulings and new legislation increasingly restricted domestic intelligence surveillance. For instance, in *National Association for the Advancement of Colored People v. Alabama* (1958), the Supreme Court ruled that the organization did not have to disclose its membership list to state authorities based on "the right of petitioner's members to pursue their lawful private interests privately and to associate freely with others."[78] In *Griswold v. Connecticut* (1965), the Supreme Court held that a state prohibition on the use of contraceptives violated "the right to marital privacy."[79] Today, debates over reproductive and sexual freedom continue to be parsed through the legal discourse of privacy.[80]

In the criminal justice and security realm, two important legal cases helped shape emerging surveillance jurisprudence. In *Katz v. United States* (1967), Charles Katz challenged his federal gambling conviction on the ground that information had been obtained by the unwarranted wiretapping of a phone booth in contravention of his Fourth Amendment rights. The Supreme Court decided in his favor, arguing that privacy attached to people, not places. The fact that federal agents did not engage in physical trespass to gain access to Katz's call did not mean he had no expectation of privacy. As the court stated:

> The Government's activities in electronically listening to and recording the petitioner's words violated the privacy upon which he justifiably relied while using the telephone booth, and thus constituted a "search and seizure" within the meaning of the Fourth Amendment. The fact that the electronic device employed to achieve that end did not happen to penetrate the wall of the booth can have no constitutional significance.[81]

Subsequently, new legislation helped codify eavesdropping rules. Title III of the Omnibus Crime Control and Safe Streets Act of 1968 specified that interception of "wire, oral, or electronic communication" is permitted only in cases of serious crimes.[82]

While *Katz* ensured changes in communications technologies could not be used to evade constitutional protections, the 1972 *Keith* decision, named for District Judge Damon Keith who made the initial ruling against the government, clarified that surveillance of domestic subversion required a warrant. The case was prompted after the attorney general authorized warrantless surveillance of individuals suspected of planning to destroy government property, one of whom actually firebombed a CIA office. The government argued that the aforementioned Title III did not infringe on the executive's constitutional powers to protect national security. The Supreme Court disagreed, finding that there was no grant to engage in warrantless domestic surveillance, that the Fourth Amendment did in fact apply to domestic security targets, and that "[t]he freedoms of the Fourth Amendment cannot properly be guaranteed if domestic security surveillances are conducted solely within the discretion of the Executive Branch without the detached judgment of a neutral magistrate." It furthermore recognized the dangers of political intelligence gathering:

> History abundantly documents the tendency of Government—however benevolent and benign its motives—to view with suspicion those who most fervently dispute its policies. Fourth Amendment protections become the more necessary when the targets

of official surveillance may be those suspected of unorthodoxy in their political beliefs. The danger to political dissent is acute where the Government attempts to act under so vague a concept as the power to protect "domestic security." Given the difficulty of defining the domestic security interest, the danger of abuse in acting to protect that interest becomes apparent.[83]

In other words, while foreign intelligence surveillance was legal and legitimate, domestic targets retained their rights even when violent subversion was at stake.

The scandals of the Nixon White House also resulted in several new laws. The Privacy Act of 1974 introduced new rules for handling public and private data.[84] That same year, the Freedom of Information Act (FOIA) was updated, permitting greater access to government documents. [85] FOIA rules made at least some aspects of government wrongdoing more difficult to conceal. The Church Committee findings contributed to several major changes to American intelligence governance. In 1976, Attorney General Levi issued the first set of Attorney General's Guidelines aimed at directing the surveillance activity of the FBI. The guidelines prohibited the FBI from investigating and disrupting the activities of Americans solely on the basis of their political beliefs as long as they did not advocate violence. They further required the FBI to initiate investigations only on the basis of "specific and articulable facts."[86] In 1983, new guidelines shifted the standard to a "reasonable indication" of criminality and permitted "limited preliminary inquiries."[87] On the foreign intelligence front, the Senate Select Committee on Intelligence and the House Permanent Select Committee on Intelligence were created in 1976 and 1977, respectively, to provide congressional oversight of intelligence agencies.

FISA, enacted in 1978, was one of Congress's most significant responses to the intelligence scandals. It supplemented Title III of the Omnibus Crime Control and Safe Streets Act of 1968, which had required warrants for criminal investigations but had permitted unconstrained surveillance for foreign intelligence purposes.[88] FISA's objective was to regulate foreign intelligence surveillance targeted at Americans. It created a Foreign Intelligence Surveillance Court (FISA Court), which could issue warrants under significantly less strenuous probable cause standards than those required in law enforcement investigations. Purely foreign intelligence operations occurring outside the United States could continue unabated, but those involving American targets would require some minimal oversight.

In order to grant a warrant, a FISA Court judge had to find that surveillance was targeted at a foreign power or agent of a foreign power, that minimization procedures were in place to prevent collection and retention of Americans' communications unrelated to foreign intelligence, and that information sought under the warrant could not reasonably be obtained by normal investigative techniques. An American or "United States person," could be considered an "agent of a foreign power" for the purposes of foreign intelligence surveillance if they knowingly engaged in clandestine intelligence gathering activities, sabotage, or international terrorism for or on behalf of a foreign power or if they aided and abetted persons in the conduct of such activities. US persons were defined as "a citizen of the United States, an alien lawfully admitted for permanent residence . . . an unincorporated association a substantial number of members of which are citizens of the United States or aliens lawfully admitted for permanent residence, or a corporation which is incorporated in the United States."[89]

Despite increasing regulation, significant gaps in the surveillance regime persisted—gaps that would be later exploited by the Bush administration. For instance, information transferred to third parties is not covered by Fourth Amendment protections. This includes information obtained by wired undercover informants. Moreover, the government has warrantless access to third-party data such as telephone, accounting, and banking records shared with third parties.[90] This was confirmed in *Smith v. Maryland* (1979),[91] in which the Supreme Court ruled that pen resisters and trap and trace devices, which detail incoming and outgoing phone numbers, were available without a warrant because the data had been voluntarily shared with a telephone company, thereby undermining any reasonable expectation of privacy.[92] Subsequent legislation required law enforcement to obtain court orders to collect various forms of third-party data, but rules remain relatively permissive.[93] As summed up by Cole, the consequences are striking: "[P]eople have no expectation of privacy when they dial phone numbers, surf the Web, make a credit card purchase, put out their garbage, or talk to people they think are their friends but are in fact informants."[94]

There are further weaknesses in the intelligence oversight system. Senate and House oversight committees were designed to be primarily reactive rather than proactive. Likewise, executive oversight via agency inspectors general is often scandal centered rather than consistently critical.[95] Fearing intelligence failures on their watch, politicians have been generally unwilling to challenge intelligence agencies. Nonetheless, the controversies of the 1970s combined with a thickened, yet still imperfect, legal regime led to declining warrantless domestic surveillance. A chastened intelligence community became increasingly concerned with legality. The systematic political spying of the pre-Church Committee era was greatly curtailed.

Growing concerns over legality did not mark an end to surveillance. Foreign intelligence surveillance continued. FISA created relatively permissive standards for monitoring US persons suspected of links to foreign threats. Changes in technology created new sources of data for domestic surveillance. While court rulings and legislation attempted to keep up with these shifts, Fourth Amendment protections did not evenly extend to all aspects of high-tech communications. On the eve of 9/11, there were no laws that prohibited American intelligence agencies or domestic law enforcement officers from spying on suspected al-Qaeda terrorists in the United States or abroad.

CULTURES OF LEGAL RATIONALIZATION: POST-9/11 SURVEILLANCE

After the 9/11 attacks, Americans feared another intelligence failure. Policymakers and pundits became increasingly preoccupied with the wall between domestic and foreign intelligence gathering, which allegedly impeded interagency cooperation to detect and preempt the hijackers. FISA restrictions on domestic spying came under attack. However, the national security establishment had learned from the scandals of past decades. Rather than rely on legal logics of exception or secrecy to justify extralegal surveillance, authorities reframed controversial intelligence programs as compliant with legal norms and sought new legislation to expand surveillance powers. While their legal rationalizations for warrantless domestic surveillance were thin, their arguments exploited permissive dimensions of American surveillance law.

In the following sections, I trace in detail post-9/11 efforts by both the Bush and Obama administrations to expand surveillance power. I discuss the adoption of the sweeping PATRIOT Act, which enhanced the intelligence gathering capacity of the FBI and NSA. I explain the Bush administration's surveillance program, which authorized the NSA to surveil Americans without a FISA Court warrant in certain circumstances. While in some ways a blatantly illegal initiative in the vein of previous covert actions, executive lawyers attempted to construct a legal basis for the program by redefining the concept of foreign surveillance, a move given ex post facto legislative approval by Congress. Finally, I address the implications of changing communications technologies, which complicate adherence to surveillance laws by blurring the line between foreign and domestic and by undermining the targeted intelligence gathering paradigm. In all these instances, authorities have been highly conscious of legal rules even when bending those rules to the breaking point.

The PATRIOT Act

The Uniting and Strengthening America by Providing Appropriate Tools Required to Intercept and Obstruct Terrorism Act of 2001, better known as the PATRIOT Act, introduced major changes to American surveillance law in the immediate aftermath of 9/11. Despite expanding surveillance powers, the act did not suspend constitutional rights or usher in a state of exception. Unlike previous security crises in which surveillance efforts explicitly targeted specific communities, section 102 clearly stated: "Arab Americans, Muslim Americans, and Americans from South Asia play a vital role in our Nation and are entitled to nothing less than the full rights of every American."[96] It sought to construct a plausibly legal basis for aggressive security initiatives that was compatible with a culture of legal rationalization.

The PATRIOT Act attempted to address barriers to domestic and foreign intelligence information exchange, which had deepened in the 1990s. After the passage of FISA, FBI agents and federal prosecutors informally shared information from FISA surveillance with an understanding that it would not be inappropriately exploited in criminal proceedings. In 1994, the trial of Soviet spy Aldrich Ames ignited concerns at the Justice Department's Office of Intelligence Policy and Review that these exchanges could be deemed abusive, thereby undermining the case. As a result, the flow of FISA-sourced information to prosecutors was limited.[97] In 1995, Attorney General Janet Reno issued further information-sharing guidelines. FBI officials misinterpreted these regulations, blocking communications between intelligence agents and criminal investigators, including information that did not rely on FISA, such as CIA and NSA foreign intelligence.[98]

While no law prohibited surveilling suspected terrorists prior to 9/11, PATRIOT Act supporters argued that restrictions on domestic and foreign intelligence prevented timely investigation of 9/11 conspirator Zacarias Moussaoui.[99] They further highlighted the case of United States-bound 9/11 hijackers Khalid al-Mihdhar and Nawaz al-Hamzi in which the CIA failed to pass on critical information to the FBI. The 9/11 Commission later reiterated these concerns.[100] Although these intelligence failures were caused by bureaucratic rivalry, human error, and technological limitations rather than simply legal regulations,[101] they inspired numerous legal reforms.

To deconstruct the domestic/foreign wall, the PATRIOT Act authorized enhanced information sharing between intelligence agents and federal law enforcement officers. Rather than having to be "the purpose" of all FISA investigations, section 218 allowed foreign intelligence gathering to be a "significant purpose" of surveillance. The majority of PATRIOT Act provisions focused on loosening restrictions on domestic surveillance. Section 505 expanded the FBI's power to issue national security letters, or secret subpoenas for telephone, credit, and financial records, without judicial oversight. Section 215 granted easier access to books, records, papers, and documents such as library and bookstore records. Section 213 authorized delayed notice of searches, permitting "sneak and peak" investigations. Section 206 created "roving wiretaps" that attached to suspects rather than physical locations, allowing authorities to surveil multiple devices without securing separate court orders.

On top of this legislation, Attorney General John Ashcroft introduced new Attorney General's Guidelines in 2002 to expand the domestic surveillance capacity of the FBI.[102] These powers were extended in 2008, "representing a direct challenge to the criminal law model of intelligence governance" by authorizing "FBI agents to engage in proactive intelligence gathering."[103] In 2004, the Intelligence Reform and Terrorist Prevention Act created a "lone wolf" provision, which allowed non-US persons suspected of planning terrorist attacks to be considered "agents of a foreign power" even where a relationship with a foreign organization or state could not be proved. Congress reauthorized the basic tenets of the PATRIOT Act and reformed the FISA framework multiple times. In 2015, President Obama signed the USA FREEDOM Act into law, which extended PATRIOT Act provisions in modified form, reflecting controversies over bulk collection activities brought to light by the Snowden leaks. There is no doubt that these reforms lifted legal barriers and restrictions on surveillance, making it easier for intelligence agencies to collect information.

While only Senator Russ Feingold voted against the initial PATRIOT Act, it eventually proved to be a highly controversial piece of legislation. Civil libertarians condemned its powers, claiming it would chill free speech and compromise the fairness of the legal system.[104] Yet, the merits of these critiques notwithstanding, the PATRIOT Act was a legitimately enacted law, publically and democratically adopted by Congress. It did not provide the state with limitless power, demonize ethnic or religious minorities, or strip American citizens of their existing constitutional rights. Rather, the PATRIOT Act expanded information sharing between agencies, exploited the longstanding third-party exception to privacy rights, and made new technologies easier to surveil. It arguably overreached in doing so, but it did not fundamentally alter the existing legal paradigm governing intelligence surveillance. The same cannot be so easily said of a variety of other post-9/11 NSA surveillance initiatives which posed a considerably greater challenge to legal norms.

Stellarwind: "A More-Than-Plausible Theory"

Eight years before Snowden's dramatic public disclosure of several contentious NSA surveillance programs in summer 2013, *New York Times* investigative reporters James Risen and Eric Lichtblau published a series of articles on what the Bush administration initially called the "Terrorist Surveillance Program" and later the "President's Surveillance Program" (PSP).[105] This warrantless wiretapping program formed one component of Stellarwind, the NSA's codename for a massive post-9/11 surveillance initiative.[106]

The President's Surveillance Program mandated the NSA, usually confined solely to foreign intelligence gathering, to spy on Americans suspected of foreign terrorist ties without obtaining a FISA Court warrant. Under the new rules, only one party to an intercepted communication was required to be a non-US person.[107] Targets could be chosen by the NSA's "operational workforce" and approved by shift supervisors.[108] To facilitate this surveillance, the Bush administration authorized the NSA to enter backdoors in the American telecommunications switching system, providing potential access to all domestic communications.[109]

Like SHAMROCK years before, the President's Surveillance Program depended on extensive cooperation from private telecommunications firms, who own the massive network of subsea fiber-optic cables through which the vast majority of American and international communications travel. As AT&T technician Mark Klein revealed, the NSA placed a splitter on the company's cables at their San Francisco facility, leading to a secret room. Interception was targeted at calls involving one non-US person. Yet by latching onto a "peering point," a hub through which a variety of regional communications passed, "many purely domestic calls were likely to get caught in the snare."[110]

There are strong echoes of both national security legal cultures of exception and of secrecy in the warrantless surveillance program. The NSA operated in a bubble of extreme secrecy, which limited scrutiny and oversight. On its face, the President's Surveillance Program was a blatantly illegal violation of FISA. Invoking the logic of exceptional necessity, the Bush administration argued that FISA was trumped by the president's commander-in-chief entitlements in war, supplemented by the Authorization for Use of Military Force enacted by Congress in the wake of 9/11. Moreover, it insisted that the Fourth Amendment requirement of reasonableness did not infer a warrant, only the unvetted belief that surveillance was targeted at a foreign power or agent of a foreign power in the interests of national security.[111]

While these arguments were first publically promulgated after journalists uncovered warrantless wiretapping, the underlying concepts had been incubating for years. According to Bush administration lawyers, the 9/11 attacks were acts of war activating the president's constitutional war powers. This war was fundamentally transnational, traversing the borders of the United States. As stated in a striking 2001 OLC memorandum by John Yoo and Robert

Delahunty, the president was fully permitted to use all necessary force to defend the country against both foreign and domestic adversaries.[112] Appropriate military actions in the face of war included "making arrests, seizing documents or other property, searching persons or places or keeping them under surveillance, intercepting electronic or wireless communications, setting up roadblocks, interviewing witnesses, and searching for suspects."[113] Following the threat, such actions could extend across national boundaries: "While, no doubt, these terrorists pose a direct military threat to the national security, their methods of infiltration and their surprise attacks on civilian and governmental facilities make it difficult to identify any front line."[114]

Because the Fourth Amendment had never applied to military actions overseas, it could not apply to domestic surveillance, according to Yoo and Delahunty:

> To apply the Fourth Amendment to overseas military operations would represent an extreme over-judicialization of warfare that would interfere with military effectiveness and the President's constitutional duty to prosecute a war successfully. . . . Our forces must be free to "seize" enemy personnel or "search" enemy quarters, papers and messages without having to show "probable cause" before a neutral magistrate, and even without having to demonstrate that their actions were constitutionally "reasonable." They must be free to use any means necessary to defeat the enemy's forces, even if their efforts might cause collateral damage to United States persons. Although their conduct might be governed by the laws of war, including laws for the protection of noncombatants, the Fourth Amendment would no more apply than if those operations occurred in a foreign theater of war.[115]

While the extreme implications of this logic allowing domestic military operations was not wholly adopted by the Bush administration, it found its way into justifications for warrantless surveillance. According to a joint interagency inspectors general investigation of the President's Surveillance Program, "it was extraordinary and inappropriate that a single Justice Department attorney, John Yoo, was relied upon to conduct the initial legal assessment of the PSP, and that the lack of oversight and review of Yoo's work, as customarily is the practice of OLC, contributed to a legal analysis of the PSP that at a minimum was factually flawed."[116]

Once warrantless wiretapping was exposed, the Department of Justice argued that the president had simply authorized the use of SIGINT in war as permitted by the Constitution.[117] The President's Surveillance Program was necessary, insisted Attorney General Alberto Gonzales, because:

> Consistent with the wartime intelligence nature of this program, the optimal way to achieve the necessary speed and agility is to leave the decisions about particular

intercepts to the judgment of professional intelligence officers, based on the best available intelligence information. They can make that call quickly. If, however, those same intelligence officers had to navigate through the FISA process for each of these intercepts, that would necessarily introduce a significant factor of DELAY, and there would be critical holes in our early warning system.[118]

As critics note, these claims were questionable at best. FISA Court proceedings were nonadversarial and ex parte, meaning that Justice Department lawyers had exclusive access to judges.[119] There was no appeal procedure for targets, only for the state. In emergencies, the government could request warrants seventy-two hours after surveillance had begun. The FISA Court rarely rejected warrant applications.[120] Between 1978 and 2002, it turned down zero requests. Through 2012, it rejected just eleven applications out of more than twenty thousand.[121] There is also limited evidence that warrantless surveillance enhanced national security. According to the inspectors general, "officials . . . had difficulty citing specific instances where PSP reporting had directly contributed to counterterrorism successes."[122]

While it embraced its expanded powers, warrantless surveillance made the NSA nervous. Former NSA Director Michael Hayden recounts telling then CIA Director George Tenet that "since the ugliness of the Church Commission, NSA had acted like it had a permanent one ball-two strike count on it. 'We don't take many close pitches.'"[123] In the prevailing national security culture of legal rationalization, the agency was risk averse:

> NSA professionals are very conservative when it comes to the privacy of US persons and are so legally attuned that they recognized immediately that what we were going to do sidestepped FISA. Without visible support, unqualified support from me, my deputy, and the legal folks (the ones who had been telling them the "thou shalt nots" for years), they wouldn't have done this.[124]

Accordingly, Stellarwind was designed "to make it absolutely clear that this was being done with the knowledge and support and under the direction of the president."[125] The NSA demanded plausible legality, not plausible deniability.

There was keen awareness within the NSA that the warrantless wiretapping program would inevitably leak and that controversy would ensue.[126] "No one expected Stellarwind to stay secret forever. Nothing does."[127] NSA counsel reviewed the administration's arguments, concluding the program was lawful. "There was no way we could play this close to the edge without a lot of legal oversight," writes Hayden.[128] However, NSA lawyers found the administration's executive power claims unnecessarily broad. For them, the foreign intelligence dimension of the President's Surveillance Program remained critical. At the core of their "more-than-plausible theory about its lawfulness"[129] was that parties targeted for surveillance were non-US persons or linked to a foreign terrorist threat. In other words, they sought to expand the meaning of foreign—and thus warrantless—surveillance. That said, certain NSA officials were more legally sensitive than others. For instance, General Keith Alexander, who led the agency after Hayden, was reportedly more amenable to pushing legal boundaries than his predecessor had been.[130]

The legitimacy of evading FISA was also contentious among members of the Bush administration itself. In 2004, the White House asked the attorney general to reauthorize warrantless wiretapping. Acting Attorney General James Comey declined to overrule the then-medically incapacitated Attorney General Ashcroft, who refused. This prompted a now-infamous hospital showdown between Comey, former OLC head Jack Goldsmith, Associate Deputy Attorney General Patrick Philbin, and FBI Director Robert Mueller on one side and senior White House officials Gonzales and Andrew Card on the other. Determined to have the program legally rubber stamped, the latter two rushed to the seriously ill Ashcroft's bedside in a last-ditch attempt to secure his sign-off. They failed, but the program was renewed anyway without standard Department of Justice authorization. The President's Surveillance Program was eventually modified after multiple threats of resignation by dissenting administration officials.[131] It was brought under FISA by 2007.

If justifications for warrantless surveillance had stopped with executive war powers arguments, it would be fair to conclude that the Bush administration and NSA had eschewed legal cover in favor of bolder invocations of exceptional necessity. Indeed, decisionistic language echoed strongly throughout several legal memoranda, especially those written by Yoo. Yet this was not the sole basis for the purported plausible legality of the President's Surveillance Program. Authorities also aimed to redefine foreign surveillance as interception of communications involving only one suspected foreign terrorist threat. Despite highly permissive OLC memos, both the Bush administration and the NSA insisted that they never targeted solely domestic communications, that they continued to use minimization procedures to avoid such collection, and that the program was focused and circumscribed. The highly secretive nature of surveillance makes it difficult to gauge the truth of these assertions, but it does not appear that the President's Surveillance Program was a domestic surveillance program akin to the Huston Plan, SHAMROCK, or COINTELPRO. It tied its substantive legitimacy not simply to presidential prerogative but to the preexisting normative acceptability of foreign surveillance. As Hayden emphasizes, "the president has inherent constitutional authority to conduct electronic surveillance without a warrant *for foreign intelligence purposes.*"[132]

Congress legislated many aspects of the President's Surveillance Program several years after it was disclosed. As revelations forced the surveillance debate into the public eye, lawmakers found themselves tasked with addressing the dilemmas raised by emerging developments. Eventually, they passed the Protect America Act of 2007, which temporarily legitimated warrantless wiretapping when one party to a communication was foreign. The act's expiration prompted an extended debate on the question of retroactive immunity for telecommunications firms that had provided private information about their customers to the NSA without a warrant.

Eventually, Congress passed the FISA Amendments Act of 2008, which protected third parties working on behalf of the state from lawsuits. Moreover, communications between a US person and a non-US person would no longer be subject to individual FISA applications.[133] Instead, section 702 allowed the attorney general and director of national intelligence to authorize surveillance of non-US persons who were reasonably believed to be located outside the United States, even if they were communicating with or about a US person. "This legislation gave the government even broader authority to intercept international communications than did the provisions of the Presidential Authorizations governing the activities that the President acknowledged in December 2005 as the Terrorist Surveillance Program," notes the interagency inspectors general report.[134] Senator Feingold argued at the time that the changes to FISA "permit the government to acquire . . . foreigners' communications with Americans inside the United States, regardless of whether anyone involved in the communication is under any suspicion of wrongdoing. . . . The result is that many law-abiding Americans who communicate with completely innocent people overseas will be swept up in this new form of surveillance, with virtually no judicial involvement."[135] Congress later reauthorized the FISA Amendments Act in 2012, extending the program.

While rejecting the Bush administration's extreme executive war powers arguments, Congress delivered at least partially similar policy outcomes. Not much changed on the surveillance front with the election of Obama. To the great disappointment of many of its supporters, the Obama administration invoked sovereign immunity claims and the state secrets privilege to block investigations of and challenges to domestic surveillance.[136]

When Snowden began leaking NSA documents in summer 2013, warrantless surveillance was subject to renewed public scrutiny. However, many of the programs Snowden disclosed were purely foreign intelligence operations. While politically and ethically contentious, they were lawful under the dichotomous legal framework governing American surveillance. The NSA is a foreign intelligence agency. Traditionally, US law primarily protects the privacy of US persons only. As previously outlined, international legal restrictions on surveillance are minimal and ambiguous. The NSA's rapacious appetite for foreign intelligence is therefore not especially shocking.

Leaked documents showed that the FISA Court granted the NSA a "warrant for the world," providing a 2010 certification that 193 countries and organizations such as the World Bank, International Monetary Fund, European Union, and International Atomic Energy Agency were potential legitimate foreign intelligence targets, thus opening them to warrantless surveillance under Section 702 of the FISA Amendments Act.[137] The United States spied on the governments, citizens, and businesses of Hong Kong and China,[138] Russia,[139] Mexico,[140] Germany,[141] France,[142] Spain,[143] Italy,[144] Brazil,[145] India,[146] Turkey,[147] and Somalia,[148] on thirty-five heads of state,[149] and even Five Eyes allies such as Britain.[150] It further surveilled the European Union,[151] OPEC,[152] the G20,[153] arms control negotiations,[154] climate negotiations,[155] international bank transactions,[156] and the al-Jazeera news network.[157] Moreover, the NSA proved "all consuming" in the scope of its data collection,[158] intercepting foreign text messages,[159] cellphone data,[160] system administrator information,[161] and even computers not linked to the Internet.[162] One program called MYSTIC saw the NSA engage in bulk collection of all calls in the Bahamas.[163] Collection systems recorded " 'every single' conversation nationwide, storing billions of records in a 30-day rolling buffer that cleared the oldest calls as new ones arrived, according to a classified summary."[164] Despite the remarkable scope of these initiatives, they are foreign operations, generally permitted by US law.

The enormity of NSA spying around the world compounds its image as a lawless agency. Yet closer scrutiny reveals that in contrast to Cold War covert programs, the post-9/11 NSA was keen to establish official authorization and legal cover. While the Bush administration invoked executive prerogative, it also asserted an expansive reinterpretation of lawful foreign surveillance. Lawyers channeled the dualistic legal norms governing foreign and domestic surveillance and the ambiguous line between the two. The President's Surveillance Program was undoubtedly an assault on FISA and, by extension, the constitutional separation of powers, but it was not a fundamental rejection of the underlying domestic/foreign dichotomy at the heart of the surveillance regime. In developing legal justifications, authorities continued to operate within, albeit at the margins of, the national security culture of legal rationalization that has shaped the United States' post-9/11 counterterrorist operations.

In addition to reconceptualizing foreign intelligence, post-9/11 American authorities argued that changing international communications architecture justified broader surveillance powers. By the turn of the millennium, new forms of networked technology made foreign and domestic communications increasingly difficult to distinguish. In particular, where communications are physically intercepted no longer determines whether they are protected. With the rise of fiber-optics, 80 percent of international communications traffic travels on subsea cables routed through a few dozen major switching stations, many of which are on American soil.[165] As computers route transmissions to uncongested networks, foreign communications transit traffic passes through American servers and switches.[166] Data packets can be broken up and sent through different channels, compounding ambiguity.[167] As Susan Landau explains:

> [C]onnections between Europe and Asia, between South America and Europe, and even between South America and South America, or Asia and Asia, went through the United States. There are any number of reasons for this geographic oddity. One was that U.S. providers underbid overpriced regional carriers .... A second cause was politics: sometimes communications could not travel between two nations, but could go through a third party (... Taiwan and China). A third reason was technology. The United States is home to many of the world's email servers (Yahoo Mail, Hotmail, Gmail). Thus email between two people in Quetta and Kabul ... may travel via a server in Oregon. If any of those communications had gone by satellite, the NSA would simply have been able to pluck the signal out of the air.[168]

Stellarwind allowed the NSA to capture foreign-foreign communications that transit the United States and that may not otherwise have been monitored.[169]

In addition to revealing numerous foreign intelligence operations, Snowden's 2013 disclosures highlighted the remarkable scope of the NSA's emerging mass surveillance capacity. Leaked documents outlined UPSTREAM, which, like the defunct President's Surveillance Program, permitted the NSA to search phone calls and Internet data from the fiber-optic telecommunications backbone.[170] Not only could agents seek communications to or from foreign targets using "selectors" such as names and email addresses, they could query information "about" these targets, including third-party communications that referenced selector terms. The leaks also identified PRISM, a cognate program that allowed the NSA to reach directly into the servers of Apple, Google, Yahoo, Facebook, Microsoft, Skype, AOL, YouTube, and other major firms. Emails, chats, videos, photos, voice-over-Internet (VoIP), files, and social media data, both stored and live, were collected. As of 2013, 77,000 intelligence reports cited PRISM data.[171] While these programs targeted non-US persons, they allowed unfettered access to trillions of domestic and international communications. Inevitably, protected American communications were also incidentally collected in the process.

Snowden could look up extensive amounts of information gathered through these programs using an XKEYSCORE search, the NSA's exceptionally powerful, all-encompassing search engine for stored and real-time data. Queries required minimal justifications. Moreover, he revealed: "In their classified internal communications, colleagues and supervisors often remind the analysts that PRISM and Upstream collection have a 'lower threshold for foreignness "standard of proof"' than a traditional surveillance warrant from a FISA judge, requiring only a 'reasonable belief' and not probable cause." For instance, speaking in a foreign language could deem a target foreign. Moreover, when FISA-authorized surveillance renewals became cumbersome, analysts would switch to permissive PRISM and UPSTREAM protocols.[172] Despite frontdoor UPSTREAM and PRISM access, the NSA also developed backdoor technologies to hack into American companies.[173] Under the RAMPART-A initiative, the NSA purportedly allowed numerous partner countries to use its capacity to tap into the Internet backbone.[174]

The extent of incidental surveillance under these programs is striking. Nine out of ten communications captured by UPSTREAM and PRISM and leaked by Snowden to the *Washington Post* were not targets of investigation. Extrapolating from this finding, the NSA's ninety thousand targets resulted in nine hundred thousand incidental collections, data that was retained anyway.[175] Of the ninety-seven billion pieces of data obtained by the NSA in March 2013 and documented by their Boundless Informant program, three billion pieces were from the United States. An NSA spokeswoman told the *Guardian*:

Current technology simply does not permit us to positively identify all of the persons or locations associated with a given communication (for example, it may be possible to say with certainty that a communication traversed a particular path within the internet. It is harder to know the ultimate source or destination, or more particularly the identity of the person represented by the TO:, FROM: or CC: field of an e-mail address or the abstraction of an IP address).[176]

Once again, these programs suggest extralegal spying. However, the NSA claimed otherwise. Section 702 of the FISA Amendments Act allowed the attorney general and director of national intelligence to certify warrantless surveillance of non-US persons abroad, even if American data was incidentally collected in the process.[177] While noting that "the unknown and potentially large scope of the incidental collection of U.S. persons' communications, the use of 'about' collection to acquire Internet communications that are neither to nor from the target of surveillance, and the use of queries to search for the communications of specific U.S. persons within the information that has been collected" pushed UPSTEAM "close to the line of constitutional reasonableness," the Privacy and Civil Liberties Oversight Board concluded that both it and PRISM were minimally lawful.[178]

In sum, the post-9/11 NSA developed extraordinary global surveillance capacity. While programs like UPSTREAM and PRISM generated extensive incidental collection of domestic communications, protected American communications were not explicitly sought by these programs. According to the NSA's legal logic, they were therefore permissible. Moreover, the NSA claimed that the changing nature of communications made them necessary. This is not to say that incidental collection was an unwanted byproduct. But domestic communications were not the target under the post-9/11 legal paradigm, which continued to rest on the longstanding legitimacy of foreign intelligence surveillance.[179]

Metadata and Data Mining

In addition to blurring lines between foreign and domestic surveillance, new technologies have also undermined traditional forms of targeted intelligence gathering. Suspected terrorists mobilize through diffuse electronic networks, constantly shifting channels of communication. Therefore, wiretapping the right person at the right time and location is almost impossible.[180] Because of this, intelligence agencies have turned to "data mining."

Data mining uses computers to scan and identify patterns in communications in order to detect suspicious behaviors. So-called dictionary computers search names, keywords, addresses, and telephone numbers.[181] This type of surveillance "tends to be divorced from the identity and location of the parties to a communication. There is no known wire linked to a known person with known characteristics."[182] In order to engage in data mining, intelligence agencies must collect vast quantities of metadata or data about communications as opposed to the content of communications. Reminiscent of the "vacuum cleaner" denounced by the Church Committee, such methods put mass surveillance before specific suspicions. Contrary to probable cause requirements for violating privacy, data mining seeks the proverbial needle in the haystack.

There have been several controversies surrounding data mining programs over the years. In the late 1990s, the Information Dominance Center at Fort Belvoir, Virginia developed a program to detect Chinese espionage by analyzing patterns in news stories, webpages, cable traffic, and intelligence reports. As a result, analysts increasingly harvested vast amounts of information about American citizens.[183] Despite legal concerns, the emergent technology was put to work in the service of Able Danger, a pre-9/11 Special Operations mission to detect and dismantle al-Qaeda. This time, the legal critiques grew strong stronger. The Department of Defense ordered analysts to delete all data on protected US persons or, as one lawyer put it, "you guys will go to jail."[184]

The macabre-sounding Total Information Awareness (TIA) program designed by the Defense Advanced Research Projects Agency followed Able Danger. Headed by Iran-Contra conspirator John Poindexter, its slogan ominously declared that "science is power" along with a graphic logo of an all-seeing eye atop a pyramid. Derided by civil liberties experts, TIA eventually caught the attention of conservative *New York Times* columnist William Safire, who criticized it. Congress subsequently quashed TIA's budget.[185] However, the program did not disappear—it was eventually quietly transferred to the NSA.

The FBI had its own unfortunately titled Carnivore system, aimed at intercepting packets of Internet communication fitting predetermined patterns.[186] Despite the huge costs involved in its production, Carnivore was rarely used and was abandoned in favor of commercial filtering soon after 9/11. In 2009, Wired.com documented a massive FBI National Security Branch Analysis Center, which collected more than 1.5 billion pieces of government and private sector information about Americans including hotel, car rental, credit card, financial, and travel records under the third-party doctrine.[187]

The 2013 Snowden disclosures revealed that along with warrantless wiretapping, Stellarwind had an extensive, previously unknown, metadata component. From 2001 until 2011, two years into the Obama administration, the NSA engaged in bulk collection of telephone and Internet metadata. The program was brought under FISA Court authorization in 2006. While the metadata collection initially focused on non-US communications or communications involving one foreign actor, in 2007 the NSA began collecting metadata associated solely with US persons.[188] Analysts could peruse the resultant databank using XKEYSCORE.

To justify these activities, authorities relied on section 215 of the PATRIOT Act, which allowed collection of business records relevant to foreign terrorist investigations, and the third-party doctrine. As I previously discussed, the latter held that data shared with corporations is not private. "Toll records, phone records like this, that don't include any content, are not covered by the fourth amendment because people don't have a reasonable expectation of privacy in who they called and when they called," claimed Deputy Attorney General James Cole. "That's something you show to the phone company. That's something you show to many, many people within the phone company on a regular basis."[189] While the third-party doctrine itself is nothing new, the volume of information held by third parties is unprecedented. Email and online browsing histories reveal considerably more detailed personal profiles than call logs.

The NSA used metadata in order to engage in "contact chaining," which mapped communications networks. NSA rules allowed up to three hops from initial targets, including hops to US persons. "That means that starting from a target's phone number, analysts can search on the phone numbers of people in contact with the target, then the numbers of people in contact with that group, and then the numbers of people in contact with that larger pool."[190] Once again, the third-party doctrine served to legitimize these practices, along with initial targeting of non-US persons.[191] As Assistant Attorney General Kenneth Wainstein noted, "NSA believes that . . . modifying its practice to chain through all telephone numbers and addresses, including those reasonably believed to be used by a United States person, will yield valuable foreign intelligence information primarily concerning non-United States persons outside the United States."[192] A 2011 NSA document on evolving metadata practice further explained: "The impact of the new procedures is two-fold. In the first place it allows NSA to discover and track connections between foreign intelligence targets and possible 2nd Party or US communicants. In the second place it enables large-scale graph analysis on very large sets of communications metadata without having to check foreignness of every node or address in the graph."[193]

Other metadata operations included EvilOlive and ShellTrumpet, which vastly increased the NSA's capability to filter metadata. In 2012, the NSA reported that ShellTrumpet had processed one trillion pieces of metadata.[194] Even more data was passed on by allied partners, such as Transient Thurible, a British program.[195] According to revelations, the NSA harvests contact and buddy lists from email, chat, and messaging services around the world.[196] Moreover, it uses commercial cookie data designed to identify Internet users for marketing purposes and "leaky" smartphone apps to track targets.[197] Metadata was stored for up to a year under in the NSA's Marina databank, including data of US persons.[198] These surveillance programs combined to form the staggering scale of NSA collection: "Leaked NSA documents show the agency sucking up data from approximately 150 collection sites on six continents. The agency estimates that 1.6 percent of all data on the Internet flows through its systems on a given day—an amount of information about 50 percent larger than what Google processes in the same period."[199]

It is not at all obvious that this massive trove of information improves national security. The NSA struggles with an "ever increasing backlog" and a terrible "gold to garbage" ratio with only one percent of collected data actually generating reports.[200] Moreover, experts warn that surveillance backdoors into new communications technologies weaken cybersecurity.[201] "In enabling eavesdropping mechanisms in the very fabric of our lives, we are building tools to catch one set of enemies. Other antagonists may well be poised to turn these tools against us . . . Rather than increasing our security, we may well be imperiling it," argues Landau.[202]

The Snowden leaks prompted extensive public and congressional debate. In December 2013, President Obama's newly formed Review Group on Intelligence and Communications Technologies issued a report highly critical of bulk collection practices, recommending "as a general rule and without senior policy review, the government should not be permitted to collect and store mass, undigested, non-public personal information about US persons for the purpose of enabling future queries and data-mining for foreign intelligence purposes."[203] Subsequently, President Obama issued Presidential Policy Directive 28 in winter 2014. It emphasized that intelligence and counterintelligence should not impede civil liberties or be used to give competitive commercial advantage to US companies. Importantly, it ordered the intelligence community to minimize personal information regardless of nationality and to disseminate and retain foreign information on a comparable basis as that applied to US persons.[204] As a result, the intelligence community adopted new minimization procedures.[205]

In 2015, Congress passed the Uniting and Strengthening America By Fulfilling Rights and Ensuring Effective Discipline Over Monitoring Act (USA FREEDOM Act), which extended section 215 of the PATRIOT Act, roving wiretaps, and lone wolf surveillance authority but ended bulk collection of metadata. Instead, it permitted the NSA to "collect from phone companies up to 'two hops' of call records related to a suspect, if the government can prove it has 'reasonable' suspicion that the suspect is linked to a terrorist organization." It further limited "the government's data collection to the 'greatest extent reasonably practical'—which means the government can't collect all data pertaining to a particular service provider or broad geographic region, such as a city or area code."[206] Telecom companies, not the NSA, were charged with storing metadata, which would be accessible by court order. Moreover, the act declassified significant FISA Court opinions and provided for a public advocate in FISA Court proceedings addressing novel legal issues.

These measures strengthened privacy protections. For the first time, the privacy interests of foreigners were acknowledged. Some limits were placed on third-party data. Not surprisingly, the intelligence community was critical. As reported by the *Washington Post*, former NSA general counsel Stewart Baker complained that the law would "make the National Security Agency risk-averse in ways that the CIA has occasionally been risk-averse . . . . They believed they were following the rules, and they got punished nonetheless."[207]

Bending and Breaking the Rules

While both the Bush and Obama administrations attempted to construct a legal basis for expanded surveillance powers and Congress provided legislative approval for these powers, it is difficult to gauge how closely surveillance conforms to legal restrictions in practice. What is evident is that the NSA is wary of accusations of illegality. In the national security culture of legal rationalization that has shaped the global war on terror, intelligence agents have sought legal cover for controversial activities. In the wake of the Snowden leaks, the NSA continually emphasized that it follows the law, is subject to extensive oversight, and protects Americans' privacy to the greatest extent possible: "NSA agents take an oath to the Constitution—not the Director, or the Agency, or the President—they take that oath very seriously."[208]

As with other counterterrorism practices discussed in this book, legal rationalizations for mass surveillance did not eliminate behaviors that went beyond legal guidance. For instance, former UN Ambassador John Bolton reportedly requested and received multiple NSA transcripts regarding American citizens working for the government in 2004–05.[209] He could hardly have been hunting al-Qaeda. Former SIGINT operators reported widespread eavesdropping on innocent Americans abroad in contravention of legal standards. Adrienne Kinne, an Arabic linguist working on Middle East satellite cuts recounted, "we could listen to all the NGOs, humanitarian aid organizations, and frigging journalists in the area—continue to even after they were identified and we knew who they were and that they weren't terrorists or terrorists affiliated."[210] Others claimed that personal conversations of Americans in the Baghdad Green Zone were constantly monitored.[211] Various investigations identified the problem of LOVINT—illegal surveillance by intelligence agents of romantic partners.[212] Moreover, the NSA reportedly monitored Wikileaks readers and supporters.[213] As revealed by the Snowden leaks, "the National Security Agency and FBI have covertly monitored the emails of prominent

Muslim-Americans—including a political candidate and several civil rights activists, academics, and lawyers—under secretive procedures intended to target terrorists and foreign spies."[214]

In April 2009, the *New York Times* reported that the NSA had engaged in unintentional but systematic "overcollection" of Americans' data. "[T]he issue appears focused in part on technical problems in the N.S.A.'s ability at times to distinguish between communications inside the United States and those overseas as it uses its access to American telecommunications companies' fiber-optic lines and its own spy satellites to intercept millions of calls and e-mail messages."[215] The Department of Justice inspector general found thousands of potentially illegal national security letter requests.[216] Leaked FISA Court documents show one of the NSA's surveillance programs collected "56,000 Internet communications . . . sent by Americans or persons in the United States with no connection to terrorism."[217] Critics such as Senator Ron Wyden have expressed concern that the NSA could exploit incidentally collected stored information through a "'back-door searches loophole' [which] allows the government to potentially go through these communications and conduct warrantless searches for the phone calls or emails of law-abiding Americans."[218] Although the USA FREEDOM Act was intended to address this concern, its precise application remains unclear.

Civil libertarians have also complained that intelligence sharing and outsourcing have eroded privacy rights. The UKUSA Five Eyes agreement created a framework for intelligence exchange, whereby one agency could volunteer information on another's nationals as long as it was not specifically requested, thus contributing to incidental collection.[219] The British Government Communications Headquarters receives extensive resources from the NSA. Because it is less regulated, it is "less constrained by NSA's concerns about compliance."[220] Domestic intelligence sharing is also potentially problematic. Despite distinct mandates, the NSA provides access to billions of pieces of metadata to twenty-three other government agencies, particularly the FBI and Drug Enforcement Agency through its ICREACH search engine architecture. "Information shared through ICREACH can be used to track people's movements, map out their networks of associates, help predict future actions, and potentially reveal religious affiliations or political beliefs."[221] While ICREACH data is culled from foreign sources, incidentally collected American data is undoubtedly included.

NGOs such as the ACLU, the Electronic Frontier Foundation, and the Electronic Privacy Information Center have pushed back against mass surveillance. The ACLU cites numerous evolving invasions of privacy from video monitoring to biometrics to DNA banks, ominously warning: "The false security of a surveillance society threatens to turn our society into a place where individuals are constantly susceptible to being trapped by data errors or misinterpretations, illegal use of information by rogue government workers, abuses by political leaders—or perhaps most insidiously expanded *legal* uses of information for all sorts of new purposes."[222] Such concerns go beyond intelligence agencies and extend to policing, consumer databases, and medical records. In this sense, the propriety of emerging surveillance powers is not just a matter of legality. Rather, these powers raise critical social and political questions. Civil libertarians and human rights advocates have had some successes in limiting domestic surveillance. The widespread public backlash that followed the Snowden leaks created political space to advocate for deeper compliance with privacy norms, resulting in legislation that checked bulk metadata collection. However, the vastness and complexity of the NSA's capacity means that technology continues to outpace law. Moreover, the contingent, nonabsolute nature of privacy norms makes them vulnerable to constant revision.

CONCLUSION

Americans have always been wary of domestic surveillance, concerns entrenched in American law. However, the same reticence has not applied to foreign intelligence surveillance, which is considered normal, necessary, and legitimate. Reflecting this state of affairs, the history of American surveillance practice has been uneven. Authorities have freely engaged in military and foreign intelligence gathering, creating a massive intelligence bureaucracy to do so. However, domestic surveillance has required various forms of probable cause and a warrant. During the Red Scares and world wars, a national security legal culture of exception encouraged violations of privacy rights. As the Cold War unfolded, a culture of secrecy facilitated blatantly illegal surveillance that could not be defended in public. Covert surveillance initiatives expanded beyond targeting demonized subversives to monitoring Americans en masse and pursuing political dirty tricks. In these contexts, *law as permit* prevailed: authorities overtly and covertly ignored legal norms in pursuit of their security agendas. In the 1970s, the Church Committee investigations revealed the extent of unlawful surveillance programs, inspiring new laws such as FISA.

After 9/11, policymakers blamed intelligence failure on legal rules. Accordingly, the PATRIOT Act loosened restrictions on intelligence gathering. At the same time, the Bush administration initiated secret programs such as Stellarwind and the President's Surveillance Program, followed by UPSTREAM, PRISM, and a host of other codenamed programs, in order to collect communications content and metadata without a FISA warrant. Many of these initiatives were inherited by the Obama administration. While accompanied by the language of sovereign decisionism, these programs were not quite as exceptional as they may initially seem. Rather, they were enacted within a national security legal culture that sought to establish legal cover for controversial activities. Instead of directly rejecting legal rules, authorities engaged the dichotomy between foreign and domestic intelligence already entrenched at the heart of the surveillance legal regime. Moreover, they exploited the third-party doctrine. The plausible legality of warrantless surveillance rested on claims that communications involving one non-US person should be classified as foreign and that metadata should not enjoy an expectation of privacy. In this sense, legal norms proved highly permissive, but at least partly constraining insofar as administration officials avoided justifying purely domestic spying.

Expecting inevitable public disclosure, these interpretive moves aimed to reassure the NSA and avoid the type of recriminations that followed the Church Committee investigations. While the 2013 Snowden leaks subjected surveillance to extensive criticism, resulting in new policy directives and legislation, legal rationales for warrantless wiretapping and other programs effectively insulated the intelligence community, as well as their private telecom partners, from formal charges of illegality. Many of these legal rationales were subsequently incorporated into congressional legislation.

Since 9/11, the scope of lawful surveillance has been rapidly expanded in the United States. Privacy norms have proved more malleable than other core human rights principles such as the torture prohibition or rights to life and liberty. While all have been subject to permissive plausibly legal reinterpretation by government lawyers, new surveillance powers enjoy much greater institutionalization and legitimacy than enhanced interrogation techniques, indefinite detention, or targeted killing. Moreover, the primarily domestic character of privacy rights, as opposed to rights also extensively codified in binding international law, has provided policymakers greater legal flexibility. FISA can be altered through domestic legal processes in ways the Convention against Torture or the Geneva Conventions cannot. In light of these trends, it is highly unlikely that the American national security establishment will be moved to embrace a *culture of human rights*—expressed as deep respect for privacy norms—anytime soon. Public outrage over the Snowden leaks temporarily created momentum for greater constraint, but there is little evidence that civil libertarians can roll back the surveillance state.

Post-9/11 American surveillance practice has in many ways strained legal rules, but it has ultimately been subject to legal rationalization. Legal arguments played a critical role in facilitating the expansion of surveillance power. More than ever before, the American intelligence community has the lawful capacity to surveil and collect almost all communications in the world.

CHAPTER 6

The Fate of Human Rights in the Global War on Terror

During the 2016 presidential campaign, then-candidate Donald J. Trump declared he would order waterboarding "in a heartbeat" and "a hell of a lot worse than waterboarding" because "only a stupid person would say it doesn't work."[1] He also pledged to kill the families of terrorists,[2] prosecute American citizens at Guantánamo Bay,[3] and ban Muslims from entering the United States.[4] "The problem is we have the Geneva Conventions, all sorts of rules and regulations, so the soldiers are afraid to fight," he said, promising to "make some changes."[5] He continued to offer similar statements after his inauguration, reiterating that "torture works" and that the United States should "fight fire with fire."[6] These sentiments are striking, not simply because they endorse human rights abuses in the name of counterterrorism, but because they so flagrantly embrace violations of American and international law. In contrast to the evasive and euphemistic legal rationalizations that have accompanied most post-9/11 counterterrorism policy, they point to efforts to push legal culture—what I define as collectively shared understandings of legal legitimacy and appropriate forms of legal practice—toward a *culture of exception*. President Trump's hostility to legal norms and judicial review are indicative of an emergent strand of Western politics outside liberal, legalistic rights culture.

Could this cultural shift occur? The capacity of law to constrain American state violence stands, I argue, at a crossroads. The Bush and Obama administrations' legal justifications for human rights violations weakened and eroded legal norms. More overt attacks on international human rights and humanitarian law may hasten this decline. However, there are also signs of the persistent grip of legal principles on American politics. While the Trump administration denounces legal constraints, human rights advocates continue to vigorously push for deeper compliance. Whether the status quo will pivot toward one of these poles remains to be seen. In this concluding chapter, I review my argument regarding the role of law in shaping American security policy as well as possible futures that may emerge from this state of affairs.

In the global war on terror, American policymakers sought to establish what I call the *plausible legality* of torture, arbitrary deprivations of life and liberty, and mass surveillance. Government lawyers played a critical role in this process, producing legal memoranda that reinterpreted the legal definition of torture to exclude enhanced interrogation techniques. They exploited alleged loopholes in and among American law, international human rights law, and international humanitarian law to permit indefinite detention, military commissions, and targeted killing. They reclassified domestic surveillance as foreign and invoked the third-party doctrine to facilitate warrantless spying and bulk metadata collection. These legal maneuvers emerged in the face of deepening legal restrictions on and intensified monitoring and criticism of the national security establishment since the 1970s. The resulting proliferation of legal justifications for contentious security policies stands in contrast to previous eras, when authorities relied on colonial and racist dehumanization and invocations of wartime exceptional necessity to legitimize state violence. The contemporary demand for legal cover also differs from the Cold War national security *culture of secrecy*, in which security agencies covertly pursued illegal practices that could not be publically justified.

In identifying pervasive post-9/11 efforts to construct plausible legality for what would otherwise be unlawful security policies, my claim is not that the torture memos or related legal arguments were legally valid or convincing. They selectively invoked legal precedents, relied heavily on contested executive power claims, and often seemed geared toward facilitating government policy rather than providing neutral analysis. They consistently interpreted legal ambiguities and lacunae to minimize human rights obligations and maximize state power. Because many of these legal opinions were formulated within a small circle of national security legal advisors, they did not benefit from interagency review or broader expert scrutiny.

At the same time, the Bush and Obama administrations' legal claims highlighted genuine instabilities in legal rules that make law vulnerable to manipulation.[7] The ambiguous definition of torture in the Convention against Torture and its distinction between torture and cruel, inhuman, and degrading treatment created room for good- and bad-faith interpretation. Because of the universal, nonderogable nature of the torture prohibition, the torture memos attempted to differentiate waterboarding, stress positioning, and other forms of violent coercion from torture, an approach informed in light of, not in spite of, the anti-torture norm.

Laws governing rights to life and liberty are rooted in overlapping layers of constitutional law, international human rights law, and international humanitarian law. In this context, American officials justified indefinite detention, trial by military commission, and targeted killing of "unlawful enemy combatants" by appealing to alleged gaps between rules covering international and noninternational armed conflicts, soldiers and civilians, and detainees held on and off American soil. Moreover, they utilized the vast discretionary powers of immigration law to undermine due process principles.

In the realm of surveillance, warrantless spying was accomplished through reclassifying as foreign communications involving one non-US person—a move predicated on the legitimacy of unconstrained foreign intelligence gathering. Moreover, authorities extended the third-party doctrine to new technologies, allowing unfettered access to corporate metadata for the purposes of data mining. Although early manifestations of these policies violated FISA, public justifications appealed to the foreign/domestic dichotomy at the heart of American surveillance law. Extralegal programs were eventually legalized through congressional legislation.

American officials took advantage of legal instabilities to authorize contentious policies. However, these authorizations were structured by existing rules, foreclosing official endorsement of practices such as overtly bloody torture, intentional targeting of civilians, or purely domestic warrantless wiretapping. Legal rules thus proved both enabling and constraining.

The role of legal norms in limiting state violence is a longstanding concern of international relations and international law scholars. As outlined in chapter 2, realists, Schmittian decisionists, and a variety of critical legal theorists emphasize the perspective of *law as permit*, noting the inevitable subordination of law to sovereign power. Especially in the realm of national security, legal rules have limited capacity to control political imperatives. In contrast, advocates of liberal and constructivist approaches understand *law as constraint*. Legal rules create rational incentives for rule following, structure international collaboration, and help shape state identity. Neither optic proves universally true; sometimes states act like scofflaws, sometimes rule followers. Accordingly, I argue that the impact of law on politics is contextually contingent on prevailing legal cultures in which political actors interpret, enact, and evade the law.

Cultures of exception and secrecy bend toward law as permit, while a yet-to-be-realized *culture of human rights* would manifest law as constraint.

The post-9/11 American *culture of legal rationalization* lies in between law as permit and law as constraint as authorities seek to expand their freedom of action without embracing overt extralegality. The dualistic nature of law as both a tool of state power and a check on policy reflects the dynamics of what I have called law as *permissive constraint*.

The remainder of this chapter examines the implications of post-9/11 American legal politics for legal rules and state practice. Plausible legality has proved a highly efficacious modality of human rights violation. While legal experts and human rights advocates have denounced American torture, indefinite detention, military commissions, targeted killing, and mass surveillance, efforts to construct legal cover for these programs have succeeded in immunizing public authorities from prosecution. This is especially notable in the case of torture, where well-documented abuses have gone unpunished.

In addition to ensuring impunity for individuals, plausible legality has weakened and even revised legal rules. In some instances, such as the attempt to legalize torture, policymakers failed to consolidate consensus around the legitimacy of enhanced interrogation techniques. However, they eroded the torture taboo, making room for renewed pro-torture arguments that emerged during the 2016 presidential election. In contrast, justifications for targeted killing and mass surveillance have secured widespread acceptance and even legislative approval. The normalization of these contentious practices demonstrates how cultures of legal rationalization can alter legal norms and open the door to bolder attacks on human rights principles in the United States and around the world.

Global political trends do not suggest that human rights activists will soon prevail in pushing states toward deeper compliance with human rights and humanitarian legal norms. Nonetheless, they continue to challenge state violence. I conclude by exploring contending approaches to achieving this end: enhanced law enforcement, legal regime redesign, and social pressure, arguing that the limitations of the first two point to the importance of the third for promoting change. NGO, social movement, judicial, and political advocacy hold promise for forging a different response to security challenges. Such efforts have borne fruit in the case of global pushback against American torture practices. But there is no inherently progressive historical trajectory toward greater respect for human rights. The fate of legal norms is contingent on ongoing struggles to defend and realize them.

IMMUNITY AND IMPUNITY

In national security cultures of legal rationalization, authorities seek plausibly legal cover in order to secure immunity from prosecution for otherwise illegal acts. There is ample evidence it has worked in this regard. Save the convictions of a handful of low-level soldiers caught on camera torturing detainees at Abu Ghraib, there have been few successful prosecutions for state authorized torture in the global war on terror. The threat of universal jurisdiction cases and civil lawsuits may prove a nuisance to the architects of enhanced interrogation techniques, but it is difficult to envision the implementation of meaningful criminal sanctions.[8] Nor are most torture victims likely to receive compensation or redress for their suffering. Ongoing indefinite detention, military commissions, targeted killing, and mass surveillance practices are even less likely to elicit significant opprobrium, let alone punishment. The Obama administration largely maintained and extended Bush administration policy in these areas. In some instances, Congress has consolidated rather than rolled back policy, entrenching the Guantánamo prison, granting immunity to CIA officers who used enhanced interrogation techniques as well as telecom companies that provided customer data to the NSA without a warrant, and legislating greater surveillance powers. Whether authorizing waterboarding, drone strikes, or warrantless wire-tapping, legal memos and legal sign-offs have wrapped their recipients in a cloak of impunity. This holds true even where legal opinions, such as the torture memos, are widely denounced as grossly fallacious.

The absence of prosecutions is significant in two regards. First, it suggests the efficacy of plausible legality as an exculpatory strategy, making it an attractive option for human rights abusers. Second, the absence of legal accountability contributes to undermining what Jutta Brunnée and Stephen Toope call a "practice of legality."[9] If legal obligation is upheld through ongoing practical interactions, it is essential to identify and sanction incongruent behavior. This is not merely because sanction serves as a rational deterrent, although it may in some cases, but because it gives life and content to positive law. Indeed, as observers of transitional justice and war crimes trials note, prosecution can serve an important didactic and transformational purpose.[10] Conversely, when norms are not enforced, they can wither and die.[11] In this sense, addressing past wrongs is a necessary component of moving forward. As Reed Brody argues, "[t]he US cannot convincingly claim to have rejected these egregious human rights violations until they are treated as crimes rather than as 'policy options.'"[12]

NORM REVISION AND EROSION

Beyond establishing impunity for human rights abuses in the global war on terror, American authorities arguably sought to revise human rights norms themselves. Policymakers and lawyers attempted to reinterpret the meaning of torture to exclude enhanced interrogation techniques. In justifying indefinite detention, military commissions, and targeted killing policy, they aimed to reduce protections for irregular fighters in international humanitarian law. They tried to shift the lines between foreign and domestic surveillance and private and public forms of data to reduce the need for warrants. Yet the degree to which these efforts succeeded is subject to debate.

The fate of the international torture prohibition has proved most contentious. On the one hand, several scholars note that the Bush administration acted as a norm entrepreneur, using tools of normative advocacy usually associated with pro-human rights and humanitarian movements to erode the anti-torture norm. For instance, Ryder McKeown suggests that the torture prohibition experienced a reverse norm life cycle or "death series," in which pro-torture advocacy gained traction, resulting in eventual norm regress.[13] Others similarly suggest that the global war on terror unleashed a "dark" form of normative argumentation that undermined human rights norms.[14] On the other hand, Kathryn Sikkink argues that counteradvocacy by human rights proponents reconsolidated the anti-torture norm, leading to policy change in the Obama administration.[15] Far from eroding the torture prohibition, this process strengthened and invigorated it.

The evidence points to mixed conclusions. Powerful states cannot unilaterally revise international norms without support from the international community.[16] The torture prohibition remains formally intact as a jus cogens legal norm. Most states continue to denounce and deny torture, war crimes trials prosecute it, and the Convention against Torture enjoys widespread ratification and support. With national variation, global public opinion opposes torture.[17] Pro-torture arguments did not result in a reverse norm cascade.[18] This is at least partly attributable to the nature of plausibly legal justifications for torture, which did not seek to explicitly overturn the torture prohibition. It is also due to extensive anti-torture advocacy by human rights NGOs, which have vigorously campaigned, lobbied, and litigated against the legalization of torture. Accordingly, OLC arguments in favor of enhanced interrogation techniques did not succeed in widely legitimizing an alternative definition of torture, as evidenced by President Obama's withdrawal of torture authorizations. However, considering ongoing impunity for torture, the anti-torture norm has certainly not been strengthened. Rather, it barely survived and remains vulnerable to renewed assaults. President Trump's open and unequivocal advocacy of torture constitutes a new front in the struggle to preserve the prohibition.

The evidence in other areas of security practice is less mixed, pointing to clearer patterns of norm erosion. In contrast to its faltering efforts to legalize torture, the Bush administration secured legislative approval for indefinite detention, military commissions, and reinterpretations of FISA. The Obama administration was unable to close Guantánamo Bay. Targeted killing enjoys bipartisan support and public popularity. Mass surveillance has been legalized. Despite some pushback from the courts, legal norms in all these areas have been significantly revised. At the international level, collective understandings of appropriate state conduct have moved to permit these practices, with real implications for human rights.

American actions have emboldened human rights abusers around the world.[19] In the wake of 9/11, the United States encouraged numerous countries, including ones with poor human rights records, to enact anti-terrorism legislation with little or no debate.[20] Much of this legislation defines terrorism extremely broadly, reduces procedural checks on law enforcement, and enhances preventative detention powers. While not all countries have utilized emerging laws for nefarious purposes, states such as China, Russia, Egypt, Syria, Malaysia, Eritrea, and Zimbabwe have employed counterterrorist rationales for repression.[21]

The United States and its allies have also advocated more aggressive counterterrorism policies in multilateral forums, pressuring states to "create an international anti-terrorism regime that mirrors the special regimes they have established at the national level."[22] After 9/11, the UN Security Council enacted multiple resolutions addressing terrorist financing, watch lists, sanctions, border control, and requirements for domestic legislation.[23] The newly created UN Counter-Terrorism Committee initially had no mandate to monitor human rights abuses.[24] Regional instruments adopted by the European Union, Organization of American States, African Union, and Association of Southeast Asian Nations have accompanied these measures, often expanding national security powers at the expense of civil liberties.

In the realm of international humanitarian law, permissive American legal interpretations of the Geneva Conventions have destabilized international rules and undermined the United States' credible commitments to the international community. Other countries are likely to let their own commitments slip in turn. As Jack Beard notes, these revisions may "impede or estop the United States from taking legal positions that it has previously relied on to support its operations and protect its personnel from violations of the laws of war," unintentionally offering adversaries "a legal model for future conflicts, with attendant negative consequences for U.S. operations."[25] As a result, states may interpret the law of armed conflict to allow increasingly lax thresholds for war initiation and the invocation of self-defense, confused standards for attributing state responsibility, looser definitions of combatants and belligerency, and greater status for nonstate actors.[26]

Targeted killing practices have diffused internationally, rapidly becoming a normalized feature of armed conflict. At least twenty countries possess armed drones, while Nigeria, Pakistan, and Iraq have joined the United States, the United Kingdom, and Israel in deploying them to kill insurgents in their ongoing civil conflicts. This expanding club is fueled by an emerging Chinese export market that makes drone technology increasingly accessible.[27] Ironically, the United States is now concerned that drones may be misused, issuing a statement with forty-eight other countries emphasizing the importance of "multilateral export control and nonproliferation regimes" and the "applicability of international law, including both the law of armed conflict and international human rights law."[28] However, it will be difficult for the United States to simultaneously defend its own track record of killing alleged terrorists outside of traditional military theatres while denouncing extrajudicial drone killings by others. In this sense, American efforts to broaden the scope of lawful killing in war have opened the floodgates as states move to enact their own interpretations of their legal obligations. The complexity of rules defining and governing armed conflict, compared to the relatively straightforward torture prohibition, makes it harder for human rights advocates to push back against growing acceptance of targeted killing in the same way they resisted the legitimation of enhanced interrogation techniques.

Already weak privacy protections have eroded around the world. As the UN Special Rapporteur on the promotion and protection of human rights and fundamental freedoms while countering terrorism observed, "Human rights standards have been tested, stretched and breached through the use of stop-and-searches; the compilation of lists and databases; the increased surveillance of financial, communications and travel data; the use of profiling to identify potential suspects; and the accumulation of ever larger databases to calculate the probability of suspicious activities and identify individuals seen as worthy of further scrutiny."[29] Accordingly, practices once associated with exceptional surveillance have become customary:

> First, States no longer limit exceptional surveillance schemes to combating terrorism and instead make these surveillance powers available for all purposes. Second, surveillance is now engrained in policymaking. Critics of unwarranted surveillance proposals must now argue why additional information must not be collected, rather than the burden of proof residing with the State to argue why the interference is necessary. Third, the quality and effectiveness of nearly all legal protections and safeguards are reduced. This is occurring even as technological change allows for greater and more pervasive surveillance powers. Most worrying, however, is that these technologies and policies are being exported to other countries and often lose even the most basic protections in the process.[30]

In the absence of a stronger international privacy consensus, these problems will be continually compounded by the growth in global intelligence information sharing and private third-party partnerships. Within the United States, congressional action has legally legitimized the erosion of FISA, enhancing state surveillance power and narrowing the constitutional right to privacy.

In sum, despite the failure of norm revisionism in the case of torture, there is evidence of norm destabilization and regress in other areas. The laws of war have been weakened, targeted killing is increasingly prevalent, and surveillance is ubiquitous. While the legitimacy of these efforts remains contested, shared understandings of appropriate state conduct are changing, both domestically and internationally. In this context, the fate of international human rights and humanitarian norms remains unsettled.

THE END OF HUMAN RIGHTS?

For Stephen Hopgood, global trends portend the "endtimes of human rights." States have hypocritically appropriated human rights discourse for ulterior purposes. International human rights advocates and institutions are out of touch with global realities. Without principled American leadership to champion human rights norms, illiberal forces threaten to roll back human rights universalism in favor of power politics and cultural relativism.[31] In the face of deepening international inequality and profound economic injustice, human rights are "not enough," argues Samuel Moyn.[32] A quarter century after Francis Fukuyama announced the "end of history," riots and uprisings, rampant poverty, genocide, and refugee flows mark a "return of history."[33] The remarkable rise of right-wing populism and authoritarianism around the world evident in the success of the anti-immigrant Brexit campaign in the United Kingdom, the rise of the European far right, and the increasing prominence of dictatorial leaders suggests human rights norms are facing critical if not terminal challenges.

Within the United States, President Trump has expressed public admiration for authoritarian leaders such as Vladimir Putin as well as sympathy for white nationalist and neofascist movements at home and abroad.[34] As I have already noted, the administration's early rhetoric and policy initiatives signal efforts to move national security culture away from legal rationalization and toward a culture of exception that openly embraces racism and extrajudicial violence. This possibility throws into relief differences from the Bush and Obama administrations, which attempted to legally justify their policies in light of extant norms. Of course, as the global war on terror makes clear, legal rationalization does not necessarily protect human rights.

Plausibly legal enhanced interrogation techniques are not better than other forms of torture. Lawful warfare can be horrifically destructive. Moreover, legal justifications for human rights violations arguably open the door to more overt attacks on human rights norms. If waterboarding is acceptable, why not "worse"? If it is okay to kill American citizens with drones, why not indefinitely detain them at Guantánamo? If the distinction between soldiers and civilians is blurred, maybe killing family members is not such a transgression? Why find legal pretexts for ethnic and racial profiling when there could simply be "a total and complete shutdown of Muslims entering the United States"?[35]

Will a culture of exception and its permissive legal politics reemerge in the United States in this context? Will American officials embrace overt extralegality? Could the law itself become an explicit instrument of racial violence, xenophobic exclusion, and ideological repression? Some observers are not optimistic. "[T]here is a strong incentive to be subordinate and compliant, because you could lose your job, lose your income, be ostracized by your friends and professional associates," writes Michael Glennon. "I don't see bureaucratic checking as a realistic way of stopping a populist authoritarian president."[36] Rosa Brooks notes that there are limited historical examples of the military resisting abusive policies. "The armed forces have a duty to disobey manifestly unlawful orders, but when top civilian lawyers at the White House and the Justice Department overrule the military's interpretation of the law, few service members persist in their opposition."[37] The Trump administration's promotion of extreme Islamophobic and anti-immigrant ideologues to formal and informal positions of power within national security circles may further weaken resistance.[38]

However, others insist that a culture of legal rationalization will constrain extralegal violence in the United States. For instance, Jack Goldsmith argues:

> I do not believe that the armed services under Trump will carry out orders to target civilians or to unwind the interrogation constraints in the Army Field Manual, because doing so would be clearly unlawful. I do not believe that the NSA career officials will—as the NSA did in the 1960s and 1970s—engage in domestic political surveillance, because doing so would be clearly unlawful. I do not believe . . . that CIA will return to waterboarding. Not only are all of these practices that people worry about unlawful, the culture and interests of these agencies would not permit these practices to occur.[39]

Michael Hayden, former director of the NSA and CIA, concurs. The national security establishment is more risk averse than ever: "Multiple investigations, grand juries, presidential condemnations, and congressional star chambers have a way of doing that to you . . . . Like the man said, if you want some-body waterboarded, bring your own damn bucket."[40] Trump administration officials such as Secretary of Defense James Mattis have publically promised to respect the torture prohibition and laws of war.[41] Demand for legal cover is likely to remain strong, particularly as tensions between the White House and the intelligence community simmer.[42] However, it is important to re-member that even if the plausible legality of waterboarding is off the table, numerous other human rights violations have and can be successfully legally authorized. Legal norms related to detention, trial, targeted killing, and sur-veillance are vulnerable to further revision and erosion.

In light of these dynamics, the Trump administration may find plau-sible legality to be a more efficient vehicle for implementing its agenda than broadly challenging legal norms. There are obstacles to forging a cul-ture of exception, from within the national security establishment itself, as well as from the judiciary. For example, in January 2017, the adminis-tration issued a hastily written executive order temporarily suspending all refugee admissions and banning travel from seven predominantly Muslim countries.[43] The immediate fallout of this sweeping action sent shock waves around the world. As the dust settled, it became clear that the White House had conducted minimal legal and interagency review. A bare-bones, one-page OLC memorandum lacking substantive legal analysis and dated the same day simply declared: "The proposed order is approved with respect to form and legality."[44] Ongoing confusion over the hugely consequential question of whether the order applied to lawful permanent residents sub-sequently forced White House counsel to issue an interpretive guidance clarifying that it did not.[45] Acting Attorney General Sally Yates was fired after refusing to defend the order in court.[46]

The Trump administration's lack of attention to legal process exposed it to legal challenges. A federal judge quickly stayed the travel ban. Because the initial executive order carelessly subsumed lawful permanent residents, it undermined their basic constitutional rights, providing grounds for additional judges to uphold the stay.[47] Moreover, the court rejected the administration's simplistic and absolutist insistence on the unreviewability of its policies.[48] The president denounced "so-called judge[s]," while White House advisor Stephen Miller ominously declared, "we have a judiciary that has taken far too much power . . . . The end result of this, though, is that our opponents, the media and the whole world will soon see as we begin to take further actions, that *the powers of the president to protect our country are very substantial and will not be questioned.*"[49] Despite the bluster, the ad-ministration was forced to revise the plan to be more legally compliant. It continues to be subject to litigation.[50] If the order was a trial balloon for aggressive challenges to legal norms, it was not particularly successful.

While human rights advocates are alarmed by the Trump administration's rhetoric and promises, they are also highly motivated to fight back, perhaps with more principled fervor than they resisted the Obama administration. Factors such as whether the Supreme Court maintains its ideological balance or tracks farther right, and whether nationalist and neofascist political parties secure electoral victories in Europe, will also contribute to the ability of judicial institutions and the international community to constrain a politics of exception. Given all this, it is premature to announce the death of human rights, which remain subject to extensive contestation.

TOWARD DEEPER HUMAN RIGHTS COMPLIANCE?

Human rights and humanitarian legal norms have been revised and eroded through strategic legal rationalization. They face growing threats from illiberal political forces. In these circumstances, can law serve as a greater and more meaningful check on state violence? Or is the status quo the best human rights advocates can hope for? In this final section, I return to this core theoretical and practical problem and argue that there are few ways to materially enforce or rationally incentivize the United States to embrace deeper compliance with its legal obligations. Rather, promoting a culture of human rights is more likely to limit abusive counterterrorism policies.

The potential for coercive enforcement of international law against the United States is extremely limited. There is no international supranational authority, such as a world court or world government, that can compel compliance. The United States has a long history of rejecting International Court of Justice rulings that contradict its positions and has eschewed participation in the International Criminal Court. Notwithstanding several limited attempts at asserting universal jurisdiction by activist prosecutors in Europe, there are no other countries willing or able to use force or sanctions to ensure American conformity with international human rights and humanitarian law. In this sense, realists are right that international law is materially unenforceable against a superpower.

That said, the United States' international legal commitments are not merely rhetorical. They are institutionalized in American law, which contains voluminous statutory restrictions on human rights abuses and war crimes. In some instances, the Supreme Court has pushed back against administration policy, requiring changes to detention and trial practices, but has generally been deferential to congressional legislation. Moreover, the architects and perpetrators of the United States' controversial post-9/11 counterterrorism programs remain hypothetically subject to prosecution in US courts, although the strategy of plausible legality is geared precisely toward evading this outcome. In this context, prosecution for torture and other crimes would upend the culture of legal rationalization that blurs the line between compliance and noncompliance and force the national security establishment to rethink its relationship to law. However, as I have argued, it is extremely unlikely that any prosecutor would attempt such a politically fraught endeavor.

Liberal and rational institutionalist approaches to international law argue that well-designed legal regimes help incentivize state compliance. As previously noted, American authorities exploited definitional ambiguities and loopholes in the law to facilitate human rights abuses in the global war on terror. It would therefore be logical to remedy these vulnerabilities. For instance, there may be room for international negotiation of rules governing detention in noninternational armed conflicts, where current guidance is lacking.[51] Targeted killing could be subject to greater international regulation. In the domestic setting, new legislation and Obama administration directives helped clarify the prohibition on torture and provided new guidelines for intelligence surveillance. Where the law is weak or vague, it can be improved. However, there are also risks to subjecting the content of legal norms to further negotiation. There is no guarantee that proponents of abusive policies would not capture these processes and institutionalize their preferred policies. It is likely that reopening the Geneva Conventions would result in more, not less, permissive rules. Domestic efforts to legislate mass surveillance have often expanded, not restricted, the state's lawful surveillance capacity.

Most importantly, even if legal norms could be formally strengthened, they would still rely on people to interpret and implement them. Seemingly powerful and universal rules such as the torture prohibition by no means guarantee compliance on their own. As Brunnée and Toope emphasize, law requires "social grounding":

> Stating a norm, even through formal means like treaty or custom, may be a step in creating law: but without the mutual engagement of social actors in a community of practice, the formal norm will not exert social influence. The prohibition on torture, for example, is contained in one of the most widely ratified treaties in the human rights domain. But the norm is constantly challenged through contrary practice and attempts at redefinition. The need for basic congruence between norms and social understandings helps explain why ambitious international regimes often founder: they have no social grounding.[52]

National security legal cultures socially ground state security practice, shaping how authorities balance legal obligations and policy preferences.

In a legal culture of human rights, the national security establishment would be substantively constrained by widely shared commitments to universal and inclusive understandings of human rights and humanitarian law as appropriate guides to action. Tensions between security imperatives and human rights norms would be resolved in favor of the latter. Lawyers would say "no" to abusive policies. Of course, greater respect for legal norms would not foreclose all state violence.[53] It would rule out torture, arbitrary deprivations of life and liberty, and more extreme forms of mass surveillance, but it would not end war, ensure equality, or guarantee social justice. Moreover, human rights are political and strategic and can be deployed for both oppressive and emancipatory ends.[54] As realists and critical theorists have long noted, moralistic security policy can lead to imprudent and imperialistic ventures, such as botched regime change and reckless democracy promotion. The United States' 1999 Kosovo bombing campaign, 2003 invasion of Iraq, and 2011 intervention in Libya are frequently criticized examples of this phenomenon. I cannot adjudicate this important issue here, but I can suggest that genuine and consistent commitment to international human rights and humanitarian law has rarely been the animating force behind such operations. Nor do international human rights advocates or international law usually support them. There is undoubtedly a potential dark side to cultures of human rights, but promoting deeper respect for human rights and humanitarian legal norms is one of—if not the only—path forward for limiting the types of abusive security practices I have documented in this study.

Changing legal culture holds most promise for ensuring greater respect for human rights and humanitarian law. However, cultural change is difficult, involving a combination of purposeful human action, shifting social norms, and major historical events. Recent trends regarding these factors do not bode well for human rights adherence. As I have argued, the global war on terror has destabilized human rights and humanitarian norms. Global political developments, such as the 2016 American presidential election as well as the growing power of reactionary social movements and authoritarian regimes around the world, have empowered human rights critics, not advocates. Fears of ISIS terrorism may further override human rights concerns. The Trump administration is actively pulling the United States toward a culture of exception. Nonetheless, international human rights activists and the international law community are pushing back. What culture prevails is largely a question of which groups in society are able to achieve a preponderance of power and influence over the national security establishment.

There are a number of well-documented ways that human rights advocates can promote their agendas. Naming and shaming are critical forms of social pressure. In this regard, NGOs, social movements, and human rights lawyers around the world have waged a relentless critique of American conduct in the global war on terror. Protests, lobbying, and litigation accusing the United States of war crimes have forced authorities to defend and in some cases abandon their permissive legal interpretations. Courts have curtailed more egregious forms of government overreach. International organizations have leveraged diplomatic pressure. While impunity reins, civil lawsuits and potential universal jurisdiction cases impose "reputational, emotional, and financial costs . . . that help to promote the human rights groups' ideological goals, even if courts never actually rule against the officials."[55] Such efforts increase policymakers' legal exposure and may limit future risk taking and norm violation. As Goldsmith notes, legal criticism "significantly influences and constrains officials, not only by direct prohibitions but also, and more significantly, by getting them to 'think twice' about what they are doing."[56] Combined, these various forms of political and legal activism could encourage authorities to take their human rights and humanitarian legal obligations more seriously.

Yet cultural change requires more than just external critique. Legal education and training and bureaucratic acculturation that emphasize human rights would help routinize deeper compliance with legal norms, even when they conflict with policy preferences. There must be space for critics, such as the military lawyers and State Department officials who expressed alarm over torture policy during the Bush administration, to make their case without fear of negative consequences. Forging a national security legal culture of human rights requires endogenous processes of reproduction within the national security establishment itself.

CONCLUSION

National security legal cultures shape how public authorities engage legal norms and pursue security policy. Such cultures can be highly permissive, legitimizing de facto and de jure legal exceptions. Colonialism, racism, and the exigencies of war justify excluding demonized targets from the protection of the law. Fulfilling realist, decisionist, and critical theoretical expectations about the subordination of law to power, cultures of exception produce numerous human rights abuses. As I have argued, exceptional legal politics have a long history in the United States. They may be emerging once again. In contrast, national security cultures of secrecy encourage authorities to do one thing and say another, to conduct their dirty work away from public purview. For instance, Cold War plausible deniability insulated American officials and facilitated unlawful clandestine and covert action.

I have argued that a national security culture of legal rationalization has shaped the global war on terror. Facing increased scrutiny and criticism, the American national security establishment sought legal cover for contentious post-9/11 policies. Government lawyers were tasked with establishing the plausible legality of torture, indefinite detention, military commissions, targeted killing, and mass surveillance in order to ensure impunity for human rights violations. In many ways, these legal opinions enabled forms of interrogation, detention, killing, and spying that might otherwise prove too risky. However, they were also limiting, authorizing policies that exploited vulnerabilities in human rights and humanitarian law without directly rejecting legal norms. In this sense, law functioned as a permissive constraint. These patterns produced a distinctive post-9/11 counterterrorism paradigm, characterized by voluminous legal memoranda, euphemistic language, and routinized repertoires of state violence.

The greatest challenge to the substantive realization of human rights and humanitarian rules in this post-9/11 context lies less in the suspension of law than in the incremental revision and erosion of legal norms. The laws that prohibit torture, arbitrary deprivations of life and liberty, and warrantless surveillance evolved gradually through time. They could eventually be undone, not just through the exercise of unmitigated sovereign power, although that remains an omnipresent possibility, but through a quiet and unexceptional process of plausibly legal reinterpretation. Throughout the global war on terror, American policymakers manipulated law to permit what it should constrain. Forging a national security legal culture that resists this logic is necessary if human rights and humanitarian law are to effectively check human rights abuses in the future.

NOTES

CHAPTER 1

1. Mark Mazzetti, Charlie Savage, and Scott Shane, "How a U.S. Citizen Came to Be in America's Cross Hairs," *New York Times*, March 9, 2013, http://www.nytimes.com/2013/03/10/world/middleeast/anwar-al-awlaki-a-us-citizen-in-americas-cross-hairs.html. The US government also killed American citizens during the Civil War, but the concept of targeted killing is new.

2. Rebecca Sanders, "Legal Frontiers: Targeted Killing at the Borders of War," *Journal of Human Rights* 13, no. 4 (2014): 512–36.

3. I have initially identified contested terminologies such as "enhanced interrogation techniques," "targeted killing," and the "global war on terror," with scare quotes. As discussed at various points throughout the text, the language of enhanced interrogation techniques euphemistically obscures the violent practices to which they refer, namely torture. The global war on terror, a term used by the Bush, but not the Obama administration, invokes a legally questionable concept of transnational armed conflict against a tactic; a conflict that is neither spatially nor temporally bounded. I use these terms throughout the book not to endorse these contested meanings but as constructs that capture the phenomena I wish to analyze. In discussing enhanced interrogation techniques, I use competing language such as "torture memos" to provide a countercharacterization. Both proponents and critics of American lethal targeting policy use the language of "targeted killing" but disagree over what this means and whether it is legal.

4. Throughout the book, I refer to a variety of political actors including American or public authorities, officials, policymakers, politicians, and leaders. Sometimes I also refer to states as actors. As will become clear in my theoretical discussion, I understand the political and legal processes I examine to be driven by human agents operating in particular normative and material environments.

5. I refer to law, legal rules, and legal norms synonymously to denote publically promulgated and binding standards of conduct for society. In domestic legal systems, law is usually codified in constitutions and legislation and institutionalized through government policy. In common law legal systems such as that of the United States, court rulings also play a role in solidifying the meaning of legal rules. International law includes legal rules created by treaties that states have ratified as well as customary international law, which is created through a combination of state practice and *opinio juris* (state beliefs about their legal obligations). Sometimes standards of conduct are broader than a specific law. In these cases, I refer to norms or social norms (e.g., Enlightenment norms). As international law becomes increasingly codified, legal and social norms frequently overlap. On occasion, I refer to regimes (e.g., the anti-torture regime) to denote the collection of domestic and international norms and laws governing an issue area.

6. I use the term national security to encompass traditional conceptualizations of military threats to states and their citizens but also more broadly to include perceived threats to governments or dominant groups from subversives or minorities. For instance, racist polities may understand national security as maintaining racial hierarchy.

7. Rebecca Sanders, "(Im)plausible Legality: The Rationalisation of Human Rights Abuses in the American 'Global War on Terror,'" *International Journal of Human Rights* 15, no. 4 (2011): 605–26.

8. Lawrence M. Friedman, *The Legal System: A Social Science Perspective* (New York: Russell Sage Foundation, 1975); Austin Sarat and Thomas R. Kearns, eds., *Law in the Domains of Culture* (Ann Arbor: University of Michigan Press, 1998); Naomi Mezey, "Law as Culture," *Yale Journal of Law and the Humanities* 13 (2001): 35–67; and Javier Couso, Alexandra Huneeus, and Rachel Sieder, eds. *Cultures of Legality: Judicialization and Political Activism in Latin America* (New York: Cambridge University Press, 2013).

9. Jutta Brunnée and Stephen J. Toope, *Legitimacy and Legality in International Law: An Interactional Account* (Cambridge: Cambridge University Press, 2010).

10. David Nelken, "Using the Concept of Legal Culture," *Australian Journal of Legal Philosophy* 29 (2004): 2.

11. Antje Wiener, "Enacting Meaning-In-Use: Qualitative Research on Norms and International Relations," *Review of International Studies* 35 (2009): 175–93.

12. Stanley Cohen, *States of Denial: Knowing about Atrocities and Suffering* (Cambridge: Polity, 2001).

13. For additional ways of conceptualizing legal culture, see David Nelken, "Thinking About Legal Culture," *Asian Journal of Law and Society* 1, no. 2 (2014): 262.

14. E.g., David Nelken and Johannes Feest, eds., *Adapting Legal Cultures* (Portland, OR: Hart, 2001); Sally Engle Merry, *Human Rights and Gender Violence: Translating International Law into Local Justice* (Chicago: University of Chicago Press, 2006); Kirsten Campbell, "The Making of Global Legal Culture and International Criminal Law," *Leiden Journal of International Law* 26 (2013): 155–72; and John Jackson and Yassin M'Boge, "The Effect of Legal Culture on the Development of International Evidentiary Practice: From the 'Robing Room' to the 'Melting Pot,'" *Leiden Journal of International Law* 26 (2013): 947–70.

15. Jeffrey W. Legro, "Which Norms Matter? Revisiting the 'Failure' of Internationalism," *International Organization* 51, no. 1 (1997): 31–63.

16. Jeremy Webber, "Culture, Legal Culture, and Legal Reasoning: A Comment on Nelken," *Australian Journal of Legal Philosophy* 29 (2004): 32.

17. E.g., Harold Koh was a leading luminary of the international human rights community before joining the national security establishment as State Department legal advisor under the Obama administration.

18. Pierre Bourdieu, "The Force of Law: Toward a Sociology of the Juridical Field," *Hastings Law Journal* 38 (1986–87): 816–18.

19. Emanuel Adler and Vincent Pouliot, eds., *International Practices* (Cambridge: Cambridge University Press, 2011).

20. Alexander L. George and Andrew Bennett, *Case Studies and Theory Development in the Social Sciences* (Cambridge: MIT Press, 2005).

21. Naomi Mezey, "Mapping a Cultural Studies of Law," in *The Handbook of Law and Society*, ed. Austin Sarat and Patricia Ewick (Malden, MA: Wiley Blackwell, 2015), 44.

22. Michael McCann, "The Unbearable Lightness of Rights: On Sociolegal Inquiry in the Global Era," *Law and Society Review* 48, no. 2 (2014): 245–73.

23. Catharine A. MacKinnon, "Women's September 11: Rethinking the International Law of Conflict," *Harvard International Law Review* 47, no. 1 (2006): 1–31.

24. Clifford Bob, *The Global Right Wing and the Clash of World Politics* (New York: Cambridge University Press, 2012) and Stephen Hopgood, *The Endtimes of Human Rights* (Ithaca, NY: Cornell University Press, 2013).

25. David Kennedy, *Of War and Law* (Princeton, NJ: Princeton University Press, 2006).

26. See Michael J. Glennon, *National Security and Double Government* (New York: Oxford University Press, 2015) for an account of the "Trumanite network."

27. Gerry Simpson, *Law, War, and Crime: War Crimes Trials and the Reinvention of International Law* (Cambridge: Polity, 2007). Simpson notes contemporary international legal mechanisms have not successfully exerted control over war initiation or aggression. In this sense, the juridification of politics has focused on individual criminal accountability.

28. Laura Dickenson, "Military Lawyers on the Battlefield: An Empirical Account of International Law Compliance," *American Journal of International Law* 104 (2010): 1–28; and Travers McCleod, *Rule of Law in War: International Law and United States Counterinsurgency Doctrine in the Iraq and Afghanistan Wars* (Oxford: Oxford University Press, 2015).

29. Jenna Johnson, "Trump Says 'Torture Works,' Backs Waterboarding and 'Much Worse,'" *Washington Post*, February 17, 2016, https://www.washingtonpost.com/politics/trump-says-torture-works-backs-waterboarding-and-much-worse/2016/02/17/4c9277be-d59c-11e5-b195-2e29a4e13425_story.html.

CHAPTER 2

1. Hans Morgenthau, *Politics Among Nations: The Struggle for Power and Peace* (New York: Alfred A. Knopf, 1963); Edward Hallett Carr, *The Twenty Years' Crisis, 1919–1939: An Introduction to the Study of International Relations* (New York: Harper and Row, 1964); John J. Mearsheimer, "The False Promise of International Institutions," *International Security* 19, no. 3 (1994–95): 5–49; Stephen D. Krasner, *Sovereignty: Organized Hypocrisy* (Princeton, NJ: Princeton University Press, 1999); Jack L. Goldsmith and Eric A. Posner, "Moral and Legal Rhetoric in International Relations: A Rational Choice Perspective," *Journal of Legal Studies* 31, no. 1 (2002): S115–S139; Jack L. Goldsmith and Stephen D. Krasner, "The Limits of Idealism," *Daedalus* 132, no. 1 (2003): 47–63; Jack L. Goldsmith and Eric A. Posner, *The Limits of International Law* (Oxford: Oxford University Press, 2005); and John Mearsheimer, *Why Leaders Lie: The Truth About Lying in International Politics* (Oxford: Oxford University Press, 2011).

2. Interestingly, Schmitt did examine international law in his later writings. In his *The Nomos of the Earth in the International Law of the* Jus Publicum Europaeum, trans. G. L. Ulmen (New York: Telos, 2003), Schmitt defends his conceptualization of the old European order against what he sees as the threat of moralistic American imperialism. However, there are some inconsistencies between his international legal theory and his writing on sovereign decisionism; see Benno Gerhard Teschke, "Fatal Attraction: A Critique of Carl Schmitt's International Political and Legal Theory," *International Theory* 3, no. 2 (2011): 197–227. Most decisionist readings of the global war on terror rely on the latter.

3. Carl Schmitt, *Political Theology: Four Chapters on the Concept of Sovereignty*, trans. George Schwab (Chicago: University of Chicago Press, 2005), 5.

4. Ibid., 6. Schmitt goes on to argue: "Because the exception is different from anarchy and chaos, order in the juristic sense still prevails even if it is not of the ordinary kind" (ibid., 12). However, as Oren Gross, "The Normless and Exceptionless Exception: Carl Schmitt's Theory of Emergency Powers and the 'Norm-Exception' Dichotomy," *Cardozo Law Review* 21, nos. 5–6 (2000): 1851 points out, this "juristic sense" is meaningless because it is based on the "unlimited authority" of the sovereign dictator. "Whatever

the sovereign decides is legitimate. There is no substantive content against which legitimacy of such actions can be measured—not even Hobbes's minimalist principle of self preservation."

5. Schmitt, *Political Theology*, 13.

6. Carl Schmitt, *The Concept of the Political*, trans. George Schwab (Chicago: University of Chicago Press, 2007), 27.

7. William E. Scheuerman, *Between the Norm and the Exception: The Frankfurt School and the Rule of Law* (Cambridge, MA: MIT Press, 1997), 22–34.

8. Schmitt, *Concept*, 33.

9. Balakrishnan Rajagopal, *International Law from Below: Development, Social Movements, and Third World Resistance* (Cambridge: Cambridge University Press, 2003); Gerry Simpson, *Great Powers and Outlaw States: Unequal Sovereigns in the International Legal Order* (Cambridge: Cambridge University Press, 2004); and Antony Anghie, *Imperialism, Sovereignty and the Making of International Law* (Cambridge: Cambridge University Press, 2005).

10. Robert Cox, "Gramsci, Hegemony, and International Relations: An Essay in Method," *Millennium* 12 (1983): 162–75 and China Miéville, *Between Equal Rights: A Marxist Theory of International Law* (Leiden: Brill, 2005).

11. Martti Koskenniemi, *The Politics of International Law* (Portland, OR: Hart, 2011) and Ian Hurd, *How to Do Things with International Law* (Princeton: Princeton University Press, 2017).

12. Michael Byers and Georg Nolte, eds., *United States Hegemony and the Foundations of International Law* (Cambridge: Cambridge University Press, 2003) and Shirley Scott, *International Law, US Power: The United States' Quest for Legal Security* (Cambridge: Cambridge University Press, 2012).

13. David Kennedy, *The Dark Side of Virtue: Reassessing International Humanitarianism* (Princeton, NJ: Princeton University Press, 2004). See also David Kennedy, *Of War and Law* (Princeton, NJ: Princeton University Press, 2006) and Nicola Perugini and Neve Gordon, *The Human Right to Dominate* (New York: Oxford University Press, 2015).

14. Robert Jervis, "Understanding the Bush Doctrine," *Political Science Quarterly* 118, no. 3 (2003): 379–80.

15. E.g., William Scheuerman, "Carl Schmitt and the Road to Abu Ghraib," *Constellations* 13, no. 1 (2006): 108–24; Derek Gregory, "The Black Flag: Guantánamo Bay and the State of Exception," *Geografiska Annaler. Series B, Human Geography* 88, no. 4 (2006): 405–27; Louiza Odysseos, *The International Political Thought of Carl Schmitt: Terror, Liberal War, and the Crisis of Global Order* (New York: Routledge, 2007); Michelle Farrell, *The Prohibition on Torture in Exceptional Circumstances* (Cambridge: Cambridge University Press, 2013); and Jason Ralph, *America's War on Terror: The State of the 9/11 Exception from Bush to Obama* (Oxford: Oxford University Press, 2013).

16. Sanford Levinson, "Torture in Iraq and the Rule of Law in America," *Daedalus* 133, no. 3 (2004): 8.

17. Scott Horton, "State of Exception: Bush's War on the Rule of Law," *Harper's*, July 2007, http://www.harpers.org/archive/2007/07/0081595.

18. Jens David Ohlin, *The Attack on International Law* (New York: Oxford University Press, 2015).

19. Giorgio Agamben, *State of Exception*, trans. Kevin Attel (Chicago: University of Chicago Press, 2005), 2. See Nasser Hussain and Melissa Ptacek, "Thresholds: Sovereignty and the Sacred," *Law and Society Review* 34, no. 2 (2000): 495–515 for an excellent overview of the complexities of Agamben's thought.

20. Giorgio Agamben, *Homo Sacer: Sovereign Power and the Bare Life*, trans. Daniel Heller-Roazen (Stanford, CA: Stanford University Press, 1998), 170.

21. Ulrich Raulff, "Interview with Giorgio Agamben—Life, A Work of Art without an Author: The State of Exception, the Administration of Disorder and Private Life," *German Law Journal* 5 (2004): 610.

22. Judith Butler, *Precarious Life: The Powers of Mourning and Violence* (London: Verso Books, 2004), 83.

23. US House of Representatives Committee on the Judiciary Majority Staff Report, *Reining in the Imperial Presidency: Lessons and Recommendations Related to the Presidency of George W. Bush*, January 13, 2009, 9, Federation of American Scientists, https://fas.org/irp/congress/2009_rpt/imperial.pdf.

24. John Yoo, *War by Other Means: An Insider's Account of the War on Terror* (New York: Atlantic Monthly, 2006), 119–20.

25. Frédéric Mégret, "From 'Savages' to 'Unlawful Combatants': A Postcolonial Look at International Law's 'Other,'" in *International Law and Its Others*, ed. Anne Orford (Cambridge: Cambridge University Press, 2006), 302.

26. Fleur Johns, "Guantánamo Bay and the Annihilation of the Exception," *European Journal of International Law* 16, no. 4 (2005): 614.

27. Nasser Hussain, "Beyond Norm and Exception: Guantánamo," *Critical Inquiry* 33, no. 4 (2007): 741.

28. For a further critique of decisionist analysis, see Ichiro Takayoshi, "Can Philosophy Explain Nazi Violence? Giorgio Agamben and the Problem of the 'Historico-Philosophical' Method," *Journal of Genocide Research* 13, nos. 1–2 (2011): 47–66.

29. Joseph Nye, *Soft Power: The Means to Success in World Politics* (New York: Public Affairs, 2004) and John G. Ikenberry, *Liberal Order and Imperial Ambition* (Cambridge: Polity, 2006).

30. Anne-Marie Slaughter, "International Law in a World of Liberal States," *European Journal of International Law* 6, no.1 (1995): 503–38 and Andrew Moravcsik, "Taking Preferences Seriously: A Liberal Theory of International Politics," *International Organization* 51, no. 4 (1997): 513–53.

31. Bruce M. Russett and John R. Oneal, *Triangulating Peace: Democracy, Interdependence, and International Organizations* (New York: Norton, 2001); Michael Doyle, "Kant, Liberal Legacies, and Foreign Affairs," *Philosophy and Public Affairs* 12 (1983): 205–35, 323–53; Beate Jahn, "Kant, Mill, and Illiberal Legacies in International Affairs," *International Organization* 59 (2005): 177–207; and Michael C. Desch, "America's Liberal Illiberalism: The Ideological Origins of Overreaction in U.S. Foreign Policy," *International Security* 32, no. 3 (2007–08): 7–43.

32. Robert O. Keohane, *After Hegemony: Cooperation and Discord in the World Political Economy* (Princeton, NJ: Princeton University Press, 1984); Kenneth W. Abbott et al., "The Concept of Legalization," *International Organization* 54 no. 3 (2000): 401–19; Andrew T. Guzman, "A Compliance-Based Theory of International Law," *California Law Review* 90 (2002): 1823–87; and Barbara Koremenos, "Institutionalism and International Law," in *Interdisciplinary Perspectives on International Law and International Relations: The State of the Art*, ed. Jeffrey L. Dunoff and Mark A. Pollack (New York: Cambridge University Press, 2013), 59–82.

33. Oona A. Hathaway, "Do Human Treaties Make a Difference?" *Yale Law Journal* 111, no. 8 (2002): 1935–2042 and Eric Neumayer, "Do International Human Rights Treaties Improve Respect for Human Rights?" *Journal of Conflict Resolution* 49, no. 6 (2005): 925–53.

34. Emilie Hafner-Burton and Kiyotero Tsutsui, "Human Rights in a Globalizing World: The Paradox of Empty Promises," *American Journal of Sociology* 110, no. 5 (2005): 1373–1411; Emilie Hafner-Burton, *Forced to Be Good: Why Trade Agreements Boost Human Rights* (Ithaca, NY: Cornell University Press, 2009); Beth A. Simmons, *Mobilizing for Human*

Rights: International Law in Domestic Politics (Cambridge: Cambridge University Press, 2009); and Jennifer Erickson, *Dangerous Trade: Conventional Arms Exports, Human Rights, and International Reputation* (New York: Columbia University Press, 2015).

35. John Ruggie, "International Regimes, Transactions, and Change: Embedded Liberalism in the Postwar Economic Order," in *International Regimes*, ed. Stephen D. Krasner (Ithaca, NY: Cornell University Press, 1983), 195–232.

36. Alexander Wendt, "Anarchy is What States Make of It: The Social Construction of Power Politics," *International Organization* 46, no. 2 (1992): 391–425.

37. James G. March and Johan P. Olsen, "The Institutional Dynamics of International Political Orders," *International Organization* 52, no. 4 (1998): 943–69 and Martha Finnemore and Stephen J. Toope, "Alternatives to Legalization: Richer Views of Law and Politics," *International Organization* 55, no. 3 (2001): 743–58.

38. Michael Barnett and Martha Finnemore, *Rules for the World: International Organizations in Global Politics* (Ithaca, NY: Cornell University Press, 2004); Emanuel Adler and Peter M. Haas, "Conclusion: Epistemic Communities, World Order, and the Creation of a Reflective Research Program," *International Organization* 46, no. 1 (1992): 367–90; Richard Price, "Reversing the Gun Sights: Transnational Civil Society Targets Land Mines," *International Organization* 52, no. 3 (1998): 613–44; Margaret Keck and Kathryn Sikkink, *Activists Beyond Borders: Advocacy Networks in International Politics* (Ithaca, NY: Cornell University Press, 1998); Thomas Risse, Stephen C. Ropp, and Kathryn Sikkink, eds., *The Power of Human Rights: International Norms and Domestic Change* (New York: Cambridge University Press, 1999); and Thomas Risse, Stephen C. Ropp, and Kathryn Sikkink, eds., *The Persistent Power of Human Rights: From Commitment to Compliance* (Cambridge: Cambridge University Press, 2013).

39. Martha Finnemore and Kathryn Sikkink, "International Norm Dynamics and Political Change," *International Organization* 52, no. 4 (1998): 887–917.

40. Harold Koh, "Why do Nations Obey International Law?," *Yale Law Journal* 106, no. 8 (1997): 2599–659; Jutta Brunnée and Stephen J. Toope, *Legitimacy and Legality in International Law: An Interactional Account* (Cambridge: Cambridge University Press, 2010); and Ryan Goodman and Derek Jinks, *Socializing States: Promoting Human Rights through International Law* (New York: Oxford University Press, 2013).

41. Jeffrey T. Checkel, "Why Comply? Social Learning and European Identity Change," *International Organization* 55, no. 3 (2001): 553–88; Jeffrey W. Legro, "Which Norms Matter? Revisiting the 'Failure' of Internationalism," *International Organization* 51, no. 1 (1997): 31–63; Antje Wiener, *The Invisible Constitution of Politics: Contested Norms and International Encounters* (Cambridge: Cambridge University Press 2008); and Wayne Sandholtz and Kendall Stiles, *International Norms and Cycles of Change* (New York: Oxford University Press, 2009).

42. George W. Bush, *Decision Points* (New York: Crown, 2010), 68.

43. Kelly M. Greenhill, *Weapons of Mass Migration: Forced Displacement, Coercion, and Foreign Policy* (Ithaca, NY: Cornell University Press, 2010), 4.

44. Ian Hurd, "Breaking and Making Norms: American Revisionism and Crises of Legitimacy," *International Politics* 44, no. 2–3 (2007): 203.

45. Thomas M. Franck, "The Power of Legitimacy and the Legitimacy of Power: International Law in an Age of Power Disequilibrium," *American Journal of International Law* 100, no. 1 (2006): 95–96.

46. David Nelken, "Using the Concept of Legal Culture," *Australian Journal of Legal Philosophy* 29 (2004): 2.

47. Finnemore and Sikkink, "International Norm Dynamics," 892.

48. E.g., Audie Klotz, *Norms in International Relations: The Struggle against Apartheid* (Ithaca, NY: Cornell University Press, 1995); Ellen L. Lutz and Kathryn Sikkink, "International

Human Rights Law and Practice in Latin America," *International Organization* 54, no. 3 (2000): 633–59; Richard Price, *The Chemical Weapons Taboo* (Ithaca, NY: Cornell University Press, 1997); Nina Tannenwald, *The Nuclear Taboo: The United States and the Non-Use of Nuclear Weapons Since 1945* (Cambridge: Cambridge University Press, 1997); Martha Finnemore, *The Purpose of Intervention: Changing Beliefs about the Use of Force* (Ithaca, NY: Cornell University Press, 2004); and Alison Brysk, *Global Good Samaritans: Human Rights as Foreign Policy* (Oxford: Oxford University Press, 2009).

49. Martti Koskenniemi, *From Apology to Utopia: The Structure of International Legal Argument* (Cambridge: Cambridge University Press, 2005).

50. Rebecca Sanders, "Human Rights Abuses at the Limits of the Law: Legal Instabilities and Vulnerabilities in the 'Global War on Terror'," *Review of International Studies* 44, no. 1 (2018): 2–23.

51. Friedrich Kratochwil, *Rules, Norms, and Decisions: On the Conditions of Practical and Legal Reasoning in International Relations and Domestic Affairs* (Cambridge: Cambridge University Press, 1989).

52. Christian Reus-Smit, "The Politics of International Law" in *The Politics of International Law*, ed. Christian Reus-Smit (Cambridge: Cambridge University Press, 2004), 41. 41.

53. Brunnée and Toope, *Legitimacy and Legality* and Lon L. Fuller, *The Morality of Law* (New Haven, CT: Yale University Press, 1964). Fuller argues an internal procedural morality allows law to function as a set of purposive rules. He notes eight necessary minimal components for this morality to operate: rules must be general, public, prospective, understandable, consistent with each other, not require powers beyond control, not change so frequently as to be unreliable, and be administered consistent with their wording.

54. Jeremy Waldron, "Torture and Positive Law: Jurisprudence for the White House," *Columbia Law Review* 105, no. 6 (2005): 1726–27.

55. Zoltán I. Búzás, "Evading International Law: How Agents Comply with the Letter of the Law but Violate its Purpose," *European Journal of International Relations* 23, no. 4 (2017): 857–83.

56. Jennifer Dixon, "Rhetorical Adaptation and Resistance to International Norms," *Perspectives on Politics* 15, no. 1 (2017): 83–99.

CHAPTER 3

1. James Ross, "A History of Torture," in *Torture: Does it Make Us Safer? Is it Ever OK? A Human Rights Perspective*, ed. Kenneth Roth and Minky Worden (New York: New Press and Human Rights Watch, 2005), 4–10.

2. Lisa Silverman, *Tortured Subjects: Pain, Truth, and the Body in Early Modern France* (Chicago: University of Chicago Press, 2001).

3. John H. Langbein, "The Legal History of Torture," in *Torture: A Collection*, ed. Sanford Levinson (Oxford: Oxford University Press, 2004), 97.

4. William Blackstone, "Of Arraignment, and its Incidents," in *Commentaries on the Laws of England,* Book 4, *Of Public Wrongs* (Oxford: Printed at the Clarendon Press, 1765–1769), http://avalon.law.yale.edu/18th_century/blackstone_bk4ch25.asp. The rack was a torture device used to dislocate victims' limbs.

5. Ibid.

6. Michel Foucault, *Discipline and Punish: The Birth of the Prison*, trans. Alan Sheridan (New York: Vintage Books, 1995), 55.

7. Helen Rawlings, *The Spanish Inquisition* (Malden, MA: Blackwell, 2006), 33; Joseph Perez, *The Spanish Inquisition: A History*, trans. Janet Lloyd (London: Profile Books, 2004), 147–48; and Jean Plaidy, *The Spanish Inquisition: Its Rise, Growth, and End* (New York: Citadel, 1969), 139.

8. Ross, "History," 10–12; Wolfgang Behringer, *Witches and Witch-Hunts: A Global History* (Cambridge: Polity, 2004) and Heinrich Kramer and James Sprenger, *Malleus Maleficarum* (1486), "The Third Part Relating to the Judicial Proceedings in Both the Ecclesiastical and Civil Courts against Witches and Indeed All Heretics," trans. Montague Summers (1948), http://www.malleusmaleficarum.org/downloads/MalleusAcrobat.pdf.

9. Alexander Gillespie, *A History of the Laws of War, Volume 1: The Customs and Laws of War with Regards to Combatants and Captives* (Portland, OR: Hart, 2011), 124–25.

10. Darius Rejali, *Torture and Democracy* (Princeton, NJ: Princeton University Press, 2007), 57.

11. Ross, "History," 3.

12. M. de Voltaire, *A Philosophical Dictionary* (Boston: J. Q. Adams, 1836), 2:256–57.

13. Quoted in Ross, "History," 13.

14. US Constitution, Amendment V (1791).

15. US Constitution, Amendment VIII (1791).

16. David Hackett Fischer, *Washington's Crossing* (New York: Oxford University Press, 2004), 379. As noted in chapter 4, humane treatment did not extend to conflict with indigenous peoples.

17. Instructions for the Government of Armies of the United States in the Field (Lieber Code), April 24, 1863, article 16, International Committee of the Red Cross, http://www.icrc.org/ihl.nsf/FULL/110?OpenDocument.

18. International humanitarian law lays out rules for legitimate belligerent conduct in armed conflict. Violations of these rules are war crimes. While it is clearly the *lex specialis* governing war, legal scholars continue to debate the extent to which it supersedes or operates in conjunction with international human rights law, which governs state obligations toward the rights of persons. Because torture is prohibited in both bodies of law, this debate is less significant in regard to torture than it is for understanding rules that govern detention and killing, the legality of which vary considerably from peace to wartime.

19. Convention (III) Relative to the Treatment of Prisoners of War (Geneva, August 12, 1949), article 3, International Committee of the Red Cross, http://www.icrc.org/ihl.nsf/WebART/375-590006.

20. UN General Assembly, International Covenant on Civil and Political Rights, December 16, 1966, entered into force March 23, 1976, United Nations Treaty Series 999:171, Refworld, http://www.unhcr.org/refworld/docid/3ae6b3aa0.html.

21. Organization of American States, *American Convention on Human Rights, "Pact of San Jose,"* Costa Rica, November 22, 1969, entered into force July 18, 1978, chapter II, article 5, Refworld, http://www.refworld.org/docid/3ae6b36510.html.

22. UN General Assembly, Convention Against Torture and Other Cruel, Inhuman or Degrading Treatment or Punishment, December 10, 1984, entered into force June 26, 1987, United Nations Treaty Series 1465:85, Refworld, http://www.unhcr.org/refworld/docid/3ae6b3a94.html.

23. UN Committee against Torture, http://www2.ohchr.org/english/bodies/cat/.

24. United Nations, Vienna Convention on the Law of Treaties, May 23, 1969, entered into force January 27, 1980, United Nations Treaty Series, 1155:331, section 3, article 31, Refworld, http://www.refworld.org/docid/3ae6b3a10.html.

25. Rome Statute of the International Criminal Court, July 17, 1998, entered into force July 1, 2002, part 2, articles 7 and 8, International Criminal Court, https://www.icc-cpi.int/resource-library/Documents/RS-Eng.pdf.

26. According to the United Nations, Vienna Convention, article 53, a peremptory or jus cogens norm of general international law "is a norm accepted and recognized by the international community of States as a whole as a norm from which no derogation is permitted

and which can be modified only by a subsequent norm of general international law having the same character."

27. R v. Bow Street Metropolitan Stipendiary Magistrate, Ex parte Pinochet Ugarte (No. 3) (2000) AC 147. This was the third in several complex and not entirely consistent legal rulings on the question. While asserting universal jurisdiction over Pinochet in a geographical sense, the decision was primarily rooted in a reading of the UN Convention against Torture, as domesticated into British law via the 1988 Criminal Justice Act rather than customary law. It thus restricted temporal jurisdiction to acts committed after 1988, thereby limiting potential prosecution to the period after Pinochet had committed his most systemic and egregious crimes. For debates over the precise legal implications of this case for head of state immunity and universal jurisdiction, see Michael Byers, "The Law and Politics of the Pinochet Case," *Duke Journal of Comparative and International Law* 10 (2000): 415–41; Campbell McLachlan, "Pinochet Revisited," *International and Comparative Law Quarterly* 51 (2002): 959–66; Philippe Sands, "International Law Transformed? From Pinochet to Congo . . . ?" *Leiden Journal of International Law* 16 (2003): 37–53; Naomi Roht-Arriaza, "Universal Jurisdiction: Steps Forward, Steps Back," *Leiden Journal of International Law* 17 (2004): 375–89; and Ed Bates, "State Immunity for Torture," *Human Rights Law Review* 7, no. 4 (2007): 651–80.

28. Uniform Code of Military Justice, 64 Stat. 109, 10 U.S.C. chapter 47, subchapter X, punitive articles, article 93, Cruelty and Maltreatment.

29. U.S. Reservations, Declarations, and Understandings, Convention Against Torture and Other Cruel, Inhuman or Degrading Treatment or Punishment, Cong. Rec. S17486-01, October 27, 1990, University of Minnesota Human Rights Library, http://www1.umn.edu/humanrts/usdocs/tortres.html.

30. Federal Anti-Torture Statute, 18 U.S.C., part 1, chapter 113C, §2340A (1994) and the War Crimes Act, 18 U.S.C., part 1, chapter 118, §2441 (1996).

31. The Torture Victim Protection Act of 1991, Pub. L. 102–256, H.R. 2092, 106 Stat. 73, March 12 1992.

32. US Department of State, Bureau of Democracy, Human Rights, and Labor, *Country Reports on Human Rights Practices*, US Department of State, http://www.state.gov/g/drl/rls/hrrpt/.

33. "An Act concerning Servants and Slaves," XXXIV, October 1705, *Encyclopedia of Virginia*, http://www.encyclopediavirginia.org/_An_act_concerning_Servants_and_Slaves_1705.

34. "An Act Directing the Trial of Slaves, Committing Capital Crimes; and for the More Effectual Punishing Conspiracies and Insurrections of Them; and for the Better Government of Negros, Mulattos, and *Indians*, Bond or Free," IV, May 1723, *Encyclopedia of Virginia*, http://www.encyclopediavirginia.org/_Act_directing_the_trial_of_Slaves_committing_capital_crimes_and_for_the_more_effectual_punishing_conspiracies_and_insurrections_of_them_and_for_the_better_government_of_Negros_Mulattos_and_Indians_bond_or_free_1723.

35. Judith Kelleher Schafer, "'Details Are of a Most Revolting Character': Cruelty to Slaves as Seen in Appeals to the Supreme Court of Louisiana," in *Slavery and the Law*, ed. Paul Finkelman (Madison, WI: Madison House, 1997), 242–67.

36. "The Unreported Case of *Humphreys v. Utz* (1856)," in Paul Finkelman, ed. *Slavery and the Law* (Madison, WI: Madison House, 1997), 270.

37. Ibid., 289–90.

38. Dred Scott v. Sandford, 60 U.S. 393 (1857).

39. Ida B. Wells, *Southern Horrors: Lynch Law in All Its Phases* (New York: The New York Age Print, 1892), The New York Public Library Digital Collections, https://digitalcollections.

nypl.org/items/868f8db7-fa74-d451-e040-e00a180630a7#/?uuid=634281e0-4abc-0134-346c-00505686a51c.

40. Lisa Cardyn, "Sexualized Racism/Gendered Violence: Outraging the Body Politic in the Reconstruction South," *Michigan Law Review* 100, no. 4 (2002): 692.

41. Ibid., 710.

42. Ibid., 714–22.

43. Lee Ann Fujii, "The Puzzle of Extra-Lethal Violence," *Perspectives on Politics* 11, no. 2 (2013): 419.

44. James W. Clarke, "Without Fear or Shame: Lynching, Capital Punishment and the Subculture of Violence in the American South," *British Journal of Political Science* 28, no. 2 (1998): 277.

45. Equal Justice Initiative, *Lynching in America: Confronting the Legacy of Racial Terror*, 3rd ed., https://lynchinginamerica.eji.org/report/.

46. Pierre Vidal Naquet, *Torture: Cancer of Democracy, France and Algeria, 1954–6*, trans. Barry Richard (Baltimore: Penguin, 1963); Henri Alleg, *The Question*, trans. John Calder (Lincoln, NE: Bison Books, 2006); Paul Aussaresses, *The Battle of the Casbah: Terrorism and Counter-Terrorism in Algeria, 1955–1957* (New York: Enigma Books, 2002); and Alistair Horne, *A Savage War of Peace: Algeria 1954–1962* (New York: New York Review of Books, 2006).

47. Caroline Elkins, *Imperial Reckoning: The Untold Story of Britain's Gulag in Kenya* (New York: Henry Holt, 2004).

48. "Lodge Committee Testimony from the *New York Times*," 1902, Wikisource, http://en.wikisource.org/wiki/Lodge_Committee_testimony_from_the_New_York_Times#Philippine_Problem_before_the_Senate.

49. "Secretary Root's Record: 'Marked Severities' in Philippine Warfare: Kennan's Investigation," Humanities Web, http://www.humanitiesweb.org/human.php?s=s&p=l&a=c&ID=1123&o.

50. Paul A. Kramer, *The Blood of Government: Race, Empire, the United States, and the Philippines* (Chapel Hill: University of North Carolina Press, 2006), 124–58.

51. Cristopher J. Einolf, *Americans in the Philippines, 1899–1902: The First Torture Scandal* (New York: Palgrave Macmillan, 2014), 95.

52. John Fabian Witt, *Lincoln's Code: The Laws of War in American History* (New York: Simon and Schuster, 2012), 358.

53. Einolf, *Americans*, 160.

54. Ibid., 171.

55. I discuss torture that occurred along with arbitrary killing during the Indian Wars in chapter 4. Other contemporaneous cases of torture include American abuses during the United States' occupation of Haiti from 1915–1934. See US Senate Select Committee on Haiti and Santo Domingo, *Inquiry into Occupation and Administration of Haiti and Santo Domingo*, 1922, https://catalog.hathitrust.org/Record/008611231.

56. Gregory Treverton, *Intelligence for an Age of Terror* (Cambridge: Cambridge University Press, 2009), 210.

57. Len Scott, "Secret Intelligence, Covert Action, and Clandestine Diplomacy," *Intelligence and National Security* 19, no. 2 (2004): 324.

58. James H. Doolittle et al., *Report on the Covert Activities of the Central Intelligence Agency*, September 30, 1954, 6–7, Central Intelligence Agency, https://www.cia.gov/library/readingroom/docs/CIA-RDP86B00269R000100040001-5.pdf.

59. Kissinger–Rogers Telecon, September 14, 1970, National Security Archive Electronic Briefing Book 255, National Security Archive, http://www.gwu.edu/~nsarchiv/NSAEBB/NSAEBB255/19700912-1215-Rogers3.pdf (italics added).

60. Danielle Ganser, "The CIA in Western Europe and the Abuse of Human Rights," *Intelligence and National Security* 21, no. 5 (2006): 760–81.

61. E.g., Stephen Kinzer, *All the Shah's Men: An American Coup and the Roots of the Middle East* (Hoboken, NJ: Wiley, 2003); Nick Cullather, *Secret History: The CIA's Classified Account of Its Operations in Guatemala, 1952–1954* (Stanford, CA: Stanford University Press, 1999); Peter Kornbluh, *Bay of Pigs Declassified: The Secret CIA Report on the Invasion of Cuba* (New York: New Press, 1998); John Prados, *Safe for Democracy: The Secret Wars of the CIA* (Chicago: Ivan R. Dee, 2006); and Tim Weiner, *Legacy of Ashes: The History of the CIA* (New York: Doubleday, 2007).

62. Central Intelligence Agency, *Family Jewels*, May 16, 1973, National Security Archive, https://nsarchive2.gwu.edu//NSAEBB/NSAEBB222/family_jewels_full_ocr.pdf and Larry Devlin, *Chief of Station, Congo: Fighting the Cold War in a Hot Zone* (New York: Public Affairs, 2007).

63. Church Committee, *Final Report, Book IV: Supplementary Detailed Staff Report*, Part 5: Conclusions, April 29, 1976, 93, Assassination Archives and Research Center, http://www.aarclibrary.org/publib/church/reports/book4/pdf/ChurchB4_5_Conclusions.pdf (italics added).

64. Alfred McCoy, *A Question of Torture: CIA Interrogation, from the Cold War to the War on Terror* (New York: Henry Holt, 2006), 63.

65. Ibid., 68.

66. Military Assistance Command Vietnam (MACV), *Pocket Card*, September 1967, Famous Trials, http://famous-trials.com/mylaicourts/1639-myl-wmac.

67. Bertrand Russell Tribunal Part II: Donald Duncan Testimony and Questioning, Roskilde, Denmark, November 20–December 1, 1967, Tuan Tran's Journal: A Vietnamese-American Experience, http://www.tuantran.org/russelltribunal/#b10.

68. Rejali, *Torture*, 581–82.

69. John Conroy, "Tools of Torture," *Chicago Reader*, February 3, 2005, http://www.chicagoreader.com/chicago/tools-of-torture/Content?oid=917876.

70. Conroy, "Tools."

71. United States Department of the Army, *Report of the Department of the Army Review of the Preliminary Investigations into the My Lai Incident. Volume I: The Report of the Investigation*, March 14, 1970, 11–14, Library of Congress, https://www.loc.gov/rr/frd/Military_Law/pdf/RDAR-Vol-I.pdf. My Lai was a hamlet of the larger village of Son My.

72. Deborah Nelson and Nick Turse, "A Tortured Past," *Los Angeles Times*, August 20, 2006, http://articles.latimes.com/2006/aug/20/nation/na-vietnam20. Also see Nick Turse, *Kill Anything that Moves: The Real American War in Vietnam* (New York: Picador, 2013).

73. "Winter Soldier Investigations, Prisoner of War Panel, Part IV," Detroit, Michigan, January 31, February 1 and 2, 1971, Sixties Project, http://www2.iath.virginia.edu/sixties/HTML_docs/Resources/Primary/Winter_Soldier/WS_26_POW.html.

74. McCoy, *Question*, 71.

75. Rejali, *Torture*, 218.

76. Ibid., 186.

77. Carlos Osorio, ed., "Nixon: 'Brazil Helped Rig the Uruguayan Elections,' 1971," National Security Archive Electronic Briefing Book 71, June 20, 2002, National Security Archive, http://www.gwu.edu/~nsarchiv/NSAEBB/NSAEBB71/.

78. Ruth Blakeley, "Still Training to Torture? US Training of Military Forces from Latin America," *Third World Quarterly* 27, no. 8 (2006): 1439–61.

79. Central Intelligence Agency, *KUBARK Counterintelligence Interrogation*, July 1963, 8, National Security Archive, http://www.gwu.edu/~nsarchiv/NSAEBB/NSAEBB27/01-01.htm. KUDOVE is a cryptonym for the CIA's Office of the Director.

80. Ibid., 85.

81. Ibid., 102.

82. McCoy, *Question*, 26.

83. Central Intelligence Agency, *Family Jewels*.

84. McCoy, *Question*, 30.

85. Ibid., 32–33. McCoy notes that the research of several major figures, including Albert Biderman, Irving Janis, Harold Wolff, Lawrence Hinkle, and Stanley Milgram, influenced (sometimes unwittingly) the emerging CIA paradigm.

86. John Marks, *The Search for the "Manchurian Candidate": The CIA and Mind Control—The Secret History of the Behavioral Sciences* (New York: Norton and Company, 1991), 10.

87. McCoy, *Question*, 59.

88. Thomas Blanton and Peter Kornbluh, "Prisoner Abuse: Patterns from the Past," National Security Archive Electronic Briefing Book 122, May 12, 2004, National Security Archive, http://www.gwu.edu/~nsarchiv/NSAEBB/NSAEBB122/#kubark.

89. Blakeley, "Still Training," 1441.

90. Jennifer Harbury, *Truth, Torture, and the American Way: The History and Consequences of U.S. Involvement in Torture* (Boston: Beacon, 2005).

91. Blakeley, "Still Training," 1449.

92. Jane Mayer, *The Dark Side: The Inside Story of How the War on Terror Turned into a War on American Ideals* (New York: Doubleday, 2008), 58.

93. Manuel Perez-Rivas, "Bush Vows to Rid the World of 'Evil-Doers,'" CNN, September 16, 2001, http://edition.cnn.com/2001/US/09/16/gen.bush.terrorism/.

94. For instance, Alan Dershowitz, *Why Terrorism Works: Understanding the Threat, Responding to the Challenge* (New Haven: Yale University Press, 2002) advocated "torture warrants" in certain scenarios.

95. For an excellent discussion of the "ticking bomb" rationale, see David Luban, "Liberalism, Torture, and the Ticking Bomb," *Virginia Law Review* 91, no. 6 (2005): 1425–61. For an examination of the discursive features of this "torture-sustaining reality," see Richard Jackson, "Language, Policy, and the Construction of a Torture Culture in the War on Terrorism," *Review of International Studies* 33 (2007): 353–71. The functions and effects of 24 are examined in Jinee Lokaneeta, *Transnational Torture: Law, Violence, and State Power in the United States and India* (New York: New York University Press, 2011).

96. Naomi Wolf, *The End of America: A Letter of Warning to a Young Patriot* (White River Junction VT: Chelsea Green, 2007), 6.

97. Scott Horton, "Through a Mirror Darkly: Applying the Geneva Conventions to a 'New Kind of Warfare,'" in *The Torture Debate in America*, ed. Karen Greenberg (New York: Cambridge University Press, 2005) and Phillippe Sands, *The Torture Team: Rumsfeld's Memo and the Betrayal of American Values* (New York: Palgrave Macmillan, 2008), 228–45.

98. Sanford Levinson, "Torture in Iraq and the Rule of Law in America," *Daedalus* 133, no. 3 (2004): 5–9; Sanford Levinson, "Constitutional Norms in a State of Permanent Emergency," *Georgia Law Review* 40, no. 3 (2006): 699–751; William Scheuerman, "Carl Schmitt and the Road to Abu Ghraib," *Constellations* 13, no. 1 (2006): 108–24; and Johan Steyn, "Guantanamo Bay: The Legal Black Hole," *International and Comparative Law Quarterly* 53 (2004): 1–15.

99. It can be difficult to untangle the theoretical beliefs of certain key individuals from the actual claims of the administration. For instance, John Yoo provocatively responded to a question as to whether any law prevented "crushing the testicles of the person's child" with "No treaty" and "I think it depends on why the president thinks he needs to do that." (Mayer, *Dark Side*, 153) While OLC memos have claimed that constitutional article II powers do permit the president to do whatever he wants in wartime, including resort to any interrogation methods deemed fit, the same memos assert that CIA techniques do not amount to torture, leaving such prerogative arguments at the purely hypothetical level.

100. Treverton, *Intelligence*, 209.
101. Richard B. Cheney, "Interview of the Vice President on Meet the Press with Tim Russert at Camp David, Maryland," September 16, 2001, American Presidency Project, http://www.presidency.ucsb.edu/ws/?pid=85598.
102. Mayer, *Dark Side*, 144.
103. Dana Priest, "Wrongful Imprisonment: Anatomy of a CIA Mistake," *Washington Post*, December 4, 2005, http://www.washingtonpost.com/wp-dyn/content/article/2005/12/03/AR2005120301476.html; Stephen Grey, *Ghost Plane: The True Story of the CIA Rendition and Torture Program* (New York: St. Martin's Griffin, 2006); and Open Society Justice Initiative, *Globalizing Torture: CIA Secret Detention and Extraordinary Rendition*, 2013, Open Society Foundations, https://www.opensocietyfoundations.org/sites/default/files/globalizing-torture-20120205.pdf.
104. For an overview of transnational governmental and judicial inquiries into this practice, see Open Society Justice Initiative, *Investigations into CIA Rendition and Torture*, November 2013, Open Society Foundations, http://www.opensocietyfoundations.org/sites/default/files/briefing-cia-investigations-roundup_0.pdf.
105. Mayer, *Dark Side*, 174–75.
106. Ibid., 250.
107. Eric Lichtblau, *Bush's Law: The Remaking of American Justice* (New York: Anchor Books, 2009), 133.
108. Rahel Gebreyes, "Will the Release of C.I.A. Torture Photos Actually Threaten National Security?" *Huffington Post*, January 6, 2015, http://www.huffingtonpost.com/2015/01/06/torture-photos-threaten-national-security_n_6424710.html.
109. Lauren Walker, "Sen. Mark Udall Contemplates Revealing CIA Torture Report," *Newsweek*, November 14, 2014, http://www.newsweek.com/sen-mark-udall-contemplates-revealing-cia-torture-report-284624.
110. US Senate Select Committee on Intelligence, *Committee Study of the Central Intelligence Agency's Detention and Interrogation Program*, April 3, 2014; redacted version December 3, 2014, 1–499, *New York Times*, http://www.nytimes.com/interactive/2014/12/09/world/cia-torture-report-document.html.
111. James M. Olson, "Intelligence and the War on Terror: How Dirty Are We Willing to Get Our Hands?" *SAIS Review* 28, no. 1 (2008): 40.
112. George W. Bush, *Decision Points* (New York: Crown, 2010), 110.
113. Jack Goldsmith, *The Terror Presidency: Law and Judgment Inside the Bush Administration* (New York: W. W. Norton, 2007), 130.
114. Goldsmith, *Terror Presidency*, 164.
115. John Yoo, *War by Other Means: An Insider's Account of the War on Terror* (New York: Atlantic Monthly, 2006), 174.
116. Mayer, *Dark Side*, 268.
117. John Rizzo, *Company Man: Thirty Years of Controversy and Crisis in the CIA* (New York: Scribner, 2014), 188.
118. US Senate Select Committee on Intelligence, *Committee Study*, 9.
119. John Yoo and Robert J. Delahunty, memorandum for William J. Haynes II, General Counsel, Department of Defense, "Application of Treaties and Laws to al Qaeda and Taliban Detainees," January 9, 2002, National Security Archive, https://nsarchive2.gwu.edu/torturingdemocracy/documents/20020109.pdf.
120. Alberto R. Gonzales, memorandum for the President, "Decision Re Application of the Geneva Convention on Prisoners of War to the Conflict with Al Qaeda and the Taliban," January 25, 2002, National Security Archive, http://www.gwu.edu/~nsarchiv/NSAEBB/NSAEBB127/02.01.25.pdf.

121. John Ashcroft, letter to the President, February 1, 2002, National Security Archive, http://nsarchive.gwu.edu/torturingdemocracy/documents/20020201.pdf.

122. William H. Taft IV, memorandum for John C. Yoo, Deputy Assistant Attorney General, Office of the Legal Counsel, Department of Justice, "Your Draft Memorandum of January 9," January 11, 2002, National Security Archive, http://nsarchive.gwu.edu/torturingdemocracy/documents/20020111.pdf.

123. Colin L. Powell, memorandum for Counsel to the President, Assistant to the President for National Security Affairs, "Draft Decision Memorandum for the President on the Applicability of the Geneva Convention to the Conflict in Afghanistan," January 26, 2002, National Security Archive, http://nsarchive.gwu.edu/torturingdemocracy/documents/20020126.pdf.

124. George W. Bush, memorandum for the Vice President, the Secretary of State, the Secretary of Defense, the Attorney General, Chief of Staff to the President, Director of Central Intelligence, Assistant to the President for National Security Affairs, and Chairman of the Joint Chiefs of Staff, "Humane Treatment of Taliban and al Qaeda Detainees," February 7, 2002, 2, Project to Enforce the Geneva Conventions, http://www.pegc.us/archive/White_House/bush_memo_20020207_ed.pdf.

125. US Senate Select Committee on Intelligence, *Committee Study*, 21. The report refers to these men by the pseudonyms "Grayson Swigert" and "Hammond Dunbar."

126. Ibid., 11.

127. Sheri Fink, "Settlement Reached in C.I.A. Torture Case," *New York Times*, August 17, 2017, https://www.nytimes.com/2017/08/17/us/cia-torture-lawsuit-settlement.html?hp&action=click&pgtype=Homepage&clickSource=story-heading&module=first-column-region&region=top-news&WT.nav=top-news.

128. US Senate Select Committee on Intelligence, *Committee Study*, 32.

129. Ibid., 35.

130. Ibid., 36.

131. Videotaped Deposition of John Rizzo in *Suleiman Abdullah Salim et al. vs. James E. Mitchell and John Jessen*, No. 2:15-cv-286-JLQ, United States District Court for the Eastern District of Washington at Spokane, March 20, 2017, 18, *New York Times*, https://static01.nyt.com/packages/pdf/us/20170620_interrogations/john-rizzo.pdf.

132. Jay S. Bybee, memorandum for Alberto R. Gonzales, Counsel to the President, "Standards of Conduct for Interrogation under 18 U.S.C. §§ 2340–2340A" (Bybee I), August 1, 2002, 1, US Department of Justice, https://www.justice.gov/olc/file/886061/download.

133. Jay S. Bybee, memorandum for John Rizzo, Acting General Counsel of the Central Intelligence Agency, "Interrogation of Al Qaeda Operative" (Bybee II), August 1, 2002, 10, US Department of Justice, https://www.justice.gov/sites/default/files/olc/legacy/2010/08/05/memo-bybee2002.pdf.

134. Ibid., 10–11.

135. Ibid., 11.

136. Ibid., 11.

137. Ibid., 11.

138. Ibid., 12.

139. Ibid., 12.

140. Ibid., 13.

141. Ibid., 15.

142. Ibid., 16.

143. Ibid., 14.

144. Bybee, memorandum for Alberto R. Gonzales (Bybee I), 28–29.

145. Ibid., 15.

146. Ibid., 19.

147. Videotaped Deposition of John Rizzo, 55.

148. Ibid., 54.

149. CIA Inspector General, *Special Review: Counterterrorism Detention and Interrogation Activities (September 2001–October 2003), 2003-7123-IG*, May 7, 2004, 21, Federation of American Scientists, https://fas.org/irp/cia/product/ig-interrog.pdf.

150. US Senate Select Committee on Intelligence, *Committee Study*,100.

151. Physicians for Human Rights, *Aiding Torture: Health Professionals' Ethics and Human Rights Violations Revealed in the May 2004 CIA Inspector General's Report*, August 31, 2009, 1–6, Physicians for Human Rights, http://physiciansforhumanrights.org/library/reports/aiding-torture-2009.html; see also "PHR Calls for Federal Probe into American Psychological Association's Role in CIA Torture Program," October 16, 2014, Physicians for Human Rights, http://physiciansforhumanrights.org/press/press-releases/phr-calls-for-federal-probe-into-american-psychological-associations-role-in-cia-torture-program.html#sthash.Mt6Os5xE.dpuf.

152. Spencer Ackerman, "Guantánamo Force-Feeding Amounts to Punishment, Detainee's Lawyers Argue," *Guardian*, October 6, 2014, http://www.theguardian.com/us-news/2014/oct/06/guantanamo-force-feeding-punishment-trial-abu-dhiab and Benedict Carey, "Nurses Urge Leniency over Refusal to Force-Feed at Guantánamo Bay," *New York Times*, November 19, 2014, http://www.nytimes.com/2014/11/20/health/nurses-urge-leniency-over-refusal-to-force-feed-at-guantnamo-bay.html?hp&action=click&pgtype=Homepage&module=second-column-region&region=top-news&WT.nav=top-news&_r=0.

153. US Senate Select Committee on Intelligence, *Committee Study*, 42.

154. International Committee of the Red Cross, Regional Delegation for United States and Canada, "ICRC Report on the Treatment of Fourteen "High Value Detainees" in CIA Custody," *New York Review of Books*, February 14, 2007, http://www.nybooks.com/media/doc/2010/04/22/icrc-report.pdf.

155. US Senate Select Committee on Intelligence, *Committee Study*, 96.

156. Ibid., 54.

157. Ibid., 85–90.

158. Central Intelligence Agency Inspector General, *Special Review*, 69.

159. Office of the Staff Judge Advocate, "Trip Report, DOD General Counsel Visit to GTMO," September 27, 2002, National Security Archive, https://nsarchive2.gwu.edu/torturingdemocracy/documents/20020927.pdf.

160. Barry A. Rhodes, email to Mark Fallon, "Counter Resistance Strategy Meeting Minutes," August 27, 2003, National Security Archive, http://nsarchive.gwu.edu/torturingdemocracy/documents/20021002.pdf.

161. Michael Dunlavey, memorandum for Commander, United States Southern Command, "Counter-Resistance Strategies," October 11, 2002, National Security Archive, http://nsarchive.gwu.edu/torturingdemocracy/documents/20021011.pdf.

162. William J. Haynes, II, action memo for Secretary of Defense, "Counter-Resistance Techniques," December 2, 2002, National Security Archive, http://www.gwu.edu/~nsarchiv/NSAEBB/NSAEBB127/02.12.02.pdf.

163. "JTF GTMO, 'SERE' Interrogation Standard Operating Procedure," December 10, 2002, National Security Archive, http://nsarchive.gwu.edu/torturingdemocracy/documents/20021210.pdf.

164. John F. Rankin and Christopher Ross, memorandum to Officer in Charge, FASOTRAGRULANT Det Brunswick, "After Action Report Joint Task Force Guantanamo Bay (JTF-GTMO) Training Evolution," January 15, 2003, National Security Archive, http://nsarchive.gwu.edu/torturingdemocracy/documents/20030115-4.pdf.

165. "Interrogation Log, Detainee O63," November 23, 2002–January 11, 2003, Center for Constitutional Rights, http://ccrjustice.org/files/Al%20Qahtani%20Interrogation%20Log.pdf.

166. al-Qahtani v. Obama, Active Cases, Center for Constitutional Rights, http://ccrjustice.org/ourcases/current-cases/al-qahtani-v.-bush,-al-qahtani-v.-gates.

167. "Interrogation Log, Detainee O63," December 16, 2002, 41.

168. US Senate Committee on Armed Services, *Inquiry into the Treatment of Detainees in U.S. Custody*, 110th Congress, 2nd Session, November 20, 2008, 136, https://www.armed-services.senate.gov/imo/media/doc/Detainee-Report-Final_April-22-2009.pdf.

169. US Senate Committee on Armed Services, *Inquiry*, 133–34.

170. Gargi Bhattacharyya, *Dangerous Brown Men: Exploiting Sex, Violence, and Feminism in the War on Terror* (London: Zed Books, 2008).

171. US Senate Committee on Armed Services, *Inquiry*, 108.

172. Military Judges Advocate General, US Department of the Air Force, Navy, and Army, "Recommendations for the Working Group," February 5–March 13, 2013, National Security Archive, http://nsarchive.gwu.edu/torturingdemocracy/documents/20030205.pdf.

173. John C. Yoo, memorandum for William J. Haynes II, General Counsel of the Department of Defense, "Military Interrogation of Alien Unlawful Combatants Held Outside the United States," March 14, 2003, National Security Archive, http://nsarchive.gwu.edu/torturingdemocracy/documents/20030314.pdf.

174. US Department of Defense, *Working Group Report on Detainee Interrogations in the Global War on Terrorism: Assessment of Legal, Historical, Policy, and Operational Considerations*, April 4, 2003, National Security Archive, http://nsarchive.gwu.edu/torturingdemocracy/documents/20030404.pdf.

175. Donald Rumsfeld, memorandum for the Commander, US Southern Command, "Counter-Resistance Techniques in the War on Terrorism (S)," April 16, 2003, National Security Archive, http://nsarchive.gwu.edu/torturingdemocracy/documents/20030416.pdf.

176. US Senate Committee on Armed Services, *Inquiry*, 132.

177. Douglas Feith, *War and Decision: Inside the Pentagon at the Dawn of the War on Terrorism* (New York: HarperCollins, 2008), 485.

178. US Senate Committee on Armed Services, *Inquiry*, 150.

179. Ibid., 151.

180. Ibid., 152.

181. Ibid., 154.

182. Ibid., 158.

183. Ibid., 159–60.

184. Ibid., 167.

185. Ibid., 191.

186. Ibid., 184–85.

187. Ibid., 201.

188. Ibid., 206.

189. Ibid., 208–16.

190. Philip Gourevitch and Errol Morris, *Standard Operating Procedure* (New York: The Penguin Press, 2008), 139.

191. US Senate Committee on Armed Services, *Inquiry*, 219–24.

192. Ibid., xxix.

193. John Hooper, "Italian Court Finds CIA Agents Guilty of Kidnapping Terrorism Suspect," *Guardian*, November 4, 2009, http://www.guardian.co.uk/world/2009/nov/04/cia-guilty-rendition-abu-omar.

194. Open Society Justice Initiative, *Globalizing Torture*, 6.
195. Grey, *Ghost Plane*, 240.
196. Dana Priest and Barton Gellman, "U.S. Decries Abuse but Defends Interrogations," *Washington Post*, December 26, 2002, http://www.washingtonpost.com/wp-dyn/content/article/2006/06/09/AR2006060901356.html.
197. Rebecca Sanders, "Norm Proxy War and Resistance through Outsourcing: The Dynamics of Transnational Human Rights Contestation," *Human Rights Review* 17, no. 2 (2016): 165–91.
198. Jay S. Bybee, memorandum for William J. Haynes, II, General Counsel, Department of Defense, "The President's Power as Commander in Chief to Transfer Captured Terrorists to the Control and Custody of Foreign Nations," March 13, 2002, 26, US Department of Justice, https://www.justice.gov/sites/default/files/olc/legacy/2009/08/24/memorandum03132002.pdf.
199. Ibid., 23.
200. US Department of State, *Second Periodic Report of the United States of America to the Committee Against Torture*, May 6, 2005, 11, US Department of State, https://www.state.gov/documents/organization/62175.pdf.
201. Daniel B. Levin, memorandum for James B. Comey, Deputy Attorney General, "Legal Standards Applicable under 18 U.S.C. §§2340–2340A," December 30, 2004, 2, GlobalSecurity.org, http://www.globalsecurity.org/security/library/policy/national/doj-dag_torture-memo_30dec2004.pdf. It is clear that Goldsmith, who resigned from the OLC, and his replacement Levin, had serious misgivings about prior memos; see Goldsmith, *Terror Presidency,* 141–76. However, formal repudiation was relatively limited.
202. Daniel B. Levin, letter to John A. Rizzo, Acting General Counsel, Central Intelligence Agency, August 6, 2004, 1–2, US Department of Justice, http://www.justice.gov/olc/docs/memo-rizzo2004.pdf and Steven Bradbury, memorandum for John A. Rizzo, Senior Deputy General Counsel, Central Intelligence Agency, "Application of 18 U.S.C. §§ 2340–2340A to Certain Techniques That May Be Used in the Interrogation of High Value al Qaeda Detainee," May 10, 2005, 1–46, US Department of Justice, http://www.justice.gov/olc/docs/memo-bradbury2005-3.pdf.
203. Steven Bradbury, memorandum for John A. Rizzo, Senior Deputy General Counsel, Central Intelligence Agency, "Application of United States Obligations under Article 16 of the Convention against Torture to Certain Techniques that May Be Used in the Interrogation of High Value al Qaeda Detainees," May 30, 2005, 1–40, US Department of Justice, http://www.justice.gov/olc/docs/memo-bradbury2005.pdf.
204. Steven Bradbury, Memorandum for John A. Rizzo, Acting General Counsel, Central Intelligence Agency, "Re: Application of Detainee Treatment Act to Conditions of Confinement at Central Intelligence Agency Detention Facilities," August 31, 2006, 1–26, US Department of Justice, http://www.justice.gov/olc/docs/memo-rizzo2006.pdf.
205. Steven Bradbury, letter to John A. Rizzo, Acting General Counsel, Central Intelligence Agency, August 31, 2006, 1–14, US Department of Justice, http://www.justice.gov/olc/docs/letter-rizzo2006.pdf.
206. Steven Bradbury, memorandum for John A. Rizzo, Acting General Counsel, Central Intelligence Agency, "Application of the War Crimes Act, the Detainee Treatment Act, and Common Article 3 of the Geneva Conventions to Certain Techniques that May be Used by the CIA in the Interrogation of High Value al Qaeda Detainees," July 20, 2007, 1–79, US Department of Justice, http://www.justice.gov/olc/docs/memo-warcrimesact.pdf.
207. Ibid., 13.
208. Bush, *Decision Points*, 111.
209. US Senate Select Committee on Intelligence, *Committee Study*, 16.

210. Barack Obama, "Executive Order 13491: Ensuring Lawful Interrogations," January 22, 2009, White House: President Barack Obama, https://obamawhitehouse.archives.gov/the-press-office/ensuring-lawful-interrogations.

211. "Guantánamo Force-feeding Timeline," Reprieve, http://reprieve.org/guantanamo-bay/guantanamo-force-feeding-timeline/.

212. Michael Ratner and the Center for Constitutional Rights, *The Trial of Donald Rumsfeld: A Prosecution by Book* (New York: New Press, 2008), 191–96.

213. Sands, *Torture Team,* 275.

214. David Cole, *The Torture Memos: Rationalizing the Unthinkable* (New York: New Press, 2009), 20.

215. Council of Europe, Parliamentary Assembly, Resolution 1507 (2006), http://assembly.coe.int/nw/xml/XRef/Xref-XML2HTML-en.asp?fileid=17454&lang=en.

216. Manfred Nowak, *Report of the Special Rapporteur on Torture and Other Cruel, Inhuman or Degrading Treatment or Punishment, Manfred Nowak: Civil and Political Rights, Including the Questions of Torture and Detention,* December 23, 2005, 11, UN Office of the High Commissioner for Human Rights, https://documents-dds-ny.un.org/doc/UNDOC/GEN/G05/168/09/PDF/G0516809.pdf?OpenElement.

217. International Commission of Jurists, *Assessing Damage, Urging Action: Report of the Eminent Jurists Panel on Terrorism, Counter-terrorism, and Human Rights,* 2009, 1–199, Refworld, http://www.refworld.org/docid/499e76822.

218. John Bellinger III, letter to Steven Bradbury, Acting Assistant Attorney General, February 9, 2007, 3, American Civil Liberties Union, https://www.aclu.org/sites/default/files/field_document/bellinger_letter_0.pdf.

219. US Justice Department Office of Professional Responsibility, *Report: Investigation into the Office of Legal Counsel's Memoranda Concerning Issues Relating to the Central Intelligence Agency's Use of "Enhanced Interrogation Techniques" on Suspected Terrorists,* July 29, 2009, 159–60, Federation of American Scientists, http://www.fas.org/irp/agency/doj/opr-final.pdf.

220. US Senate Committee on Armed Services, *Inquiry.*

221. Detainee Treatment Act of 2005, H.R. 2863, Title X, December 30, 2005, (italics added).

222. Peter Finn and Julie Tate, "Justice Department to Investigate Deaths of Two Detainees in CIA Custody," *Washington Post,* June 30, 2011, http://www.washingtonpost.com/politics/federal-prosecutor-probes-deaths-of-2-cia-held-detainees/2011/06/30/AGsFmUsH_story.html.

223. Scott Shane, "No Charges Filed on Harsh Tactics Used by the C.I.A.," *New York Times,* August 30, 2012, http://www.nytimes.com/2012/08/31/us/holder-rules-out-prosecutions-in-cia-interrogations.html?pagewanted=all&_r=0.

224. Hooper, "Italian Court." See also Jonathan S. Landay, "U.S. Allowed Italian Kidnap Prosecution to Shield Higher-Ups, Ex-CIA Officer Says," *McClatchy DC,* July 27, 2013, http://www.mcclatchydc.com/2013/07/27/197823/us-allowed-italian-kidnap-prosecution.html.

225. Michael Slackman, "Officials Pressed Germans on Kidnapping by C.I.A.," *New York Times,* December 8, 2010, http://www.nytimes.com/2010/12/09/world/europe/09wikileaks-elmasri.html.

226. Giles Tremlett, "Wikileaks: US Pressured Spain Over CIA Rendition and Guantánamo Torture," *Guardian,* December 1, 2010, http://www.guardian.co.uk/world/2010/nov/30/wikileaks-us-spain-guantanamo-rendition.

227. Julie Deisher, "Supreme Court Rejects Rumsfeld Torture Suit Appeal," *Jurist,* June 11, 2013, http://jurist.org/paperchase/2013/06/supreme-court-rejects-rumsfeld-torture-suit-appeal.php.

228. David Cole, "They Did Authorize Torture, But . . . ," *New York Review of Books*, March 10, 2010, http://www.nybooks.com/blogs/nyrblog/2010/mar/10/they-did-authorize-torture-but/.

229. US Department of Justice, Office of Professional Responsibility, *Investigation*, 254.

230. Ibid., 259.

231. David Margolis, memorandum for the Attorney General and the Deputy Attorney General, "Memorandum of Decision Regarding the Objections to the Findings of Professional Misconduct in the Office of Professional Responsibility's Report of Investigation into the Office of Legal Counsel's Memoranda Concerning Issues Relating to the Central Intelligence Agency's Use of 'Enhanced Interrogation Techniques' on Suspected Terrorists," January 5, 2010, 68, Federation of American Scientists, http://www.fas.org/irp/agency/doj/opr-margolis.pdf.

CHAPTER 4

1. Frédéric Mégret, "A Cautionary Tale from the Crusades? War and Prisoners in Situations of Normative Incommensurability," in *Prisoners in War*, ed. Sibylle Scheipers (Oxford: Oxford University Press, 2010), 23–38.

2. Peter H. Wilson, "Prisoners in Early Modern European Warfare," in ibid., 39–56.

3. Stephen C. Neff, "Prisoners of War in International Law: The Nineteenth Century," in ibid., 57–58.

4. Magna Carta (1215), Clause 39, British Library, http://www.bl.uk/treasures/magnacarta/translation/mc_trans.html.

5. "Charles I, 1640: An Act for the [Regulating the Privie Councell and for taking away the Court commonly called the Star Chamber," *Statutes of the Realm: Volume 5*, 1628–80, ed. John Raithby (1819), 110–12, British History Online, http://www.british-history.ac.uk/report.aspx?compid=47221 and "Charles II, 1679, An Act for the better secureing the Liberty of the Subject and for Prevention of Imprisonments beyond the Seas," *Statutes of the Realm: Volume 5*, 1628–80, ed. John Raithby (1819), 935–38, British History Online, http://www.british-history.ac.uk/report.aspx?compid=47484.

6. John Adams, Diary Entry, March 5, 1773, Famous Trials, http://law2.umkc.edu/faculty/projects/ftrials/bostonmassacre/diaryentries.html.

7. Alexander Hamilton, "The Federalist No. 84," in *The Federalist with Letters of "Brutus"*, ed. Terence Ball (Cambridge: Cambridge University Press, 2003), 418.

8. US Constitution, article I, section 9 (1787).

9. US Constitution, Amendment V (1791).

10. US Constitution, Amendment VI (1791).

11. US Constitution, Amendment VIII (1791).

12. US Constitution, Amendment XIV, section 1 (1868).

13. UN General Assembly, Universal Declaration of Human Rights, December 10, 1948, articles 9 and 10, Refworld, http://www.unhcr.org/refworld/docid/3ae6b3712c.html.

14. UN General Assembly, *International Covenant on Civil and Political Rights*, December 16, 1966, entered into force March 23, 1976, United Nations Treaty Series 999:171, part III, articles 9, 14, and 15, Refworld, http://www.unhcr.org/refworld/docid/3ae6b3aa0.html.

15. Instructions for the Government of Armies of the United States in the Field (Lieber Code), April 24, 1863, article 16, International Committee of the Red Cross, http://www.icrc.org/ihl.nsf/FULL/110?OpenDocument.

16. Ibid., article 22.

17. Ibid., article 43.

18. Ibid., article 56.

19. Ibid., article 82.

20. Ibid., article 24.

21. Charter of the United Nations, 1945, http://www.un.org/en/charter-united-nations/.

22. Gary D. Solis, *The Law of Armed Conflict: International Humanitarian Law in War* (New York: Cambridge University Press, 2010).

23. Ibid., 270.

24. Ibid., 273.

25. Frédéric Mégret, "From 'Savages' to 'Unlawful Combatants': A Postcolonial Look at International Humanitarian Law's 'Other,'" in *International Law and Its Others*, ed. Anne Orford (Cambridge: Cambridge University Press, 2006), 265–317.

26. Peter H. Maguire, *Law and War: An American Story* (New York: Columbia University Press, 2000), 22.

27. Andrew Jackson, "Fifth Annual Message," December 3, 1833, American Presidency Project, http://www.presidency.ucsb.edu/ws/index.php?pid=29475.

28. Sand Creek Massacre National Historic Site Colorado, "The Life of Silas Soule," January 25, 2017, National Park Service, https://www.nps.gov/sand/learn/historyculture/the-life-of-silas-soule.htm.

29. Ibid.

30. Tony Horwitz, "The Horrific Sand Creek Massacre Will Be Forgotten No More," *Smithsonian Magazine*, December 2014, http://www.smithsonianmag.com/history/horrific-sand-creek-massacre-will-be-forgotten-no-more-180953403/#Mh3b50ec7MjB58le.99.

31. Theodore Roosevelt, *The Winning of the West: An Account of the Exploration and Settlement of our Country from the Alleghenies to the Pacific* (New York: G. P. Putnam's Sons, 1917), 2:56–57 (italics added).

32. Lieber Code, Article 29.

33. Brooks D. Simpson and Jean V. Berlin, eds., *Sherman's Civil War: Selected Correspondence of William T. Sherman, 1860–1865* (Chapel Hill: University of North Carolina Press, 1999), 708. Confederate forces also committed crimes, but I focus on the Union as the predecessor to future American governments.

34. Christopher Andrew, *For the President's Eyes Only: Secret Intelligence and the American Presidency from Washington to Bush* (New York: HarperCollins, 1996), 16.

35. Ex parte Merryman, 17 F. Cas. 144 (1861).

36. Ex parte Milligan, 71 U.S. 2 (1866).

37. Detlev F. Vagts, "Military Commissions: A Concise History," *American Journal of International Law* 101, no. 1 (2007): 38–39.

38. Crystal Nicole Feimster, *Southern Horrors: Women and the Politics of Rape and Lynching* (Cambridge, MA: Harvard University Press, 2009). While only some perpetrators were prosecuted, mostly for raping white rather than black women (although the latter were primarily targeted), experts on these courts-martial emphasize that the Union took these crimes unusually seriously. Moreover, Union officials accepted the legal testimony of black women against white men, a phenomenon unheard of at the time. For further distinctions between countercivilian violence between the Indian Wars and Civil War see Helen M. Kinsella, *The Image Before the Weapon: A Critical History of the Distinction between Combatant and Civilian* (Ithaca, NY: Cornell University Press, 2011), 101–103.

39. Douglas A. Blackmon, *Slavery by Another Name: The Re-Enslavement of Black Americans from the Civil War to World War II* (New York: Doubleday, 2008).

40. David Cole, *Enemy Aliens: Double Standards and Constitutional Freedoms in the War on Terrorism* (New York: New Press, 2003), 92.

41. Ibid., 109.

42. Remsen Crawford, "New Immigration Net: How Other Causes Have Anticipated Effect of the Dillingham Act," *New York Times*, July 10, 1921, http://query.nytimes.com/mem/archive-free/pdf?res=9900E5DE173EEE3ABC4852DFB166838A639EDE.

43. Geoffrey R. Stone, *Perilous Times: Free Speech in Wartime from the Sedition Act of 1798 to the War on Terrorism* (New York: W. W. Norton, 2004), 140.

44. Cole, *Enemy Aliens*, 92.

45. Ibid., 111–12.

46. Ibid., 120.

47. Ibid., 122.

48. Elizabeth Glendower Evans, "Foreigners," in *Sacco and Vanzetti: Rebel Lives*, ed. John Davis (Melbourne: Ocean Press, 2004), 57.

49. Tami Davis Biddle, "Strategic Bombardment: Expectation, Theory, and Practice in the Early Twentieth Century," in *The American Way of Bombing*, ed. Matthew Evangelista and Henry Shue (Ithaca, NY: Cornell University Press, 2014), 45.

50. Solis, *Law*, 256.

51. This changed after Vietnam, as scandalous abuses such as the My Lai massacre became indicative of ethical degeneration. The subsequent rise of operational law from the late 1970s on meant an increasingly prominent role for lawyers in military decision making. See Jack Goldsmith, *Power and Constraint: The Accountable Presidency After 9/11* (New York: W. W. Norton, 2012), 125–35.

52. Cole, *Enemy Aliens*, 93.

53. Adam Klein and Benjamin Wittes, "Preventative Detention in American Theory and Practice," *Harvard National Security Journal* 2 (2011): 106.

54. Cole, *Enemy Aliens*, 97.

55. Hirabayashi v. United States, 320 U.S. 81 (1943); Yasui v. United States, 320 U.S. 115 (1943); and Korematsu v. United States, 323 U.S. 214 (1944).

56. Jerry Kang, "Watching the Watchers: Enemy Combatants in the Internment's Shadow," *Law and Contemporary Problems* 68, no. 2 (2005): 255–83.

57. J. Murphy, dissenting opinion, Korematsu v. United States, 323 U.S. 214 (1944), Legal Information Institute, http://www.law.cornell.edu/supct/html/historics/USSC_CR_0323_0214_ZD1.html.

58. R. Jackson, dissenting opinion, Korematsu v. United States, 323 U.S. 214 (1944), Legal Information Institute, http://www.law.cornell.edu/supct/html/historics/USSC_CR_0323_0214_ZD2.html.

59. Cole, *Enemy Aliens*, 101–2.

60. Ibid., 131–32.

61. Ibid., 149.

62. Joseph Wershba, "Murrow vs. McCarthy: See it Now," *New York Times*, March 4, 1979, http://www.nytimes.com/1979/03/04/archives/murrow-vs-mccarthy-see-it-now.html.

63. "Have You No Sense of Decency?" US Senate Historical Office, https://www.senate.gov/artandhistory/history/minute/Have_you_no_sense_of_decency.htm.

64. Cole, *Enemy Aliens*, 149.

65. Mary L. Dudziak, *Cold War Civil Rights: Race and the Image of American Democracy* (Princeton, NJ: Princeton University Press, 2000). As Dudziak notes, the Cold War both enabled and constrained the advance of civil rights. On the one hand, racial injustice was a source of international criticism and embarrassment for the United States. On the other, anti-Communism limited the ability of civil rights activists to engage in radical critiques of the relationship between race and class in America.

66. For an extensive discussion of Western collusion with violence in the global south, see Ruth Blakeley, *State Terrorism and Neoliberalism: The North in the South* (New York: Routledge, 2009).

67. UN Human Rights Council, *Joint Study on Global Practices in Relation to Secret Detention in the Context of Countering Terrorism of the Special Rapporteur on the Promotion and Protection of Human Rights and Fundamental Freedoms while Countering Terrorism, Martin Scheinin; the Special Rapporteur on Torture and Other Cruel Inhuman or Degrading Treatment or Punishment, Manfred Nowak; the Working Group on Arbitrary Detention Represented by its Vice Chair, Shaheen Sardar Ali; and the Working Group on Enforced or Involuntary Disappearances Represented by its Chair, Jeremy Sarkin*, May 20, 2010, 30, UN Digital Library, https://digitallibrary.un.org/record/677500/files/A_HRC_13_42-EN.pdf.

68. J. Patrice McSherry, *Predatory States: Operation Condor and Covert War in Latin America* (Lanham, MD: Rowman and Littlefield, 2005), 241–42.

69. Ibid., 243–44.

70. Carlos Osorio and Peter Kornbluh, eds., "Operation Condor: Officials of Amnesty International Targeted for 'Liquidation,'" National Security Archive Electronic Briefing Book 572, December 14, 2016, National Security Archive, http://nsarchive.gwu.edu/NSAEBB/NSAEBB572-Declassified-files-show-Operation-Condor-targets-for-assassination/.

71. McSherry, *Predatory States*, 248.

72. Church Committee, *Interim Report: Alleged Assassination Plots Involving Foreign Leaders*, 1975, Assassination Archives and Research Center, http://www.aarclibrary.org/publib/church/reports/ir/html/ChurchIR_0001a.htm. It is now well known that the United States also assisted coups against Mohammad Mosaddegh of Iran, Jacobo Árbenz Guzmán of Guatemala, and Salvador Allende of Chile.

73. Central Intelligence Agency, "Covert Action, the Loss of Life, and the Prohibition on Assassination, 1976–96," *Studies in Intelligence* 40, no. 2 (1996): 15–25, http://www.gwu.edu/~nsarchiv/NSAEBB/NSAEBB431/docs/intell_ebb_001.PDF.

74. "Backgrounder: The President's Quotes on Islam," White House: President George W. Bush, http://georgewbush-whitehouse.archives.gov/infocus/ramadan/islam.html.

75. Natsu Taylor Saito, *From Chinese Exclusion to Guantánamo Bay: Plenary Power and the Prerogative State* (Boulder: University Press of Colorado, 2007), 26.

76. Glenn A. Fine, *The September 11 Detainees: A Review of the Treatment of Aliens Held on Immigration Charges in Connection with the Investigation of the September 11 Attacks*, April 2003, 1–2, US Department of Justice, Office of the Inspector General, http://www.justice.gov/oig/special/0306/full.pdf.

77. Ibid., 2.

78. Ibid., 196.

79. Ibid., 2.

80. Louise Cainkar, "Post-9/11 Policies Affecting U.S. Arabs and Muslims: A Brief Overview," *Comparative Studies of South Asia, Africa and the Middle East* 24, no. 1 (2004): 245.

81. Ibid., 245.

82. Ibid., 245.

83. Ibid., 246.

84. Ibid., 246.

85. Nasser Hussain, "Beyond Norm and Exception: Guantánamo," *Critical Inquiry* 33, no. 4 (2007): 747–48.

86. Ibid., 747.

87. For example, anti-terrorism legislation in Britain authorized detention without charge for twenty-eight days; see Dominic Casciani, "Q&A: Anti-Terrorism Legislation," *BBC News*, January 23, 2008, http://news.bbc.co.uk/2/hi/uk_news/6729027.stm.

88. Human Rights Watch, *Witness to Abuse: Human Rights Abuses Under the Material Witness Law Since September 11, Human Rights Watch* 17, no. 2 (G), June 2005, American Civil Liberties Union, http://www.aclu.org/FilesPDFs/materialwitnessreport.pdf.

89. Adam Liptak, "Supreme Court to Hear Material Witness Case," *New York Times*, February 11, 2011, http://www.nytimes.com/2011/02/21/us/politics/21witness. html?pagewanted=1&sq=material%20witness&st=cse&scp=1.

90. "Indefensible Detention," *New York Times*, March 10, 2011, http://www.nytimes.com/ 2011/03/11/opinion/11fri1.html?hp.

91. Ashcroft v. al-Kidd, U.S.C No. 10–98 (2011).

92. American Civil Liberties Union, "Terrorist Watch List Hits One Million Names," July 14, 2008, https://www.aclu.org/news/terrorist-watch-list-hits-one-million-names?redirect= cpredirect/35968. Related to concerns about watch lists are complaints that terrorist financing laws are unfair. The Department of the Treasury also used "material support" rules to shut down charities suspected of aiding terrorists. Like watch lists, targeting standards are unclear and evidence is secret and uncontestable. The ACLU suggests that Muslim charities have been harassed and slandered, as well as unduly closed during pending investigations, and that Muslim donors have been deterred from engaging in Islamic charity, or *zakat*. Such actions resulted in the denial of free speech and religious freedom, reputational harm, and irreversible damage to accused charities and their aid recipients. See American Civil Liberties Union, *Blocking Faith, Freezing Charity: Chilling Muslim Charitable Giving in the "War on Terrorism Financing,"* June 2009, American Civil Liberties Union, http://www.aclu.org/files/pdfs/humanrights/blockingfaith.pdf#page=2.

93. Authorization for Use of Military Force (AUMF) (2001), https://www.congress.gov/ 107/plaws/publ40/PLAW-107publ40.pdf.

94. Geneva Convention (I) for the Amelioration of the Condition of the Wounded and Sick in Armed Forces in the Field (August 12, 1949), International Committee of the Red Cross, http://www.icrc.org/ihl.nsf/FULL/365?OpenDocument; Geneva Convention (II) for the Amelioration of the Condition of Wounded, Sick and Shipwrecked Members of Armed Forces at Sea, (August 12, 1949), 75 UNTS 85, International Committee of the Red Cross, http://www.icrc.org/ihl.nsf/FULL/370?OpenDocument; Geneva Convention (III) Relative to the Treatment of Prisoners of War (August 12, 1949), International Committee of the Red Cross, http://www.icrc.org/ihl.nsf/FULL/ 375; and Geneva Convention (IV) Relative to the Protection of Civilian Persons in Time of War (August 12, 1949), 75 UNTS 287, International Committee of the Red Cross, http://www.icrc.org/ihl.nsf/FULL/380?OpenDocument.

95. Nils Melzer, *Interpretive Guidance on the Notion of Direct Participation in Hostilities Under International Humanitarian Law* (Geneva: International Committee of the Red Cross, 2009), 21, https://www.icrc.org/en/publication/0990-interpretive-guidance-notion-direct-participation-hostilities-under-international.

96. Ibid., 20. A *levée en masse* refers to "the inhabitants of a territory which has not been occupied, who on the approach of the enemy spontaneously take up arms to resist the invading troops without having had time to organize themselves into regular armed forces." See International Committee of the Red Cross, https://casebook.icrc.org/glossary/levee-en-masse.

97. Geneva Convention (III), article 4.

98. Ibid.

99. UN Human Rights Council, *Joint Study*, 27–28.

100. Protocol Additional to the Geneva Conventions of 12 August 1949, and relating to the Protection of Victims of International Armed Conflicts (Additional Protocol I), June 8, 1977, article 1, International Committee of the Red Cross, http://www.icrc.org/ihl.nsf/ full/470?opendocument.

101. Ibid., article 75.

102. Michael J. Matheson, "Remarks on the United States' Position on the Relation of Customary International Law to the 1977 Protocols Additional to the 1949 Geneva

Conventions," reprinted in Martin P. Dupuis, John Q. Heywood, and Michéle Y. F. Sarko, "The Sixth Annual American Red-Cross Washington College of Law Conference on International Humanitarian Law: A Workshop on Customary International Law and the 1977 Protocols Additional to the 1949 Geneva Conventions," *American University Journal of International Law and Policy* 2, no. 2 (1987), 419, http://digitalcommons.wcl.american.edu/cgi/viewcontent.cgi?article=1660&context=auilr.

103. Geneva Convention (III), article 3.

104. Melzer, *Interpretive Guidance*, 24–25.

105. Ibid., 83–84.

106. Geneva Convention (IV), article 27.

107. Protocol Additional to the Geneva Conventions of 12 August 1949, and relating to the Protection of Victims of Non-International Armed Conflicts (Additional Protocol II), June 8, 1977, International Committee of the Red Cross, https://ihl-databases.icrc.org/ihl/INTRO/475?OpenDocument. Additional Protocol II addresses noninternational armed conflicts, but only covers situations in which states are engaged in conflict on their territory with nonstate actors who control portions of that territory. Its provisions are vaguer than Additional Protocol I governing international armed conflicts. It has not been ratified by the United States.

108. Oona Hathaway et al., "The Power to Detain: Detention of Terrorism Suspects after 9/11," *Yale Journal of International Law* 38 (2013): 158.

109. "US: Prolonged Indefinite Detention Violates International Law," January 24, 2011, Human Rights Watch, https://www.hrw.org/news/2011/01/24/us-prolonged-indefinite-detention-violates-international-law.

110. International Committee of the Red Cross, *Strengthening Legal Protection for Persons Deprived of their Liberty in relation to Non-International Armed Conflict, Regional Consultations 2012-13: Background Paper*, 14, International Committee of the Red Cross, https://www.icrc.org/eng/assets/files/2013/strengthening-legal-protection-detention-consultations-2012-2013-icrc.pdf.

111. Robin Geiss and Michael Siegrist, "Has the Armed Conflict in Afghanistan Affected the Rules on the Conduct of Hostilities?" *International Review of the Red Cross* 93, no. 881 (2011): 13.

112. Jay S. Bybee, memorandum for Alberto R Gonzales, Counsel to the President, and William J. Haynes, II, General Counsel of the Department of Defense, "Application of Treaties and Laws to al Qaeda and Taliban Detainees," January 22, 2002, 10, US Department of Justice, http://www.justice.gov/olc/docs/memo-laws-taliban-detainees.pdf.

113. Ibid., 22.

114. Ibid., 31–32.

115. Geoffrey S. Corn, "What Law Applies to the War on Terror?" in *The War on Terror and the Laws of War: A Military Perspective*, eds Michael Lewis et al. (Oxford: Oxford University Press, 2009), 3.

116. Bybee, memorandum for Alberto R Gonzales, Counsel to the President, and William J. Haynes II, General Counsel of the Department of Defense, 6–9.

117. Richard B. Cheney and Liz Cheney, *In My Time: A Personal and Political Memoir* (New York: Threshold Editions, 2011), 355.

118. William H. Taft IV, memorandum to Counsel to the President, "Comments on Your Paper on the Geneva Convention," February 2, 2002, 1–2, National Security Archive, http://www.gwu.edu/~nsarchiv/NSAEBB/NSAEBB127/02.02.02%20DOS%20Geneva.pdf.

119. George W. Bush, memorandum for the Vice President, the Secretary of State, the Secretary of Defense, the Attorney General, Chief of Staff to the President, Director of Central Intelligence, Assistant to the President for National Security Affairs, and

Chairman of the Joint Chiefs of Staff, "Humane Treatment of Taliban and al Qaeda Detainees," February 7, 2002, 2, Project to Enforce the Geneva Conventions, http://www.pegc.us/archive/White_House/bush_memo_20020207_ed.pdf.

120. Military Commissions Act of 2006, P.L. 109–366, 2006, §948a (2006). Definitions.

121. Rumsfeld v. Padilla, 542 U.S. 426, 430–32 (2004). In this case, the Supreme Court relied on jurisdictional arguments to avoid substantively ruling on the merits of Padilla's detention.

122. Richard H. Fallon Jr. and Daniel J. Meltzer, "Habeas Corpus Jurisdiction, Substantive Rights, and The War on Terror," *Harvard Law Review* 120, no. 8 (2007): 2076.

123. James A. Schoettler, Jr., "Detention of Combatants and the Global War on Terror," in *The War on Terror and the Laws of War: A Military Perspective*, ed. Michael Lewis et al. (Oxford: Oxford University Press, 2009), 78.

124. Guantanamo Review Task Force, *Final Report*, January 22, 2010, 1, *Washington Post*, http://media.washingtonpost.com/wp-srv/nation/pdf/GTMOtaskforcereport_052810.pdf.

125. Amy Kaplan, "Where is Guantánamo?" *American Quarterly* 57, no. 3 (2005): 831–32.

126. Agreement for the Lease to the United States of Lands in Cuba for Coaling and Naval Stations, U.S.-Cuba, Art. 111, T.S. No. 418 (February 23, 1903).

127. Treaty Between the United States of America and Cuba Defining Their Relations, U.S.-Cuba, Art. 111, T.S. No. 866 (May 29, 1934).

128. Gerald L. Neuman, "Anomalous Zones," *Stanford Law Review* 48, no. 5. (1996): 1228.

129. Ibid., 1198–99.

130. Ibid., 1232.

131. Ibid., 1200. See also Cuban Am. Bar Ass'n, Inc. v. Christopher, 43 F.3d 1412, 1426 (11th Cir. 1995) and Harold Koh, "The Case Against Military Commissions," *American Journal of International Law* 96, no. 2 (2002): 342.

132. Neuman, "Anomalous Zones," 1201.

133. Patrick F. Philbin and John C. Yoo, memorandum for William Haynes II, General Counsel, Department of Defense, "Possible Habeas Jurisdiction over Aliens Held in Guantanamo Bay, Cuba," December 28, 2001, 1–2, National Security Archive, http://nsarchive2.gwu.edu/torturingdemocracy/documents/20011228.pdf.

134. Ibid., 1.

135. Ibid., 8–9 (italics added).

136. Johan Steyn, "Guantanamo Bay: The Legal Black Hole," *International and Comparative Law Quarterly* 53 (2004): 1–15.

137. Koh, "Case," 339.

138. Franklin D. Roosevelt, "Order Establishing a Military Commission to Try Eight Captured German Saboteurs," July 2, 1942, ed. Gerhard Peters and John T. Woolley, American Presidency Project, http://www.presidency.ucsb.edu/ws/?pid=16280.

139. Ex parte Quirin, 317 U.S. 1 (1942).

140. Condoleezza Rice, *No Higher Honor: A Memoir of My Years in Washington* (New York: Crown, 2011), 105.

141. George W. Bush, "Military Order—Detention, Treatment, and Trial of Certain Non-Citizens in the War Against Terrorism," November 13, 2001, Federation of American Scientists, https://fas.org/irp/offdocs/eo/mo-111301.htm.

142. Ibid.

143. Ibid.

144. US Department of Defense, *Military Commissions Order No. 1: Procedures for Trials by Military Commissions of Certain Non-United States Citizens in the War Against Terrorism*, March 21, 2002, GlobalSecurity.org, http://www.globalsecurity.org/security/library/policy/dod/d20020321ord.pdf.

145. Karen Greenberg, *The Least Worst Place: Guantanamo's First 100 Days* (Oxford: Oxford University Press, 2009), 3.

146. Hamdi v. Rumsfeld, 542 U.S. 507 (2004).

147. Fallon and Meltzer, "Habeas," 2045–47.

148. Rasul v. Bush, 542 U.S. 466 (2004).

149. Robert M. Chesney, "Boumediene v. Bush," *American Journal of International Law* 102, no. 4 (2008): 848.

150. Sonia R. Farber, "Forgotten at Guantánamo: The Boumediene Decision and Its Implications for Refugees at the Base under the Obama Administration," *California Law Review* 98 (2010): 1006.

151. Hamdan v. Rumsfeld, 548 U.S. 557 (2006).

152. Corn, "What Law," 12.

153. Jack M. Beard, "The Geneva Boomerang: The Military Commissions Act of 2006 and U.S. Counterterror Operations," *American Journal of International Law* 101, no. 1. (2007): 58.

154. Farber, "Forgotten," 1006.

155. George W. Bush, *Decision Points* (New York: Crown, 2010), 114. Rice, *No Higher Honor*, 502 writes that she played a role in convincing the president in this regard.

156. Hamdan v. Rumsfeld, 548 U.S. 557 (2006), Concurrence (Stephen J. Breyer).

157. Bush, *Decision Points*, 114.

158. Beard, "Geneva Boomerang," 62.

159. Ibid., 61.

160. Military Commissions Act of 2006, § 948b (g) (2006).

161. Boumediene v. Bush, 553 U.S. 723 (2008).

162. Farber, "Forgotten," 1007–8.

163. Chesney, "Boumediene v. Bush," 852.

164. Ibid., 853.

165. Al Maqaleh v. Gates, 604 F. Supp. 2d 205 (D.D.C. 2009).

166. Al Maqaleh v. Gates, 605 F. 3d 84 (D.C. Cir. 2010).

167. Goldsmith, *Power*, 194.

168. Harold Koh, "The Obama Administration and International Law," Annual Meeting of the American Society of International Law, Washington, DC, March 25, 2010, U.S. Department of State, https://2009-2017.state.gov/s/l/releases/remarks/139119.htm.

169. Mary Ellen O'Connell, "The Choice of Law against Terrorism," *Journal of National Security Law and Policy* 4 (2010): 357.

170. Guantanamo Review Task Force, *Final Report*.

171. Vanessa R. Brinkman, letter to Charles Savage, June 17, 2013, *New York Times*, https://www.documentcloud.org/documents/714599-savage-final-response.html.

172. Office of the Press Secretary, "Remarks by the President on National Security," May 21, 2009, White House: President Barack Obama, https://obamawhitehouse.archives.gov/the-press-office/remarks-president-national-security-5-21-09. According to the Guantánamo Review Task Force, there are forty-eight prisoners who cannot be released or prosecuted.

173. "The Guantánamo Docket," *New York Times*, February 22, 2017, http://projects.nytimes.com/guantanamo.

174. Goldsmith, *Power*, 193.

175. Military Commissions Act of 2009, Title XVIII of the National Defense Authorization Act for Fiscal Year 2010, Pub.L. 111–84, H.R. 2647, 123 Stat. 2190, October 28, 2009.

176. Andrea Prasow, "Khadr's Plea Agreement and Sentencing: Questions Never to be Answered," *Jurist*, November 5, 2010, http://www.hrw.org/en/news/2010/11/05/khadrs-plea-agreement-and-sentencing.

177. "Cases," United States Department of Defense, Office of Military Commissions, http://www.mc.mil/CASES.aspx.

178. Robert Chesney, "Military Commission Proceeding Against the 9/11 Defendants (KSM and Others) Inches Closer," *Lawfare* (blog), May 31, 2011, http://www.lawfareblog.com/2011/05/military-commission-proceeding-against-the-911-defendants-ksm-and-others-inches-closer/.

179. Mark Lander, "After Struggle on Detainees, Obama Signs Defense Bill," *New York Times*, December 31, 2011, http://www.nytimes.com/2012/01/01/us/politics/obama-signs-military-spending-bill.html.

180. "CCR Condemns President Obama's Lifting of Stay in Military Tribunals," March 7, 2011, Center for Constitutional Rights, http://ccrjustice.org/newsroom/press-releases/ccr-condemns-president-obama's-lifting-of-stay-military-tribunals.

181. James Joyner, "Why We Should Be Glad the Haditha Massacre Marine Got No Jail Time," *Atlantic*, January 25, 2012, https://www.theatlantic.com/international/archive/2012/01/why-we-should-be-glad-the-haditha-massacre-marine-got-no-jail-time/251993/.

182. Philip Alston, *Report of the Special Rapporteur on Extrajudicial, Summary, or Arbitrary Executions, Philip Alston, Addendum: Study on Targeted Killings*, May 28, 2010, 3, UN Office of the High Commissioner for Human Rights, https://documents-dds-ny.un.org/doc/UNDOC/GEN/G10/137/53/PDF/G1013753.pdf?OpenElement.

183. Seymour M. Hersh, "Target Qaddafi," *New York Times Magazine*, February 22, 1987, http://www.nytimes.com/1987/02/22/magazine/target-qaddafi.html?pagewanted=all&src=pm.

184. Jane Mayer, *The Dark Side* (New York: Doubleday, 2008), 19. See also National Commission on Terrorist Attacks Upon the United States, *The 9/11 Commission Report: Final Report of the National Commission on Terrorist Attacks upon the United States* (New York: W. W. Norton, 2004), 126–34.

185. Barton Gellman, "CIA Weighs 'Targeted Killing' Missions," *Washington Post*, October 28, 2001, https://www.washingtonpost.com/archive/politics/2001/10/28/cia-weighs-targeted-killing-missions/92d127df-aa07-48d5-9cab-306e6922c229/?utm_term=.3ec5daa67895.

186. Andrew Callam, "Drone Wars: Unmanned Aerial Vehicles," *International Affairs Review* 18, no. 3 (2010), http://www.iar-gwu.org/node/144.

187. Alston, *Report*, 7.

188. The New America Foundation. Drone Strikes: Pakistan, February 2018, https://www.newamerica.org/in-depth/americas-counterterrorism-wars/pakistan/.

189. The Bureau of Investigative Journalism, *CIA and US Military Drone Strikes in Pakistan, 2004 to Present*, https://docs.google.com/spreadsheets/d/1NAfjFonM-Tn7fziqiv33HlGt09wgLZDSCP-BQaux51w/edit#gid=1000652376. For discussion of the controversy over casualty statistics, see Stanford International Human Rights and Conflict Resolution Clinic and The Global Justice Clinic at New York University School of Law, *Living under Drones: Death, Injury and Trauma to Civilians from US Drone Practices in Pakistan*, 2012, http://chrgj.org/wp-content/uploads/2012/10/Living-Under-Drones.pdf and Micah Zenko, "How Many Terrorists Have Been Killed by Drones?" *Council on Foreign Relations* (blog), February 20, 2013, http://blogs.cfr.org/zenko/2013/02/20/how-many-terrorists-have-been-killed-by-drones/.

190. Greg Miller, "Why CIA Drone Strikes Have Plummeted," *Washington Post*, June 16, 2016, https://www.washingtonpost.com/world/national-security/cia-drone-strikes-plummet-as-white-house-shifts-authority-to-pentagon/2016/06/16/e0b28e90-335f-11e6-8ff7-7b6c1998b7a0_story.html?utm_term=.0d863acdf176.

191. Office of the Press Secretary, "Press Briefing by Press Secretary Jay Carney, 5/3/2011," May 3, 2011, White House: President Barack Obama, https://obamawhitehouse. archives.gov/the-press-office/2011/05/03/press-briefing-press-secretary-jay-carney-532011; Office of the Press Secretary, "Press Briefing by Press Secretary Jay Carney, 5/4/2011," May 4, 2011, White House: President Barack Obama, https:// obamawhitehouse.archives.gov/the-press-office/2011/05/04/press-briefing-press-secretary-jay-carney-542011.

192. Scott Shane, "U.S. Approves Targeted Killing of American Cleric," *New York Times,* April 6, 2010, http://www.nytimes.com/2010/04/07/world/middleeast/07yemen.html.

193. UN General Assembly, *International Covenant,* article 6.

194. David Kretzmer, "Targeted Killing of Suspected Terrorists: Extra-Judicial Executions or Legitimate Means of Defence?" *European Journal of International Law* 16, no. 2 (2005): 176.

195. Françoise Hampson, "Direct Participation in Hostilities and the Interoperability of the Law of Armed Conflict and Human Rights Law," in *International Law and the Changing Character of War,* ed. Raul A. Pedrozo and Daria P. Wollschlaeger, International Law Studies 87 (Newport, RI: Naval War College, 2011).

196. Koh, "Obama Administration."

197. Eric Holder, "Remarks as Prepared for Delivery by Attorney General Eric Holder at Northwestern University School of Law," Chicago, March 5, 2012, US Department of Justice, https://www.justice.gov/opa/speech/attorney-general-eric-holder-speaks-northwestern-university-school-law.

198. US Department of Justice, *White Paper: Lawfulness of a Lethal Operation Directed Against a U.S. Citizen Who is a Senior Operational Leader of Al-Qa'ida or an Associated Force,* November 8, 2011, 3, US Department of Justice, https://www.justice.gov/sites/default/files/oip/legacy/2014/07/23/dept-white-paper.pdf.

199. Ibid., 7.

200. Ibid., 8.

201. Ibid., 8.

202. Nils Melzer, *Interpretive Guidance on the Notion of Direct Participation in Hostilities Under International Humanitarian Law* (Geneva: International Committee of the Red Cross, May 2009), 46, https://www.icrc.org/eng/assets/files/other/icrc-002-0990.pdf.

203. Ibid., 53.

204. Ibid., 62.

205. Ibid., 34.

206. Dapo Akande, "Clearing the Fog of War? The ICRC's Interpretive Guidance on Direct Participation in Hostilities," *International and Comparative Law Quarterly* 59 (2010): 180–92; Michael N. Schmitt, "Deconstructing Direct Participation in Hostilities: The Constitutive Elements," *NYU Journal of International Law and Politics* 42 (2009–10): 697–739; and Kenneth Watkin, "Opportunity Lost: Organized Armed Groups and the ICRC 'Direct Participation in Hostilities' Interpretive Guidance," *NYU Journal of International Law and Politics* 42 (2009–10): 641–95.

207. US Department of Justice, *White Paper: Lawfulness,* 16.

208. Cora Currier, "How Does the U.S. Mark Unidentified Men in Pakistan and Yemen as Drone Targets?" *ProPublica,* March 1, 2013, http://www.propublica.org/article/how-does-the-u.s.-mark-unidentified-men-in-pakistan-and-yemen-as-drone-targ.

209. Stanford International Human Rights and Conflict Resolution Clinic and The Global Justice Clinic at New York University School of Law, *Living under Drones,* chapter 1.

210. Alston, *Report,* 21.

211. Jeh Charles Johnson, "National Security Law, Lawyers and Lawyering in the Obama Administration," Dean's Lecture at Yale Law School, February 22, 2012, *Lawfare* (blog), http://www.lawfareblog.com/2012/02/jeh-johnson-speech-at-yale-law-school/.

212. Holder, "Remarks."

213. Johnson, "National Security Law."

214. Eric Holder, letter to Representative Rand Paul, March 4, 2013, Rand Paul, http://paul.senate.gov/files/documents/BrennanHolderResponse.pdf and Eric Holder, letter to Representative Rand Paul, March 7, 2013, *Politico*, http://www.politico.com/story/2013/03/attorney-general-eric-holder-drone-letter-to-sen-rand-paul-88572.html.

215. Mary Louise Kelly, "When the U.S. Military Strikes, White House Points to a 2001 Measure," *NPR*, September 6, 2016, http://www.npr.org/sections/parallels/2016/09/06/492857888/when-the-u-s-military-strikes-white-house-points-to-a-2001-measure.

216. John B. Bellinger III, "Legal Issues Related to Armed Conflict with Non-State Groups," in *Prisoners in War*, ed. Sibylle Scheipers (Oxford: Oxford University Press, 2010), 259.

CHAPTER 5

1. SIGINT may take the form of communications intelligence (COMINT) that captures voice communications or electronic intelligence (ELINT) that uses sensors. There are also a variety of other technologically dependent phenomena such as imagery intelligence (IMINT) and measurement and signature intelligence (MASINT) often used by the military.

2. Semayne's Case, 77 Eng. Rep. 194; 5 Co. Rep. 91 (1604).

3. Leonard W. Levy, "Origins of the Fourth Amendment," *Political Science Quarterly* 114, no. 1 (1999): 81.

4. Ibid., 82.

5. Susan Landau, *Surveillance or Security? The Risks Posed by New Wiretapping Technologies* (Cambridge, MA: MIT Press, 2010), 66.

6. Levy, "Origins," 84.

7. Ibid., 85.

8. Orin S. Kerr, "The Fourth Amendment and New Technologies: Constitutional Myths and the Case for Caution," *Michigan Law Review* 102, no. 5 (2004): 809.

9. Entick v. Carrington and Ors, EWHC KB J98 (1765).

10. US Constitution, Amendment IV (1791).

11. Ex parte Jackson, 96 U.S. 727 (1878); Landau, *Surveillance*, 66.

12. Boyd v. United States, 116 U.S. 616 (1886).

13. Peter P. Swire, "Katz Is Dead. Long Live Katz," *Michigan Law Review* 102, no. 5 (2004): 907.

14. Olmstead v. United States, 277 U.S. 438, 48 S. Ct. 564, 72 L. Ed. 944 (1928).

15. Landau, *Surveillance*, 67.

16. Christopher Andrew, *For the President's Eyes Only: Secret Intelligence and the American Presidency from Washington to Bush* (New York: HarperCollins, 1995), 11.

17. Ibid., 19–20.

18. David Kahn, *The Reader of Gentlemen's Mail: Herbert O. Yardley and the Birth of American Codebreaking* (New Haven, CT: Yale University Press, 2004), 98.

19. Matthew M. Aid, *The Secret Sentry: The Untold History of the National Security Agency* (New York: Bloomsbury, 2009), 8.

20. John Keegan, *Intelligence in War: The Value—and Limitations—of What the Military Can Learn About the Enemy* (Toronto: Vintage Canada, 2004).

21. National Security Act of 1947, P.L. 80-235, 61 Stat 496 (1947), section 102 d (3).

22. Harry S. Truman, Memorandum for the Secretary of State, the Secretary of Defense, "Subject: Communications Intelligence Activities," October 24, 1952, 2 (b), National Security Archive, http://www.gwu.edu/~nsarchiv/NSAEBB/NSAEBB23/02-01.htm. Congress later passed the National Security Agency Act, Pub. L. 86-36, May 29, 1959, 73 Stat. 63 (1959), which made the NSA the agency responsible for SIGINT.

23. Aid, *Secret Sentry*, 12.
24. UN General Assembly, *Universal Declaration of Human Rights*, December 10, 1948, article 12, United Nations, http://www.un.org/en/universal-declaration-human-rights/index.html.
25. UN General Assembly, *International Covenant on Civil and Political Rights*, December 16, 1966; entered into force March 23, 1976, United Nations Treaty Series 999:171, article 17, Refworld, http://www.unhcr.org/refworld/docid/3ae6b3aa0.html.
26. *European Convention for the Protection of Human Rights and Fundamental Freedoms*, November 4, 1950, entered into force September 3, 1950, Council of Europe Treaty Series 5, article 8, Refworld, http://www.unhcr.org/refworld/docid/3ae6b3b04.html.
27. Simon Chesterman, "The Spy Who Came in From the Cold War: Intelligence in International Law," *Michigan Journal of International Law* 27 (2006): 1074–75.
28. Ibid., 1081.
29. Ibid., 1083–85.
30. Ibid., 1088.
31. Mark Mazzetti, "U.S. Expands Role of Diplomats in Spying," *New York Times*, November 28, 2010, http://www.nytimes.com/2010/11/29/world/29spy.html.
32. Chesterman, "Spy," 1097.
33. Interim Agreement Between the United States of America and the Union of Soviet Socialist Republics on Certain Measures with Respect to the Limitation of Strategic Offensive Arms, May 26, 1972; entered into force October 3, 1972, article V, US Department of State, http://www.state.gov/t/isn/4795.htm.
34. Chesterman, "Spy," 1091.
35. Ibid., 1112–21.
36. Stephen D. Krasner, *Sovereignty: Organized Hypocrisy* (Princeton, NJ: Princeton University Press, 1999).
37. Andrew, *For the President's Eyes*, 54–57.
38. John Bach McMaster, *The United States in the World War 1914–1918, Volume II* (New York: P. Appleton, 1920), 45.
39. Ibid., 48 and Andrew, *For the President's Eyes*, 48.
40. Athan Theoharis, "The FBI and the Politics of Anti-Communism 1920–1945: A Prelude to Power," in *Little 'Red Scares': Anti-Communism and Political Repression in the United States 1921–1946*, ed. Robert Justin Goldstein (Burlington, VT: Ashgate, 2014), 24.
41. Regin Schmidt, *Red Scare: FBI and the Origins of Anti-Communism in the United States, 1919–1943* (Copenhagen: Museum Tusculanum, 2000), 150.
42. Ibid., 163.
43. Samuel J. Rascoff, "Domesticating Intelligence," *Southern California Law Review* 83 (2010): 600.
44. Ibid., 601.
45. Daniel J. Solove, Marc Rotenberg, Paul M. Schwartz, *Privacy, Information, and Technology* (New York: Aspen, 2007), 83.
46. Church Committee, *Hearings, Volume 5: The National Security Agency and Fourth Amendment Rights*, November 6, 1975, 58, Assassination Archives and Research Center, http://www.aarclibrary.org/publib/church/reports/vol5/html/ChurchV5_0031a.htm.
47. Landau, *Surveillance*, 68.
48. Solove, Rotenberg, and Schwartz, *Privacy*, 84.
49. Andrew, *For the President's Eyes*, 74.
50. Frederick A. O. Schwarz, Jr., "The Church Committee and a New Era of Intelligence Oversight," *Intelligence and National Security* 22, no. 2 (2007): 281.
51. Nora K. Breglio, "Leaving FISA Behind: The Need to Return to Warrantless Foreign Intelligence Surveillance," *Yale Law Journal* 113, no. 1 (2003): 182.

52. David Cole, *Enemy Aliens: Double Standards and Constitutional Freedoms in the War on Terrorism* (New York: New Press, 2003), 157.
53. Church Committee, *Hearings, Volume 2: Huston Plan, Tuesday September 23, 1975*, 9, Assassination Archives and Research Center, http://www.aarclibrary.org/publib/church/reports/vol2/html/ChurchV2_0008a.htm.
54. Ibid., 401, exhibit 65.
55. Church Committee, *Hearings, Volume 3: Internal Revenue Service*, October 2, 1975, 2, Assassination Archives and Research Center, http://www.aarclibrary.org/publib/church/reports/vol3/html/ChurchV3_0003b.htm.
56. Ibid., 2.
57. Church Committee, *Hearings, Volume 4: Mail Opening*, October 21, 1975, 31, Assassination Archives and Research Center, http://www.aarclibrary.org/publib/church/reports/vol4/html/ChurchV4_0003a.htm.
58. Ibid., 2.
59. Ibid., 22.
60. Ibid., 7.
61. Ibid., 17–18.
62. Church Committee, *Hearings, Volume 5: The National Security Agency and Fourth Amendment Rights*, October 29, 1975, 9, Assassination Archives and Research Center, http://www.aarclibrary.org/publib/church/reports/vol5/html/ChurchV5_0007a.htm.
63. Ibid., 10.
64. Matthew M. Aid and Robert Burr, "Secret Cold War Documents Reveal NSA Spied on Senators," *Foreign Policy*, September 25, 2013, http://foreignpolicy.com/2013/09/25/secret-cold-war-documents-reveal-nsa-spied-on-senators/.
65. Ibid.
66. Church Committee, *Hearings, Volume 5*, October 29, 1975, 59.
67. Ibid., 60.
68. Ibid., 62.
69. Tim Weiner, *Legacy of Ashes: The History of the CIA* (New York: Doubleday, 2007), 330.
70. Church Committee, *Hearings, Volume 6: Federal Bureau of Investigation*, November 18, 1975, 8, Assassination Archives and Research Center, http://www.aarclibrary.org/publib/church/reports/vol6/html/ChurchV6_0006a.htm.
71. Ibid., 16.
72. Ibid., 6.
73. Cole, *Enemy Aliens*, 157.
74. Ibid., 155.
75. Church Committee, *Hearings, Volume 6*, 13.
76. Church Committee, *Final Report, Book II: Intelligence Activities and the Rights of Americans*, April 29, 1976, Introduction and Summary, 15, Assassination Archives and Research Center, http://www.aarclibrary.org/publib/church/reports/book2/html/ChurchB2_0016a.htm.
77. Ibid., 289.
78. National Association for the Advancement of Colored People v. Alabama, 357 U.S. 449 (1958).
79. Griswold v. Connecticut, 381 U.S. 479 (1965).
80. The right to privacy formed an important cornerstone of Roe v. Wade, 410 U.S. 113 (1973), which decriminalized abortion and Lawrence v. Texas, 539 U.S. 558 (2003), which decriminalized homosexual sodomy.
81. Katz v. United States, 389 U.S. 347 (1967).
82. Title III of the Omnibus Crime Control and Safe Streets Act of 1968, 18 U.S.C. §§2510–22 (1968).

83. United States v. United States District Court (Keith), 407 U.S. 297 (1972).

84. Privacy Act of 1974, 5 U.S.C. §552a, Public Law No. 93-579 (1974).

85. Freedom of Information Act (FOIA) Amendments of 1974, Public Law No. 93-502, 88 Stat. 1561 (1974).

86. "The Attorney General's Guidelines," Electronic Privacy Information Center, http:// epic.org/privacy/fbi/.

87. Ibid.

88. Matt Bedan, "Echelon's Effect: The Obsolescence of the U.S. Foreign Intelligence Legal Regime," *Federal Communications Law Journal* 59, no. 2 (2007): 427.

89. Foreign Intelligence Surveillance Act of 1978, 50 U.S.C. §1801 (i) (1978).

90. Orin S. Kerr, "The Case for the Third-Party Doctrine," *Michigan Law Review* 107 (2009): 567–69.

91. Smith v. Maryland, 442 U.S. 735, 744 (1979).

92. Swire, "Katz," 908.

93. Ibid., 910.

94. David Cole, *Justice at War: The Men and Ideas That Shaped America's War on Terror* (New York: New York Review of Books, 2008), 74.

95. Mary DeRosa, "Privacy in the Age of Terror," *Washington Quarterly* 26, no. 3 (2003): 35.

96. Uniting and Strengthening America by Providing Appropriate Tools Required to Intercept and Obstruct Terrorism (USA PATRIOT ACT) Act of 2001, H.R 3162, Pub. L. 107-56, Title I, §102 (2001).

97. *The 9/11 Commission Report: Final Report of the National Commission on Terrorist Attacks Upon the United States* (New York: W. W. Norton, 2004), 78.

98. Ibid., 79.

99. John Yoo, *War by Other Means: An Insider's Account of the War on Terror* (New York: Atlantic Monthly, 2006), 80.

100. *9/11 Commission Report*, 269–71.

101. Kate Martin, "Domestic Intelligence and Civil Liberties," *SAIS Review* 24, no. 1 (2004): 12; James Bamford, *The Shadow Factory: The Ultra-Secret NSA from 9/11 to the Eavesdropping on America* (New York: Doubleday, 2008), 18–21; and Aid, *Secret Sentry*, 212.

102. "Attorney General's Guidelines."

103. Rascoff, "Domesticating Intelligence," 599.

104. Sharon H. Rackow, "How the USA Patriot Act Will Permit Government Infringement upon the Privacy of Americans in the Name of 'Intelligence' Investigations," *University of Pennsylvania Law Review* 150, no. 5 (2002): 1690; Katherine Wong, "Recent Developments: The NSA Terrorist Surveillance Program," *Harvard Journal on Legislation* 43 (2006): 530; and Whitfield Diffie and Susan Landau, *Privacy on the Line: The Politics of Wiretapping and Encryption* (Cambridge, MA: MIT Press, 2007), 282.

105. The terminology of the Terrorist Surveillance Program was invented by the Bush administration undoubtedly to draw attention to the threat of terrorism. It was retitled the President's Surveillance Program in the process of review by the inspectors general and Congress. See Offices of the Inspectors General of the Department of Defense, Department of Justice, Central Intelligence Agency, National Security Agency, and Office of the Director of National Intelligence, *Unclassified Report on the President's Surveillance Program*, July 10, 2009, 10, Federation of American Scientists, http://www. fas.org/irp/eprint/psp.pdf.

106. As early as 2010, Aid, *Secret Sentry*, 287–88 wrote that the NSA runs ten to twelve unacknowledged programs associated with warrantless SIGINT, including Stellarwind, a "parallel data-mining" operation.

107. Michael V. Hayden, "Address to the National Press Club: What American Intelligence and Especially the NSA Have Been Doing to Defend the Nation," January 23, 2006, 1–11, National Security Archive, http://www.gwu.edu/~nsarchiv/NSAEBB/NSAEBB178/surv40.pdf.

108. Wong, "Recent Developments," 519; Michael V. Hayden, *Playing to the Edge: American Intelligence in the Age of Terror* (New York: Penguin, 2016), 108.

109. James Risen, *State of War: The Secret History of the CIA and the Bush Administration* (New York: Free Press, 2006), 51.

110. Landau, *Surveillance*, 90.

111. Alberto R. Gonzales, "Intercepting Al Qaeda: A Lawful and Necessary Tool for Protecting America," Georgetown University Law Center, Washington, DC, January 24, 2006, 6, National Security Archive, http://nsarchive2.gwu.edu//NSAEBB/NSAEBB178/surv41.pdf; Wong, "Recent Developments," 522.

112. John C. Yoo and Robert J. Delahunty, memorandum for Alberto R. Gonzales and William J. Haynes, II, "Authority for Use of Military Force to Combat Terrorist Activities Within the United States," October 23, 2001, 13, US Department of Justice, http://www.justice.gov/olc/docs/memomilitaryforcecombatus10232001.pdf.

113. Ibid., 18.

114. Ibid., 25.

115. Ibid., 25–26.

116. Offices of the Inspectors General, *Unclassified Report*, 30.

117. *Legal Authorities Supporting the Activities of the National Security Agency Described by the President* (January 19, 2006), US Department of Justice, http://www.justice.gov/opa/whitepaperonnsalegalauthorities.pdf.

118. Gonzales, "Intercepting Al Qaeda," 12–13.

119. Bedan, "Echelon's Effect," 432.

120. Ibid., 432 and Breglio, "Leaving FISA Behind," 189.

121. Glenn Greenwald, *No Place to Hide: Edward Snowden, the NSA, and the U.S. Surveillance State* (New York: Metropolitan Books, 2014), 128.

122. Offices of the Inspectors General, *Unclassified Report*, 40.

123. Hayden, *Playing*, 68.

124. Ibid., 73.

125. Ibid., 72.

126. Ibid., 69.

127. Ibid., 76.

128. Ibid., 70.

129. Ibid., 69.

130. Shane Harris, "The Cowboy of the NSA," *Foreign Policy*, September 9, 2013, http://foreignpolicy.com/2013/09/09/the-cowboy-of-the-nsa/?wp_login_redirect=0.

131. Ibid., 21–29.

132. Hayden, *Playing*, 71.

133. Landau, *Surveillance*, 93.

134. Offices of the Inspectors General, *Unclassified Report*, 35.

135. Russ Feingold, "Statement in Opposition to the Flawed FISA Bill," December 17, 2007, Common Dreams, https://www.commondreams.org/views/2007/12/18/statement-opposition-flawed-fisa-bill.

136. David Kravets, "Obama Claims Immunity, As New Spy Case Takes Center Stage," *Wired*, July 15, 2009, http://www.wired.com/threatlevel/2009/07/jewel/.

137. Ellen Nakashima and Barton Gellman, "Court Gave NSA Broad Leeway in Surveillance, Documents Show," *Washington Post*, June 30, 2014, https://www.washingtonpost.com/

world/national-security/court-gave-nsa-broad-leeway-in-surveillance-documents-show/
2014/06/30/32b872ec-fae4-11e3-8176-f2c941cf35f1_story.html.

138. Lana Lam, "Edward Snowden: US Government Has Been Hacking Hong Kong
and China for Years," *South China Morning Post*, June 13, 2013, http://www.scmp.
com/news/hong-kong/article/1259508/edward-snowden-us-government-has-
been-hacking-hong-kong-and-china and "Targeting Huawei: NSA Spied on Chinese
Government and Networking Firm," *Spiegel Online*, March 22, 2014, http://www.
spiegel.de/international/world/nsa-spied-on-chinese-government-and-networking-
firm-huawei-a-960199.html.

139. Ewen MacAskill et al., "G20 Summit: NSA Targeted Russian President Medvedev
in London," *Guardian*, June 17, 2013, https://www.theguardian.com/world/2013/
jun/16/nsa-dmitry-medvedev-g20-summit and "Snowden Files Reveal Swedish-
American Surveillance of Russia," *SVT*, December 5, 2013, http://www.svt.se/ug/
snowden-files-reveale-swedish-american-surveillance-of-russia.

140. "Inside TAO: Documents Reveal Top NSA Hacking Unit," *Spiegel Online*, December
29, 2013, http://www.spiegel.de/international/world/the-nsa-uses-powerful-toolbox-
in-effort-to-spy-on-global-networks-a-940969-2.html.

141. Jacob Appelbaum et al., "Berlin Complains: Did US Tap Chancellor Merkel's Mobile
Phone?" *Spiegel Online*, October 23, 2013, http://www.spiegel.de/international/world/
merkel-calls-obama-over-suspicions-us-tapped-her-mobile-phone-a-929642.html; Ryan
Gallagher, "Der Spiegel: NSA Put Merkel on List of 122 Targeted Leaders," *Intercept*,
March 29, 2014, https://theintercept.com/2014/03/29/der-spiegel-nsa-ghcq-hacked-
german-companies-put-merkel-list-122-targeted-leaders/; and Laura Poitras, Marcel
Rosenbach, and Holger Stark, "Partner and Target: NSA Snoops on 500 Million German
Data Connections," *Spiegel Online*, June 30, 2013, http://www.spiegel.de/international/
germany/nsa-spies-on-500-million-german-data-connections-a-908648.html.

142. Jacques Follorou and Glenn Greenwald, "France in the NSA's Crosshair: Phone
Networks Under Surveillance," *Le Monde*, October 21, 2013, http://www.lemonde.
fr/technologies/article/2013/10/21/france-in-the-nsa-s-crosshair-phone-networks-
under-surveillance_3499741_651865.html#6W11qDumiXRsOgLg.99.

143. Miguel González, "NSA Revelations: Spain also a Victim of US Espionage," *El Pais*,
October 25, 2013, http://elpais.com/elpais/2013/10/25/inenglish/1382703360_
329586.html.

144. Glenn Greenwald and Stefania Maurizi, "Revealed: How the NSA Targets Italy,"
L'Espresso, December 5, 2013, http://espresso.repubblica.it/inchieste/2013/12/05/
news/revealed-how-the-nsa-targets-italy-1.144428.

145. "NSA Documents Show United States Spied Brazilian Oil Giant," *Globo*, September 8,
2013, http://g1.globo.com/fantastico/noticia/2013/09/nsa-documents-show-united-
states-spied-brazilian-oil-giant.html.

146. Glenn Greenwald and Shobhan Saxena, "India Among Top Targets of Spying by NSA,"
Hindu, September 23, 2013, http://www.thehindu.com/news/national/india-among-
top-targets-of-spying-by-nsa/article5157526.ece.

147. Laura Poitras et al., "A Two-Faced Friendship: Turkey Is 'Partner and Target' for the
NSA," *Spiegel Online*, August 31, 2014, http://www.spiegel.de/international/world/
documents-show-nsa-and-gchq-spied-on-partner-turkey-a-989011.html.

148. Steven Derix and Huib Modderkolk, "The Secret Role of the Dutch in the American
War on Terror," *NRC*, March 5, 2013, http://www.nrc.nl/nieuws/2014/03/05/
the-secret-role-of-the-dutch-in-the-american-war-on-terror-a1426677.

149. James Ball, "NSA Monitored Calls of 35 World Leaders after US Official Handed Over
Contacts," *Guardian*, October 25, 2013, https://www.theguardian.com/world/2013/
oct/24/nsa-surveillance-world-leaders-calls.

150. James Ball, "US and UK Struck Secret Deal to Allow NSA to 'Unmask' Britons' Personal Data," *Guardian*, November 20, 2013, https://www.theguardian.com/world/2013/nov/20/us-uk-secret-deal-surveillance-personal-data.

151. Laura Poitras et al., "Attacks from America: NSA Spied on European Union Offices," *Spiegel Online*, June 29, 2013, http://www.spiegel.de/international/europe/nsa-spied-on-european-union-offices-a-908590.html.

152. "Oil Espionage: How the NSA and GCHQ Spied on OPEC," *Spiegel Online*, November 11, 2013, http://www.spiegel.de/international/world/how-the-nsa-and-gchq-spied-on-opec-a-932777.html.

153. Greg Weston, Glenn Greenwald, and Ryan Gallagher, "New Snowden Docs Show U.S. Spied During G20 in Toronto," *CBC*, November 27, 2013, http://www.cbc.ca/news/politics/new-snowden-docs-show-u-s-spied-during-g20-in-toronto-1.2442448.

154. Leonardo Souza and Raphael Gomide, "Spies of the Digital Age," *Época*, July 27, 2013, http://epoca.globo.com/tempo/noticia/2013/07/spies-bdigital-ageb.html.

155. Kate Sheppard and Ryan Grim, "Snowden Docs: U.S. Spied on Negotiators at 2009 Climate Summit," *Huffington Post*, January 29, 2014, http://www.huffingtonpost.com/2014/01/29/snowden-nsa-surveillance-_n_4681362.html.

156. Laura Poitras, Marcel Rosenbach and Holger Stark, "'Follow the Money': NSA Monitors Financial World," *Spiegel Online*, September 16, 2013, http://www.spiegel.de/international/world/how-the-nsa-spies-on-international-bank-transactions-a-922430.html.

157. "Snowden Document: NSA Spied on Al Jazeera Communications," *Spiegel Online*, August 31, 2013, http://www.spiegel.de/international/world/nsa-spied-on-al-jazeera-communications-snowden-document-a-919681.html.

158. Scott Shane, "No Morsel Too Minuscule for All-Consuming N.S.A.," *New York Times*, November 2, 2013, http://www.nytimes.com/2013/11/03/world/no-morsel-too-minuscule-for-all-consuming-nsa.html.

159. James Ball, "NSA Collects Millions of Text Messages Daily in 'Untargeted' Global Sweep," *Guardian*, January 16, 2014, https://www.theguardian.com/world/2014/jan/16/nsa-collects-millions-text-messages-daily-untargeted-global-sweep.

160. Barton Gellman and Ashkan Soltani, "NSA Tracking Cellphone Locations Worldwide, Snowden Documents Show," *Washington Post*, December 4, 2013, https://www.washingtonpost.com/world/national-security/nsa-tracking-cellphone-locations-worldwide-snowden-documents-show/2013/12/04/5492873a-5cf2-11e3-bc56-c6ca94801fac_story.html.

161. Ryan Gallagher and Peter Maas, "Inside the NSA's Secret Efforts to Hunt and Hack System Administrators," *Intercept*, March 20, 2014, https://theintercept.com/2014/03/20/inside-nsa-secret-efforts-hunt-hack-system-administrators/.

162. David E. Sanger and Thom Shanker, "N.S.A. Devises Radio Pathway into Computers," *New York Times*, January 14, 2014, http://www.nytimes.com/2014/01/15/us/nsa-effort-pries-open-computers-not-connected-to-internet.html.

163. Ryan Devereaux, Glenn Greenwald, and Laura Poitras, "Data Pirates of the Caribbean," *Intercept*, May 19, 2014, https://theintercept.com/2014/05/19/data-pirates-caribbean-nsa-recording-every-cell-phone-call-bahamas/.

164. Barton Gellman and Ashkan Soltani, "NSA Surveillance Program Reaches 'Into the Past' to Retrieve, Replay Phone Calls," *Washington Post*, March 18, 2014, https://www.washingtonpost.com/world/national-security/nsa-surveillance-program-reaches-into-the-past-to-retrieve-replay-phone-calls/2014/03/18/226d2646-ade9-11e3-a49e-76adc9210f19_story.html.

165. Bamford, *Shadow Factory*, 175.

166. Diffie and Landau, *Privacy*, 302.

167. Bamford, *Shadow Factory*, 161–62.
168. Landau, *Surveillance*, 87.
169. Hayden, *Playing*, 75.
170. Privacy and Civil Liberties Oversight Board, *Report on the Surveillance Program Operated Pursuant to Section 702 of the Foreign Intelligence Surveillance Act*, July 2, 2014, 7, Privacy and Civil Liberties Oversight Board, https://www.pclob.gov/library/702-Report.pdf#page=41.
171. Glenn Greenwald and Ewen MacAskill, "NSA Prism Program Taps in to User Data of Apple, Google, and Others," *Guardian*, June 7, 2013, https://www.theguardian.com/world/2013/jun/06/us-tech-giants-nsa-data.
172. Barton Gellman, Julie Tate, and Ashkan Soltani, "In NSA-Intercepted Data, Those Not Targeted Far Outnumber the Foreigners Who Are," *Washington Post*, July 5, 2014, https://www.washingtonpost.com/world/national-security/in-nsa-intercepted-data-those-not-targeted-far-outnumber-the-foreigners-who-are/2014/07/05/8139adf8-045a-11e4-8572-4b1b969b6322_story.html.
173. Barton Gellman and Ashkan Soltani, "NSA Infiltrates Links to Yahoo, Google Data Centers Worldwide, Snowden Documents Say," *Washington Post*, October 30, 2013, https://www.washingtonpost.com/world/national-security/nsa-infiltrates-links-to-yahoo-google-data-centers-worldwide-snowden-documents-say/2013/10/30/e51d661e-4166-11e3-8b74-d89d714ca4dd_story.html.
174. Anton Geist et al., "NSA 'Third Party' Partners Tap the Internet Backbone in Global Surveillance Program," *Information*, June 19, 2014, https://www.information.dk/udland/2014/06/nsa-third-party-partners-tap-the-internet-backbone-in-global-surveillance-program.
175. Gellman, Tate, and Soltani, "In NSA-Intercepted Data."
176. Glenn Greenwald and Ewan MacAskill, "Boundless Informant: The NSA's Secret Tool to Track Global Surveillance Data," *Guardian*, June 11, 2013, https://www.theguardian.com/world/2013/jun/08/nsa-boundless-informant-global-datamining.
177. "Tapping Fiber-Optic Cables: 'Leverage Unique Key Corporate Partnerships,'" *Guardian*, November 1, 2013, http://www.theguardian.com/world/interactive/2013/nov/01/nsa-tapping-cables-document.
178. Privacy and Civil Liberties Oversight Board, *Report*, 9.
179. Greenwald, *No Place*, 127.
180. Diffie and Landau, *Privacy*, 295–301.
181. Lawrence D. Sloan, "ECHELON and the Legal Restraints on Signals Intelligence: A Need for Reevaluation," *Duke Law Journal* 50, no. 5 (2001): 1481.
182. Orin S. Kerr, "Updating the Foreign Intelligence Surveillance Act," *University of Chicago Law Review* 75, no. 1 (2008): 234.
183. Shane Harris, *The Watchers: The Rise of America's Surveillance State* (New York: Penguin, 2010), 110.
184. Ibid., 130.
185. Yoo, *War*, 110.
186. Diffie and Landau, *Privacy*, 269–70.
187. Ryan Singel, "Newly Declassified Files Detail Massive FBI Data-Mining Project," *Wired*, September 23, 2009, http://www.wired.com/threatlevel/2009/09/fbi-nsac/.
188. Glenn Greenwald and Spencer Ackerman, "NSA Collected US Email Records in Bulk for More Than Two Years Under Obama," *Guardian*, June 27, 2013, https://www.theguardian.com/world/2013/jun/27/nsa-data-mining-authorised-obama.
189. Ibid.
190. Ellen Nakashima and Sari Horwitz, "Newly Declassified Documents on Phone Records Program Released," *Washington Post*, July 31, 2013, https://www.washingtonpost.

com/world/national-security/governments-secret-order-to-verizon-to-be-unveiled-at-senate-hearing/2013/07/31/233fdd3a-f9cf-11e2-a369-d1954abcb7e3_story.html?tid=a_inl.

191. James Risen and Laura Poitras, "N.S.A. Gathers Data on Social Connections of U.S. Citizens," *New York Times,* September 28, 2013, http://www.nytimes.com/2013/09/29/us/nsa-examines-social-networks-of-us-citizens.html.

192. Greenwald and Ackerman, "NSA Collected US Email Records."

193. "Documents on N.S.A. Efforts to Diagram Social Networks of U.S. Citizens," *New York Times,* September 28, 2013, http://www.nytimes.com/interactive/2013/09/29/us/documents-on-nsa-efforts-to-diagram-social-networks-of-us-citizens.html.

194. Glenn Greenwald and Spencer Ackerman, "How the NSA is Still Harvesting Your Online Data," *Guardian,* June 27, 2013, https://www.theguardian.com/world/2013/jun/27/nsa-online-metadata-collection.

195. Ibid.

196. Barton Gellman and Ashkan Soltani, "NSA Collects Millions of Email Books Globally," *Washington Post,* October 14, 2013, https://www.washingtonpost.com/world/national-security/nsa-collects-millions-of-e-mail-address-books-globally/2013/10/14/8e58b5be-34f9-11e3-80c6-7e6dd8d22d8f_story.html.

197. James Ball, "Angry Birds and 'Leaky' Phone Apps Targeted by NSA and GCHQ for User Data," *Guardian,* January 28, 2014, https://www.theguardian.com/world/2014/jan/27/nsa-gchq-smartphone-app-angry-birds-personal-data.

198. James Ball, "NSA Stores Metadata of Millions of Web Users for up to a Year, Secret Files Show," *Guardian,* September 30, 2013, https://www.theguardian.com/world/2013/sep/30/nsa-americans-metadata-year-documents.

199. Harris, "Cowboy."

200. Aid, *Secret Sentry,* 304.

201. Jeff Larson, Nicole Perlroth, and Scott Shane, "Revealed: The NSA's Secret Campaign to Crack, Undermine Internet Security," *ProPublica,* September 5, 2013, https://www.propublica.org/article/the-nsas-secret- campaign-to- crack-undermine-internet-encryption.

202. Landau, *Surveillance,* 9.

203. President's Review Group on Intelligence and Communications Technologies, *Liberty and Security in a Changing World,* December 12, 2013, White House: President Barack Obama, https://obamawhitehouse.archives.gov/sites/default/files/docs/2013-12-12_rg_final_report.pdf.

204. Office of the Press Secretary, "Presidential Policy Directive 28—Signals Intelligence Activities," January 17, 2014, White House: President Barack Obama, https://obamawhitehouse.archives.gov/the-press-office/2014/01/17/presidential-policy-directive-signals-intelligence-activities.

205. Lauren Bateman, "NSA, CIA, and FBI Implementation of PPD-28," *Lawfare* (blog), February 9, 2015, https://www.lawfareblog.com/nsa-cia-and-fbi-implementation-ppd-28.

206. "USA Freedom Act: What's In, What's Out," *Washington Post,* June 2, 2015, https://www.washingtonpost.com/graphics/politics/usa-freedom-act/.

207. Ellen Nakashima, "Congressional Action on NSA is a Milestone in the Post-9/11 World," *Washington Post,* June 2, 2015, https://www.washingtonpost.com/world/national-security/congressional-action-on-nsa-is-a-milestone-in-the-post-911-world/2015/06/02/f46330a2-0944-11e5-95fd-d580f1c5d44e_story.html.

208. Pamela N. Phillips, letter to Mr. Leopold, October 17, 2013, *al-Jazeera,* http://www.documentcloud.org/documents/813055-nsa-talking-points.html.

209. Matthew M. Aid, "Prometheus Embattled: A Post-9/11 Report Card on the National Security Agency," *Intelligence and National Security* 21, no. 6 (2006): 994.

210. Bamford, *Shadow Factory,* 131.

211. Ibid., 133.

212. Barton Gellman, "NSA Broke Privacy Rules Thousands of Times Per Year, Audit Finds," *Washington Post*, August 15, 2013, https://www.washingtonpost.com/world/national-security/nsa-broke-privacy-rules-thousands-of-times-per-year-audit-finds/2013/08/15/3310e554-05ca-11e3-a07f-49ddc7417125_story.html and Siobhan Gorman, "NSA Officers Spy on Love Interests," *Wall Street Journal*, August 23, 2013, http://blogs.wsj.com/washwire/2013/08/23/nsa-officers-sometimes-spy-on-love-interests/.

213. Glenn Greenwald and Ryan Gallagher, "Snowden Documents Reveal Covert Surveillance and Pressure Tactics Aimed at Wikileaks and Its Supporters," *Intercept*, February 18, 2014, https://theintercept.com/2014/02/18/snowden-docs-reveal-covert-surveillance-and-pressure-tactics-aimed-at-wikileaks-and-its-supporters/.

214. Glenn Greenwald and Murtaza Hussain, "Meet the Muslim-American Leaders the FBI and NSA Have Been Spying On," *Intercept*, July 9, 2014, https://theintercept.com/2014/07/09/under-surveillance/.

215. Eric Lichtblau and James Risen, "Officials Say U.S. Wiretaps Exceeded Law," *New York Times*, April 15, 2009, http://www.nytimes.com/2009/04/16/us/16nsa.html?pagewanted=2&fta=y.

216. R. Jeffrey Smith, "FBI Violations May Number 3,000, Official Says," *Washington Post*, March 21, 2007, http://www.washingtonpost.com/wp-dyn/content/article/2007/03/20/AR2007032000921.html.

217. "NSA Illegally Collected Thousands of US Emails Annually," *al-Jazeera America*, August 21, 2013, http://america.aljazeera.com/articles/2013/8/21/nsa-collected-tensofthousandsofuscommunications.html.

218. James Ball and Spencer Ackerman, "NSA Loophole Allows Warrantless Search for US Citizens' Emails and Phone Calls," *Guardian*, August 9, 2013, https://www.theguardian.com/world/2013/aug/09/nsa-loophole-warrantless-searches-email-calls.

219. Bedan, "Echelon's Effect," 439 and Sloan, "ECHELON," 1504.

220. Nick Hopkins and Julian Borger, "NSA pays £100m in Secret Funding for GCHQ," *Guardian*, August 1, 2013, https://www.theguardian.com/uk-news/2013/aug/01/nsa-paid-gchq-spying-edward-snowden.

221. Ryan Gallagher, "The Surveillance Engine: How the NSA Built Its Own Secret Google," *Intercept*, August 25, 2014, https://theintercept.com/2014/08/25/icreach-nsa-cia-secret-google-crisscross-proton/.

222. Jay Stanley and Barry Steinhardt, *Even Bigger, Even Weaker: The Emerging Surveillance Society: Where Are We Now?* September 2007, 9, American Civil Liberties Union, http://www.aclu.org/pdfs/privacy/bigger_weaker.pdf.

CHAPTER 6

1. Jenna Johnson, "Trump Says 'Torture Works,' Backs Waterboarding and 'Much Worse,'" *Washington Post*, February 17, 2016, https://www.washingtonpost.com/politics/trump-says-torture-works-backs-waterboarding-and-much-worse/2016/02/17/4c9277be-d59c-11e5-b195-2e29a4e13425_story.html.

2. Nick Gass, "Trump: We Have to Take Out ISIL Members' Families," *Politico*, December 2, 2015, http://www.politico.com/story/2015/12/trump-kill-isil-families-216343.

3. Charlie Savage, "Donald Trump 'Fine' With Prosecuting U.S. Citizens at Guantánamo," *New York Times*, August 13, 2016, http://www.nytimes.com/2016/08/13/us/politics/donald-trump-american-citizens-guantanamo.html?_r=0.

4. Jenna Johnson, "Donald Trump is Expanding His Muslim Ban, Not Rolling It Back," *Washington Post*, July 24, 2016, https://www.washingtonpost.com/news/post-politics/wp/2016/07/24/donald-trump-is-expanding-his-muslim-ban-not-rolling-it-back/.

5. Ben Shreckinger, "Trump Calls Geneva Conventions 'the Problem,'" *Politico*, March 3, 2016, http://www.politico.com/blogs/2016-gop-primary-live-updates-and-results/2016/03/donald-trump-geneva-conventions-221394.

6. Matthew Weaver and Spencer Ackerman, "Trump Claims Torture Works but Experts Warn of Its 'Potentially Existential' Costs," *Guardian*, January 26, 2017, https://www.theguardian.com/us-news/2017/jan/26/donald-trump-torture-absolutely-works-says-us-president-in-first-television-interview.

7. Rebecca Sanders, "Human Rights Abuses at the Limits of the Law: Legal Instabilities and Vulnerabilities in the 'Global War on Terror,'" *Review of International Studies* 44, no. 1 (2018): 2–23.

8. According to *No More Excuses: A Roadmap to Justice for CIA Torture*, November 2015, Human Rights Watch, https://www.hrw.org/report/2015/12/01/no-more-excuses/roadmap-justice-cia-torture: "US officials who played a role in the process of creating, authorizing, and implementing the CIA program should be among those investigated for conspiracy to torture as well as other crimes. They include: Acting CIA General Counsel John Rizzo, Assistant Attorney General for Office of Legal Counsel (OLC) Jay Bybee, OLC Deputy Assistant Attorney General John Yoo, an individual identified as 'CTC Legal' in the Senate Summary, CIA Director George Tenet, National Security Legal Advisor John Bellinger, Attorney General John Ashcroft, White House Counsel Legal Advisor Alberto Gonzales, Counsel to the Vice President David Addington, Deputy White House Counsel Timothy Flanigan, National Security Advisor Condoleezza Rice, Defense Department General Counsel William Haynes II, Vice President Dick Cheney, and President George W. Bush. In addition, James Mitchell and Bruce Jessen, CIA psychologist contractors who devised the program, proposed it to the CIA, and helped carry it out, should also be investigated for their role in the initial conspiracy."

9. Jutta Brunnée and Stephen J. Toope, *Legitimacy and Legality in International Law: An Interactional Account* (Cambridge: Cambridge University Press, 2010).

10. Ruti G. Teitel, *Transitional Justice* (Oxford: Oxford University Press, 2000).

11. Diana Panke and Ulrich Pertersohn, "Why International Norms Disappear Sometimes," *European Journal of International Relations* 18, no. 4 (2012): 719–42.

12. Reed Brody, *Getting Away with Torture: The Bush Administration and Mistreatment of Detainees*, July 2011, 5, Human Rights Watch, www.hrw.org/sites/default/files/reports/us0711webwcover.pdf.

13. Ryder McKeown, "Norm Regress: US Revisionism and the Slow Death of the Torture Norm," *International Relations* 23, no. 1 (2009): 10–11.

14. Regina Heller, Martin Kahl, and Daniela Pisiou, "The 'Dark Side' of Normative Argumentation—the Case of Counterterrorism Policy," *Global Constitutionalism* 1, no. 2 (2012): 278–312.

15. Kathryn Sikkink, "The United States and Torture: Does the Spiral Model Work?" in *The Persistent Power of Human Rights: From Commitment to Compliance*, ed. Thomas Risse, Stephen C. Ropp, and Kathryn Sikkink (Cambridge: Cambridge University Press, 2013), 148.

16. Wayne Sandholtz, *Prohibiting Plunder: How Norms Change* (New York: Oxford University Press, 2007).

17. International Committee of the Red Cross, *People on War: Perspectives from 16 Countries*, December 2016, International Committee of the Red Cross, https://www.icrc.org/en/document/people-on-war. The report found that 46 percent of Americans supported torture to gain information from enemy combatants, one of the highest levels of support found among countries surveyed.

18. Adriana Sinclair, *International Relations Theory and International Law: A Critical Approach* (Cambridge: Cambridge University Press, 2010), 159.

19. David P. Forsythe, *The Politics of Prisoner Abuse: The United States and Enemy Prisoners After 9/11* (New York: Cambridge University Press, 2011).

20. *In the Name of Security: Counterterrorism Laws Worldwide Since September 11*, June 29, 2012, Human Rights Watch, https://www.hrw.org/report/2012/06/29/name-security/counterterrorism-laws-worldwide-september-11 and Beth Elise Whitaker, "Exporting the Patriot Act? Democracy and the 'War on Terror' in the Third World," *Third World Quarterly* 28, no. 5 (2007): 1019.

21. Whitaker, "Exporting the Patriot Act?" 1028.

22. Daniel Moeckli, "The Emergence of Terrorism as a Distinct Category of International Law," *Texas International Law Journal* 45 (2008): 177.

23. For instance, see UN Security Council, Resolution 1373 (2001): On Threats to International Peace and Security Caused by Terrorist Acts, September 28, 2001, United Nations, http://www.un.org/en/sc/ctc/specialmeetings/2012/docs/United%20Nations%20Security%20Council%20Resolution%201373%20(2001).pdf.

24. UN Security Council Counter-Terrorism Committee, "Protecting Human Rights While Countering Terrorism," September 10, 2015, United Nations, http://www.un.org/en/sc/ctc/rights.html.

25. Jack M. Beard, "The Geneva Boomerang: The Military Commissions Act of 2006 and U.S. Counterterror Operations," *American Journal of International Law* 101, no. 1 (2007): 66.

26. Mary Ellen O'Connell, "Enhancing the Status of Non-State Actors Through a Global War on Terror?" *Columbia Journal of Transnational Law* 43 (2004–2005): 434–58 and Eric L. Heinze, "The Evolution of International Law in Light of the 'Global War on Terror,'" *Review of International Studies* 37 (2011): 1069–94.

27. W. J. Hennigan, "A Fast Growing Club: Countries that Use Drones for Killing by Remote Control," *Los Angeles Times*, February 22, 2016, http://www.latimes.com/world/africa/la-fg-drone-proliferation-2-20160222-story.html and Eric Lin-Greenberg, "New Declaration on UAV Exports Unlikely to Reduce Drone Proliferation," *Lawfare* (blog), November 20, 2016, https://www.lawfareblog.com/new-declaration-uav-exports-unlikely-reduce-drone-proliferation.

28. "Joint Declaration for the Export and Subsequent Use of Armed or Strike-Enabled Unmanned Aerial Vehicles (UAVs)," October 5, 2016, US Department of State, https://www.state.gov/t/pm/rls/fs/2017/274817.htm.

29. UN Human Rights Council, *Report of the Special Rapporteur on the Promotion and Protection of Human Rights and Fundamental Freedoms while Countering Terrorism, Martin Scheinin*, December 28, 2009, 10, UN Office of the High Commissioner for Human Rights, https://documents-dds-ny.un.org/doc/UNDOC/GEN/G09/178/04/PDF/G0917804.pdf?OpenElement.

30. Ibid., 20.

31. Stephen Hopgood, *The Endtimes of Human Rights* (Ithaca, NY: Cornell University Press, 2013).

32. Samuel Moyn, *Not Enough: Human Rights in an Unequal World* (Cambridge, MA: Harvard University Press, 2018).

33. Alain Badiou, *The Rebirth of History: Times of Riots and Uprisings*, trans. Gregory Elliott (London: Verso Books, 2012); Jennifer Welsh, *The Return of History: Conflict, Migration, and Geopolitics in the Twenty-First Century* (Toronto: House of Anansi, 2016).

34. Abby Phillip, "O'Reilly Told Trump that Putin is a Killer. Trump's Reply: 'You Think Our Country is so Innocent?'" *Washington Post*, February 4, 2017, https://www.washingtonpost.com/news/post-politics/wp/2017/02/04/oreilly-told-trump-that-putin-is-a-killer-trumps-reply-you-think-our-countrys-so-innocent/?utm_

term=.45bdd252f6d0 and Glenn Thrush and Maggie Haberman, "Trump Gives White Supremacists an Unequivocal Boost," *New York Times*, August 15, 2017, https://www.nytimes.com/2017/08/15/us/politics/trump-charlottesville-white-nationalists.html.

35. Jenna Johnson, "Trump Calls for 'Total and Complete Shutdown of Muslims Entering the United States,'" *Washington Post*, December 7, 2015, https://www.washingtonpost.com/news/post-politics/wp/2015/12/07/donald-trump-calls-for-total-and-complete-shutdown-of-muslims-entering-the-united-states/?utm_term=.dcd18ef98279.

36. Leon Neyfakh, "Can the 'Secret Government' Save Us?" *Slate*, November 14, 2016, http://www.slate.com/articles/news_and_politics/politics/2016/11/can_the_secret_government_save_us_from_donald_trump.html.

37. Rosa Brooks, "The Military Wouldn't Save Us from President Trump's Illegal Orders," *Washington Post*, March 4, 2016, https://www.washingtonpost.com/opinions/the-military-wouldnt-save-us-from-president-trumps-illegal-orders/2016/03/04/9ef8fd44-e0ea-11e5-846c-10191d1fc4ec_story.html?utm_term=.ce77356fecdd.

38. Such figures include former National Security Advisor Michael Flynn, former chief strategist Stephen K. Bannon, former counterterrorism advisor Sebastian Gorka, and a variety of individuals associated with Frank Gaffney's Center for Security Policy and John Tanton's Federation for American Immigration Reform.

39. Jack Goldsmith, "Libertarian Panic, Unlawful Action, and the Trump Presidency," *Lawfare* (blog), November 22, 2016, https://www.lawfareblog.com/libertarian-panic-unlawful-action-and-trump-presidency.

40. Quoted in Ken Dilanian, "Trump Needs His 'Own Damn Bucket' to Waterboard: Ex-CIA Chief," *NBC News*, February 22, 2016, http://www.nbcnews.com/news/us-news/trump-needs-his-own-damn-bucket-waterboard-ex-cia-chief-n523576.

41. Sheri Fink and Helene Cooper, "Inside Trump Defense Secretary Pick's Efforts to Halt Torture," *New York Times*, January 2, 2017, https://www.nytimes.com/2017/01/02/us/politics/james-mattis-defense-secretary-trump.html. As of May 2018, Gina Haspel, who was associated with black site interrogations, has been nominated to head the CIA. Her position on torture remains unclear at the time of writing.

42. Daniel Benjamin, "How Trump's Attacks on U.S. Intelligence Will Come Back to Haunt Him," *Politico Magazine*, January 11, 2017, http://www.politico.com/magazine/story/2017/01/how-trumps-attacks-on-us-intelligence-will-come-back-to-haunt-him-214622.

43. Donald J. Trump, "Executive Order: Protecting the Nation from Foreign Terrorist Entry into the United States," January 27, 2017, White House: President Donald J. Trump, https://www.whitehouse.gov/the-press-office/2017/01/27/executive-order-protecting-nation-foreign-terrorist-entry-united-states.

44. Curtis E. Gannon, memorandum, "Proposed Executive Order Entitled, 'Protecting the Nation from Foreign Terrorist Entry into the United States,'" January 27, 2017, *Lawfare* (blog), https://assets.documentcloud.org/documents/3442905/EO-Foreign-Terrorist-Entry.pdf.

45. Donald F. McGahn, II, memorandum to the Acting Secretary of State, the Acting Attorney General, and the Secretary of Homeland Security, "Authoritative Guidance on Executive Order Entitled 'Protecting the Nation from Foreign Terrorist Entry into the United States,'" January 27, 2017," February 1, 2017, *Lawfare* (blog), https://assets.documentcloud.org/documents/3442906/Sub-Buzz-20267-1486076420-31.pdf.

46. Michael D. Shear et al., "Trump Fires Acting Attorney General Who Defied Him," *New York Times*, January 30, 2017, https://www.nytimes.com/2017/01/30/us/politics/trump-immigration-ban-memo.html.

47. Jane Chong, "How the Ninth Circuit Did It: Due Process Sinkhole Swallows Trump's Executive Order Whole," *Lawfare* (blog), February 10, 2017, https://www.lawfareblog.com/how-ninth-circuit-did-it-due-process-sinkhole-swallows-trumps-executive-order-whole.

48. Jennifer Rubin, "The 9th Circuit Deals a Blow to the Imperial—and Incompetent—President," *Washington Post*, February 9, 2017, https://www.washingtonpost.com/blogs/right-turn/wp/2017/02/09/the-9th-circuit-deals-a-blow-to-the-imperial-and-incompetent-president/?utm_term=.169721376104.

49. Quoted in Aaron Blake, "Stephen Miller's Authoritarian Declaration: Trump's National Security Actions 'Will Not Be Questioned,'" *Washington Post*, February 13, 2017, https://www.washingtonpost.com/news/the-fix/wp/2017/02/13/stephen-millers-audacious-controversial-declaration-trumps-national-security-actions-will-not-be-questioned/?utm_term=.1e2a27159339 (italics added).

50. Joel Rose and Bill Chappell, "Federal Judge in Maryland Blocks Trump's Latest Travel Ban Attempt," *NPR*, October 18, 2017, http://www.npr.org/sections/thetwo-way/2017/10/18/558501163/federal-judge-in-maryland-blocks-trumps-latest-travel-ban-attempt.

51. The ICRC has spearheaded international discussion of international humanitarian law rules governing detention in noninternational armed conflicts. See "Strengthening IHL Protecting Persons Deprived of their Liberty in Relation to Armed Conflict," April 1, 2017, International Committee of the Red Cross, https://www.icrc.org/en/document/detention-non-international-armed-conflict-icrcs-work-strengthening-legal-protection-0.

52. Brunnée and Toope, *Legitimacy and Legality*, 351.

53. Jinee Lokaneeta, *Transnational Torture: Law, Violence, and State Power in the United States and India* (New York: New York University Press, 2011) and Neta C. Crawford, *Accountability for Killing: Moral Responsibility for Collateral Damage in America's Post-9/11 Wars* (New York: Oxford University Press, 2013).

54. Ruth Blakeley, "Human Rights, State Wrongs, and Social Change: The Theory and Practice of Emancipation," *Review of International Studies* 39 (2013): 599–619; Hopgood, *The Endtimes of Human Rights*.

55. Jack Goldsmith, *Power and Constraint: The Accountable Presidency After 9/11* (New York: W. W. Norton, 2012), 200.

56. Ibid., 230.

BIBLIOGRAPHY

Abbott, Kenneth W., Robert O. Keohane, Andrew Moravcsik, Anne-Marie Slaughter, and Duncan Snidal. "The Concept of Legalization." *International Organization* 54, no. 3 (2000): 401–19.

Adler, Emanuel, and Peter M. Haas. "Conclusion: Epistemic Communities, World Order, and the Creation of a Reflective Research Program." *International Organization* 46, no. 1 (1992): 367–90.

Adler, Emanuel, and Vincent Pouliot, eds. *International Practices*. Cambridge: Cambridge University Press, 2011.

Agamben, Giorgio. *Homo Sacer: Sovereign Power and the Bare Life*. Translated by Daniel Heller-Roazen. Stanford, CA: Stanford University Press, 1998.

––––––. *State of Exception*. Translated by Kevin Attel. Chicago: University of Chicago Press, 2005.

Aid, Matthew M. "Prometheus Embattled: A Post-9/11 Report Card on the National Security Agency." *Intelligence and National Security* 21, no. 6 (2006): 980–98.

––––––. *The Secret Sentry: The Untold History of the National Security Agency*. New York: Bloomsbury, 2009.

Akande, Dapo. "Clearing the Fog of War? The ICRC's Interpretive Guidance on Direct Participation in Hostilities." *International and Comparative Law Quarterly* 59 (2010): 180–92.

Alleg, Henri. *The Question*. Translated by John Calder. Lincoln, NE: Bison Books, 2006.

Andrew, Christopher. *For the President's Eyes Only: Secret Intelligence and the American Presidency from Washington to Bush*. New York: HarperCollins, 1995.

Anghie, Antony. *Imperialism, Sovereignty, and the Making of International Law*. Cambridge: Cambridge University Press, 2005.

Aussaresses, Paul. *The Battle of the Casbah: Terrorism and Counter-Terrorism in Algeria, 1955–1957*. New York: Enigma Books, 2002.

Badiou, Alain. *The Rebirth of History: Times of Riots and Uprisings*. Translated by Gregory Elliott. London: Verso Books, 2012.

Bamford, James. *The Shadow Factory: The Ultra-Secret NSA from 9/11 to the Eavesdropping on America*. New York: Doubleday, 2008.

Barnett, Michael, and Martha Finnemore. *Rules for the World: International Organizations in Global Politics*. Ithaca, NY: Cornell University Press, 2004.

Bates, Ed. "State Immunity for Torture." *Human Rights Law Review* 7, no. 4 (2007): 651–80.

Beard, Jack M. "The Geneva Boomerang: The Military Commissions Act of 2006 and U.S. Counterterror Operations." *American Journal of International Law* 101, no. 1 (2007): 56–73.

Bedan, Matt. "Echelon's Effect: The Obsolescence of the U.S. Foreign Intelligence Legal Regime." *Federal Communications Law Journal* 59, no. 2 (2007): 425–44.

Behringer, Wolfgang. *Witches and Witch-Hunts: A Global History.* Cambridge: Polity, 2004.

Bellinger, John B., III. "Legal Issues Related to Armed Conflict with Non-State Groups." In *Prisoners in War*, edited by Sibylle Scheipers, 251–62. Oxford: Oxford University Press, 2010.

Bhattacharyya, Gargi. *Dangerous Brown Men: Exploiting Sex, Violence, and Feminism in the War on Terror.* London: Zed Books, 2008.

Biddle, Tami Davis. "Strategic Bombardment: Expectation, Theory, and Practice in the Early Twentieth Century." In *The American Way of Bombing*, edited by Matthew Evangelista and Henry Shue, 27–46. Ithaca, NY: Cornell University Press, 2014.

Blackmon, Douglas A. *Slavery by Another Name: The Re-Enslavement of Black Americans from the Civil War to World War II.* New York: Doubleday, 2008.

Blakeley, Ruth. "Human Rights, State Wrongs, and Social Change: The Theory and Practice of Emancipation." *Review of International Studies* 39 (2013), 599–619.

_____. *State Terrorism and Neoliberalism: The North in the South.* New York: Routledge, 2009.

_____. "Still Training to Torture? US Training of Military Forces From Latin America." *Third World Quarterly* 27, no. 8 (2006): 1439–61.

Bob, Clifford. *The Global Right Wing and the Clash of World Politics.* New York: Cambridge University Press, 2012.

Bourdieu, Pierre. "The Force of Law: Toward a Sociology of the Juridical Field." *Hastings Law Journal* 38 (1986–87): 805–53.

Breglio, Nora K. "Leaving FISA Behind: The Need to Return to Warrantless Foreign Intelligence Surveillance." *Yale Law Journal* 113, no. 1 (2003): 179–217.

Brunnée, Jutta, and Stephen J. Toope. *Legitimacy and Legality in International Law: An Interactional Account.* Cambridge: Cambridge University Press, 2010.

Brysk, Alison. *Global Good Samaritans: Human Rights as Foreign Policy.* Oxford: Oxford University Press, 2009.

Bush, George W. *Decision Points.* New York: Crown, 2010.

Butler, Judith. *Precarious Life: The Powers of Mourning and Violence.* London: Verso Books, 2004.

Búzás, Zoltán I. "Evading International Law: How Agents Comply with the Letter of the Law but Violate Its Purpose." *European Journal of International Relations* 23, no. 4 (2017): 857–83.

Byers, Michael. "The Law and Politics of the Pinochet Case." *Duke Journal of Comparative and International Law* 10 (2000): 415–41.

Byers, Michael, and Georg Nolte, eds. *United States Hegemony and the Foundations of International Law.* Cambridge: Cambridge University Press, 2003.

Cainkar, Louise. "Post-9/11 Policies Affecting U.S. Arabs and Muslims: A Brief Overview." *Comparative Studies of South Asia, Africa and the Middle East* 24, no. 1 (2004): 245–48.

Callam, Andrew. "Drone Wars: Unmanned Aerial Vehicles." *International Affairs Review* 18, no. 3 (2010). http://www.iar-gwu.org/node/144.

Campbell, Kirsten. "The Making of Global Legal Culture and International Criminal Law." *Leiden Journal of International Law* 26 (2013): 155–72.

Cardyn, Lisa. "Sexualized Racism/Gendered Violence: Outraging the Body Politic in the Reconstruction South." *Michigan Law Review* 100, no. 4 (2002): 675–867.

Carr, Edward Hallett. *Twenty Years' Crisis, 1919–1939: An Introduction to the Study of International Relations.* New York: Harper and Row, 1964.

Checkel, Jeffrey T. "Why Comply? Social Learning and European Identity Change." *International Organization* 55, no. 3 (2001): 553–88.

Cheney, Richard B., and Liz Cheney. *In My Time: A Personal and Political Memoir.* New York: Threshold Editions, 2011.

Chesney, Robert M. "Boumediene v. Bush." *American Journal of International Law* 102, no. 4 (2008): 848–54.

Chesterman, Simon. "The Spy Who Came in From the Cold War: Intelligence in International Law." *Michigan Journal of International Law* 27 (2006): 1071–1130.

Clarke, James W. "Without Fear or Shame: Lynching, Capital Punishment and the Subculture of Violence in the American South." *British Journal of Political Science* 28, no. 2 (1998): 269–89.

Cohen, Stanley. *States of Denial: Knowing about Atrocities and Suffering*. Cambridge: Polity 2001.

Cole, David. *Enemy Aliens: Double Standards and Constitutional Freedoms in the War on Terrorism*. New York: New Press, 2005.

_____. *Justice at War: The Men and Ideas That Shaped America's War on Terror*. New York: New York Review of Books, 2008.

_____. *The Torture Memos: Rationalizing the Unthinkable*. New York: New Press, 2009.

Corn, Geoffrey S. "What Law Applies to the War on Terror?" In *The War on Terror and the Laws of War: A Military Perspective*, edited by Michael Lewis, Eric Jensen, Geoffrey Corn, Victor Hansen, Richard Jackson, and James Schoettler, 1–36. Oxford: Oxford University Press, 2009.

Couso, Javier, Alexandra Huneeus, and Rachel Sieder, eds. *Cultures of Legality: Judicialization and Political Activism in Latin America*. New York: Cambridge University Press, 2013.

Cox, Robert. "Gramsci, Hegemony, and International Relations: An Essay in Method." *Millennium* 12 (1983): 162–75.

Crawford, Neta C. *Accountability for Killing: Moral Responsibility for Collateral Damage in America's Post-9/11 Wars*. New York: Oxford University Press, 2013.

Cullather, Nick. *Secret History: The CIA's Classified Account of Its Operations in Guatemala, 1952–1954*. Stanford, CA: Stanford University Press, 1999.

DeRosa, Mary. "Privacy in the Age of Terror." *Washington Quarterly* 26, no. 3 (2003): 27–41.

Dershowitz, Alan. *Why Terrorism Works: Understanding the Threat, Responding to the Challenge*. New Haven, CT: Yale University Press, 2002.

Desch, Michael C. "America's Liberal Illiberalism: The Ideological Origins of Overreaction in U.S. Foreign Policy." *International Security* 32, no. 3 (2007–08): 7–43.

Devlin, Larry. *Chief of Station, Congo: Fighting the Cold War in a Hot Zone*. New York: Public Affairs, 2007.

Dickenson, Laura. "Military Lawyers on the Battlefield: An Empirical Account of International Law Compliance." *American Journal of International Law* 104 (2010): 1–28.

Diffie, Whitfield, and Susan Landau. *Privacy on the Line: The Politics of Wiretapping and Encryption*. Cambridge, MA: MIT Press, 2007.

Dixon, Jennifer. "Rhetorical Adaptation and Resistance to International Norms." *Perspectives on Politics* 15, no. 1 (2017): 83–99.

Doyle, Michael. "Kant, Liberal Legacies, and Foreign Affairs." *Philosophy and Public Affairs* 12 (1983): 205–35, 323–53.

Dudziak, Mary L. *Cold War Civil Rights: Race and the Image of American Democracy*. Princeton, NJ: Princeton University Press, 2000.

Einolf, Cristopher J. *Americans in the Philippines, 1899–1902: The First Torture Scandal*. New York: Palgrave Macmillan, 2014.

Elkins, Caroline. *Imperial Reckoning: The Untold Story of Britain's Gulag in Kenya*. New York: Henry Holt, 2004.

Erickson, Jennifer. *Dangerous Trade: Conventional Arms Exports, Human Rights, and International Reputation*. New York: Columbia University Press, 2015.

Evans, Elizabeth Gower. "Foreigners." In *Sacco and Vanzetti: Rebel Lives*, edited by John Davis, 53–57. Melbourne: Ocean Press, 2004.

Fallon, Richard H., Jr., and Daniel J. Meltzer. "Habeas Corpus Jurisdiction, Substantive Rights, and the War on Terror." *Harvard Law Review* 120, no. 8 (2007): 2029–2112.

Farber, Sonia R. "Forgotten at Guantánamo: The Boumediene Decision and Its Implications for Refugees at the Base under the Obama Administration." *California Law Review* 98 (2010): 989–1022.

Farrell, Michelle. *The Prohibition on Torture in Exceptional Circumstances.* Cambridge: Cambridge University Press, 2013.

Feimster, Crystal Nicole. *Southern Horrors: Women and the Politics of Rape and Lynching.* Cambridge, MA: Harvard University Press, 2009.

Feith, Douglas. *War and Decision: Inside the Pentagon at the Dawn of the War on Terrorism.* New York: HarperCollins, 2008.

Finkelman, Paul, ed. *Slavery and the Law.* Madison, WI: Madison House, 1997.

Finnemore, Martha. *The Purpose of Intervention: Changing Beliefs about the Use of Force.* Ithaca, NY: Cornell University Press, 2004.

Finnemore, Martha, and Kathryn Sikkink. "International Norm Dynamics and Political Change." *International Organization* 52, no. 4 (1998): 887–917.

Finnemore, Martha, and Stephen J. Toope. "Alternatives to Legalization: Richer Views of Law and Politics." *International Organization* 55, no. 3 (2001): 743–58.

Fischer, David Hackett. *Washington's Crossing.* New York: Oxford University Press, 2004.

Foot, Rosemary. "Torture: The Struggle over a Peremptory Norm in a Counter-Terrorist Era." *International Relations* 20, no. 2 (2006): 131–51.

Forsythe, David P. *The Politics of Prisoner Abuse: The United States and Enemy Prisoners After 9/11.* New York: Cambridge University Press, 2011.

Foucault, Michel. *Discipline and Punish: The Birth of the Prison.* Translated by Alan Sheridan. New York: Vintage Books, 1995.

Franck, Thomas M. "The Power of Legitimacy and the Legitimacy of Power: International Law in an Age of Power Disequilibrium." *American Journal of International Law* 100, no. 1 (2006): 88–106.

Friedman, Lawrence M. *The Legal System: A Social Science Perspective.* New York: Russell Sage Foundation, 1975.

Fujii, Lee Ann. "The Puzzle of Extra-Lethal Violence." *Perspectives on Politics* 11, no. 2 (2013): 410–26.

Fuller, Lon L. *The Morality of Law.* New Haven, CT: Yale University Press, 1964.

Ganser, Danielle. "The CIA in Western Europe and the Abuse of Human Rights." *Intelligence and National Security* 21, no. 5 (2006): 760–81.

Geiss, Robin, and Michael Siegrist. "Has the Armed Conflict in Afghanistan Affected the Rules on the Conduct of Hostilities?" *International Review of the Red Cross* 93, no. 881 (2011): 11–46.

George, Alexander L., and Andrew Bennett. *Case Studies and Theory Development in the Social Sciences.* Cambridge, MA: MIT Press, 2005.

Gillespie, Alexander. *A History of the Laws of War, Volume 1: The Customs and Laws of War with Regards to Combatants and Captives.* Portland, OR: Hart, 2011.

Glennon, Michael J. *National Security and Double Government.* New York: Oxford University Press, 2015.

Goldsmith, Jack. *Power and Constraint: The Accountable Presidency after 9/11.* New York: W. W. Norton, 2012.

_____. *The Terror Presidency: Law and Judgment inside the Bush Administration.* New York: W. W. Norton, 2007.

Goldsmith, Jack L., and Eric A. Posner. *The Limits of International Law.* Oxford: Oxford University Press, 2005.

_____. "Moral and Legal Rhetoric in International Relations: A Rational Choice Perspective." *Journal of Legal Studies* 31, no. 1 (2002): S115–S139.

Goldsmith, Jack L., and Stephen Krasner. "The Limits of Idealism." *Daedalus* 132, no. 1 (2003): 47–63.

Goodman, Ryan, and Derek Jinks. *Socializing States: Promoting Human Rights through International Law.* New York: Oxford University Press, 2013.

Gourevitch, Philip, and Errol Morris. *Standard Operating Procedure.* New York: Penguin, 2008.

Greenberg, Karen. *The Least Worst Place: Guantánamo's First 100 Days.* Oxford: Oxford University Press, 2009.

Greenhill, Kelly M., *Weapons of Mass Migration: Forced Displacement, Coercion and Foreign Policy.* Ithaca, NY: Cornell University Press, 2010.

Greenwald, Glenn. *No Place to Hide: Edward Snowden, the NSA, and the U.S. Surveillance State.* New York: Metropolitan Books, 2014.

Gregory, Derek. "The Black Flag: Guantánamo Bay and the State of Exception." *Geografiska Annaler. Series B, Human Geography* 88, no. 4 (2006): 405–27

Grey, Stephen. *Ghost Plane: The True Story of the CIA Rendition and Torture Program.* New York: St. Martin's Griffin, 2006.

Gross, Oren. "The Normless and Exceptionless Exception: Carl Schmitt's Theory of Emergency Powers and the 'Norm-Exception' Dichotomy." *Cardozo Law Review* 21, nos. 5–6 (2000): 1825–68.

Guzman, Andrew T. "A Compliance-Based Theory of International Law." *California Law Review* 90 (2002): 1823–87.

Hafner-Burton, Emilie. *Forced to Be Good: Why Trade Agreements Boost Human Rights.* Ithaca, NY: Cornell University Press, 2009.

Hafner-Burton, Emilie, and Kiyotero Tsutsui. "Human Rights in a Globalizing World: The Paradox of Empty Promises." *American Journal of Sociology* 110, no. 5 (2005): 1373–1411.

Hamilton, Alexander. "The Federalist No. 84." In *The Federalist with Letters* of "Brutus," edited by Terence Ball. Cambridge: Cambridge University Press, 2003.

Hampson, Françoise. "Direct Participation in Hostilities and the Interoperability of the Law of Armed Conflict and Human Rights Law." In *International Law and the Changing Character of War*, edited by Raul A. Pedrozo and Daria P. Wollschlaeger. International Law Studies 87. Newport, RI: Naval War College, 2011.

Harbury, Jennifer. *Truth, Torture, and the American Way: The History and Consequences of U.S. Involvement in Torture.* Boston: Beacon, 2005.

Harris, Shane. *The Watchers: The Rise of America's Surveillance State.* New York: Penguin, 2010.

Hathaway, Oona A. "Do Human Rights Treaties Make a Difference?" *Yale Law Journal* 111, no. 8 (2002): 1935–2042.

Hathaway, Oona, Samuel Adelsberg, Spencer Amdur, Philip Levitz, Freya Pitts, and Sirine Shebaya. "The Power to Detain: Detention of Terrorism Suspects after 9/11." *Yale Journal of International Law* 38 (2013): 123–77.

Hayden, Michael V. *Playing to the Edge: American Intelligence in the Age of Terror.* New York: Penguin, 2016.

Heinze, Eric L. "The Evolution of International Law in Light of the 'Global War on Terror.'" *Review of International Studies* 37 (2011): 1069–94.

Heller, Regina, Martin Kahl, and Daniela Pisiou. "The 'Dark Side' of Normative Argumentation—the Case of Counterterrorism Policy." *Global Constitutionalism* 1, no. 2 (2012): 278–312.

Hopgood, Stephen. *The Endtimes of Human Rights.* Ithaca, NY: Cornell University Press, 2013.

Horne, Alistair. *A Savage War of Peace: Algeria 1954–1962.* New York: New York Review of Books, 2006.

Horton, Scott. "Through a Mirror Darkly: Applying the Geneva Conventions to a 'New Kind of Warfare.'" In *The Torture Debate in America*, edited by Karen Greenberg, 136–50. New York: Cambridge University Press, 2005.

Hurd, Ian. "Breaking and Making Norms: American Revisionism and Crises of Legitimacy." *International Politics* 44, no. 2–3 (2007): 194–213.

_____. *How to Do Things with International Law*. Princeton: Princeton University Press, 2017.

Hussain, Nasser. "Beyond Norm and Exception: Guantánamo." *Critical Inquiry* 33, no. 4 (2007): 734–53.

Hussain, Nasser, and Melissa Ptacek. "Thresholds: Sovereignty and the Sacred." *Law and Society Review* 34, no. 2 (2000): 495–515.

Ignatieff, Michael. "American Exceptionalism and Human Rights." In *American Exceptionalism and Human Rights*, edited by Michael Ignatieff, 1–26. Princeton, NJ: Princeton University Press, 2005.

Ikenberry, John G. *Liberal Order and Imperial Ambition*. Cambridge: Polity, 2006.

Jackson, John, and Yassin M'Boge. "The Effect of Legal Culture on the Development of International Evidentiary Practice: From the 'Robing Room' to the 'Melting Pot.'" *Leiden Journal of International Law* 26 (2013): 947–70.

Jackson, Richard. "Language, Policy and the Construction of a Torture Culture in the War on Terrorism." *Review of International Studies* 33 (2007): 353–71.

Jahn, Beate. "Kant, Mill, and Illiberal Legacies in International Affairs." *International Organization* 59 (2005): 177–207.

Jervis, Robert. "Understanding the Bush Doctrine." *Political Science Quarterly* 118, no. 3 (2003): 365–88.

Johns, Fleur. "Guantánamo Bay and the Annihilation of the Exception." *European Journal of International Law* 16, no. 4 (2005): 613–35.

Kahn, David. *The Reader of Gentlemen's Mail: Herbert O. Yardley and the Birth of American Codebreaking*. New Haven, CT: Yale University Press, 2004.

Kang, Jerry. "Watching the Watchers: Enemy Combatants in the Internment's Shadow." *Law and Contemporary Problems* 68, no. 2 (2005): 255–83.

Kaplan, Amy. "Where is Guantánamo?" *American Quarterly* 57, no. 3 (2005): 831–58.

Keck, Margaret, and Kathryn Sikkink. *Activists Beyond Borders: Advocacy Networks in International Politics*. Ithaca, NY: Cornell University Press, 1998.

Keegan, John. *Intelligence in War: The Value—and Limitations—of What the Military Can Learn About the Enemy*. Toronto: Vintage Canada, 2004.

Kennedy, David. *The Dark Side of Virtue: Reassessing International Humanitarianism*. Princeton, NJ: Princeton University Press, 2004.

_____. *Of War and Law*. Princeton, NJ: Princeton University Press, 2006.

Keohane, Robert O. *After Hegemony: Cooperation and Discord in the World Political Economy*. Princeton, NJ: Princeton University Press, 1984.

Kerr, Orin S. "The Case for the Third-Party Doctrine." *Michigan Law Review* 107 (2009): 561–602.

_____. "The Fourth Amendment and New Technologies: Constitutional Myths and the Case for Caution." *Michigan Law Review* 102, no. 5 (2004): 801–88.

_____. "Updating the Foreign Intelligence Surveillance Act." *University of Chicago Law Review* 75, no. 1 (2008): 225–43.

Kinsella, Helen M. *The Image Before the Weapon: A Critical History of the Distinction between Combatant and Civilian*. Ithaca, NY: Cornell University Press, 2011.

Kinzer, Stephen. *All the Shah's Men: An American Coup and the Roots of the Middle East*. Hoboken, NJ: Wiley, 2003.

Klein, Adam, and Benjamin Wittes. "Preventative Detention in American Theory and Practice." *Harvard National Security Journal* 2 (2011): 85–191.

Klotz, Audie. *Norms in International Relations: The Struggle against Apartheid.* Ithaca, NY: Cornell University Press, 1995.

Koh, Harold. "Why do Nations Obey International Law?" *Yale Law Journal* 106, no. 8 (1997): 2599–659.

———. "The Case Against Military Commissions." *American Journal of International Law* 96, no. 2 (2002): 337–44.

Koremenos, Barbara. "Institutionalism and International Law." In *Interdisciplinary Perspectives on International Law and International Relations: The State of the Art,* edited by Jeffrey L. Dunoff and Mark A. Pollack, 59–82. New York: Cambridge University Press, 2013.

Kornbluh, Peter. *Bay of Pigs Declassified: The Secret CIA Report on the Invasion of Cuba.* New York: New Press, 1998.

Koskenniemi, Martti. *From Apology to Utopia: The Structure of International Legal Argument.* Cambridge: Cambridge University Press, 2005.

———. *The Politics of International Law.* Portland, OR: Hart, 2011.

Kramer, Paul A. *The Blood of Government: Race, Empire, the United States and the Philippines.* Chapel Hill: University of North Carolina Press, 2006.

Krasner, Stephen D. *Sovereignty: Organized Hypocrisy.* Princeton, NJ: Princeton University Press, 1999.

Kratochwil, Friedrich. *Rules, Norms, and Decisions: On the Conditions of Practical and Legal Reasoning in International Relations and Domestic Affairs.* Cambridge: Cambridge University Press, 1989.

Kretzmer, David. "Targeted Killing of Suspected Terrorists: Extra-Judicial Executions or Legitimate Means of Defence?" *European Journal of International Law* 16, no. 2 (2005): 171–212.

Landau, Susan. *Surveillance or Security? The Risks Posed by New Wiretapping Technologies.* Cambridge, MA: MIT Press, 2010.

Langbein, John H. "The Legal History of Torture." In *Torture: A Collection,* edited by Sanford Levinson, 93–104. Oxford: Oxford University Press, 2004.

Legro, Jeffrey W. "Which Norms Matter? Revisiting the 'Failure' of Internationalism." *International Organization* 51, no. 1 (1997): 31–63.

Levinson, Sanford. "Constitutional Norms in a State of Permanent Emergency." *Georgia Law Review* 40, no. 3 (2006): 699–751.

———. "Torture in Iraq and the Rule of Law in America." *Daedalus* 133, no. 3 (2004): 5–9.

Levy, Leonard W. "Origins of the Fourth Amendment." *Political Science Quarterly* 114, no. 1 (1999): 79–101.

Lichtblau, Eric. *Bush's Law: The Remaking of American Justice.* New York: Anchor Books, 2009.

Lokaneeta, Jinee. *Transnational Torture: Law, Violence, and State Power in the United States and India.* New York: New York University Press, 2011.

Luban, David. "Liberalism, Torture, and the Ticking Bomb." *Virginia Law Review* 91, no. 6 (2005): 1425–61.

Lutz, Ellen L., and Kathryn Sikkink. "International Human Rights Law and Practice in Latin America." *International Organization* 54, no. 3 (2000): 633–59.

MacKinnon, Catharine A., "Women's September 11: Rethinking the International Law of Conflict." *Harvard International Law Review* 47, no. 1 (2006): 1–31.

Maguire, Peter H. *Law and War: An American Story.* New York: Columbia University Press, 2000.

March, James G., and Johan P. Olsen. "The Institutional Dynamics of International Political Orders." *International Organization* 52 (1998): 943–69.

Marks, John. *The Search for the "Manchurian Candidate": The CIA and Mind Control—The Secret History of the Behavioral Sciences.* New York: Norton, 1991.

Martin, Kate. "Domestic Intelligence and Civil Liberties." *SAIS Review* 24, no. 1 (2004): 7–21.

Mayer, Jane. *The Dark Side: The Inside Story of How the War on Terror Turned into a War on American Ideals*. New York: Doubleday, 2008.

McCann, Michael. "The Unbearable Lightness of Rights: On Sociolegal Inquiry in the Global Era." *Law and Society Review* 48, no. 2 (2014): 245–73.

McCleod, Travers. *Rule of Law in War: International Law and United States Counterinsurgency Doctrine in the Iraq and Afghanistan Wars*. Oxford: Oxford University Press, 2015.

McCoy, Alfred. *A Question of Torture: CIA Interrogation, from the Cold War to the War on Terror*. New York: Henry Holt, 2006.

McKeown, Ryder. "Norm Regress: US Revisionism and the Slow Death of the Torture Norm." *International Relations* 23, no. 1 (2009): 5–25.

McLachlan, Campbell. "Pinochet Revisited." *International and Comparative Law Quarterly* 51 (2002): 959–66.

McMaster, John Bach. *The United States in the World War 1914–1918, Volume II*. New York: P. Appleton, 1920.

McSherry, J. Patrice. *Predatory States: Operation Condor and Covert War in Latin America*. Lanham, MD: Rowman and Littlefield, 2005.

Mearsheimer, John J. "The False Promise of International Institutions." *International Security* 19, no. 3 (1994–95): 5–49.

_____. *Why Leaders Lie: The Truth About Lying in International Politics*. Oxford: Oxford University Press, 2011.

Mégret, Frédéric. "A Cautionary Tale from the Crusades? War and Prisoners in Situations of Normative Incommensurability." In *Prisoners in War*, edited by Sibylle Scheipers, 23–38. Oxford: Oxford University Press, 2010.

_____. "From 'Savages' to 'Unlawful Combatants': A Postcolonial Look at International Humanitarian Law's 'Other.'" In *International Law and Its Others*, edited by Anne Orford, 265–317. Cambridge: Cambridge University Press, 2006.

Merry, Sally Engle. *Human Rights and Gender Violence: Translating International Law into Local Justice*. Chicago: University of Chicago Press, 2006.

Mezey, Naomi. "Law As Culture." *Yale Journal of Law and The Humanities* 13 (2001): 35–67.

_____. "Mapping a Cultural Studies of Law." In *The Handbook of Law and Society*, edited by Austin Sarat and Patricia Ewick, 39–55. Malden, MA: Wiley Blackwell, 2015.

Miéville, China. *Between Equal Rights: A Marxist Theory of International Law*. Leiden: Brill, 2005.

Moeckli, Daniel. "The Emergence of Terrorism as a Distinct Category of International Law." *Texas International Law Journal* 45 (2008): 157–83.

Moravcsik, Andrew. "Taking Preferences Seriously: A Liberal Theory of International Politics." *International Organization* 51, no. 4 (1997): 513–53.

Morgenthau, Hans. *Politics Among Nations: The Struggle for Power and Peace*. New York: Alfred A. Knopf, 1963.

Moyn, Samuel. *Not Enough: Human Rights in an Unequal World*. Cambridge, MA: Harvard University Press, 2018.

National Commission on Terrorist Attacks Upon the United States. *The 9/11 Commission Report: Final Report of the National Commission on Terrorist Attacks upon the United States*. New York: W. W. Norton, 2004.

Neff, Stephen C. "Prisoners of War in International Law: The Nineteenth Century." In *Prisoners in War*, edited by Sibylle Scheipers, 57–73. Oxford: Oxford University Press, 2010.

Nelken, David. "Thinking About Legal Culture." *Asian Journal of Law and Society* 1, no. 2 (2014): 255–74.

_____. "Using the Concept of Legal Culture." *Australian Journal of Legal Philosophy* 29 (2004): 1–26.

Nelken, David, and Johannes Feest, eds. *Adapting Legal Cultures*. Portland, OR: Hart, 2001.

Neuman, Gerald L. "Anomalous Zones." *Stanford Law Review* 48, no. 5 (1996): 1197–234.

Neumayer, Eric. "Do International Human Rights Treaties Improve Respect for Human Rights?" *Journal of Conflict Resolution* 49, no. 6 (2005): 925–53.

Nye, Joseph. *Soft Power: The Means to Success in World Politics*. New York: Public Affairs, 2004.

O'Connell, Mary Ellen. "The Choice of Law against Terrorism." *Journal of National Security Law and Policy* 4 (2010): 343–68.

———. "Enhancing the Status of Non-State Actors Through a Global War on Terror?" *Columbia Journal of Transnational Law* 43 (2004–05): 434–58.

Odysseos, Louiza. *The International Political Thought of Carl Schmitt: Terror, Liberal War and the Crisis of Global Order*. New York: Routledge, 2007.

Ohlin, Jens David. *The Attack on International Law*. New York: Oxford University Press, 2015.

Olson, James M. "Intelligence and the War on Terror: How Dirty Are We Willing to Get Our Hands?" *SAIS Review* 28, no. 1 (2008): 37–45.

Panke, Diana, and Ulrich Pertersohn. "Why International Norms Disappear Sometimes." *European Journal of International Relations* 18, no. 4 (2012): 719–42.

Perez, Joseph. *The Spanish Inquisition: A History*. Translated by Janet Lloyd. London: Profile Books, 2004.

Perugini, Nicola, and Neve Gordon. *The Human Right to Dominate*. New York: Oxford University Press, 2015.

Plaidy, Jean. *The Spanish Inquisition: Its Rise, Growth, and End*. New York: Citadel, 1969.

Prados, John. *Safe for Democracy: The Secret Wars of the CIA*. Chicago: Ivan R. Dee, 2006.

Price, Richard. *The Chemical Weapons Taboo*. Ithaca, NY: Cornell University Press, 1997.

———. "Reversing the Gun Sights: Transnational Civil Society Targets Land Mines." *International Organization* 52, no. 3 (1998): 613–44.

Rackow, Shannon H. "How the USA Patriot Act Will Permit Governmental Infringement upon the Privacy of Americans in the Name of 'Intelligence' Investigations." *University of Pennsylvania Law Review* 150, no. 5 (2002): 1651–96.

Rajagopal, Balakrishnan. *International Law from Below: Development, Social Movements, and Third World Resistance*. Cambridge: Cambridge University Press, 2003.

Ralph, Jason. *America's War on Terror: The State of the 9/11 Exception from Bush to Obama*. Oxford: Oxford University Press, 2013.

Rascoff, Samuel J. "Domesticating Intelligence." *Southern California Law Review* 83 (2010): 575–648.

Ratner, Michael, and the Center for Constitutional Rights. *The Trial of Donald Rumsfeld: A Prosecution by Book*. New York: New Press, 2008.

Raulff, Ulrich. "Interview with Giorgio Agamben—Life, A Work of Art without an Author: The State of Exception, the Administration of Disorder and Private Life." *German Law Journal* 5 (2004): 609–14.

Rawlings, Helen. *The Spanish Inquisition*. Malden, MA: Blackwell, 2006.

Rejali, Darius. *Torture and Democracy*. Princeton, NJ: Princeton University Press, 2007.

Reus-Smit, Christian. "The Politics of International Law." In *The Politics of International Law* edited by Christian Reus-Smit, 14–44. Cambridge: Cambridge University Press, 2004.

Rice, Condoleeza. *No Higher Honor: A Memoir of My Years in Washington*. New York: Crown, 2011.

Risen, James. *State of War: The Secret History of the CIA and the Bush Administration*. New York: Free Press, 2006.

Risse, Thomas, Stephen C. Ropp, and Kathryn Sikkink, eds. *The Persistent Power of Human Rights: From Commitment to Compliance*. Cambridge: Cambridge University Press, 2013.

———, eds. *The Power of Human Rights: International Norms and Domestic Change*. New York: Cambridge University Press, 1999.

Rizzo, John. *Company Man: Thirty Years of Controversy and Crisis in the CIA*. New York: Scribner, 2014.

Roht-Arriaza, Naomi. "Universal Jurisdiction: Steps Forward, Steps Back." *Leiden Journal of International Law* 17 (2004): 375–89.

Roosevelt, Theodore. *The Winning of the West: An Account of the Exploration and Settlement of our Country from the Alleghenies to the Pacific.* 4 vols. New York: G. P. Putnam's Sons, 1917.

Ross, James. "A History of Torture." In *Torture: Does it Make Us Safer? Is it Ever OK? A Human Rights Perspective,* edited by Kenneth Roth and Minky Worden, 3–17. New York: New Press and Human Rights Watch, 2005.

Ruggie, John Gerard. "International Regimes, Transactions, and Change: Embedded Liberalism in the Postwar Economic Order." In *International Regimes,* edited by Stephen D. Krasner, 195–232. Ithaca, NY: Cornell University Press, 1983.

Russett, Bruce M., and John R. Oneal. *Triangulating Peace: Democracy, Interdependence, and International Organizations.* New York: Norton, 2001.

Saito, Natsu Taylor. *From Chinese Exclusion to Guantánamo Bay: Plenary Power and the Prerogative State.* Boulder: University Press of Colorado, 2007.

Sanders, Rebecca. "Human Rights Abuses at the Limits of the Law: Legal Instabilities and Vulnerabilities in the 'Global War on Terror.'" *Review of International Studies* 44, no. 1 (2018): 2–23.

_____. "(Im)plausible Legality: The Rationalisation of Human Rights Abuses in The American 'Global War On Terror.'" *International Journal of Human Rights* 15, no. 4 (2011): 605–26.

_____. "Legal Frontiers: Targeted Killing at the Borders of War." *Journal of Human Rights* 13, no. 4 (2014): 512–36.

_____. "Norm Proxy War and Resistance through Outsourcing: The Dynamics of Transnational Human Rights Contestation." *Human Rights Review* 17, no. 2 (2016): 165–91.

Sandholtz, Wayne. *Prohibiting Plunder: How Norms Change.* New York: Oxford University Press, 2007.

Sandholtz, Wayne, and Kendall Stiles. *International Norms and Cycles of Change.* New York: Oxford University Press, 2009.

Sands, Philippe. "International Law Transformed? From Pinochet to Congo . . . ?" *Leiden Journal of International Law* 16 (2003): 37–53.

_____. *The Torture Team: Rumsfeld's Memo and the Betrayal of American Values.* New York: Palgrave Macmillan, 2008.

Sarat, Austin, and Thomas R. Kearns, eds. *Law in The Domains of Culture.* Ann Arbor: University of Michigan Press, 2000.

Schafer, Judith Kelleher. "'Details Are of a Most Revolting Character': Cruelty to Slaves as Seen in Appeals to the Supreme Court of Louisiana." In *Slavery and the Law,* edited by Paul Finkelman, 242–67. Madison, WI: Madison House, 1997.

Scharf, Michael, and Paul Williams. *Shaping Foreign Policy in Times of Crisis: The Role of International Law and the State Department Legal Advisor.* New York: Cambridge University Press, 2010.

Scheuerman, William E. *Between the Norm and the Exception: The Frankfurt School and the Rule of Law.* Cambridge, MA: MIT Press, 1997.

_____. "Carl Schmitt and the Road to Abu Ghraib." *Constellations* 13, no. 1 (2006): 108–24.

Schmidt, Regin. *Red Scare: FBI and the Origins of Anti-Communism in the United States, 1919– 1943.* Copenhagen: Museum Tusculanum, 2000.

Schmitt, Carl. *The Concept of the Political.* Translated by George Schwab. Chicago: University of Chicago Press, 2007.

_____. *The Nomos of the Earth in the International Law of the Jus Publicum Europaeum.* Translated by G. L. Ulmen. New York: Telos, 2003.

_____. *Political Theology: Four Chapters on the Concept of Sovereignty.* Translated by George Schwab. Chicago: University of Chicago Press, 2005.

Schmitt, Michael N. "Deconstructing Direct Participation in Hostilities: The Constitutive Elements." *NYU Journal of International Law and Politics* 42 (2009–10): 697–739.

Schoettler, James A., Jr. "Detention of Combatants and the Global War on Terror." In *The War on Terror and the Laws of War: A Military Perspective*, edited by Michael Lewis, Eric Jensen, Geoffrey Corn, Victor Hansen, Richard Jackson, and James Schoettler, 67–124. Oxford: Oxford University Press, 2009.

Schwarz, Frederick A. O., Jr. "The Church Committee and a New Era of Intelligence Oversight." *Intelligence and National Security* 22, no. 2 (2007): 270–97.

Scott, Len. "Secret Intelligence, Covert Action, and Clandestine Diplomacy." *Intelligence and National Security* 19, no. 2 (2004): 322–41.

Scott, Shirley. *International Law, US Power: The United States' Quest for Legal Security.* Cambridge: Cambridge University Press, 2012.

Sikkink, Kathryn. "The United States and Torture: Does the Spiral Model Work?" In *The Persistent Power of Human Rights: From Commitment to Compliance*, edited by Thomas Risse, Stephen C. Ropp, and Kathryn Sikkink, 145–64. Cambridge: Cambridge University Press, 2013.

Silverman, Lisa. *Tortured Subjects: Pain, Truth, and the Body in Early Modern France.* Chicago: University of Chicago Press, 2001.

Simmons, Beth A. *Mobilizing for Human Rights: International Law in Domestic Politics.* Cambridge: Cambridge University Press, 2009.

Simpson, Brooks D., and Jean V. Berlin, eds. *Sherman's Civil War: Selected Correspondence of William T. Sherman, 1860–1865.* Chapel Hill: University of North Carolina Press, 1999.

Simpson, Gerry. *Great Powers and Outlaw States: Unequal Sovereigns in the International Legal Order.* Cambridge: Cambridge University Press, 2004.

————. *Law, War and Crime: War Crimes Trials and the Reinvention of International Law.* Cambridge: Polity, 2007.

Sinclair, Adriana. *International Relations Theory and International Law: A Critical Approach.* Cambridge: Cambridge University Press, 2010.

Slaughter, Anne-Marie. "International Law in a World of Liberal States." *European Journal of International Law* 6 (1995): 503–38.

Sloan, Lawrence D. "ECHELON and the Legal Restraints on Signals Intelligence: A Need for Reevaluation." *Duke Law Journal* 50, no. 5 (2001): 1467–510.

Solis, Gary D. *The Law of Armed Conflict: International Humanitarian Law in War.* New York: Cambridge University Press, 2010.

Solove, Daniel J., Marc Rotenberg, and Paul M. Schwartz. *Privacy, Information, and Technology.* New York: Aspen, 2007.

Steyn, Johan. "Guantanamo Bay: The Legal Black Hole." *International and Comparative Law Quarterly* 53 (2004): 1–15.

Stone, Geoffrey R. *Perilous Times: Free Speech in Wartime from the Sedition Act of 1798 to the War on Terrorism.* New York: W. W. Norton, 2004.

Swire, Peter P. "Katz Is Dead. Long Live Katz." *Michigan Law Review* 102, no. 5 (2004): 904–32.

Takayoshi, Ichiro. "Can Philosophy Explain Nazi Violence? Giorgio Agamben and the Problem of the 'Historico-Philosophical' Method." *Journal of Genocide Research* 13, nos. 1–2 (2011): 47–66.

Tannenwald, Nina. *The Nuclear Taboo: The United States and the Non-Use of Nuclear Weapons Since 1945.* Cambridge: Cambridge University Press, 1997.

Teitel, Ruti G. *Transitional Justice.* Oxford: Oxford University Press, 2000.

Teschke, Benno Gerhard. "Fatal Attraction: A Critique of Carl Schmitt's International Political and Legal Theory." *International Theory* 3, no. 2 (2011): 197–227.

Theoharis, Athan. "The FBI and the Politics of Anti-Communism 1920–1945: A Prelude to Power." In *Little 'Red Scares': Anti-Communism and Political Repression in the United States 1921–1946*, edited by Robert Justin Goldstein, 23–45. Burlington, VT: Ashgate, 2014.

Treverton, Gregory. *Intelligence for an Age of Terror*. Cambridge: Cambridge University Press, 2009.

Turse, Nick. *Kill Anything that Moves: The Real American War in Vietnam*. New York: Picador, 2013.

Vagts, Detlev F. "Military Commissions: A Concise History." *American Journal of International Law* 101, no. 1 (2007): 35–48.

Vidal Naquet, Pierre. *Torture: Cancer of Democracy, France and Algeria, 1954–6*. Translated by Barry Richard. Baltimore: Penguin, 1963.

Voltaire, M. de. *A Philosophical Dictionary*. 2 vols. Notes by Abner Kneeland. Boston: J. Q. Adams, 1836.

Waldron, Jeremy. "Torture and Positive Law: Jurisprudence for the White House." *Columbia Law Review* 105, no. 6 (2005): 1681–750.

Watkin, Kenneth. "Opportunity Lost: Organized Armed Groups and the ICRC 'Direct Participation in Hostilities' Interpretive Guidance." *NYU Journal of International Law and Politics* 42 (2009–10): 641–95.

Webber, Jeremy. "Culture, Legal Culture, and Legal Reasoning: A Comment on Nelken." *Australian Journal of Legal Philosophy* 29 (2004): 28–36.

Weiner, Tim. *Legacy of Ashes: The History of the CIA*. New York: Doubleday, 2007.

Welsh, Jennifer. *The Return of History: Conflict, Migration, and Geopolitics in the Twenty-First Century*. Toronto: House of Anansi, 2016.

Wendt, Alexander. "Anarchy is What States Make of It: The Social Construction of Power Politics." *International Organization* 46, no. 2 (1992): 391–425.

Whitaker, Beth Elise. "Exporting the Patriot Act? Democracy and the 'War on Terror' in the Third World." *Third World Quarterly* 28, no. 5 (2007): 1017–32.

Wiener, Antje. "Enacting Meaning-In-Use: Qualitative Research on Norms and International Relations." *Review of International Studies* 35 (2009): 175–93.

———. *The Invisible Constitution of Politics: Contested Norms and International Encounters*. Cambridge: Cambridge University Press 2008.

Wilson, Peter H. "Prisoners in Early Modern European Warfare." In *Prisoners in War*, edited by Sibylle Scheipers, 39–56. Oxford: Oxford University Press, 2010.

Witt, John Fabian. *Lincoln's Code: The Laws of War in American History*. New York: Simon and Schuster, 2012.

Wolf, Naomi. *The End of America: A Letter of Warning to a Young Patriot*. White River Junction, VT: Chelsea Green, 2007.

Wong, Katherine. "Recent Developments: The NSA Terrorist Surveillance Program." *Harvard Journal on Legislation* 43 (2006): 517–34.

Yoo, John. *War by Other Means: An Insider's Account of the War on Terror*. New York: Atlantic Monthly, 2006.

INDEX

AT&T, 136
Australia, 121
Authorization for Use of Military
    Force (AUMF)
  broad discretion granted to executive branch
    in, 113, 136
  Foreign Intelligence Surveillance Act
    and, 136
  Islamic State and, 114
  law of war paradigm and, 110
  Obama Administration and, 105
  unlawful enemy combatant designations
    and, 92–93, 103
al-Awlaki, Anwar, 1, 109, 111

Bagram air base (Afghanistan), 62, 105
The Bahamas, 141
Baker, Howard, 127
Beaver, Diane, 59
Beccaria, Cesare, 36
Bell, James, 42
Bellinger, John, 68, 115
Bernstein, Carl, 125
Bill of Rights, 7, 10, 76, 99, 119–20. *See also*
    specific amendments
Bin Laden, Osama, 108–9
"black sites," 50, 58, 70, 103
Blackstone, William, 34, 76
Bolton, John, 148
Boumediene v. Bush, 104–5
Boundless Informant program (National
    Security Agency), 143
Bourdieu, Pierre, 6
Boyd v. United States, 120
Bradbury, Steven, 66–67, 70
Brandeis, Louis, 120
Brown v. Board of Education, 86
Brussels Declaration on Laws and Customs of
    War (1874), 78
Buchwald, Art, 127
Bureau of Investigation (BI), 123–24. *See also*
    Federal Bureau of Investigation
Burge, Jon, 46
Burr, Robert, 127
Bush, George W.
  Abu Ghraib abuses denounced by, 61
  culture of legal rationalization and, 2, 14, 23,
    51, 53–54, 73, 153–54, 161
  culture of secrecy and, 51–52
  enhanced interrogation techniques and,
    52–66, 69, 71, 157
  extraordinary rendition policies and,
    64–65, 68

Foreign Intelligence Surveillance Act and,
    136, 139, 158–59
  Geneva Conventions and, 54, 57, 96–98,
    101, 103, 112
  immigration and deportation policies
    under, 89–91
  indefinite detention policies and, 72–73,
    97–98, 158–59
  military commissions and, 72,
    101–5, 158–59
  National Security Agency and, 133, 136,
    141, 150
  President's Surveillance Program and,
    136–39, 150
  surveillance practices and, 117, 132–33,
    136–41, 148, 150
  targeted killings and, 72, 88–89,
    108–9, 157
  torture and, 1, 22, 24, 28–29, 33, 50–69, 73,
    154–55, 157–58, 167
  unlawful enemy combatant distinctions and,
    72, 97–98, 112
  waterboarding and, 51–52, 55, 58–59, 67
Bybee, Jay, 55, 57, 70

Calley, William, 47
Cameron, Eugene, 48
Camp Nama (Iraq), 51
Canada, 106, 121
Card, Andrew, 139
Castro, Fidel, 45, 87
Central America, 13, 45, 48–49, 87
Central Intelligence Agency (CIA)
  assassinations and, 28, 45, 87–88
  "black sites" and, 50, 58, 70, 103
  CHAOS (domestic spying program)
    and, 128
  Church Committee reports on, 45, 125–27
  Cold War and, 87–88
  Congressional grants of immunity to
    members of, 157
  culture of secrecy and, 28, 154
  detention policies and, 53–54
  domestic surveillance prohibited for, 121
  drone warfare and, 1, 108–9
  electoral manipulation in foreign
    countries by, 45
  enhanced interrogation and, 53–55, 57–59,
    61–67, 69–70
  extraordinary rendition and, 51, 64–65, 68
  illegal mail opening campaign by, 125–27
  lack of torture-related criminal prosecutions
    of members of, 69–70

MK Ultra hallucinogenic drug program
(1960s) and, 48
National Security Act of 1947 and, 121
PATRIOT Act and, 134
plausible deniability and, 12, 127
September 11, 2001 terrorist attacks
and, 134
SERE interrogation program and, 54–55
surveillance practices and, 121, 125–28,
134, 148
torture and, 5, 28, 47–48, 50–52,
54–55, 57–58
Uniform Code of Military Justice and, 54
waterboarding and, 51, 55, 58–59
CHAOS (Central Intelligence Agency domestic
spying program), 128
Cheney, Dick, 51, 64, 97, 101
Cheyenne Indians, 80–81
Chile, 38, 45, 88
China, 100, 141–42, 159–60
Chinese Exclusion Act (1882), 83
Chivington, John, 80–81
Church, Frank, 125
Church Committee
assassination plots uncovered by, 13, 45
Central Intelligence Agency abuses
documented by, 45, 87, 125–27
Congressional intelligence committees
created following, 48, 131
Foreign Intelligence Surveillance Act as a
consequence of, 116, 131
on surveillance abuses, 13, 125–27, 129,
131–32, 144, 150–51
Cipher Bureau, 120, 124
Civil War
abuse of civilians in, 82
Atlanta campaign (1864) and, 81
habeas corpus suspended during, 82
Lieber Code and, 36, 42, 77, 80–82
military commissions and, 82
prisoners of war in, 77, 82
Clinton, Bill, 108
COINTELPRO (FBI counterintelligence
program), 128–29, 139
Coke, Sir Edward, 118
Cold War
authoritarian anti-Communist regimes and,
11–12, 28, 44–45, 47–49, 73, 87
Central Intelligence Agency and, 87–88
clandestine intelligence operations and,
44–45, 71, 87, 114, 167
culture of secrecy and, 3, 6, 13, 27, 33,
44–47, 70–71, 73, 87, 125, 150, 167

due process denials during, 86–87
plausible deniability and, 6, 12, 44–45,
71, 167
proxy wars and, 12–13, 44–49
second Red Scare and, 85–86, 92
surveillance practices and, 122, 125, 128,
141, 150
torture and, 28, 45–49, 87
Cole, James, 146
collateral damage, 78–79, 110, 137
colonialism
culture of exception and, 3, 10, 42–43, 80–
82, 123, 167
culture of human rights and, 9, 80
Indian Wars and, 80–82
torture and, 42–44, 80
Combatant Status Review Tribunals, 103, 105
Comey, James, 139
common article 2 (Geneva Conventions), 96, 103
common article 3 (Geneva Conventions)
Al Qaeda and Taliban prisoners under, 54,
97, 113
enhanced interrogation methods and, 68
Hamdan v. Rumsfeld and, 66, 103
international armed conflicts and, 96, 103
Military Commissions Act of 2006 and, 104
noninternational armed conflicts and, 94,
96, 103
torture prohibition in, 36
Congo, 45, 87
Congress. *See also* Church Committee; *specific
legislation*
Authorization for Use of Military Force
(AUMF) and, 110, 113, 136
FISA Amendments Act of 2008 and,
140, 161
Guantánamo Bay and, 157
immigration law and, 83
indefinite detention laws and, 103
intelligence agency oversight and, 48, 52,
131–33, 157
military commissions and, 104
PATRIOT Act and, 135
President's Surveillance Program and, 140
Total Information Awareness Program
and, 145
USA FREEDOM Act and, 147
constructivism
law as constraint and, 3, 15, 18, 20, 23,
25–26, 28, 31, 155
law as permissive constraint and, 28
sociological dimensions of political and legal
behavior in, 19

Convention against Torture (1984)
  Bush Administration interpretation of, 65
  cruel and inhuman punishment prohibited
    under, 37–38, 66
  extraditions and, 37, 65
  prosecution of violations of, 24, 37, 57
  torture defined in, 37–38, 55, 154
  United States and, 38–39, 151
convict leasing, 73, 82–83
Cuba, 45, 87, 99, 123. *See also* Guantánamo Bay
    detention center
culture of exception
  African Americans brutalized under, 3, 11,
    33, 40–42, 70, 82–83, 114
  authoritarian regimes and, 27
  Civil War and, 81–82
  colonialism and, 3, 10, 42–43, 80–82,
    123, 167
  culture of legal rationalization
    compared to, 23
  discourses of necessity and, 26–27
  due process and, 11, 73, 79–80
  human rights and, 4, 7, 10, 13, 27, 30, 40, 52,
    86–87, 167
  immigrant populations in, 83–85
  immigration law and, 83
  Indian Wars and, 73, 80–82, 93
  law as permit and, 15, 18–19, 23, 26–28, 31,
    71, 88, 155
  national emergencies and, 40
  racism and, 40–43, 73, 81, 123, 167
  second Red Scare and, 85–86, 150
  segregation and, 27, 86
  slavery and, 7, 10, 27, 40–41
  state violence facilitated through,
    18, 39–40
  "subversives" and, 3, 10, 80, 123–24
  torture and, 3, 10
  Trump and, 3, 14–15, 19, 31, 71, 115,
    153–54, 161–63, 166
  U.S. surveillance practices and, 116, 123–24,
    136, 150–51
culture of human rights. *See also* human rights
  colonialism and, 9, 80
  culture of secrecy and, 11, 17–18, 30, 43, 52
  The Enlightenment and emergence of, 8–9
  law as constraint and, 27–28, 31, 155–56
  minorities and, 9
  nongovernmental organizations' promotion
    of, 5, 16, 166–67
  transnational nature of, 5, 8, 24
  U.S. international law commitments
    and, 164–65

U.S. national security establishment and,
    30–31, 151, 165–66
  women and, 9
culture of legal rationalization. *See also* plausible
    legality
  culture of exception compared to, 23
  enhanced interrogation and, 117,
    158–59, 162
  human rights abuses and, 8, 12, 14, 19, 30,
    50, 52, 161–62, 165
  indefinite detention and, 4, 17, 156, 158–59
  law as permissive constraint and, 16, 19, 27–
    29, 31, 53, 71, 156
  law as permit and, 23, 27, 156
  National Security Agency (NSA) and, 2–3,
    138, 141, 148, 152
  surveillance practices and, 3, 117, 151–52,
    154–56, 158–59
  targeted killing and, 4, 14, 17, 156, 158–59
  torture and, 4, 17, 39, 50, 53, 156, 163
  torture memos and, 16, 22
  U.S. national security establishment in post-
    9/11 era and, 4, 18, 30, 33, 50, 52, 71, 73,
    88–89, 91–92, 98, 100, 133, 154, 167–68
  waterboarding and, 30, 157, 162–63
culture of secrecy
  Central Intelligence Agency and, 28, 154
  Cold War and, 3, 6, 13, 27, 33, 44–47, 70–71,
    73, 87, 125, 150, 167
  extraordinary rendition and, 51, 64–65, 68
  human rights and, 11, 17–18, 30, 43, 52
  law as permit and, 27–28, 71, 88
  National Security Agency and, 116, 136
  Nixon Administration and, 125
  plausible deniability and, 17, 27
  U.S. counterterrorism policy and, 51
  warrantless surveillance and, 136

Damiens, Robert-Francois, 34
data mining, 144–45, 155
Debs, Eugene, 83
decisionism
  intergroup competition and, 26
  interwar Europe and, 20
  law as permit and, 3, 28, 31, 155
  law subordinated to power in, 21, 167
  surveillance programs and, 139, 151
Declaration of Independence, 41, 113
Defense Advanced Research Projects
    Agency, 145
Delahunty, Robert J., 54, 136–37
Detainee Treatment Act of 2005, 66, 69, 103–4
Donovan, "Wild Bill," 120

International Committee of the Red
        Cross (ICRC) (*cont.*)
    on law enforcement in non-armed conflicts, 94
    on preventative detention of civilians, 95
    reports on U.S. detention and interrogation
        practices by, 58
    on targeted killing of civilians directly
        engaged in hostilities and, 111–12
International Covenant on Civil and Political
        Rights, 36–38, 76–77, 122
International Criminal Court, 37, 79, 164
International War Crimes Tribunal, 45
Iran, 45
Iran Contra scandal, 13, 49
Iraq
    drone warfare and targeted killings in, 108, 160
    enhanced interrogations at U.S. facilities in,
        61–64, 69
    plausible legality and the U.S. invasion
        (2003) of, 78, 166
    prisoners of war in, 63
    torture at detention facilities in, 50–51
    U.S. massacres of civilians in, 107
    U.S. surveillance in, 123
Islamic State in Iraq and al-Sham (ISIS),
        114, 166
Israel, 160
Italy, 70, 141
ITT World Communications, 127

Jackson, Andrew, 80
Jackson, Robert, 85
Japanese-American internment (Second World
        War), 73, 84–85, 89, 102
Jefferson, Thomas, 119
Jessen, John "Bruce," 54–55
Johnson, Jeh, 113
Johnson, Lyndon, 128
Johnson v. Eisentrager, 100
Jordan, 64
judge advocates general (JAGs), 60–61, 68
Justice Department
    culture of legal rationalization and, 2–3
    military commissions and, 101
    Muslim visa holders interviewed and
        detained by, 90–91
    Office of Legal Counsel and, 53–55, 57–59,
        61, 63–70, 96–97, 100–1, 136–37, 139,
        158, 163
    Office of Professional Responsibility
        and, 68, 70
    surveillance practices and, 137, 139, 149
    targeted killings policies and, 111–14

Katz v. United States, 130
Keith decision, 130–31
Kennedy, Robert, 91
Kenya, 42
Khadr, Omar, 106
King Jr., Martin Luther, 127–28
Kinne, Adrienne, 148
Klein, Mark, 136
Koh, Harold, 101, 110
Korean War, 48
Korematsu v. United States, 84–85
Kosovo bombing campaign (1999), 166
KUBARK Counterintelligence Training Manual
        (1963), 47–48
Ku Klux Klan (KKK), 41, 128

law as constraint
    constructivism and, 3, 15, 18, 20, 23, 25–26,
        28, 31, 155
    culture of human rights and, 27–28,
        31, 155–56
    "hypocrisy costs" and, 24
    indefinite detention and, 27
    law's ability to shape state practice and, 3, 23
    liberalism and, 3, 15, 18, 20, 23, 25, 28,
        31, 155
    targeted killing and, 27
    torture and, 27–28
law as permissive constraint
    constructivism and, 28
    culture of legal rationalization and, 16, 19,
        27–29, 31, 53, 71, 156
    definition of, 3
    human rights and, 16, 19, 32
    liberalism and, 28
    plausible legality and, 32, 115
    realities of political power acknowledged in,
        29, 155
    states' reputational concerns and, 29
    torture and, 53
    U.S. national security practices and, 27, 168
law as permit
    American exceptionalism and, 21
    culture of legal rationalization and, 23,
        27, 156
    culture of secrecy and, 27–28, 71, 88
    cultures of exception and, 15, 18–19, 23,
        26–28, 31, 71, 88, 155
    decisionism and, 3, 28, 31, 155
    executive power and, 22
    realism and, 3, 18, 20–21, 28, 31, 155
    supremacy of sovereign power over law and,
        3, 21, 31

surveillance and, 28, 150
torture and, 28
lawful enemy combatants, 97
law of war paradigm, 109–11
League of Nations, 20
legal cultures. *See also* specific legal cultures
collectively shared understandings of, 4–5
contested nature of, 4, 6
contextual nature of, 26, 31
definition of, 2, 4
historical evolution of, 8–15
human agency and, 5–6, 26
LeMay, Curtis, 84
Levi, Edward, 125–26, 131
Levin, Daniel, 66
liberalism
individual rights and freedoms in, 23
international law and, 23, 165
law as constraint and, 3, 15, 18, 20, 23, 25, 28, 31, 155
law as permissive constraint and, 28
neoliberalism and, 23
Libya, 64, 109, 114, 166
Lichtblau, Eric, 136
Liddy, G. Gordon, 125
Lieber Code
human rights norms promoted under, 77–78, 80
on the intensity and duration of wars, 81
torture prohibited under, 36, 42, 77
Lincoln, Abraham, 82, 120
Lumumba, Patrice, 45, 87
lynchings, 11, 41–42, 83, 89

Magna Carta, 75
Mahmudiyah gang rape (Iraq), 107
Malaysia, 159
Manifest Destiny, 80
Marina databank (National Security Agency), 146
el-Masri, Khaled, 70
material witness laws, 72, 89–90, 92, 98, 115
Mattis, James, 163
McCarran Act (1950), 85
McCarran-Walter Act (1952), 85
McCarthy, Joseph, 73, 85–86. *See also* second Red Scare
McKinley, William, 43
metadata
data mining and, 144–45, 155
legislation limiting the collection of, 150
National Security Agency Programs to collect, 146–47, 149

plausible legality and the collection of, 154
privacy and, 151
Stellarwind program and, 145–46
Mexico, 141
al-Mihdhar, Khalid, 134
military commissions
Al Qaeda suspects and, 102
Bush Administration counterterrorism policy and, 72, 101–5, 158–59
Civil War and, 82
culture of legal rationalization and, 4, 17, 156, 158–59
due process considerations and, 101–4
evidentiary standards at, 72
Geneva Conventions and, 104
law as permissive constraint and, 28
law of war paradigm and, 110
Military Commissions Act of 2006 and, 97, 104
national security information and, 102
Obama Administration counterterrorism policies and, 105–6, 157
plausible legality and, 29, 73, 89, 114–15, 154–55, 168
Second World War and, 101–2
terrorism-related trials at, 72
torture memos and, 1
unlawful enemy combatants tried at, 97, 101–2, 104
Miller, Geoffrey, 62
Miller, Stephen, 163
MINARET (National Security Agency electronic monitoring program), 127–28
Mitchell, James, 54–55
Mitrione, Dan, 47
MKUltra program (Central Intelligence Agency hallucinogenic drugs program of 1960s), 48
Mohammed, Khalid Sheik, 58–59, 106
Mora, Alberto, 61
Morocco, 64
Moussaoui, Zacarias, 134
Mueller, Robert, 139
Murphy, Frank, 84–85
Muslim immigration and travel ban (Trump administration), 15, 92, 153, 162–63
My Lai massacre (Vietnam War), 46
MYSTIC (National Security Agency surveillance program), 141

Nasr, Osama Moustafa Hassan, 64
National Association for the Advancement of Colored People v. Alabama, 129

National Defense Authorization Act of 2012, 106–7
National Security Act of 1947, 121, 128
National Security Agency (NSA)
  Boundless Informant Program and, 143
  Bush Administration counterterrorism policies and, 133, 136, 141, 150
  Church Committee reports on, 125, 127–28, 138
  Congress and, 157
  culture of legal rationalization and, 2–3, 138, 141, 148, 152
  culture of secrecy and, 116, 136
  EvilOlive metadata operation and, 146
  Federal Bureau of Investigation and, 149
  Foreign Intelligence Surveillance Act and, 134, 141, 143
  foreign intelligence *versus* domestic intelligence and, 141, 143, 162
  Fourth Amendment and, 128
  Marina databank, 146
  MINARET electronic monitoring program and, 127–28
  MYSTIC surveillance program and, 141
  PATRIOT Act and, 133–35
  plausible legality and, 138
  President's Surveillance Program and, 137–39
  PRISM surveillance program and, 142–44, 151
  prominent Muslim-Americans monitored by, 148–49
  RAMPART-A surveillance program, 143
  SHAMROCK telegram monitoring program and, 127–28, 136, 139
  ShellTrumpet metadata gathering program and, 146
  signals intelligence as purview of, 121
  Snowden disclosures regarding, 116, 135, 140, 147, 150–51
  Stellarwind surveillance initiative and, 136–38, 142, 145, 150
  technological changes and, 142–44
  UPSTREAM surveillance program and, 142–44, 151
  USA Freedom Act and, 147, 149
  warrantless surveillance and, 138–39
  XKEYSCORE search engine and, 143, 145
National Security Entry and Exit Registry System, 91
necessity principle, 78–79, 110
neoliberalism, 23
New Zealand, 121

Nigeria, 160
Nisour Square massacre (Iraq), 107
Nixon, Richard, 13, 22, 47, 125–26, 131
NKVD manual, 45–46
No Fly List, 92
noninternational armed conflicts
  civilians engaged in "continuous combat function" in, 112
  civilians engaged in "direct participation in hostilities" in, 111–12
  common article 3 and, 94, 96, 103
  detention of civilians in, 95, 165
  Geneva Conventions and, 93–94, 98, 115
  human rights case law and, 79
NSC 1012, 44
Nuremberg Trials (1940s), 44, 79

Obama, Barack
  Authorization for Use of Military Force and, 105
  Bin Laden raid (2011) and, 109
  culture of legal rationalization and, 2, 14, 23, 51, 73, 153–54, 161
  culture of secrecy and, 51–52
  decision not to pursue torture-related prosecutions by, 69
  enhanced interrogation techniques repudiated by, 106
  Guantánamo Bay facility maintained by, 72, 106–7, 159
  indefinite detention policies and, 105–6, 157
  military commissions and, 105–6, 157
  National Defense Authorization Act of 2012 and, 107
  National Security Agency and, 145, 151
  Review Group on Intelligence and Communications Technologies and, 147
  Senate Select Committee on Intelligence report (2014) and, 52
  surveillance practices and, 117, 133, 135, 140, 145, 147–48, 151, 157, 165
  targeted killings and, 1, 72, 88–89, 105, 108–10, 115, 157
  torture memos rescinded by, 67, 158, 165
  USA FREEDOM Act (2015) and, 135, 147, 149
Office of Legal Counsel (OLC)
  enhanced interrogation and, 53, 55–59, 61, 63–64, 66, 158, 180–81n99
  extraordinary rendition policies and, 65
  on Geneva Conventions and counterterrorism, 54, 96–97
  Guantánamo Bay detentions and, 100

privacy
  civil libertarians' concerns about surveillance
      and, 149–50
  culture of legal rationalization and, 16
  domestic *versus* foreign persons and, 141
  international erosions in, 160–61
  international law regarding, 121–22
  mail communications and, 126–27
  metadata and, 151
  multiple domains of, 117–18
  National Security Agency's professions of
      concern regarding, 138
  physical trespass as a consideration in, 120
  post-Snowden efforts to improve protections
      for, 148
  property rights and, 119
  reasonable expectation criterion and, 132
  search warrants as means of
      protecting, 118–19
  Supreme Court case law regarding, 129–31
  third-party exceptions and, 135, 146,
      148, 154
  U.S. civil liberties tradition and, 116–17
  U.S. constitutional protections of, 119–20
Privacy Act of 1974, 131
Project HTLINGUAL, 126–27
Project MINARET (National Security Agency
    electronic monitoring program), 127–28
Project SHAMROCK (National Security
    Agency telegram monitoring program),
    127–28, 136, 139
Project X (Pentagon interrogation program), 47
Protect America Act of 2007, 140
Providing Appropriate Tools Required to
    Intercept and Obstruct Terrorism Act of
    2001. *See* PATRIOT Act

al-Qahtani, Mohammed, 59–61

Rahman, Gul, 58
RAMPART-A (National Security Agency
    surveillance program), 143
Rasul v. Bush, 103
RCA Global, 127
Reagan, Ronald, 49, 108
realism
  intergroup competition and, 26
  international law critiqued in, 20–21, 23, 164
  law as permit and, 3, 18, 20–21, 28, 31, 155
  law subordinated to power in, 20–21, 71, 167
  moralistic security policy criticized by, 166
  new realism and, 21
  torture and, 21

Red Scare. *See* first Red Scare; second Red Scare
Reno, Janet, 108, 134
Review Group on Intelligence and
    Communications Technologies (Obama
    Administration), 147
Rice, Condoleezza, 55, 101
Risen, James, 136
Rizzo, John, 53, 55, 57, 59
Rogers, William, 45
Rome Statute of the International Criminal
    Court, 37
Roosevelt, Franklin Delano, 84, 101, 124
Roosevelt, Theodore, 81
Rules of Land Warfare (Glenn), 43, 46
Rumsfeld, Donald, 59, 61–64, 66, 68, 103
Russell, Bertrand, 45
Russia, 141, 159. *See also* Soviet Union
Rwanda, 79

Sacco, Nicola, 84
Safire, William, 145
Saint Petersburg Declaration (1868), 78
Salem witchcraft trials (1690s), 35
Sanchez, Ricardo, 63
Sand Creek massacre (1864), 80–81
Sartre, Jean-Paul, 45
Saudi Arabia, 67
Schmitt, Carl, 18, 20–22, 50, 155, 171n2
Schneider, Rene, 88
School of the Americas (SOA), 47, 49. *See also*
    Institute for Security Cooperation
Schwarz Jr., Frederick A. O., 126
second Red Scare (1950s), 73, 85–86, 92, 150
Second World War
  alien detention case law and, 100
  civilians as target of attacks in, 84
  Japanese American internment during, 73,
      84–85, 89, 102
  military commissions and, 101–2
  surveillance practices during, 120–21, 124
Sedition Act of 1918, 83
Senate Select Committee on Intelligence report
    (2014), 52, 58, 67
September 11, 2001 terrorist attacks,
    50, 133–34
sexual violence and humiliation, 9, 41, 60, 82,
    104, 107, 188n38
SHAMROCK (National Security Agency
    telegram monitoring program), 127–28,
    136, 139
ShellTrumpet (National Security Agency
    metadata gathering program), 146
Sherman, William Tecumseh, 81

signals intelligence (SIGINT), 118, 120–21, 137, 148
Sixth Amendment, 76
slavery
  in ancient societies, 34, 74
  culture of exception and, 7, 10, 27, 40–41
  human rights violated under, 33, 40–41
  torture and, 28, 34, 40
  United States and, 7, 11, 40–41
Smith Act, 85
Smith v. Maryland, 132
Snowden, Edward
  impact of National Security Agency program disclosures by, 116, 135, 140, 147, 150–51
  PRISM program revealed by, 142–43
  on Stellarwind's metadata component, 145
  surveillance of prominent Muslim-Americans revealed by, 148–49
  UPSTREAM program revealed by, 142
Somalia, 109, 141
Soule, Silas S., 80–81
South Africa, 87
Southern Christian Leadership Conference, 128
Soviet Union, 44, 71, 87, 122, 126. *See also* Cold War
Spain, 38, 141
Spanish-American War, 99
Spanish Inquisition, 35
Star Chamber court (England), 75
State Department
  annual human rights review by, 39
  culture of legal rationalization and, 2–3
  enhanced interrogations and, 68, 167
  Geneva Conventions and, 54, 68, 97
  military commissions and, 101
  visa policies and, 90
Stellarwind (National Security Agency surveillance initiative), 136–38, 142, 145, 150
Stimson, Henry, 120
Stone, Harlan Fiske, 124
Strategic Arms Limitation Talks, 122
"subversives"
  Central Intelligence Agency spying on, 128
  culture of exception and abuses of, 3, 10, 80, 123–24
  Federal Bureau of Investigation's targeting of and spying on, 85, 128
  First World War and, 123–24
  law as permit and surveillance of, 28
  surveillance of, 123–25, 129, 150

surveillance. *See also* warrantless surveillance
  American Revolutionary War and, 120
  Bush Administration counterterrorism policies and, 117, 132–33, 136–41, 148, 150
  Central Intelligence Agency and, 121, 125–28, 134, 148
  Church Committee on abuses in, 13, 125–27, 129, 131–32, 144, 150–51
  civil libertarians' complaints regarding, 149–50, 152
  Civil War, 120
  Cold War and, 122, 125, 128, 141, 150
  culture of exception and, 116, 123–24, 136, 150–51
  culture of legal rationalization and, 3, 117, 151–52, 154–56, 158–59
  cybersecurity potentially weakened by, 147
  first Red Scare and, 119
  First World War and, 120
  foreign *versus* domestic forms of, 12, 117–18, 120–21, 123, 127, 129–33, 150–51, 155, 158
  human intelligence (HUMINT) and, 118, 120–21
  Internal Revenue Service and, 126
  international law regarding, 121–23
  law as permissive constraint and, 28
  law as permit and, 28, 150
  mail and, 119–20, 125–28
  military conflicts and, 120–21
  Nixon and, 125–26
  norm erosions and international expansions in, 160–61, 163
  Obama Administration and, 117, 133, 135, 140, 145, 147–48, 151, 157, 165
  Office of Legal Counsel and, 136–37, 139
  PATRIOT Act and, 133–35, 145–47, 150
  plausible legality and, 14, 29, 117, 133, 151, 157, 168
  Second World War and, 120–21, 124
  signals intelligence (SIGINT) and, 118, 120–21, 137, 148
  of "subversives," 123–25, 129, 150
  technological changes and, 132–33, 142–44
  telegrams and, 120, 124–25, 127–28, 136, 139
  treaty-based monitoring of, 122–23
  wiretapping and, 120, 130
Survival, Evasion, Resistance, and Escape (SERE) program, 54–56, 59, 62–63
Syria, 64, 109, 114, 159

Taft, William, 97
The Taliban, 54, 95–97, 106–10
Taney, Roger, 82
targeted killing
    Al Qaeda suspects and, 1, 109, 111–14
    assassinations compared to, 88
    Bin Laden raid (2011) and, 109
    Bush Administration and, 72, 88–89,
        108–9, 157
    civilian deaths and, 107, 109
    culture of exception and, 3
    culture of legal rationalization and, 4, 14, 17,
        156, 158–59
    drone warfare and, 1, 108–9
    due process protections and, 1, 72,
        75, 109–10
    Geneva Convention on targeting civilians
        and, 111–12
    international law and, 165
    Islamic State and, 114
    law as constraint and, 27
    law as permissive constraint and, 28
    law of war paradigm and, 109–13
    norm erosion and international expansion in,
        160–61, 163
    Obama Administration and, 1, 72, 88–89,
        105, 108–10, 115, 157
    plausible legality and, 29, 73, 114–15, 151,
        154–55, 168
    "signature strikes" and, 113
    U.S. citizens as targets in, 109
Tenet, George, 53–54
Third Amendment, 113
Third Geneva Convention, 36, 93
torture. See also torture memos
    Bush Administration and, 1, 22, 24, 28–29,
        33, 50–69, 73, 154–55, 157–58, 167
    canon law and, 35
    Central Intelligence Agency and, 5, 28,
        47–48, 50–52, 54–55, 57–58
    Cold War and, 28, 45–49, 87
    colonialism and, 42–44, 80
    Convention against Torture and, 24, 37–39,
        55, 57, 65, 151, 154, 158
    culture of exception and, 3, 10
    culture of legal rationalization and, 4, 17, 39,
        50, 53, 156, 163
    death threats as form of, 38
    The Enlightenment's condemnation of,
        34–36, 40, 43
    extraordinary renditions and, 64–65
    as human rights violation, 33–34

history of, 8, 33–35, 74
Indian Wars and, 80–82
international law's prohibition of, 33–34,
    36–38, 72, 160–61, 163, 166, 168. See also
    Geneva Conventions
in Latin America, 47, 49, 87
law as constraint and, 27–28
law as permissive constraint and, 53
law as permit and, 28
Lieber Code's prohibition of, 36, 42, 77
lynchings and, 28, 41–42
manuals outlining methods of, 47–48
military commission cases and evidence
    obtained by, 104
necessity principle and, 79
norm erosion regarding, 158
plausible legality and, 29, 34, 67, 154–55
prisoners of war and, 35
prosecuting perpetrators of, 24, 37, 39, 57,
    69–70, 115, 156–57, 165
psychological dimensions of, 38, 48,
    56–57, 60, 62
as punishment for treason, 34–35
slavery and, 28, 34, 40
Torture Victim Protection Act (1991)
    and, 39
Trump's endorsement of, 14, 34, 153, 158
U.S. legal prohibitions against, 38–39,
    54, 116
witch trials and, 35
torture memos (Bush Administration)
on confinement boxes, 56–57
criticism of, 14, 67–69, 157
culture of legal rationalization and, 16, 22
enhanced interrogation and, 1, 55–58, 61,
    64, 69–70
indefinite detention and, 1
Justice Department post-facto reviews
    of, 68, 70
law as constraint and, 24
law as permissive constraint and, 28
on mental pain and suffering, 56–57
military commissions and, 1
Obama Administration's rescinding of, 67,
    158, 165
Office of Legal Counsel's role in drafting, 53,
    55, 67–69
permissive atmosphere at detention facilities
    created by, 59, 66
plausible legality and, 29, 33, 68–69, 71, 154
surveillance methods and, 1
waterboarding and, 1, 56, 155

Total Information Awareness Program
(Defense Advanced Research Projects
Agency), 145
Tower, John, 126
Tower of London, 34
Transient Thurible (British metadata collection
program), 146
Treaty of Relations (United States and Cuba,
1934), 99
Trujillo, Rafael, 45, 88
Truman, Harry, 85
Trump, Donald
authoritarian leaders praised by, 161
culture of exception and, 3, 14–15, 19, 31,
71, 115, 153–54, 161–63, 166
culture of legal rationalization and, 3, 14–15
human rights norms threatened by, 16, 153,
164, 166
Muslim immigration and travel ban of, 15,
92, 153, 162–63
sympathy for white nationalism expressed
by, 161
torture endorsed by, 14, 34, 153, 158
Tunisia, 64
Turkey, 141

Ultra (British intelligence program of Second
World War), 121
Uniform Code of Military Justice, 38, 54, 64, 78
unitary executive theory, 22
United Kingdom
Afghanistan War and, 96
Brexit vote (2016) and, 161
drone warfare and, 160
Kenyan colonial regime and, 42
Pinochet No. 3 case in, 38
surveillance practices in, 118–19, 121, 146, 149
torture in history of, 35
United Kingdom-United States Agreement,
121, 141, 149
United Nations
Article 51 on collective defense and, 78
Chapter VII Security Council resolution, 78
Convention against Torture and, 24, 37–39,
55, 57, 65, 151, 154, 158
Counter-Terrorism Committee at, 159
founding of, 9, 11
Special Rapporteur on extrajudicial,
summary, or arbitrary executions, 108
Special Rapporteur on the promotion
and protection of human rights and
fundamental freedoms, 160

Special Rapporteur on torture and, 68
surveillance data presented at, 123
Universal Declaration of Human Rights and,
36, 39, 44, 76, 122
Voluntary Fund for the Victims of Torture
and, 39
United States Agency for International
Development, 39, 45
Universal Declaration of Human Rights (1948),
36, 39, 44, 76, 122
unlawful enemy combatants
Authorization for Use of Military Force
(AUMF) and, 92–93
Bush Administration counterterrorism
policies and, 72, 97–98, 112
Combatant Status Review Tribunals and,
103, 105
Detainee Treatment Act of 2005 and, 103
due process considerations and, 88–89,
92–93, 100–103
Geneva Convention rights denied to,
97–99, 112
Guantánamo Bay detention center and, 72,
89, 98–101, 103
indefinite detention and, 97–101
military commission trials and, 97,
101–2, 104
Obama Administration's semantic change
regarding, 106
U.S. citizens designated as, 98
UPSTREAM (National Security Agency
surveillance program), 142–44, 151
Uruguay, 47
USA FREEDOM Act (2015), 135, 147, 149
Utz, Henry, 40–41

Vanzetti, Bartolomeo, 84
Vienna Convention on Diplomatic Relations,
37, 122, 177n26
Vietnam War, 13, 45–47, 51, 87–88, 126
Voltaire, 36

Wainstein, Kenneth, 146
War Bonnet (Sand Creek massacre victim), 81
War Crimes Act (1996), 39, 54, 66, 104
warrantless surveillance. *See also* surveillance
Church Committee reports
regarding, 125–26
Congress and, 157
culture of legal rationalization and, 4, 17
FISA Amendments Act and, 143–44
plausible legality and, 14, 29, 151, 155, 157, 168

warrantless surveillance (*cont.*)
  President's Surveillance Program
    and, 136–39
  Protect America Act of 2007 and, 140
  public scrutiny of, 140–41
Washington, George, 36, 80, 120
watch lists, 92, 127, 159
waterboarding
  Bush Administration counterterrorism
    policy and, 51–52, 55, 58–59, 67
  Central Intelligence Agency and, 51,
    55, 58–59
  culture of legal rationalization and, 30,
    157, 162–63
  Office of Legal Counsel and, 66
  Philippine War and, 42–43
  Spanish inquisition and, 35
  torture memos and, 1, 56, 155
  Trump's endorsement of, 153
Watergate scandal, 13, 125
Welch, Joseph, 86
Western Union International, 127
White Antelope (Sand Creek massacre
    victim), 81

Wicker, Tom, 127
Wilson, Woodrow, 83
witch trials, 35, 75
Wood, Carolyn, 62–63
Woodward, Bob, 125
Wounded Knee massacre (1890), 81

Yardley, Herbert O., 120
Yates, Sally, 163
Yemen, 1, 108–9
Yoo, John
  Abu Ghraib scandal and, 64
  on Afghanistan conflict and Geneva
    Conventions protections, 54
  on enhanced interrogations, 55–57, 61, 70,
    180–81n99
  on executive power and foreign affairs, 22
  Guantánamo Bay facility and, 100
  surveillance practices and, 136–37, 139
Young, Whitney, 127
Yugoslavia, 79

Zimbabwe, 159
Zubaydah, Abu, 54–56, 58